The Sword and the Cross

The Medieval and Early Modern Iberian World

Edited by

Larry J. Simon (*Western Michigan University*)
Gerard Wiegers (*University of Amsterdam*)
Arie Schippers (*University of Amsterdam*)
Isidro J. Rivera (*University of Kansas*)
Mercedes García-Arenal (*CCHS/CSIC*)
Montserrat Piera (*Temple University*)

VOLUME 77

The titles published in this series are listed at *brill.com/memi*

The Sword and the Cross

Castile-León in the Era of Fernando III

Edited by

Edward L. Holt
Teresa Witcombe

BRILL

LEIDEN | BOSTON

Cover illustration: fourteenth-century illumination of Fernando III in the *Compendio de crónicas de reyes* (Madrid, Biblioteca Nacional de España, MSS/7415, f. 40r). © Biblioteca Nacional de España.

Library of Congress Cataloging-in-Publication Data
Names: Holt, Edward L., editor. | Witcombe, Teresa, editor.
Title: The sword and the cross : Castile-León in the era of Fernando III / Edward L. Holt, Teresa Witcombe.
Other titles: Castile-León in the era of Fernando III
Description: Leiden ; Boston : Brill, [2020] | Series: The medieval and early modern Iberian world, 1569-1934 ; vol. 77 | Includes bibliographical references and index.
Identifiers: LCCN 2020002367 (print) | LCCN 2020002368 (ebook) | ISBN 9789004427624 (hardback) | ISBN 9789004428287 (ebook)
Subjects: LCSH: Castile (Spain)--History--Ferdinand III, 1217-1252.
Classification: LCC DP140.S95 2020 (print) | LCC DP140 (ebook) | DDC 946/.302--dc23
LC record available at https://lccn.loc.gov/2020002367
LC ebook record available at https://lccn.loc.gov/2020002368

Typeface for the Latin, Greek, and Cyrillic scripts: "Brill". See and download: brill.com/brill-typeface.

ISSN 1569-1934
ISBN 978-90-04-42762-4 (hardback)
ISBN 978-90-04-42828-7 (e-book)

Copyright 2020 by Koninklijke Brill NV, Leiden, The Netherlands.
Koninklijke Brill NV incorporates the imprints Brill, Brill Hes & De Graaf, Brill Nijhoff, Brill Rodopi, Brill Sense, Hotei Publishing, mentis Verlag, Verlag Ferdinand Schöningh and Wilhelm Fink Verlag.
All rights reserved. No part of this publication may be reproduced, translated, stored in a retrieval system, or transmitted in any form or by any means, electronic, mechanical, photocopying, recording or otherwise, without prior written permission from the publisher.
Authorization to photocopy items for internal or personal use is granted by Koninklijke Brill NV provided that the appropriate fees are paid directly to The Copyright Clearance Center, 222 Rosewood Drive, Suite 910, Danvers, MA 01923, USA. Fees are subject to change.

This book is printed on acid-free paper and produced in a sustainable manner.

Printed by Printforce, United Kingdom

Contents

Acknowledgments VII
List of Figures and Tables VIII
Abbreviations IX
Notes on Contributors X

Fernando III and His World 1
  Edward L. Holt and Teresa Witcombe

1 Empire and Crusade under Fernando III 15
   Carlos de Ayala Martínez

2 The Man "Who Broke and Destroyed All of His Enemies": The Military Action of Fernando III 44
   Francisco García Fitz

3 Fernando III and Muḥammad I of Granada: A Time of Collaboration between Two "Incompatible Worlds" 61
   Bárbara Boloix-Gallardo

4 *In exercitu loco eius pontificalia exercet*: Warrior Clerics in the Era of Fernando III 85
   Kyle C. Lincoln

5 *Dilecta consanguinea mea*: Fernando III's Donation to a Nun of Fontevraud 105
   Martín Alvira

6 *Laudes regiae*: Liturgy and Royal Power in Thirteenth-century Castile-León 140
   Edward L. Holt

7 "At the Command of the Infantas": Royal Women at Las Huelgas in the Thirteenth Century 165
   Janna Bianchini

8 Family and Friends: Women at the Court of Fernando III 193
   Miriam Shadis

9   The Peculiarities of Frontier Religious Authority in the Age of
    Fernando III   224
      Francisco García-Serrano

10 Literary Expressions of Pastoral Reform during the Reign of
    Fernando III   241
      Cristina Catalina

    Index   261

Acknowledgments

This book began as a series of conference papers at the Madrid campus of Saint Louis University in October 2017. That year marked the eight-hundredth anniversary of the accession of Fernando III to the throne of Castile. We are tremendously grateful for the financial help received from the Center for Medieval and Renaissance Studies, Saint Louis University, Office of the Dean, Saint Louis University, Madrid, Office of the Dean of Arts and Sciences, Saint Louis University, and the Department of History, Saint Louis University, which allowed the conference organizers (Edward Holt, Damian Smith, and Francisco García-Serrano) to assemble an international team of experts on the theme of Fernando's reign. We are grateful to the contributors for sharing their work for publication here, and to all those who have imparted advice in the process of compiling this volume, especially Damian Smith and Edward Sutcliffe. We would also like to thank the board of The Medieval and Early Modern Iberian World series, Marcella Mulder, and the anonymous reviewers for their comments and support throughout the publication process. Finally, we want to acknowledge one of the original conference participants: Professor Simon Barton. Simon's tragic and unexpected death shortly after the event has been a sore loss for medieval scholarship and has deprived many of us of a dear colleague, friend, and mentor. Simon's presentation, a study of the nobility of Fernando III, was, as always, rigorous, incisive, and highly engaging, and some of his rich insights and comments can be found in the chapters to follow. This volume is dedicated to his memory.

Figures and Tables

Figures

5.1 *Vidimus* (1250, January 5) of the donation of Fernando III to the nun Alix of Blois (1220, March 31. Toledo). Biblioteca de Catalunya (Barcelona), Parchments, no. 343, reg. 15196 (*recto*). Photo reprinted with kind permission of the Biblioteca de Catalunya, Barcelona   106

5.2 Seal of Adelaide of Brittany, Abbess of Fontevraud (1210): SIGILLUM ADILIDIS, [ABBATISSE BEA]TE MARIE FONTIS [EBRALDI]. AD Maine-et-Loire (Angers) 240 H 1, no. 3. © Archives départementales de Maine-et-Loire (Photo: Martín Alvira)   114

5.3 Great seal of Alix of Blois, Abbess of Fontevraud (1235): [SIGILLUM] ADILIDIS, ABBATISSE BE[ATE] MARIE FONTIS E[BRALDI]. AD Aube (Troyes), 42 Fi 200; AN (Paris), sc/Ch 2813 -2813bis and sc/D 9205 -9205bis. © Département de l'Aube, Noël Mazières. Photo reprinted by kind permission of the Archives départementales de l'Aube, Troyes   117

5.4 *Vidimus* (1250, January 5) of the donation of Fernando III to the nun Alix of Blois (1220, March 31. Toledo). Biblioteca de Catalunya (Barcelona), Parchments, no. 343, reg. 15196 (*verso*). Photo reprinted with kind permission of the Biblioteca de Catalunya, Barcelona   122

Tables

5.1 List of Abbesses of Fontevraud   111
6.1 Comparison of Castilian *Missa Pro Rege* Prayers   145

Abbreviations

Alfonso VIII González, Julio. *El reino de Castilla en la época de Alfonso VIII*, 3 vols. Madrid: CSIC, 1960.

Cantigas Kulp-Hill, Kathleen, trans. *Songs of Holy Mary of Alfonso X, the Wise: A Translation of the Cantigas de Santa María*. Tempe, AZ: Center for Medieval and Renaissance Studies, 2000.

CM Lucas of Tuy. *Chronicon mundi*. Ed. Emma Falque Rey. Vol. 74 of *Corpus Christianorum: Continuatio mediaeualis*. Turnhout: Brepols, 2003.

DrH Rodrigo Jiménez de Rada. *Historia de rebus Hispanie, sive Historia Gothica*. Ed. Juan Fernández Valverde. Vol. 72 of *Corpus Christianorum: Continuatio mediaeualis*. Turnhout: Brepols, 1987.

Fernando III González, Julio, ed. *Reinado y diplomas de Fernando III*, 3 vols. Córdoba: Monte de Piedad y Caja de Ahorros de Córdoba, 1980–1986.

PCG *Primera crónica general de España*. Ed. Ramón Menéndez Pidal et al. Madrid: Gredos, 1955.

CLRC Charlo Brea, Luis, ed. *Chronica latina regum Castellae*. In *Chronica Hispana Saeculi XIII,* ed. Luis Charlo Brea, Juan Estévez Sola and Rocío Carande Herrero. Vol. 73 of *Corpus Christianorum: Continuatio medievalis*, 7–118. Turnhout: Brepols, 1997.

Notes on Contributors

Martín Alvira
is a Profesor Titular in the Department of Medieval History at the Universidad Complutense in Madrid. His works include *Las Navas de Tolosa, 1212: Idea, liturgia, y memoria de la batalla* (Madrid, 2012) and *Muret 1213: La batalla decisiva de la Cruzada contra los Cataros* (Barcelona, 2008), as well as the edition of the documents of Peter II of Aragón (6 vols., Zaragoza, 2010).

Carlos de Ayala Martínez
holds a chair in Medieval History in the Department of Ancient and Medieval History, Paleography, and Diplomatic at the Universidad Autónoma de Madrid. He is the author of many monographs including *Las órdenes militares hispánicas en la Edad Media* (Madrid, 2003) and *Sacerdocio y reino en la España Altomedieval* (Madrid, 2008), as well as co-editor of multiple volumes including, with Ríos Saloma, *Fernando III, tiempo de cruzada* (Madrid, 2012), with Henriet and Palacios Ontalva, *Orígenes y desarrollo de la guerra santa en la Península Ibérica* (Madrid, 2016), with Palacios Ontalva, *Hombres de religión y guerra: Cruzada y guerra santa en la Edad Media peninsular (siglos X–XV)* (Madrid, 2018), and with Fernandes and Palacios Ontalva, *La Reconquista: Ideología y justificación de la Guerra Santa peninsular* (Madrid, 2019).

Janna Bianchini
is an Associate Professor of History at the University of Maryland and the author of *The Queen's Hand: Power and Authority in the Reign of Queen Berenguela of Castile* (Philadelphia, 2012). Her articles have appeared widely in such journals as *Early Medieval Europe*, the *Journal of Medieval Iberian Studies*, and the *Journal of Medieval History*.

Bárbara Boloix-Gallardo
is Associate Professor of Arabic and Islamic Studies in the Department of Semitic Studies at the University of Granada. Her main research interests concern the history of the Nasrid Kingdom of Granada (13th–15th centuries), to which she has devoted several publications and papers in both national and international publications and conferences. Among her main publications are *De la taifa de Arjona al Reino nazarí de Granada (1232–1246)* (Jaén, 2006), *Las Sultanas de la Alhambra. Las grandes desconocidas del Reino Nazarí de Granada (siglos XIII–XV)* (Granada, 2013), "The Genealogical Legitimization of the

Nasrid Dynasty (13th–15th Centuries): The Alleged Anṣārī Origins of the Banū Naṣr" (2014), *Ibn al-Aḥmar. Vida y reinado del primer sultán de Granada (1195–1273)*, (Granada, 2017).

Cristina Catalina
teaches in the Department of Philosophy and Society at the Universidad Complutense in Madrid. She was previously a pre-doctoral research grant holder with the Institute of History at the CSIC and received her PhD from the Universidad Complutense. Her work combines methodologies and analytical perspectives from history, philosophy, and historical sociology and has appeared in such journals as the *Journal of Medieval Iberian Studies* and the *Anales del seminario de historia de la filosofía*.

Francisco García Fitz
is a Professor of Medieval History at the Universidad de Extremadura. He is the author of many monographs, including *Ejércitos y actividades guerreras en la Edad Media europea* (Madrid, 1998), *Castilla y León frente al Islam: Estrategias de expansión y tácticas militares (siglos XI al XIII)* (Seville, 1998), *La Edad Media, Guerra e ideología: Justificaciones religiosas y jurídicas* (Madrid, 2003), *Las Navas de Tolosa* (Barcelona, 2005), *La Reconquista*, (Granada, 2010), as well as co-editor with Feliciano Novoa of *Cruzados en la Reconquista* (Madrid, 2014).

Francisco García-Serrano
is a Professor of History in the Department of Humanities at Saint Louis University, Madrid Campus. He also serves as the Director of Ibero-American Studies. He has published *Preachers of the City: The Expansion of the Dominican Order in Castile, 1217–1348* (New Orleans, 1997), and edited the volume *The Friars and their Influence in Medieval Spain* (Amsterdam, 2018). His scholarly research focuses on the influence of the Mendicant Orders in Iberia during the late Middle Ages and on social relations, religious identity and interfaith relations and can be found in several recent edited volumes.

Edward L. Holt
is an Assistant Professor of History at Grambling State University and a 2019–2020 Fellow with the Madrid Institute for Advanced Study. His articles have appeared in *al-Masaq*, the *Bulletin for Spanish and Portuguese Historical Studies, Crusades*, and *English Language Notes* and have received the Best Early Career Article Prize from ASPHS and the Bernard Hamilton Essay Prize from the

SSCLE. He is currently working on a monograph on royal leadership and political liturgy in medieval Iberia.

Kyle C. Lincoln

is an Associate Lecturer of History at the University of Wisconsin-La Crosse. He co-edited *King Alfonso VIII: Government, Family, and War* (New York, 2019), and is finishing a monograph on the episcopate in the kingdom of Castile during the reign of Alfonso VIII of Castile. He also is currently revising two medieval studies textbook projects for the Reacting to the Past Consortium, on the topics of the Fourth Crusade and the Conquest of Granada in 1492. His articles have appeared in the *Journal of Medieval History, eHumanista, Crusades*, the *Bulletin of Medieval Canon Law*, and the *Revista Chilena de Estudios Medievales*, as well as in several edited volumes.

Miriam Shadis

is Associate Professor of History at Ohio University. She is the author of *Berenguela of Castile (1180–1246) and Her Family: Political Women in the High Middle Ages* (New York, 2009) and her articles have appeared in edited volumes and journals such as *History Compass* and the *Journal of Medieval Iberian Studies*.

Teresa Witcombe

is a Leverhulme Visiting Research Fellow at the Universidad Autónoma de Madrid, also affiliated with the CSIC-CCHS. She was previously a Junior Research Fellow at the Institute of Historical Research in London, and received her PhD from the University of Exeter. She works on the intellectual, cultural and religious history of Castile in the twelfth and thirteenth centuries, and has articles published in the *Journal of Medieval Iberian Studies* and the *Bulletin for Spanish and Portuguese Historical Studies*. She is in the process of publishing a monograph on Bishop Maurice of Burgos.

Fernando III and His World

Edward L. Holt and Teresa Witcombe

> Here lies the most illustrious King Fernando of Castile, and of Toledo, León, Galicia, Seville, Córdoba, Murcia, and Jaén, who conquered all *Hispania*...
> TOMB of FERNANDO III, Seville Cathedral[1]

∴

If, by the end of his life, King Fernando III could be remembered thus by his descendants, such success could hardly have been imagined in the late summer of 1217, when, as a teenager, he was whisked away from the court of his father, Alfonso IX of León, to be declared king of Castile. Fernando faced considerable opposition throughout the early years of his reign: first, from his father in León, and then from his own discontented nobility, who, in the early 1220s, went so far as to invite Louis VIII of France to take over the Castilian throne.[2] It was an inauspicious start to a reign that was to become without doubt one of the most celebrated in medieval Spanish history.

The thirty-five years of Fernando's rule, from his accession in 1217 until his death in 1252, was a period of substantial, and at times, dramatic political and cultural change across the Iberian Peninsula. Fernando was the son of Berenguela of Castile and Alfonso IX of León, and heir to two kingdoms that he would ultimately unite after almost a century of conflict. However his reign is best known for the series of military victories led by Fernando into al-Andalus, the territory of the Almohad Empire, lands which had lain under Islamic rule since the eighth century. It was for this territorial expansion to the south and the accompanying extension of the Church into the lands of Islam that

---

1 *Hic iacet illustrissimus rex Ferrandus Castelle et Toleti, Legionis, Gallizie, Sibillie, Cordube, Murcie et Iaheni, qui totam Hispaniam conquisivit*: Latin text as reproduced in Dodds, Menocal and Krasner, *The Arts of Intimacy*, 200; see also Nickson, "Remembering Fernando," 180–1.
2 Hernández, "La corte de Fernando III," 103–56, esp. 110–9; Rodríguez López, "Quod alienus regnet." Simon Barton spoke further about the instability of Fernando's early years at the conference *San Fernando and His Age*, at which many of these papers were first read in Madrid in October 2017.

Fernando would be lionized at the court of his son, Alfonso X.³ The resulting cult culminated in his canonization in 1671 by Pope Clement X, on which occasion Fernando was eulogized for his propagation of the Catholic faith through military conquest.⁴

Whether precipitated by divine inspiration (as the *Latin Chronicle of the Kings of Castile* would have it) or by the need to unite a fractious nobility at a moment of Almohad weakness, there can be no doubt that the wars embarked upon by Fernando in July 1224 were to fundamentally reshape the geopolitical landscape of the Iberian Peninsula.⁵ By the time of his death, Fernando had conquered Jaén, Murcia, Córdoba and Seville, and the remaining bastion of Islamic power in the south, the Nasrid kingdom of Granada, was ruled by Fernando's ally, Muḥammad I. The imagery of a triumphant, Christian conquest – the twin victories of the sword and the cross – is one that came, much later, to be elaborated upon in historiographical discussions of "Reconquista," the echoes of which have dominated popular and academic discourse surrounding medieval Spain until relatively recently.⁶ The thirteenth century marked a turning point in the series of territorial wars that had unfolded on the borders between Castile and her Islamic neighbors. A succession of Castilian victories, from the battle of Las Navas de Tolosa in 1212, led by Fernando's grandfather Alfonso VIII, heralded this as a period of permanent conquest and

---

3 The bibliography on Fernando's legacy at the court of Alfonso X is vast; see especially Szpeich, "Founding Father to Pious Son"; Nickson, "Remembering Fernando"; González Jiménez, *Alfonso X*; Salvador Martínez, *Alfonso X*; O'Callaghan, *The Learned King*; idem, *Alfonso X*; Doubleday, *Wise King*.

4 Janna Bianchini has pointed out that this "made him a figure of such cultural stature that it can be difficult to tease the historical fact of his life away from its mythos." Bianchini, *The Queen's Hand*, 1. For the canonization of Fernando III, see Rodríguez Lopez, "Fernando III." It should be noted that this entry was changed with the promulgation of a new Roman Martyrology in 2001, revised in light of the decrees of the Second Vatican Council. For the revised entry, see *Martyrologium Romanum* (2001), 295. For the relevant decree of the Second Vatican Council, see Pope Paul VI, *Sacrosanctum concilium*, §92c, promulgated December 4, 1963. San Fernando is today patron saint of Seville, among many other places, as well as of the Spanish army's Engineering Corps.

5 CLRC, 62. There can be no doubt that Fernando was taking advantage of a moment of crisis in the Almohad succession; see Lomax, *Reconquest of Spain*, 134–54.

6 The historiographical narratives surrounding the theory of "Reconquista" have been comprehensively deconstructed in modern scholarship, and there is a vast bibliography on the subject. For a summary of the term and its legacy, see Kosto, "Reconquest, Renaissance and the Histories of Iberia," 93–116; and Barton, *Brides and Concubines*, 8–12; Linehan, *History and the Historians*; idem, "The invention of Toledo," 123–41; Garcia Sanjuán, "Rejecting Al-Andalus," 127–45; Powers, *Society*; and Fletcher, "Reconquest and Crusade in Spain," 31–47, as well as the recent survey by Fancy, "The new *convivencia*," concerning the debates between Emilio González Ferrín and Alejandro García Sanjuán.

expansion to the south. Yet even if, as was noted recently by Teófilo Ruiz, "Las Navas de Tolosa opened the door for Christian hegemony in the Peninsula,"[7] this much can hardly have been clear to the Castilian knights chastised just one year later, in 1213, by the archbishop of Toledo for selling their military services to the Muslims.[8] Fernando's own success relied, at times, on the cooperation of Muslim allies, as Francisco García Fitz and Bárbara Boloix-Gallardo discuss in the chapters ahead. Recent scholarship has raised important questions about Fernando's aims and ambition in al-Andalus, and, especially, the extent to which Castilian attitudes towards Islam were influenced by extra-peninsular notions of crusade, propagated by the papacy.[9] It is one of the aims of this volume to bring the light of fresh scholarship to bear on Fernando's military endeavors, his motivations and goals, and the ever-shifting networks of power and patronage upon which his military success was built.

Fernando's world was dynamic, multi-lingual, and expanding, not just to the south but also in the north of the Iberian Peninsula. Arabic continued to be widely spoken and written in Toledo, and elsewhere, Romance (medieval Castilian) came increasingly to appear in written documents, in addition to Latin. Territories to the north east of Castile on the Navarrese border had only recently been secured by Alfonso VIII, and Fernando would go much further. He acceded to the Leonese Crown on his father's death in 1230, permanently uniting the two kingdoms as Castile-León and thereby neutralizing one of the most serious threats to Castile's northern borders.[10] Moreover, on a dynastic level, the Castilian Crown sustained family networks that stretched far beyond the Peninsula and spread roots into the major royal houses of medieval Europe. Lasting ties were established with the French royal house when, in 1204, Alfonso VIII's daughter Blanca (Fernando's aunt) was sent to the Parisian court to marry Louis VIII, thereby becoming the powerful Queen Blanche.[11] Further French connections, this time between Fernando and the abbey of Fontevraud, will become apparent in Martín Alvira's essay in this volume. In November 1219, following the ambassadorial delegation of Bishop Maurice of Burgos,

---

7   Ruiz, "Alfonso VIII: An Introduction," 4. For more on the battle and the events surrounding it, see Alvira, *Las Navas de Tolosa*.
8   Pick, *Conflict and Coexistence*, 211–2.
9   For the most important publications on this question, see Pick, *Conflict and Coexistence*; Smith, "'Soli Hispani'? Innocent III and Las Navas de Tolosa," 487–513; idem, "Las Navas and the restoration of Spain," 39–43; Ayala Martínez and Palacios Ontalva, *Hombres de religión y guerra*; Ayala Martínez and Ríos Saloma, *Fernando III: tiempo de cruzada*; García Fitz, *Relaciones políticas*; and Lomax, *Reconquest*.
10 For more on these events, see Bianchini, *The Queen's Hand*, 180–208.
11 See the recent biography by Grant, *Blanche of Castile*.

Fernando himself married into two imperial lineages by taking the hand of Princess Beatriz, daughter of Philip of Swabia and granddaughter of the Byzantine Emperor Isaac II Angelos. Beatriz would bear him at least ten children, including seven sons. Following her death, Fernando married again in 1237, this time into the French aristocracy, in the person of Juana, heir of the counts of Ponthieu. Yet another international match was made in 1224, when Fernando's sister, Berenguela, was married to John of Brienne, king of Jerusalem. It was within these networks of powerful women and men, spanning much of medieval Europe, that the Castilian king negotiated his own royal identity. The construction and curation of regal power through royal individuals and institutions such as the monastery of Las Huelgas in Burgos, and also by means of the liturgy, is another key theme that is explored in the pages to come, notably in the essays of Edward Holt, Janna Bianchini, and Miriam Shadis.

Another central thread running throughout this volume is the development of the Castilian Church during the reign of Fernando. Whilst he was extending the limits of the Church to the south, he was also squeezing the churches and cathedrals of the north to fund his endeavors.[12] Nonetheless, this was a time of rapid cultural change in the religious life of the Peninsula. When the Leonese chronicler Lucas of Tuy commented on the splendor of the new buildings around him, he was referring to the kingdom's first Gothic cathedrals, founded in Burgos in 1221 and Toledo in 1226.[13] Masons, artists, musicians and craftsmen swelled the long-established stream of pilgrims traversing northern Castile-León along the Camino de Santiago. Scholars from across medieval Europe had been drawn to the Iberian Peninsula during the twelfth century, but it was not until the early thirteenth that the *studia* of Palencia and Salamanca emerged as important intellectual centers.[14] Some of the most senior clergy to serve the Castilian Church and court, such as Archbishop Rodrigo of Toledo (1209–1247) and Bishop Maurice of Burgos (1213–1238), maintained regular political, cultural and intellectual ties with the ultramontane world.[15] The mendicant orders also established themselves in the kingdom; their role in populating the

---

12 For the most important scholarship on the Castilian Church in the thirteenth century, see Linehan, *The Spanish Church and the Papacy*, as well as idem, *Spanish Church and Society*.

13 *CM*, IV.95. On these foundations, see Karge, *La catedral de Burgos*; Nickson, *Toledo Cathedral*; Abella, "Opus francigenum," 69–104; Catalunya, "Thirteenth-Century *Organistae*," 105–40; and Witcombe, "Building Heaven on Earth," 46–60.

14 The *studium* at Palencia was founded by Alfonso VIII of Castile, see Rucquoi, "La double vie"; the one in Salamanca was founded by Alfonso IX of León in 1218, see Martín Martín, "Origen y desarrollo."

15 See Pick, *Conflict and Coexistence*; idem, "Michael Scot"; Ayala Martínez, *Ibn Tumart*.

newly conquered territories is discussed by Francisco García-Serrano in this volume.¹⁶ Fernando had come to the throne just two years after the Fourth Lateran Council, held under Pope Innocent III in 1215. This was one of the most important events in the history of the medieval Church, and in its aftermath, the papacy made every effort to tighten its grip over the regional churches of the Latin West, although this agenda was met with an undoubtedly muted reception in Castile-León.¹⁷ Nonetheless, traffic between Rome and the Peninsula did show signs of increasing under Fernando, especially in terms of appeals to the papal court and the appointment of judges-delegate. An alternative perspective on the reception of papal reform in Castile is provided by Cristina Catalina in the final essay in this volume.

The essays presented here provide a series of new perspectives on Fernando III and the political, cultural and religious history of Castile-León during his lifetime, bringing together scholars from Spain, the US, and the UK, and, from departments of history, and also medieval languages, and philosophy. They add an important and much-needed voice to scholarly debates on Fernando, who, despite his importance, is yet to be the subject of a modern scholarly biography, unlike his mother and aunt, and several other of his royal predecessors.¹⁸ A key publication for our understanding of Fernando remains the magisterial *Reinado y diplomas de Fernando III* by Julio González, published between 1980 and 1986, including a collection of charters that is fundamental to modern scholarship on the monarch, although in need of updating.¹⁹ More recently, Ana Rodríguez López, Francisco Hernández, Carlos de Ayala Martínez and Martín Ríos Saloma, among others, have provided crucial analyses of the political history of the reign.²⁰ Similarly, Janna Bianchini's research

---

16   See also García-Serrano, *The Friars and their Influence*.
17   On the impact of the Lateran Council in Castile-León, see Linehan, "Councils and Synods"; idem, *The Spanish Church and the Papacy*, 4–19; idem, "A Papal Legation and its aftermath," 236–56; O'Callaghan, "Innocent III," 317–35; and García y García, "Innocent III," 337–50.
18   On Berenguela: Shadis, *Berenguela of Castile*; Bianchini, *The Queen's Hand*. On Blanche: Grant, *Blanche of Castile*. For earlier comparisons, see the publications of Reilly, *The Kingdom of León-Castilla under Queen Urraca*; idem, *The Kingdom of León-Castilla under Alfonso IV*; and likewise, idem, *The Kingdom of León-Castilla under Alfonso VII*; Smith, Gómez, and Lincoln, *Alfonso VII*. It should be noted that there are numerous works of popular history dedicated to Fernando, such as González Jiménez, *Fernando III el Santo* and Mena, *Entre la cruz y la espada: San Fernando*.
19   *Fernando III*.
20   See Rodríguez López, *La consolidación territorial*; idem, "Linajes nobiliarios"; idem, "Quod alienus regnet"; idem, "La preciosa transmisión"; Hernández, "La corte de Fernando III";

into Berenguela, Fernando's mother, has supplied an alternative perspective onto Fernando's court and the nature of his rule in the first half of the thirteenth century.[21] A conference held in León in 2001 to celebrate the eight-hundredth anniversary of Fernando's birth brought together many of the key voices in thirteenth-century Castilian history, whilst more recently, a special issue of the *Bulletin for Spanish and Portuguese Historical Studies* was dedicated to the reign of Fernando.[22]

The essays in the present volume build upon the important work of these scholars, while also integrating new methodologies and fresh interpretative lenses, including sociological and literary history, intercultural interactions, the history of gender and power networks, and the study of liturgy. The volume is structured loosely around the two central themes of the "sword" and the "cross," the two bulwarks of Fernando's reign that interwove continually in underpinning the Castilian-Leonese Crown throughout the first half of the thirteenth century. Fernando stands at the center of this book, but the authors have approached his reign from a variety of perspectives, drawing widely on sources that include Arabic chronicles and poetry, liturgical documents, clerical verse in Romance, and a previously unknown *vidimus*, as well as the narrative and diplomatic sources that are more familiar to scholars of this period. Together, these essays raise thought-provoking new questions about Fernando's reign, and invite the reader to re-evaluate and re-contextualize the central ideas that have defined and shaped the historiographical discourse of this period.

The focus of these essays is decidedly on the kingdom of Castile (and, after 1230, León) in the lifetime of Fernando III, but nonetheless it is hoped that the issues discussed here will allow for broader comparisons. One of the most important conclusions to emerge from the present collection is the ease with which people and ideas crossed geopolitical and cultural boundaries and the breadth and depth of the connections – dynastic, cultural, religious and political – between Castile and the world around it in the early thirteenth century; not only its peninsular neighbors, including the Islamic rulers to the south, but also across Latin Christendom, including France, the papal curia, the Holy Roman Empire, and England. By the same token, it is hoped that scholars of medieval Europe will find much that is of value in the essays

---

      Ayala Martínez and Ríos Saloma, *Fernando III: tiempo de cruzada*; Holt, "*In eo tempore*"; Nieto Soria, "La monarquía fundacional de Fernando III"; Metzeltin, "Fernando III."

21 Bianchini, *The Queen's Hand*.

22 *Fernando III y su tiempo (1201–1252)*; the relevant issue of the *Bulletin for Spanish and Portuguese Historical Studies* is vol. 42, no. 1 (2017).

presented here, especially on the themes of medieval kingship, the thirteenth-century Church, Christian-Muslim relations, and religious and cultural borderlands in the middle ages.

Fernando's military endeavors against the Almohads – and the intentions and political strategies that underpinned them – lie at the heart of the first three essays presented in this volume. In Chapter One, "Empire and Crusade under Fernando III," Carlos de Ayala Martínez explores the ways in which Hispanic imperial ambitions were awakened under Fernando, and married to the new crusading ideas that came increasingly to influence the rhetoric around war with the Islamic south. These combined concepts reached their zenith towards the end of Fernando's life through his proposed crusade to North Africa, thus effectively reimagining the Castilian-Leonese policy of conquest in line with the aims of Pope Innocent IV towards conversion in North Africa.

Francisco García Fitz's contribution in Chapter Two explores the question of how Fernando III perceived the Andalusi Muslims who were to serve as both his enemies and at times also his allies throughout the course of his reign. In "The Man 'Who Broke and Destroyed All of His Enemies': The Military Action of Fernando III," García Fitz problematizes the historiographical legacy of Fernando as inscribed in stone in the king's funerary epitaphs in Seville cathedral. By comparing the rhetoric of conquest, generated in the political discourse surrounding Fernando's legacy, with the realities of the king's reliance on mutually beneficial treatises with Muslim rulers, as seen in the Castilian-Leonese chronicles, this chapter juxtaposes ideological discourse with the political reality of Fernando's rule.

A view of Iberian politics "from right to left" is provided by Bárbara Boloix-Gallardo in Chapter Three. Her essay, "Fernando III and Muḥammad I: A Time of Collaboration between Two 'Incompatible Worlds'," investigates the same set of military and political developments, however, approached through the Arabic sources pertaining to the Almohad south. From this perspective, Boloix-Gallardo sheds an important light on the relationship between the Nasrid emir, Muḥammad I, and the Castilian Crown between 1232 and 1252, thereby reformulating scholarly discussions about Fernando's interactions with Muslim polities to the south and the complexity of Muslim-Christian relations in the Peninsula more generally.

Bringing together both sword and cross, Kyle Lincoln's essay, "*In exercitu loco eius pontificalia exercet*: Warrior Clerics in the Era of Fernando III" in Chapter Four explores the role of bishops and secular clergy in the wars against al-Andalus, focusing on the physical place of the warrior-bishop in the armies of Fernando III. Using legal, narrative, and diplomatic sources, he investigates the ways in which military organization was inflected by clerical participation, and how changes in the nature of conquest in Fernando's era altered the ways in which clerics could participate.

Fernando III's connections with the abbey of Fontevraud are the subject of Martín Alvira's contribution in Chapter Five, "*Dilecta consanguinea mea*: Fernando III's Donation to a Nun of Fontevraud." This chapter not only sheds light on Fernando's relationship with a nun of that house, Alix of Blois, but also on the depth and variety of the connections between the Castilian Crown and the imperial and royal dynasties of Latin Europe, as well as bringing new information to bear on the history of Fontevraud itself. In this chapter, Alvira analyzes a previously unknown document – a *vidimus*, or attested copy, made in 1250, of a donation from Fernando III to Alix of Blois at Fontevraud in 1220. A transcription of this important document is included as an appendix to the chapter.

The strength of the monarch was underpinned by precisely such links between Crown and Church. In Chapter Six, "*Laudes Regiae*: Liturgy and Royal Power in Thirteenth-Century Castile-León," Edward Holt brings a new perspective to the construction and legitimization of regal power in Castile through his examination of the ways in which the liturgy manifested both a performance of regal power and a space within which that power could be negotiated. Through his analysis of the *Missa pro rege* (the Mass in favor of the king) and the remembrance of deceased monarchs, Holt argues for the need to examine liturgical performances as a means to understand one of the more regular interfaces of the monarchical image with both the Church and the wider public.

The creation of tradition and royal legitimization in Castile is a theme that is also explored in Chapter Seven, "'At the Command of the Infantas': Royal Women at Las Huelgas in the Thirteenth Century." In this chapter, Janna Bianchini investigates the often highly important political roles held by three royal women, the Castilian infantas, housed at the monastery of Las Huelgas in Burgos. Historians have generally considered many of these roles lost with the dissolution of the Infantazgo in the twelfth century, yet, as Bianchini demonstrates, during the thirteenth century, the infantas Constanza II, Constanza III, and Berenguela Fernández – respectively, an aunt, sister, and daughter of Fernando III – each exercised lordship in the royal monastery of Las Huelgas de Burgos. This chapter considers these three infantas' authority at Las Huelgas as a vestige of royal women's sacral and lordly roles in the Infantazgo.

In "Family and Friends: Women at the Court of Fernando III," Miriam Shadis further explores the networks of regal power established at the court of Fernando by considering the many roles of the women whose lives were intertwined with the major events of this period, and whose connections and influence not only supported Castilian regal power but constituted a key element of it. Chapter Eight surveys the numerous women who were present at or interacted with the court of Fernando III, including not only the queens (his mother, Berenguela, his wives, Beatriz and Juana), other royal and noble women (his many sisters and the wives of his male followers), religious women (notably the abbesses of San Andrés de Arroyo and Las Huelgas de Burgos), but also, the many women who counted among the workers at the court, bringing to the fore voices that have been often overwritten both in modern scholarship and in the sources themselves.

Chapter Nine, "The Peculiarities of Frontier Religious Authority in the Age of Fernando III" by Francisco García-Serrano, considers the effects of the territorial expansion of Fernando's reign on the Castilian Church through a study of the developing mendicant orders and their place in the society of Castile. The followers of both St Francis and St Dominic lost no time in establishing their respective orders in Castile from the earliest years of their development. On the kingdom's southern frontier, however, they faced quite unique circumstances; newly conquered lands without pre-existing parochial networks and close to the ever-present threat of Islam. These were circumstances that shaped the development of the mendicant orders in the Peninsula, whilst, at the same time, establishing them as key players in Fernando III's efforts to expand his control to the south.

Finally, in Chapter Ten, Cristina Catalina sheds an important new light on the reception of papal ideas in Castile under Fernando III in her paper entitled "Literary Expressions of Pastoral Reform during the Reign of Fernando III." In a period when the Roman pontiff was extending his reach into regional churches around Latin Europe, this chapter explores new literary routes for the integration of pastoral reform ideas in Castile, and the manifestation of these ideas in the vernacular lyric poetry of the *Mester de Clerecía*, the "Craft of the Clergy," of which one of the key proponents was Gonzalo de Berceo (c.1197–c.1264). Through her sociological approach to the reception of pastoral reform, Catalina provides a valuable new perspective on the development of moral theology and pastoral care in Castile during this period.

Works Cited

Primary Sources (Published)

Charlo Brea, Luis, ed. *Chronica latina regum Castellae*. In *Chronica Hispana Saeculi XIII*, ed. Luis Charlo Brea, Juan Estévez Sola and Rocío Carande Herrero. Vol. 73 of *Corpus Christianorum: Continuatio medievalis*, 7–118. Turnhout: Brepols, 1997.

Lucas of Tuy. *Chronicon mundi*. Ed. Emma Falque Rey. Vol. 74 of *Corpus Christianorum: Continuatio mediaeualis*. Turnhout: Brepols, 2003.

Martyrologium Romanum. Rome: C.L.V. Edizioni liturgiche, 1998.

Martyrologium Romanum. Città del Vaticano: Libreria editrice vaticana, 2001.

Pope Paul VI. *Sacrosanctum concilium*, §92c, promulgated December 4, 1963.

Secondary Sources

Abella, P. "Opus francigenum en el Iter francorum: el fecundo siglo XIII y la nueva arquitectura de Castilla." *Portium: Revista d'Estudis Medievals* 1 (2011): 69–104.

Alvira, Martín. *Las Navas de Tolosa, 1212: Idea, liturgia y memoria de la batalla*. Madrid: Sílex, 2012.

Ayala Martínez, Carlos de and Martín Ríos Saloma. *Fernando III: tiempo de cruzada*. Madrid: Sílex, 2012.

Ayala Martínez, Carlos de. *Ibn Tumart, el Arzobispo Jiménez de Rada, y la "Cuestion sobre Dios."* Madrid: Ediciones de La Ergástula, 2017.

Ayala Martínez, Carlos de. "La realeza en a la cronística castellano-leonesa del siglo XIII: La imagen de Fernando III." In *Monarquía, crónicas, archivos, y cancillerías en los reinos hispano-cristianos: siglos XIII–XV*, ed. Esteban Sarasa Sánchez, 247–276. Zaragoza: Insitución Fernando el Católico, 2014.

Ayala Martínez, Carlos de and J. Santiago Palacios Ontalva, eds. *Hombres de guerra y de religión: Cruzada y guerra santa en la Edad Media peninsular (siglos x–xv)*. Madrid: Sílex, 2018.

Barton, Simon. *Conquerors, Brides, and Concubines: Interfaith Relations and Social Power in Medieval Iberia*. Philadelphia: University of Pennsylvania Press, 2015.

Bianchini, Janna. *The Queen's Hand: Power and Authority in the Reign of Berenguela of Castile*. Philadelphia: University of Pennsylvania Press, 2012.

Bulletin for Spanish and Portuguese Historical Studies 42, no. 1 (2017).

Catalunya, David. "Thirteenth-Century *Organistae* in Castile." *Orgelpark Research Reports* 4 (2017): 105–140.

Dodds, Jerrilynn, María Rosa Menocal and Abigail Krasner Balbale. *The Arts of Intimacy: Christians, Jews, and Muslims in the Making of Castilian Culture*. New Haven: Yale University Press, 2009.

Doubleday, Simon. *The Wise King: A Christian prince, Muslim Spain, and the Birth of the Renaissance*. New York: Basic Books, 2015.

Fancy, Hussein. "The new convivencia." *Journal of Medieval Iberian Studies* 11, no. 3 (2019): 295–305.

Fernando III y su tiempo (1201–1252). León: Fundación Sánchez Albornoz, 2003.

Fletcher, Richard. "Reconquest and Crusade in Spain 1050–1150." *Transactions of the Royal Historical Society* 5, no. 37 (1987): 31–47.

García Fitz, Francisco. *Relaciones políticas y guerra. La experiencia castellano-leonesa frente al Islam. Siglos XI–XIII*. Seville: Universidad de Sevilla, 2002.

García y García, Antonio. "Innocent III and the Kingdom of Castile." In *Innocent III and his world*, ed. John C. Moore, 337–350. Aldershot: Ashgate, 1999.

García-Sanjuán, Alejandro. "Rejecting al-Andalus, exalting the Reconquista: historical memory in contemporary Spain." *Journal of Medieval Iberian Studies* 10, no. 1 (2018): 127–145.

García-Serrano, Francisco, ed. *The Friars and their Influence in Medieval Spain*. Amsterdam: Amsterdam University Press, 2018.

González Jiménez, Manuel. *Alfonso X: El Sabio*. Barcelona: Ariel, 2004.

González Jiménez, Manuel. *Fernando III, el santo*. Seville: Fundación José Manuel Lara, 2011.

González, Julio. *El reino de Castilla en la época de Alfonso VIII*, 3 vols. Madrid: CSIC, 1960.

González, Julio, ed. *Reinado y diplomas de Fernando III*, 3 vols. Córdoba: Monte de Piedad y Caja de Ahorros de Córdoba, 1983.

Grant, Lindy. *Blanche of Castile, Queen of France: Power, Religion and Culture in the Thirteenth Century*. New Haven: Yale University Press, 2016.

Hernández, Francisco. "La corte de Fernando III y la casa real de Francia: documentos, crónicas, monumentos." In *Fernando III y su tiempo (1201–1252): VIII Congreso de Estudios Medievales*, 103–156. León: Fundación Sánchez Albornoz, 2003.

Holt, Edward L. "*In eo tempore*: The Circulation of News and Reputation in the Charters of Fernando III." *Bulletin for Spanish and Portuguese Historical Studies* 42, no. 1 (2017): 3–22. DOI: https://doi.org/10.26431/0739-182X.1253.

Karge, Henrik. *La catedral de Burgos y la arquitectura del siglo XIII en Francia y España*. Valladolid: Junta de Castilla y León, 1995.

Kosto, Adam. "Reconquest, Renaissance and the Histories of Iberia, c. 1000–1200." In *European Transformations: The Long Twelfth Century*, ed. Thomas Noble and John van Engen, 93–116. Notre Dame: University of Notre Dame Press, 2012.

Linehan, Peter. "Columpna firmissima: D. Gil Torres, the cardinal of Zamora." In *Cross, Crescent and Conversion: Studies on Medieval Spain and Christendom in Memory of Richard Fletcher*, ed. Simon Barton and Peter Linehan, 241–262. Leiden: Brill, 2008.

Linehan, Peter. "Councils and Synods in Thirteenth-Century Castile and Aragon." *Studies in Church History* 7 (1971): 101–111.

Linehan, Peter. *History and Historian of Medieval Spain*. Oxford: Oxford University Press, 1993.

Linehan, Peter. *Spain, 1157–1300: a Partible inheritance*. Oxford: Blackwell Publishing, 2008.

Linehan, Peter. *The Spanish Church and the Papacy in the Thirteenth Century*. Cambridge: Cambridge University Press, 1971.

Linehan, Peter, and Francisco Hernández. *The Mozarabic Cardinal: The life and times of Gonzalo Pérez Gudiel.* Florence: Edizioni del Galluzzo, 2004.

Linehan, Peter and José Carlos de Lera Maíllo. *Las postrimerías de un obispo alfonsino: Don Suero Pérez, el de Zamora.* Zamora: Semuret, 2003.

Lomax, Derek. *The Reconquest of Spain.* New York: Longman, 1978.

Martin, Georges. *Les juges de Castille: mentalités et discours historique dans l'Espane médiévale.* Paris: Klincksieck, 1992.

Martín Martín, José Luis. "Origen y desarrollo de la Universidad de Salamanca, siglos XIII–XIV." In *La Universidad de Salamanca: ochocientos años,* ed. Luis Enrique Rodríguez-San Pedro Bezares, 13–50. Salamanca: Universidad de Salamanca, 2018.

Mena, José María. *Entre la cruz y la espada: San Fernando.* Sevilla: R. C. Editor, 1990.

Metzeltin, Michael. "Fernando III: la imagen cronística de un rey." In *Homenaje Carlos Alvar,* ed. Sarah Finci et al., 251–268. San Millán de Cogolla: Cilengua, 2016.

Nickson, Tom. "Remembering Fernando: Multilingualism in Medieval Iberia." In *Viewing Inscriptions in the Late Antique and Medieval World,* ed. Anthony Eastmond, 170–186. Cambridge: Cambridge University Press, 2015.

Nickson, Tom. *Toledo Cathedral: Building Histories in Medieval Castile.* University Park: Pennsylvania State University Press, 2015.

Nieto Soria, José Manuel. "La monarquía fundacional de Fernando III." In *Fernando III y su tiempo (1201–1252): VIII Congreso de Estudios Medievales,* 31–66. León: Fundación Sánchez Albornoz, 2003.

O'Callaghan, Joseph. *Alfonso X, the Justinian of His Age: Law and Justice in Thirteenth-Century Castile.* Ithaca: Cornell University Press, 2019.

O'Callaghan, Joseph. "Innocent III and the Kingdoms of Castile and Leon." In *Innocent III and his world,* ed. John C. Moore, 317–335. Aldershot: Ashgate, 1999.

O'Callaghan, Joseph. *The Learned King: The Reign of Alfonso X of Castile.* Philadelphia: University of Pennsylvania Press, 1993.

O'Callaghan, Joseph. *Reconquest and Crusade in Medieval Spain.* Philadelphia: University of Pennsylvania Press, 2003.

Pick, Lucy. *Conflict and Coexistence: Archbishop Rodrigo and the Muslims and Jews of Medieval Spain.* Ann Arbor: University of Michigan, 2004.

Pick, Lucy. "Michael Scot in Toledo: *Natura Naturens* and the Hierachy of Being." *Traditio* 53 (1998): 93–116.

Powers, James. *A Society Organized for War: The Iberian Municipal Militias in the Central Middle Ages, 1000–1284.* Berkeley: University of California Press, 1988.

Reilly, Bernard F. *The Kingdom of León-Castilla under King Alfonso VI 1065–1109.* Princeton: University of Princeton Press, 1988.

Reilly, Bernard F. *The Kingdom of León-Castilla under King Alfonso VII 1126–1157.* Philadelphia: University of Pennsylvania Press. 1998.

Reilly, Bernard F. *The Kingdom of León-Castilla under Queen Urraca, 1109–1126*. Princeton: University of Princeton Press, 1982.

Ríos Saloma, Martín. "La figura de Fernando III en la historiografía moderna y contemporánea." In *Fernando III: tiempo de cruzada*, ed. Carlos de Ayala Martínez and Martín Ríos Saloma, 491–518. Madrid: Sílex, 2012.

Rodríguez López, Ana. "Fernando III el Santo (1217–1252). Evolución historiográfica, canonización, y utilización política." In *Miscel·lania en homenatge al padre Agustí Altisent*, ed. Facultad de Filosofía y Letras de Barcelona, 573–588. Tarragona: Diputación de Tarragona, 1991.

Rodríguez López, Ana. *La consolidación territorial de la monarquía feudal castellana: Expansión y fronteras durante el reinado de Fernando III (1217–1252)*. Madrid: CSIC, 1994.

Rodríguez López, Ana. "La política eclesiástica de la monarquía castellano-leonesa durante el reinado de Fernando III." *Hispania* 48 (1998): 7–48.

Rodríguez López, Ana. "La preciosa transmisión: Memoria y Curia Regia en Castilla en la primera mitad del siglo XIII." In *La construcción medieval de la memoria regia*, ed. Pascual Martínez Sopena and Ana Rodríguez López, 295–304. Valencia: Universidad de Valencia, 2011.

Rodríguez López, Ana. "Linajes nobiliarios y monarquía castellano-leonesa en la primera mitad del siglo XIII." *Hispania* 53, no. 185 (1993): 841–859.

Rodríguez López, Ana. "'Quod alienus regnet et heredes expelatur': L'offre de trone de Castille au roi Louis VIII de France." *Le Moyen Age* 105 (1999): 109–128.

Rucquoi, Adeline. "La double vie de l'université de Palencia 1180–1250." *Studia Gratiana* 19 (1998): 723–774.

Ruiz, Teófilo. "Alfonso VIII: An Introduction." In *King Alfonso VIII of Castile: Government, Family, and War*, ed. Miguel Gómez, Damian Smith and Kyle C. Lincoln, 1–9. New York: Fordham University Press, 2019.

Ruiz-Gálvez Priego, Estrella. "'De reyes y de santos': San Fernando, de las crónicas de la edad media a las hagiografías del siglo XVII: permanencia y adaptación de una imagen." In *Homenaje a Henri Guerreiro: La hagiografía entre historia y literatura en la España de la Edad Media y el Siglo de Oro*, ed. Marc Vitse, 1015–1031. Madrid: Vervuert, 2005.

Salvador Martínez, H. *Alfonso X, el Sabio*. Trans. Odile Cisneros. Leiden: Brill, 2010.

Shadis, Miriam. *Berenguela of Castile and political women in the High Middle Ages*. New York: Palgrave, 2009.

Smith, Damian. "Las Navas and the restoration of Spain." *Journal of Medieval Iberian Studies* 4 (2012): 39–43.

Smith, Damian. "'Soli Hispani'? Innocent III and Las Navas de Tolosa." *Hispania Sacra* 51 (1999): 487–513.

Smith, Damian, Miguel D. Gómez and Kyle C. Lincoln. *King Alfonso VIII of Castile: Government, Family, and War*. New York: Fordham University Press, 2019.

Szpeich, Ryan. "From Founding Father to Pious Son: Filiation, Language, and Royal Inheritance in Alfonso X, the Learned." *Interfaces* 1 (2015): 209–235.

Witcombe, Teresa. "Building Heaven on Earth: Bishop Maurice and the *novam fabricam* of Burgos cathedral." *Bulletin for Spanish and Portuguese Historical Studies* 42, no. 1 (2017): 46–60. DOI: https://doi.org/10.26431/0739-182X.1252.

CHAPTER 1

Empire and Crusade under Fernando III

Carlos de Ayala Martínez

1   The Hispanic Imperial Project[1]

The imperial project that took shape in Hispania, a subject of intense historiographical controversy, was a political reality in the kingdom of León from the early tenth century until the mid-twelfth century.[2] It was a concept that passed through several iterations, and one that could hardly be considered either coherent or stable at any point throughout this period. However, it is possible to determine three key moments which illustrate its evolution over the course of these 250 years.

In the tenth century, the imperial idea was no more than theoretical, unconnected to any other reality beyond that of effective lordship, without entailing within this lordship any pretension towards assuming a title equivalent to that of a crowned emperor, in accordance with Roman-Carolingian tradition. Understood in this way, *imperium* was devoid of any hegemonic pretensions that might extend beyond effective lordship; it was never a title that kings attributed to themselves, and similar instances of this formula can be found outside of the Iberian Peninsula.[3]

Towards the end of the tenth century and throughout the first third of the eleventh, in the final phase of the Leonese kingdom, it is possible to detect a

---

1   The present study is part of the research project I+D *Violencia religiosa en la Edad Media peninsular: guerra, discurso apologético y relato historiográfico (ss. X–XV)*, funded by the *Agencia Estatal de Investigación del Ministerio de Economía y Competitividad del Gobierno de España* (referencia: HAR2016-74968-P).
2   This historiographical controversy has been comprehensively discussed by Hélène Sirantoine in her recent monograph on the subject: Sirantoine, *Imperator Hispaniae*. A general overview can be found in Bartolomé Bellón, "La *idea imperial* leonesa."
3   For instance, in Anglo-Saxon Britain where already in the eighth century, Bede the Venerable was using the verb *imperare* or the term *imperium* to describe the effective power that some Anglo-Saxon kings had begun to exercise over other kingdoms since the seventh century, kings who were to be referred to later by the ninth-century Anglo Saxon Chronicle as "bretwaldas" but never "emperors." Fanning, "Bede, Imperium and the Bretwaldas," 1–26. In France, Adalberon of Laon in his celebrated "Poem to King Robert" alludes to the *imperium* held by the Capetian kings, since they had descended from kings and emperors. Sirantoine, *Imperator Hispaniae*, 61.

conscious shift towards an imperial ideal which has a political context. It was a moment of intense neo-gothicization in which, by their employment of the *regnum-imperium* formula, not commonly used by the royal chancery,[4] the kings of León expressed a growing desire to identify their own power with lordship over the Peninsula as a whole, an argument central to neo-Visigothic ideology.[5] This wider politicization of what continued to be an amorphous imperial ambition would become more concrete under Alfonso VI (r. 1065–1109), who, in 1077, was the first ruler to adopt the title of *imperator totius Hispaniae*.[6] Alfonso's political ambition lies at the heart of the second key stage in the evolution of the Hispanic imperial project, one that would be difficult to understand without taking into account the pan-Hispanic experience of his grandfather, Sancho III of Pamplona, known as *rex ibericus* in 1030,[7] and of his father Fernando I, king of León and count of Castile, who embraced the definitive identification of the Isidorian neo-Visigothic tradition with León, by translating the relics of St. Isidore from Seville to their resting place in the basilica dedicated to the saint in León.[8] Alfonso VI was able to reconcile the diverse imperial traditions of León with a more hegemonic program strongly anchored in a neo-Visigothic tradition that incorporated the whole of the Peninsula, including al-Andalus.[9]

---

4   Sánchez Candeira, *El "regnum-imperium" leonés*. For a critical and well-documented contribution to this issue, see Isla Frez, *Realezas hispánicas*, 73–94.
5   In a document of Vermudo II, granted in 996 to the monastery of San Pelayo de Oviedo, we read the following: *Veremudus rex, dum possideret regnum Spanie et regeret universas urbes et provincias usque finibus terrae*. Fernández Conde, Torrente Fernández, and De la Noval Menéndez, *El Monasterio de San Pelayo de Oviedo*, I: no. 1. The king is aware that his power, derived from the Visigothic inheritance, is projected over the *regnum Spanie*. Was the *regnum-imperium* expression which started to appear during his reign also an indication of this? Later on, and under his successor Alfonso V, during whose reign the expression became more wide-spread, we read in the preamble of the "Fuero de León" o "Leyes leonesas" de 1017: ... *in presentia regis domni Adefonsi (...) omnes pontifices, abbates et obtimates regni Ispanie...* Martínez Díez, "La tradición manuscrita," 159.
6   Gambra, *Alfonso VI*, II: no. 50.
7   Sancho was described thus by Abbot Oliba. See Jimeno and Pescador, *Colección documental de Sancho Garcés III*, no. 67.
8   Ayala Martínez, "Fernando I y la sacralización," 88–95.
9   The *Historia Silense*, an unfinished work conceived of as a panegyric for the king, makes its neo-Visigothic roots abundantly clear. Ayala Martínez, "Obispos, guerra santa y cruzada," 228; idem, *Órdenes militares*, 272–3. Regarding the inclusion of al-Andalus in the vision of Alfonso VI, although we are aware that the problems involved are far from having been definitively resolved, it is well-known that, following the conquest of Toledo, Alfonso VI had been attributed the title of "Emperor of the two religions" (*al-Imbratūr dhū-l-Millatayn*) or similar in various documents addressed to different Muslim authorities, specifically the Sevillian King al-Muʿtamid and the Almoravid Emir Yūsuf ibn Tāsufīn. To the later and unreliable anonymous

These Alfonsine imperial designs remained unchanged in the decades following the death of the first, self-styled "emperor of Spain," and this despite the political turmoil in the reign of Urraca (r. 1109–1126) that led to open warfare with her husband, Alfonso "the Battler" of Aragón and Pamplona. However, the imperial idea did not truly blossom until the reign of Alfonso VII (r. 1126–1157), grandson of Alfonso VI, when it was reformulated not only in political and rhetorical terms, but also in a strictly institutional sense; for it was Alfonso VII who instituted the exceptional and previously unheard of imperial coronation ceremony of 1135. Although Alfonso VII certainly recognized the inheritance of his grandfather, he added new and important nuances that mark out this moment as being the third stage in the evolution of the complex political concept of imperialism. The imperial title expressed, as it had in the past, an unambiguous desire for peninsular hegemony, but its means of legitimization had been transformed from that of the "reconqueror" of neo-Visigothic tradition, to that of "crusade," the military conquest of land for spiritual, salvific purposes. Without doubt, the idea of crusade, rooted as it was in the spiritual arsenal of the papacy, would strengthen the imperial ideal, once it had overcome the resistance of the Church to a concept that, despite its exclusive connection to the Peninsula, it nonetheless initially regarded with suspicion.

---

chronicle which contains these alleged letters–*al-Hulal al-Mawshiyya*- (Huici Miranda, "*Al-Hulal al Mawsiyya*," 52–3 and 56–7), we must add a second Arabic source, namely an Egyptian one, also later but independent and much more reliable, which serves to confirm the veracity of such a title. See MacKay and Benaboud, "Alfonso VI of León and Castile"; Benaboud and MacKay, "The authenticity of Alfonso VI's letter"; MacKay and Benaboud, "Yet again Alfonso VI." The title is certainly debatable. These Arabic sources were no doubt far removed from the rubric of the Latin chancery of the king of Castile, though perhaps they were not so far from the spirit of it. The use for the first time of *Hispania-Spania* in the royal, and above all, imperial intitulation of Alfonso VI constituted a clear extension of a Peninsular reality that, of course, did not exclude Islamic domains. They are implicit in the well-known and numerous formulae of which *imperator super omnes Spanie nationes* is only one, albeit, one of the most significant. This formula was used for the first time in 1087; see Gambra, *Alfonso VI*, II: no. 89. Gambra's comprehensive view of the impact of the royal-imperial title in the Peninsula is quite clear. (Gambra, *Alfonso VI*, I: 683ss.) The linking of ideas about an *Imperio Hispánico* that, from the 1070s, would drive these ambitions for sovereignty over the Islamic domains had previously been suggested by Estepa Díez, *El reinado de Alfonso VI*, 26; and in any case, we know that some private documents of the reign, whose authenticity has not been questioned, include similar phrases such as the well-known: *regnante rex domno Adefonsus in Toleto et imperante christianorum quam et paganorum omnia Hispanie regna* from a Sahagun document of 1098: Herrero de la Fuente, *Colección diplomática del monasterio de Sahagún*, III: no. 1022. Nor did formulae utilized in private documents, such as *imperante Adefonsus principis Toleto et tota Spania*, seek to express anything different (Ibid., nos. 886, 927, 955), a fact to which Menéndez Pidal drew attention: Menéndez Pidal, *La España del Cid*, II: 730–1.

Although the pope certainly never addressed Alfonso VII as "emperor," he nevertheless recognized the imperial project legitimized behind the notion of crusade.[10] Nonetheless, this papal reticence in recognizing the title goes some way towards explaining the disintegration of this imperial ideology following the death of Alfonso VII. Neither his sons, Sancho III and Fernando II, nor his grandsons, Alfonso VIII and Alfonso IX, nor indeed his great-grandchildren, Enrique I and Berenguela, claimed the imperial title nor tried to do so, although there are occasional references, above all in literary sources, to imperial allusions concerning some of them.[11] In no case, however, did these imperial whims go beyond the use of the title *rex Hispaniarum*.

Aside from this papal reticence, a variety of other factors go some way towards explaining the extinction of the use of the imperial title, namely: an awareness of the failures of the imperial program in the last years of Alfonso VII's life;[12] the reluctance of the nobility to lose their dominance;[13] and, above all, the rise and consolidation of the other Christian kingdoms within the Peninsula.[14] However, the idea of an imperial title associated with a hegemony established through crusade did not disappear. Rather, it would return to be reinvigorated during the reign of Fernando III. It is to Fernando III and his reign from 1217 to 1252 that we shall now turn, in an effort to reconstruct the imperial ideology of the Saint-King, an ideology that was to be inextricably bound up with the concept of crusade.

2 Fernando III and the Imperial Idea

Although the imperial idea and its association with crusading hegemony had not been forgotten, nonetheless, in the years immediately following Fernando III's accession to the Castilian throne in 1217, in the midst of serious political tension, the concept became somewhat blurred. Alfonso VIII had been the exemplary exponent of a peninsular form of crusading that was far removed

---

10 Crucial to this recognition is the recurring presence of the pontifical legate Guido de Vico in the imperial lands and at signings of the cross, such as in the Burgos court of 1136. Ayala Martínez, "Religiosidad Militar y Cancillería Regia," 50–5.
11 Sirantoine, *Imperator Hispaniae*, 379–84.
12 Especially when it comes to crusade leadership. See Ayala Martínez, "Los inicios," 226.
13 The thirteenth-century chronicle blames the division on the influential counsel of two nobles: the Galician count Fernando Pérez de Traba and the Castilian noble Manrique de Lara. For the allusion to this see *CLRC*, 41; *DrH*, 229. See Sirantoine, *Imperator Hispaniae*, 376.
14 See Ladero Quesada, "Unidad y diversidad," 17–39.

from any idea of imperialism. As a result, having lost its crusading dimension, the concept had become assimilated with mere territorial ambition. This is apparent from the description by the chronicler Juan of Osma of King Alfonso IX of León, who, whilst in the process of occupying Castilian lands, was attempting to stymie the recent royal proclamation of his son, Fernando. The chronicler, who declares himself to be expressing the widely-held opinion of the moment – *sicut dicebatur* – informs us that the Leonese monarch had let himself be led by a vain desire to seize the empire.[15]

However, it seems that it was not long before Fernando III began to consider reviving the dormant imperial ideas of Alfonso VII. And indeed, the responsibility for this, although certainly indirect, may well be ascribed in some way to the figure of Pope Honorius III. Among the extensive list of crusading pontiffs, Honorius III occupies a place of some distinction. His preoccupation with this matter led him, upon his accession to the pontifical throne, to proclaim himself to be chosen by God to oversee the recovery of Jerusalem, a claim that, it appears, had considerable success in mobilizing the faithful.[16] In any case, he lost no time; in a circular letter sent in July 1216, to, among many others, the archbishops and bishops of Hispania communicating the news of his election, he also exhorted them to encourage crusaders from their respective dioceses.[17] Indeed, it was this pope who, at the outbreak of strife between the new Castilian king and his Leonese father in July 1218, hastened to undo the stain of illegitimacy that weighed on Fernando III as son of a union annulled by the Church, and recognized him not only as the legitimate king of Castile but also as the future heir to the throne of León.[18]

---

15   ... *elatus uento inanis glorie, quam conceperat, sicut dicebatur, de imperio habendo, transiuit Pisorgam...*: CLRC, 79.
16   This claim was made in the famous sermon that the pope addressed to the Romans, recounting the legendary anecdote according to which Saint Peter himself had foreseen these same events. The anecdote is recorded in the writings of the contemporary Buchard von Ursberg. Sayers, *Papal Government*, 10–1. Smith, "The Iberian Legations," 81–2; Claverie, *Honorius III et l'Orient*, 24–5.
17   The last paragraph of the letter expresses it in these terms: "For this purpose, we wish and command that you firmly encourage the crusaders (*crucesignatos*) of your diocese, so that the death of our predecessor should not cause consternation in their hearts and nor should they weaken, thus hindering aid to the Holy Land (*Terre Sancte succursus*); for, although our predisposition may seem to appear weaker, nonetheless, we aspire towards its liberation (*liberationem*) with no less desire, so that the Lord, who never abandons those who trust in him, should grant strength in a way that our own capacity could not achieve, just as he dispenses his grace." Mansilla, *Honorio III*, no. 1.
18   Mansilla, *Honorio III*, no. 171.

Yet why such a quick strategic move, reversing the strict policy of his predecessor? Without a doubt, the answer lies in his obsession with crusade. At that very moment, Honorius's eastern front was already advancing. A year earlier, in the summer of 1217, he had named the Spanish Cardinal Pelayo de Albano as the head of the crusade,[19] and before the year was out, the first news had reached Castile of the actions of the crusaders in Syria.[20] Peace in the West was an indispensable requirement for the success of the crusade. This was especially true as the Iberian Peninsula constituted a second crusading front, for which in January 1218 Honorius named a specific legate, the archbishop of Toledo, Rodrigo Jiménez de Rada.[21]

Faced with this reality, it was necessary to settle quickly upon a political solution that would guarantee peace between the two kingdoms, León and Castile, which had been in conflict for so long; indeed, a solution capable of guaranteeing peace and of fomenting the desire for combat against the Muslims. For the pope, it was clear that Alfonso IX, who until this point had been unreliable, could not provide this solution. A far more likely prospect, however, was his son, who was also descended from Berenguela, the first-born of Alfonso VIII, protected by the Holy See,[22] a woman with close links to the crusading champion in the Peninsula, the archbishop Jiménez de Rada.[23] Together, they

---

19   Claverie, *Honorius III et l'Orient*, 46.
20   On November 24, 1217, Honorius III addressed the archbishop, bishops, and prelates of the province of Toledo, informing them of the recent arrival in the Holy Land of the king of Hungary and the dukes of Austria and Merania, as well as the penitential demonstrations in support of the expedition that had been assembled in Rome. In line with these, the pope ordered the leaders of the Toledan church to organize similar processions in their provinces, and also to urge crusaders to join the expedition. ACT, O.3.C.1.53; published in Ayala Martínez, "De nuevo."
21   On January 30, 1218, he informed the Archbishop of Tarragona, and his suffragens, as well as the suffragens of the province of Toledo and the bishops of Burgos, Ávila, and Plasencia, of the appointment. Mansilla, *Honorio III*, no. 148; Goñi, *Historia de la bula*, 142–3.
22   He had taken her, her children, and goods under apostolic protection in November 2016. Mansilla, *Honorio III*, no. 7. On that occasion, he did the same with Teresa of Portugal, so that apostolic protection covered the two wives of Alfonso IX, whose marriages had been dissolved by canonical imperative. Ibid., no. 6.
23   Honorius III had high expectations of the archbishop. On the same day that he informed him of his legatial appointment, January 30, 1218, he commanded him to impose peace and truce among the peninsular kings as decreed in the Fourth Lateran Council in order to guarantee victory against the infidels. Mansilla, *Honorio III*, no. 149; Goñi, *Historia de la bula*, 142. The next day, the pope granted the archbishop the authority to confer on all the territories of his legation the benefits which corresponded to the Holy See *specialiter pro christianorum finibus, auxiliante Domino, dilatandis...*, and another document of the same date authorized the archbishop to absolve those involved in violence against clerics or committing fraud in the payment of the twentieth. Mansilla, *Honorio III*, nos. 151–2;

could no doubt inflame the soul of the young king to relight the torch of crusade that his grandfather Alfonso VIII had brandished with such success.[24] And so it was not in vain that the miraculous victory at Las Navas five years before had announced the imminent triumph of the "Lord of the Armies."[25]

Moreover, the pope saw with pleasure the marriage that was being arranged between the young king and the princess Beatriz of Swabia, a granddaughter of Frederick Barbarossa and cousin of the king of the Romans, Frederick II, who at that time, constituted, albeit ephemerally, the papacy's great hope for a strong and successful crusade. The marriage took place in Burgos in November 1219, just one year before the imperial coronation of Frederick II at Saint Peter's in Rome.[26] In the eyes of the pope, the two great leaders of crusade were thus linked.

The pope's confidence in Frederick II was about to come to an abrupt end, but not so his faith in Fernando III,[27] whose own propaganda, established following the assemblies at Muñó and Carrión in 1224,[28] presented him as the

---

Goñi, *Historia de la bula*, 142. Finally, also from January 31, is the papal letter which ordered Alfonso IX of León to attend to the initiatives of the apostolic legate in all that was related to the combat against the Saracens and peace amongst Christian princes, since, according to the pope, the presence of the Saracens *in Yspania* relied more on the disunity of the Christians than on the strength of their own forces. Mansilla, *Honorio III*, no. 155; Goñi, *Historia de la bula*, 142.

24   It is to Alfonso VIII that Pope Honorius alludes directly in two letters that he wrote just one month after the recognition of Fernando III as heir to the Leonese throne; the first to the Castilian monarch himself, taking him and his kingdom under apostolic protection, and the second, to the archbishop of Toledo and to the bishops of Palencia and Burgos urging them to stem any resistance to the young monarch and his intentions. In both cases, he invoked the memory of the *preclaris inclite recordationis A[lfonsi] regis Castelle, avi sui*. Mansilla, *Honorio III*, nos. 185–6.

25   This is alluded to in the papal letter informing the Hispanic bishops of the naming of Jiménez de Rada as papal legate for the crusade: ... *agarenos cum miraculo illius victorie, quam Dominus exercituum anno nunc quinto celitus ministravit*. Mansilla, *Honorio III*, no. 148.

26   Diago Hernando, "La monarquía castellana y los Staufer," 65–6; Rodríguez López, "El Reino de Castilla y el Imperio germánico," 614–5; Colmenero López, "La boda"; Estepa Díaz, "El reino de Castilla y el imperio," 252–9.

27   Barely a year after the coronation of Frederick II, the news of the fall of Damietta reached the West, but the new emperor, engaged by the uprising of the Sicilian Muslims, could not attend to the urgent requests of the pope, who began to consider the dilatory excuses of the Staufen to be breaching of the crusade vow. In this context of German-papal distancing, Honorius III had no problem in August 1222 confirming the dowry that Fernando III had given his wife Beatriz of Swabia. Mansilla, *Honorio III*, no. 411.

28   We are indebted to the most "official" of the royal chroniclers, Juan de Osma, for the theatrical description the formal declaration of war against the Muslims, undertaken by the king within the solemn framework of the court at Muñó held between Easter and

perfect leader for a crusade. It was an image that would be endorsed by Pope Honorius III barely a year later through a series of bulls which consecrated Fernando as champion of the Christian faith in Spain.[29]

In this way, even before the definitive union of Castile with León, the pope had put in place a plan destined to convert Fernando III into the most powerful of the peninsular monarchs and the undisputed leader of a Hispanicized crusade. At this stage, very probably, the Castilian court itself was already revitalizing the imperial idea which would shape a program of peninsular hegemony legitimized by the discourse of crusade. Undoubtedly, the pope never had such a thing in mind, but his favorable attitude towards Fernando III was surely one of the most important props in the materialization of the imperial dreams of the king.

However, what can we know of the existence of these dreams? We have two sources of information which historians have pointed to for corroboration.[30] The first is the notice provided by the monk Alberic, a Cistercian of the abbey of Trois-Fontaines in Champagne, who was normally well-informed and who was strictly contemporaneous when providing news from the year 1234. In that year, King Fernando had brought before the Roman Curia a formal request for the recognition of the imperial title and the corresponding blessing,

---

Pentecost of 1224. *CLRC*, 85–7. The court, which would move to Carrión in the following month of July, is well-known and has been discussed on numerous occasions, including by the author; see Ayala Martínez, "Fernando III," 45–6; idem, "La realeza," 258–9.

29   In fact, even when the anti-Islamic offensives of the king still only consisted of interventions in favor of one faction in the civil war at the end the Almohad caliphate, Honorius III addressed two letters to Fernando III written in unequivocally crusading language. The first, dated September 25, 1225, contains the protection conceded by the pope to the king, his family, and the kingdom in support of the *negotium* which the king had decided to embark on *contra sarracenos Ispanie,* as a "devout and Catholic prince" moved by the "zeal of his faith." Mansilla, *Honorio III,* no. 574. The second, dated the following day, emphasizes with special intensity the role of Fernando in the fight against the infidel in the Iberian Peninsula, affirming that, although the battle against the Saracens of *Ispanie* is something that was to be accomplished for the whole of Christianity, it particularly affected Fernando and the *alios Ispaniarum reges,* victims of an unjust Islamic occupation of their land. The pope continues by proclaiming that, since Fernando's zeal had constituted the most seemly response against Islam, therefore, with his prayers, he granted to those who decide to engage in the aforementioned *negotium* in Spain, the same indulgences that have been granted to the *crucesignatis* in the Holy Land, also extending to them papal protection. He finally announced the appointment of two *protectores,* Archbishop Rodrigo of Toledo and Bishop Maurice of Burgos, who were to announce and administer the aforementioned indulgence. Ibid., nos. 575–6.

30   They have been assembled on various occasions. See González Jiménez, *Fernando III,* 130–2, and more recently Sirantoine, *Imperator Hispaniae,* 384–6.

something that already had been held by some of his predecessors.³¹ The second appears to be a confirmation of the first, provided by Alfonso X, in the *Setenario*, although it does not specify contact with Rome nor the date. After praising the excellent and pious initiatives of his father, Alfonso alludes to the fame that radiated "over the people, not only those in Spain, but those in all the other lands," a fame that came to justify the identification of his *sennorio* not with a kingdom, but an empire.³²

We do not know exactly when the *Setenario* was redacted,³³ but there is no doubt that it was a work that was highly personal to the king, and produced by Alfonso at his father's bidding, as the text itself indicates, to provide something of a moral reference-point at the royal court.³⁴ We are faced, therefore, with an unusual "mirror of princes," in which the natural recipient is recast as the work's author, thus presenting a "subtle scheme" used by Alfonso to justify his own goals.³⁵

Modern historians readily admit the historicity of Fernando's pretensions. Joseph O'Callaghan suggests, in effect, that the Castilian-Leonese king requested the recognition of the title from the pope and that the latter refused or simply deferred.³⁶ Before this the king would have desisted, although not his chroniclers, who left a record of the imperial pretensions of the monarch, as Jiménez de Rada did in the royal dedication with which he opens his chronicle, using epithets that convey a clear imperial message: "Most serene and unconquered and always august our Lord Fernando."³⁷ Manuel González Jiménez

---

31 ... *In curia Romana talem petitionem proposuit rex Castelle Fernandus, quod nomen imperatoris et benedictionem volebat habere, sicut habuerunt quidam antecessores eius...*: Alberic of Trois-Fontaines, *Chronica Alberici*, 936.

32 *sobre las otras gentes, non tan solamiente de Espanna, mas aun en todas las otras tierras; e que fuese él coronado por enperador segunt lo fueron otros de su linage*: Alfonso X, *Setenario*, 21–2.

33 Fernando Gómez Redondo affirms that, in reality, there were two redactions of the *Setenario*, owing to the presence of the "Elogio de Fernando III" in the complex years at the beginning of the reign: Gómez Redondo, *Historia de la prosa medieval*, 304–30. For arguments pertaining to the end of his reign, see Craddock, "El *Setenario*," 441–66; Martin, "De nuevo."

34 *se viesen siempre como en espejo para saber enmendar los sus yerros en los de los otros e endereçar sus fechos e saberlos fazer bien e complidamente*: Alfonso X el Sabio, *Setenario*, 25.

35 Gómez Redondo, *Historia de la prosa medieval*, 313.

36 O'Callaghan, *El Rey Sabio*, 189–90.

37 *Serenissimo et inuicto et semper augusto domino suo Fernando*: DrH, 3. See O'Callaghan, *El Rey Sabio*, 189–90. The author alludes, moreover, to the characterization of Fernando III as "vicar of the kingdom of the Spaniards," attributed to Lucas of Tuy according to the later Romance version of the *Chronicon Mundi*.

also affirms the imperial pretensions of Fernando III.[38] The definitive union of Castile and León in 1230 created the perfect scenario upon which to build a solid basis for the hegemonic project of Fernando III. It provided confirmation that his peninsular leadership, facilitated by ideas about crusade and secured with papal blessing, could be translated into an explicit recognition that would revitalize the old imperial Leonese tradition, which he had inherited along with the kingdom.

Fernando's privileged relationship with Emperor Frederick II must also have stimulated in the king of Castile his own imperial longing. Their relations are marked by a series of diplomatic contacts and personal missives throughout the reign of Fernando III. These had begun with the negotiation of Fernando's marriage to Beatriz of Swabia in 1219, and in the years immediately afterwards some Castilian-German contact was maintained through Abbot Pedro of San Pedro de Gumiel, who had travelled to German lands in 1223.[39] These relations intensified when, following the death of Beatriz in 1235, diplomatic exchanges focused on the duchy of Swabia and the presumed Castilian rights to the territory. In the days following the death of the queen, the *Annales Colonienses Maximi* inform us that Frederick II, after a meeting of the imperial Diet in Augsburg on November 1, 1235, in which he had delivered 10,000 marks of silver to the king of Bohemia to secure rights to the duchy of Swabia that belonged by hereditary right to his wife,[40] wintered at Haginhowe castle, and it was there that a group of ambassadors from the queen of *Hyspania* appeared before the emperor with magnificent gifts.[41] The embassy arrived after

---

38   The endorsement of the date by the monk Alberic permits Manuel González to describe it as *"perfectamente documentado."* González Jiménez, *Fernando III*, 131.

39   The letter of Archbishop Engelbert of Cologne which informs us of the embassy, specifies that the Abbot Pedro *pro regni sui negocio Castelle quod gerebat*. However, it was not an embassy directly promoted by Fernando IIII, but rather more connected with questions related to the Order of Calatrava and its projects in German lands. See Ferreiro Alemparte, "España y Alemania." The author, however, states that the embassy "had as its main objective the moral and material support of the Empire with regard to the military ventures that the Castilian king was already ambitiously planning for these years (*tendría como principal objetivo alcanzar el apoyo moral y material del Imperio para las empresas militares que el rey castellano planeaba ya por estos años con miras muy ambiciosas*)." Ibid., 509. See also Rodríguez López, "El Reino de Castilla y el Imperio germánico," 617–22.

40   ...*In festo omnium sanctorum imperator conventum principum habuit apud Augustam, ubi rex Bohemie affuit, recipiens ab imperatore 10 milia marcarum pro parte Suevie, que iure hereditario suam uxorem contigit*: "Annales Colonienses Maximi," 844. Indeed, the wife of King Wenceslaus I of Bohemia (r. 1230–1253) was Cunegunda, daughter of Philip of Swabia and Irene Angelus, sister therefore to Beatriz, the queen of Castile.

41   ... *Ibidem nuncii regine Hyspanie affuerunt, qui pulcherrimus dextrarios et magnifica munera cesari attulerunt*: "Annales Colonienses Maximi," 845. According to Estepa, these

the queen had died, and the *Annales* say that very soon after the embassy, the emperor received news of her death.

It is impossible to determine the motives behind this enigmatic embassy from Queen Beatriz, although Ana Rodríguez connects it with the 1234 request for recognition of the imperial title mentioned by Alberic of Trois-Fontaines. Such a request to the pope, in the context of 1235, she suggests, could only have been for the reclamation of the duchy of Swabia, taking advantage of the vacancy caused by the titular ruler, the king of the Romans, Henry, son of Frederick II, who revolted against his father in 1234 and one year later was deposed and imprisoned.[42] It is not easy to accept this interpretation, for, on the one hand, it necessitates a detailed and immediate knowledge of the events in Germany, and on the other, it would hardly have been logical to attempt, at that moment, a reclamation of the duchy, associated in these years with the title of the Germanic kingdom,[43] to which Beatriz only possessed limited rights, similar to those also recently held by her sister Cunegunda.[44] In reality, it would not be until 1239 that the Castilian court formally tried to claim these rights in an attempt to mediate between Frederick II and Gregory IX at a moment of high tension.[45]

---

magnificent presents were fruit of the treasure obtained from the Muslims. Estepa Díaz, "El reino de Castilla y el imperio," 259.

42 Rodríguez López, "El Reino de Castilla y el Imperio germánico," 622 and 630, fn. 43.

43 Carlos Estepa, following Helmut Maurer, has highlighted the special political significance of the duchy of Swabia and its connection to the exercise of royal authority in the Germanic kingdom. Estepa Díaz, "El reino de Castilla y el imperio," 259.

44 Diago Hernando, "La monarquía castellana y los Staufer," 66–8.

45 We know that in the first months of 1230, more or less coinciding with the second excommunication of the emperor, Fernando III had sent an embassy bearing gifts and horses, which in August of that year, Frederick II thanked by means of an interesting missive in which, emphasizing the ties of kinship with the Castilians, he congratulated Fernando on his military successes against the *rebellibus vestris*, in what seems to be a curious amalgamation of the Muslim enemies of the king of Castile with those of the Emperor incited by the Pope. Huillard-Bréholles, *Historia Diplomatica Frederici Secundi*, V: Pt. 1, pp. 370–1; Rodríguez López, "El reino de Castilla y el Imperio germánico," 624. The backdrop to this exchange is undoubtedly that of the Castilian claims of rights that might correspond with a Castilian dynasty in the Duchy of Swabia, but, in any case, this represents a significant contact at a delicate moment, taken advantage of by the emperor for the purposes of propaganda. As such, it is noteworthy that a few months later, in December, and while the reclamation of rights in the Duchy of Swabia remained a priority for Castile, Fernando III sent the abbot of Sahagún as his emissary to Gregory IX with the purpose of mediating in the conflict between the Pope and Emperor. *Fernando III*, III: no. 659. See also Ibid., nos. 660–661. Probably, Frederick II was pleased with the attitude of the Castilian king. In any case, in the spring of 1240, Fadrique, the Castilian infante destined to represent the Swabian claim, would move to the court of the excommunicated emperor, and remain there

Aside from the influence that this close link between Fernando III and the Germanic court may have exercised over a particular approach to the idea of empire, there was certainly no lack of theorists within the Peninsula putting forward the image of a radically free Hispania – *omnimoda libertas* – a place with its own full jurisdictional autonomy, whose kings were not subject to any temporal empire. Lucas of Tuy wrote in these terms in the preface to the *Chronicon mundi*, a work completed around the year 1238.[46] In it he expressed the concept of "full sovereignty," ultimately claiming an authentic imperial *auctoritas*. Others went further and advocated for the validity in the Iberian Peninsula of a notion of empire, considered to be both natural and rooted in historical precedent. The case of the canonist Vincentius Hispanus is well known.[47] Traditionally, he has been assumed to have been of Portuguese origin, although this has not been proven beyond doubt.[48] This renowned decretalist, who would later become bishop, is the author of an important gloss on Innocent III's *Venerabilem* following its publication in 1234 as part of the *Decretales* of Gregory IX, also known as the *Liber Extra*. The bull alluded to – and recognized – the historicity of the *translatio imperii* from the hands of the "Greeks" to those of the Germans thanks to the will of the pope. In his commentary, Vincentius Hispanus affirmed that the Germans had lost their empire due to their own stupidity – *busnardiam* –, but that the Spanish had obtained their empire through their virtue. After all, they had been able to oppose the invasion of Charlemagne and had inherited from the Visigothic kings a unified territory that, by their own virtues, they had expanded.[49] Curiously, Vincentius

---

until June 1245; in September 1240, Frederick II would write to Fernando III giving news as to the presence of his son, referred to by the emperor as *nepote nostro*. Huillard-Bréholles, *Historia Diplomatica Frederici Secundi*, V: Pt. 2, p. 1047; Rodríguez López, "El reino de Castilla y el Imperio germánico," 625–6.

46 *Prefulget etiam omnimoda libertate Yspania, cum in agendis causis ciuilibus propriis utitur legibus et Yspanorum rex nulli subditur imperio temporali*: *CM*, praef. 9. See Fernández-Ordóñez, "La denotación de 'España'," 70–1.

47 Nieto Soria, "La monarquía fundacional," 61. Sirantoine, *Imperator Hispaniae*, 385–6.

48 Post, *Studies in Medieval Legal Thought*, 484. The chapter which Post devotes to the figure of Vincentius corresponds with an article by the author (Post, "*Blessed Lady Spain*"), which, in revised form, was added to Post, *Studies in Medieval Legal Thought*, 434. Questions about the Portuguese origin of Vicentius have been raised by Ochoa Sanz, *Vincentius Hispanus*, 11–22; the author is inclined to reject his position as bishop of Idanha-Duarda and to support that of Zaragoza. Ibid., 9–112.

49 Gaines Post published the text of the gloss and the commentary on the same in Post, *Studies in Medieval Legal Thought*, 489–90. For a fairly well-founded criticism of Post's interpretation of "Blessed Lady Spain," see Gil, "A apropiação da ideia de Império," 17–8. Gil points out, rightly, that the expression refers not to the "Blessed Lady Spain" but to the

Hispanus does not explicitly address the matter of "reconquest," but the idea of expansion driven by virtue is implicit throughout his discourse, an idea that would ultimately serve to justify Hispanic imperial ambitions. It was a notion hardly distinct from the territorial designs put forward by the propagandists of Fernando III, to be carried out at the expense of the enemies of the faith. But would this empire, bastion of crusade and increasingly dominant power within the Peninsula, be claimed by the king of Castile?

Everything pointed in that direction; the most powerful king of the Peninsula, propelled by crusade, was able to consolidate his power across his territories, whilst this same crusade concurrently facilitated the expansion of his lordship, permitting him to be at the head of the ensemble of Hispanic kingdoms, as their natural leader, indeed, as their "emperor." From the 1230s, Fernando III oversaw unparalleled territorial expansion, beginning with the addition of just over 100,000 square kilometers.[50] His milestones are well known – Córdoba (1236), Murcia (1243), Jaén (1246), and Seville (1248) –, yet the imperial title, despite the propaganda of the chronicles to which we have alluded, would never materialize.

The key to this is, without a doubt, the reluctant attitude of the pope to recognize the title which, in addition to being held by his worst enemy, the German Emperor, also stood somewhat in defiance of the *verus imperator*, as the *Decretum* termed the pope himself.[51] Nonetheless, we would like to put forward, as a mere hypothesis, the possibility that not only did Fernando III refuse to renounce his imperial ideals, but also that he continued to pursue pontifical blessing for it through his program of territorial conquest that would reach the very limits of the Peninsula, thereby obliging the pope to provide that long-awaited recognition. We are referring to what, some years later, Alfonso X would call the *fecho de allende*; the expansion of conquest into Africa.

---

vendidas señoras hispanas, alluding to the complex marriage politics of the Castilian dynasty since the time of Alfonso VIII, which afforded the kingdom an extra-Penisular presence until then unprecedented.

50   *Fernando III*, I: 9. For more on the extent of Fernando's conquests, see in this volume García Fitz, Chp. 2.

51   This epithet appears in glosses on the famous *Decretum* of Gratian (ca. 1140), dated to as early as the second half of the twelfth century, such as the *Summa Coloniensis* and the *Summa Parisiensis*. Carlyle and Carlyle, *A History of Mediaeval Political Theory in the West*, II: 224. Of course, one does not dare to attribute such to Gratian, although without a doubt his doctrinal positions made such derivations inevitable. See Chodorow, *Christian political theory*, 133ff; Robinson, *The Papacy*, 145, 299.

3 The African Project

There has been much speculation about the so-called African project, conceived of by Fernando III towards the end of his reign and continued by his son. Two key sources refer to the project. The most explicit is a later testimony, contained in the so-called *Estoria de España*, in what is considered to be an insertion into the section related to the government of Fernando III, known as the *Crónica particular de san Fernando*, a text that has been dated to the beginning of the fourteenth century.[52] It informs us that, having completed the

---

[52] Over fifty years ago, Diego Catalán argued that "neither during the life of Alfonso X, nor after the death of the Wise King, did the Alfonsine historiographical school succeed in concluding the planned *Estoria de España* (*el taller historiográfico alfonsí, ni en vida de Alfonso X, ni después de muerto el rey Sabio, llegó a concluir la proyectada* Estoria de España)," and that the *Primera crónica general de España* – edited and thus named by Menéndez Pidal – "could not be identified with the *Estoria de España* of Alfonso X." Catalán, "El taller historiográfico alfonsí"; idem, *La Estoria de España de Alfonso X*, 47. In fact, the entire section that runs between the reigns of Alfonso VII and the year 1243, in which culminates the main text of *De rebus Hispaniae* by Jiménez de Rada, was no more than a translation of the archbishop's work pending revision – being, from the start of the reign of Alfonso VIII no more than a transcription of the *De rebus Hispaniae* –, and that it remained as a draft, without being included in the unfinished *Estoria de España*, with the years of Fernando's reign from 1243 until his death, that is to say, those of the glorious conquests that culminate in the taking of Seville, being simply "an artifice of the fourteenth century." Ibid., 50–3. This work is known as the *Seguimiento del Toledano*, of the *Crónica particular de san Fernando*. Catalán, "Alfonso X"; idem, *La Estoria de España de Alfonso X*, 81. Years later, and with these considerations in mind, Fernando Gómez Redondo reflected that the historiographical cut-off point that has been imagined within the Alfonsine tradition, namely the appearance of a new genre of an individualized "royal chronicle," born out of an ideological context that has come to be known as "Molinism," a doctrine based on a certain aristocratic logic that aimed to influence the development of the monarchy, defending the values of unity and political centralization during the turbulent years of the minorities of Fernando IV and Alfonso XI. The first manifestation of this ideology inspired by the political genius of María de Molina, would be the so-called *Crónica particular de san Fernando*, a moral reference point for this political regenerative drive. This chronicle can be identified, as we have mentioned, with the *Seguimiento del Toledano*, but also includes the archbishop's *De rebus Hispaniae*, translated into Romance and conveniently inserted within the text. From it results a coherent whole, whose composition can be situated in the final years of the reign of Fernando IV. Gómez Redondo, *Historia de la prosa medieval*, II: 1225–48. Recently, Luis Fernández Gallardo has returned to this question in an exhaustive work, which relates the appearance of this text to the context of the stimulus attributed to the composition of the *Vie de saint Louis de Joinville*, in 1309, from which the *Crónica particular de san Fernando* would emerge in a form of "emulatory response." Fernández Gallardo, "La *Crónica particular de San Fernando*," I: 248. There is a second part of this work. Its contents are summarized in Fernández Gallardo, "La crónica real," 285–8.

conquest of the Islamic lands in the Peninsula, in which enterprise he was aided by God, the king cast his eyes to the opposing shore and ordered the construction of various types of ships with the purpose of conquering "many great lands."[53] The second testimony, in this case a strict contemporary, the monk-chronicler Matthew Paris, of the English abbey of St Albans, provides information from near the end of Fernando's reign, in 1250; namely, the news that King Fernando, who throughout the pages is repeatedly called "the most victorious king of Castile Alfonso (*Andefulsus*)" and who has amassed thirteen victories over the Muslims, is summoning a crusade with the intention to go to the Holy Land out of pity for the Franks.[54] Later, the same chronicler, in an entry attributed to the year 1251, informs us that an ambassador of the king of Castile, "an eloquent and elegant knight," had encouraged the king of England to undertake a crusade, avoiding the errors of the king of the Franks, and the vanity of his people, but organizing instead an expedition alongside the Castilian monarch, who would accompany him as a tireless ally. The text does not allude to the destination of the expedition, but it specifies that, following the conquest of Seville, the Castilian king had under his control "nearly all of Hispania" (*tota fere Hispania*). It also mentions the king of Morocco as being a beneficiary of the sizeable income received from the wealthy city of Seville before its Castilian conquest.[55] It is conceivable that the destination of this crusade may have been North Africa, given the old image of the *via hispanica* as a better and more secure crusading route by which to reach the Levant. In any case, this project, frustrated by the death of the Castilian king, was immediately taken up by his son Alfonso X, reflected in a treaty with the king of England made in April 1253.[56]

---

53 *Allen mar tenie oio para pasar, et conquerir lo dalla desa parte que la morisma ley tenie, ca los daca por en su poder los tenie, que asy era. Galeas et baxeles mandaua fazer et labrar a grant priesa et guisar naues, auiendo grant fiuza et gran esperança en la grant merçed quel Dios aca fazie; teniendo que sy alla pasase, que podría conquerir muy grandes tierras si la uida le durase unos días*: PCG, 770.

54 ... *Haec cum audisset victoriosissimus rex Castellae Andefulsus, qui jam plusquam tredecim dietas super sarracenos adquisivit, compassus Francorum miseriae, cruce signatus est, dignius reputans Terram Sanctam Christo subjugare quam aliam*: Matthew Paris, *Chronica Majora*, V: 170. See Goodman, "Alfonso X and the English Crown," 40–1.

55 Matthew Paris, *Chronica Majora*, V: 231–2. This relatively long fragment is reproduced in Lomax, "La conquista de Andalucía," 48.

56 In the Anglo-Castilian accord signed on April 20, 1254, Henry III promised Alfonso X to ask the pope about the possibility of directing his crusade army to Morocco, and in the case of the pope agreeing, to go to their aid dividing between both parts the loot and territory obtained. Rymer, *Foedera, conventiones, litterae*, I: 1, pp. 180–1. See Ayala Martínez, *Directrices fundamentales*, 67–70.

As such, there is no reason to doubt the reality of Fernando's project to wage crusade in Africa, even though it was ultimately to be more dream than reality. Historians affirm that the Sevillian dockyards, traditionally associated with this endeavor, were the work of Alfonso X. This appears to be corroborated by the *Estoria de España*.[57] However, it is evident that the project had an earlier phase. Otherwise, it would not be easy to explain why, in October 1252, Pope Innocent IV confirmed for the benefit of Alfonso X a number of *compositiones* that the Castilian monarch had negotiated "with the Saracens of Africa," which the pope recognized as royal efforts "to the glory of God, and the honor of the Church, and also of the Christian people."[58] It seems logical to consider that these negotiations were not initiated by Alfonso X. And perhaps something similar can account for another pontifical letter from the same month, October 1252, authorizing the absolution of all clergy and laymen who had the intention of participating in the expedition to Saracen Africa which was already being organized.[59] Everything points to a project initiated by Fernando III that was subsequently inherited by his son.

However, what was this project? We must start by highlighting the fact that it received firm papal support. Furthermore, it was a project that aimed to combine military intervention with negotiated settlements. Behind this operation looms the figure of Innocent IV, who Fernando III wished to accommodate in line with his own political interests. Benjamin Z. Kedar has attributed to Innocent IV, who, before his accession, was known as the great canonist Sinibaldo dei Fieschi, the establishment of the spiritual solution connecting the need for Christian holy war with the imperative for conversion of the infidel. Innocent IV maintained, of course, the idea of crusades and the indulgences attached to both the recovery of the Holy Land or other territories unjustly overtaken by infidels (or, indeed, by the great enemy of the Church, Frederick II). What holy war could never provide, however, was the coercive means to achieve the conversion of the infidel: preaching and coercion were simply incompatible. Innocent IV also dealt with the legality of war waged to facilitate the work of preachers in a hostile territory, especially when this work had been hindered or impeded. In this case, war, duly authorized by the pope, is not only legitimate but necessary, since the authority of the "Vicar of God," knows no territorial limits, and therefore must also preside equally over the lands of

---

57 González Jiménez, *Fernando III*, 257.
58 ...*cum sarracenis de Africa ... ad Dei gloriam, honorem Ecclesie ac populi christiani...*: Quintana Prieto, *Inocencio IV*, no. 803.
59 Ibid., no. 807.

infidels. Such a doctrine was reflected in a commentary – or *apparatus* – on the decretals of Gregory IX, published shortly after 1245.[60]

Kedar speculates whether this doctrine of sanctifying war destined to facilitate missionary activity, a doctrine with clear antecedents,[61] was influential in the development of later crusading initiatives, that is to say, in the expeditions of St. Louis, the first of which went to the Levant in 1248–1254. Kedar concludes that this operation, despite securing the interest of the Capetian monarch in the conversion of infidels, was adjusted almost entirely to the crusading norms of conquest and defense and was not, therefore, a campaign aimed at compelling Muslim authorities to permit preaching in their territories.[62] Nonetheless, it remains to be considered whether the first field test consciously designed by the pope in order to exercise his ideas along these lines was that of the African crusading project of King Fernando III.

Indeed, and quite independent of the missionary attempts that the popes, especially Honorius III[63] and Gregory IX,[64] developed in the Almohad territory

---

60   Kedar, *Crusade and Mission*, 159–60. The text of the *apparatus* in Ibid., 217. See also Tyerman, *How to Plan a Crusade*, 36–7.
61   The most immediate was the treatist and preacher of the Fifth Crusade, Oliver of Cologne, who was responsible for the formulation of the letter addressed to Sultan al-Kāmil of Egypt which invited him to convert. He was not the only ecclesiastic who did not think exclusively in crusading terms when dealing with the Muslims. For Oliver of Cologne (or of Paderborn) and his precedents, see Kedar, *Crusade and Mission*, 131–5, 160.
62   Ibid., 161, 165.
63   In the final years of his pontificate, Honorius III gave a considerable boost to the missionary efforts of the Church in North Africa, seemingly coinciding with a notable policy of tolerance on the part of the Almohad authorities. In this context, the recently formed mendicant orders were destined to undertake the mission to convert the Saracens. Kedar, *Crusade and Mission*, 136–58. In June 1225, the pope gave instructions to the Dominicans and Franciscans about the mission in the lands of *Miramamolin*. Mansilla, *Honorio III*, no. 562. The instructions were repeated in October of the same year. Ibid., no. 579. At this time there was already a bishopric ruled by Dominicans in the Almohad lands. Ibid., nos. 588, 590. This missionary work depended on the primate of Hispania, Archbishop Rodrigo of Toledo, whom the pope commissioned in February 1226 to give new impetus to the evangelizing work of the Dominicans and Franciscans in Morocco, urging him, if necessary, to appoint new bishops. Ibid., no. 595; Gorosterratzu, *Don Rodrigo*, 245–51. Only a month later, Honorius III authorized the receipt of alms by those Dominicans and Franciscans engaged in the evangelization of Morocco, in order to support them in their efforts. Mansilla, *Honorio III*, no. 596.
64   In May 1233, Gregorio IX addressed an interesting letter to the Almohad Caliph al-Rashīd (r. 1232–1242) inviting him to convert and asking him, among other things, to attend diligently to the Franciscans sent, among them *fray* Agnello, who had been appointed bishop of Fez; and informing him that this favorable attitude toward them and the broader ensemble of Maghrebi Christians must be maintained if the caliph did not wish the Apostolic See to prohibit these same Christians from rendering their services. Mas Latrie, *Traités de paix et de commerce*, Documents, x, 10. These Christians constituted a significant number

in North Africa, it is evident that Innocent IV clearly raised the importance of missionary intervention in the region from 1245. Unquestionably, the pope considered as providential the conversion of one *Zeid Aaron, rex Zale ilustris* to Christianity and the delivery of the African *regnum* which would be governed by the Holy See, a delivery that was transferred in September 1245 to the military order of Santiago in return for an annual *censo* of forty maravedís.[65] The identification of this person or his "kingdom" is not entirely clear, but Joseph O'Callaghan has reasonably proposed an identification with the *sayyid* or prince al-Hasan, one of the sons of Abū Zayd, the last king of Valencia who ultimately converted to Christianity. Being the son-in-law of the Almohad Caliph, who governed the strategic Atlantic stronghold of Salé, this must subsequently be the *regnum* to which the papal document alludes; the governor would have committed a seditious act by converting to Christianity and this would have been the cause of his execution, ordered by the caliph, and which Ibn Idhārī situates in 1243–1244.[66] It is clear that the issue of Salé encapsulates perfectly the missionary crusading approach of Innocent IV: reinforcing Christianization with the martial support of the military order. The aforementioned document alludes to the importance of this acquisition in the spread of the Christian cult, and the pope's insistence on the policy of constructing churches and hospitals that, without restrictions, remained entrusted to the Order of Santiago from this new operational base in Africa.

4   The Diocese of Morocco

In step with this fortuitous event, Innocent IV poured his efforts into attempting to consolidate control over the somewhat ethereal diocese of Morocco,

---

of Castilian troops that had transferred to Morocco at the initiative of Fernando III during the caliphate of al-Ma'mūn, the father of al-Rashīd (see below fn. 81). In order to attend to them, the pope in that same year of 1233 widened the pastoral powers of the Dominicans who came to preach in the land of the Saracens, allowing them not only to absolve the Christians residing there, but also to lift any sentences of excommunication they might have incurred. Domínguez Sánchez, *Gregorio IX*, no. 309. Some years later, in June 1237, Gregory IX sent a new bishop to preside over the Moroccan church *inter hostes Christi posita*. Mas Latrie, *Traités de paix et de commerce*, Documents, xii: 11–2; O'Callaghan, *Reconquest and Crusade*, 118. More interestingly, the papal bull of March 1238 equates the merit of the traditional crusade project with the missionary labor of the Dominicans and Franciscans, for whose development the bull also grants an indulgence decreed by the Fourth Lateran Council: Kedar, *Crusade and Mission*, 142; the bull is published in Ibid., 213.

65   Quintana, *Inocencio IV*, no. 216.
66   Ibn 'Idhārī, *Al-Bayan*, II: 153; O'Callaghan, *Reconquest and Crusade*, 119.

delivering it in 1246 into the care of an especially capable ecclesiastic, the Franciscan Lope Fernández de Ain, a man close to the throne.[67] Throughout the final months of that year, the pope dictated a series of measures in support of the new bishop and requested all kinds of support for him and his men: from his new flock of the faithful,[68] from the coastal councils of the peninsular maritime coast, including those of northern Castile,[69] from Jaime I of Aragón,[70] from the Franciscans themselves and their religious family,[71] from the Santiagans,[72] and from the Calatravans,[73] and also from the emir of Tunis, Abū Zakariyā' Yaḥyā I, formally independent of the Almohads since 1237,[74] as well as from those responsible for the governing of Ceuta and of Bugía.[75] The pope also addressed the Almohad Caliph himself – at this point, al-Sa'īd al Mu'taḍid – celebrating his successes, congratulating him on his treatment of Christians, and exhorting him to continue along these lines. Nor did the pope hesitate to inform the caliph of the possibility of conversion to the Christian faith and

---

[67] He had been a soldier in his youth and later became a canon in the Basilica of Nuestra Señora del Pilar in Zaragoza. Becoming prior of the same place, he supported the development in the city of a community of the newly founded order of Franciscan mendicants, in 1221. He went on to represent the Spanish province of the order at the pontifical curia, and there won the trust of Gregory IX and, later, Innocent IV. He was a beneficiary in the *repartimiento* of Seville, and in the first years of Alfonso X, he carried out important diplomatic tasks, such as in 1255, when he was named the apostolic delegate for Africa and general preacher of crusade in the same territory. He died in 1260. Castellanos, *Apostolado seráfico en Marruecos*, 134–62; López, *Obispos de África*; MacDonald, *Espéculo*, 498. A papal dispensation from 1247 informs us of his irregular family origins. Quintana, *Inocencio IV*, no. 357.

[68] Quintana, *Inocencio IV*, no. 333.

[69] Ibid., no. 318. The circular also addressed the prelates responsible for the Mediterranean port dioceses potentially connected to North Africa.

[70] Ibid., no. 322. We also know that letters of the same tenor were addressed to the kings Fernando III of Castile, Teobald I of Navarre, and Alfonso III of Portugal. Wading, *Annales minorum*, III: 154; Sbaralea, *Ad Bullarium Franciscanum*, I: 435; Mas Latrie, *Traités de paix et de commerce*, Documents, 16; Tisserant and Wiet, "Une lettre de l'almohade Murtaḍā," 27, fn. 1.

[71] Quintana, *Inocencio IV*, nos. 323, 326, 338–9, 340–1.

[72] Ibid., no. 328.

[73] Sbaralea, *Ad Bullarium Franciscanum*, 436. Tisserant and Wiet, "Une lettre de l'almohade," 26, fn. 5.

[74] Quintana, *Inocencio IV*, no. 325. It was not the first time that the pontificate addressed the government of Tunis. Two years before the formal "declaration of independence," in 1235, Gregory IX had done so precisely in response to the Tunisian authorities, in order to establish regular contact through a Franciscan friar by the name of Juan. Mas Latrie, *Traités de paix et de commerce*, Documents, XI: 11.

[75] Ceuta and Bugía had also become isolated from the Almohad regime and moved closer to Hafsid-controlled Tunis. See Mosquera Merino, *La señoría de Ceuta*, 134–5.

subsequently of placing his kingdom under apostolic protection.[76] He requested, in any case, that Christians in the caliph's service should have a security that they had not always enjoyed and that for this, the caliph should provide them with fortified places and even some ports, always under caliphal sovereignty, to provide, if necessary, a refuge for them or a means of gathering reinforcements.[77] Bishop Lope served as the intermediary for all of these requests to the caliph and for this mission the bishop received special disciplinary powers,[78] a dispensation not to attend the Roman Curia for ten years,[79] and, above all, in April 1247, an indulgence similar to those obtained by pilgrims to the Holy Land for the benefit of all who, being lay members of the bishop's "household," chose to collaborate actively with the prelate.[80]

This papal activity, although in principle far from the goals of Fernando III, would ultimately converge with them. The king had long had his sights set on Morocco. The definitive disintegration of the Almohad Caliphate from 1228 posed interesting prospects for Fernando III in relation to North Africa,[81]

---

76   It was not the first time that the pope had invited an Almohad caliph to convert. Innocent III already had invited al-Nāsir to the Christian faith in 1199 in what was no doubt a formal use of the pontifical chancellery. Mansilla, *Inocencio III*, no. 182.
77   Quintana, *Inocencio IV*, no. 332.
78   Namely, dispensations of consanguinity. Ibid., no. 340.
79   Wading, *Annales minorum*, 468; Mas Latrie, *Traités de paix et de commerce*, Documents, 16.
80   Quintana, *Inocencio IV*, no. 372.
81   When the governor of Seville, Abū l-'Alā, staged a coup and proclaimed himself caliph under the name al-Ma'mūn in September of 1227 [Ibn Idhārī, I: 297, 301,] Fernando III wasted little time in reaching an agreement with him that would enable him to withdraw from al-Andalus and further his cause in Morocco. Without a doubt, it was the end of Almohad rule in the Peninsula. Although some of the terms of this agreement, which can be found in the *Rawd al-qirtās*, have been called into question, there is much to indicate that they consisted of the delivery to the Castilian king of substantial sums of money, as well as a sizable collection of border fortresses in al-Andalus and the improvement of conditions for the Christians resident in Morocco, including the construction in Marrakesh of a church that could sound its bells, and all this in exchange for effective military assistance in the shape of a permanent corps of Christian soldiers that would function in Africa under the caliph's orders. Ibn Abī Zar', *Rawd al-qirtās*, II: 485–6. The editor is reluctant to accept the terms of the pact as transmitted by the *Rawd al-qirtās*; this position is also reflected in Ibn Idhārī, I: 313, fn. 1. See Fierro, "La religion," 506, 528. With regard to the church in Marrakesh, see Cenival, "L'église chretienne de Marrakech," 69–83. Such pro-Christian measures should come as no surprise from a Caliph who had renounced the Almohad dogma and proclaimed in a letter reproduced by Ibn Idhārī that "we have rejected that which is false and we have made known the truth, and that there is no other

although it is true that the conquest of Andalusia and Murcia kept him engrossed in Andalusi territory until after the occupation of Seville in 1248. Nonetheless, it was an occurrence that had an international resonance, and one that must have corresponded with Fernando's own inclinations towards political hegemony and peninsular superiority. In his *Chronica Majora,* Matthew Paris described the distress of the French king upon the news of the death of the Castilian monarch; it was an occasion on which Fernando was referred to as the *rex Hispaniae totius,* on account of his having been responsible for a series of grand deeds of conquest against the infidels, so many and so mighty that they would require their own great tome.[82]

Such words came to confirm the imperial strategy that Fernando III had mooted years ago, and that, hypothetically, perhaps now as a corollary of a long process, he was able to raise once again. Conquest on the other side of the Strait of Gibraltar would be opportune at a time when the connection between the Atlantic and the Mediterranean was beginning to take on special strategic importance, and furthermore, would guarantee peninsular integrity in the face of expansionist activities from North Africa. However, above all, such a move could be justified by none other than the old ideology of "Reconquista"; after all, Mauritania Tingitana had once been part of the diocese of Hispania ruled by the Goths.[83] It was, as such, a possible means by which to rethink such imperial objectives, especially if, as the evidence suggests, there was a convergence of interests with the pope, whose mixed policy of preaching and military pressure continued in the years immediately after the conquest of Seville.

It was not until June 1250 that the new figure in charge of the moribund Almohad Caliphate decided to answer the requests of the pope, as articulated

---

Mahdī than Jesus, son of Mary, who was only called al-Mahdī because he spoke of the right path, and we have suppressed this – Almohad – innovation and may God help us in the mission entrusted to us (*hemos rechazado lo falso y hemos publicado la verdad y que no hay más Mahdī que Jesús, hijo de María, el cual solamente se llamó al-Mahdī porque habló de la buena dirección y esta innovación – almohade – la hemos suprimido y Dios nos ayuda en la misión que se nos ha confiado*)." Furthermore, his wife Habbāba, mother of the caliph al-Rasīd, was herself a Christian. Ibn Idhārī, I: 319, 338. See also Ibn Abī Zarʿ, *Rawd al-qirṭās,* II: 487–8. Finally, the sources do not agree about the troops that Fernando III decided to send to Africa in support of the Caliph. The exaggerated number of 12,000 that we find in *Rawd al-qirṭās* cannot be accepted; much more realistic is the number provided by Ibn ʿIdhārī: 500 knights. Ibn ʿIdhārī, *Al-Bayan,* I: 313, fn. 1. See Barton, "Traitors to faith?," 23–45; García Sanjuán, "Mercenarios cristianos," 435–47; Albarrán Iruela, "De la conversión."

82 ... *illustris rex Castellae Andefulsus, qui dicitur propter sui eminentiam rex Hispaniae totius, post praeclara gesta sua et super infideles Hispaniae conquisitiones máximas, quae diffusos et speciales tractatus exigerent...*: Matthew Paris, *Chronica Majora,* V: 311.

83 O'Callaghan, *Reconquest and Crusade,* 117.

by Bishop Lope in October 1246. The letter had been received by al-Saʿīd al-Muʿtaḍīd, but it was his successor al-Murtaḍā (r. 1248–1266) who responded to it. Al-Murtaḍā, governor of Salé, succeeded al-Saʿīd as a result of the defeat and death of the latter in an unsuccessful operation to subdue Tlemcen,[84] his death there itself informing us of the ephemeral Christian control of this strategic Atlantic port. The new caliph was an Almohad prince whose power, surrounded by Marinid pressure, barely surpassed Marrakesh in its radius of influence. His weakened position was largely dependent on Christian mercenaries of Castilian origin who allowed him to remain on the throne.[85] Despite this, his response to the pope vacillated between haughtiness and evasion. While it recognized the supreme jurisdiction of the Roman pontiff over all of Christianity, it quickly became a lecture on Islamic doctrine with blatant contempt for the Christian Trinity, signaling all but a refusal to the papal invitation to conversion. Regarding the request for strongholds for the protection of Christians, the answer is shrouded in the most impenetrable vagueness, perhaps because al-Murtaḍā was not in a position to politically compromise a sovereignty that was being snatched from him.[86]

It was at this point that the pope's attitude changed towards the African project of Fernando III.[87] Although in March 1251 Innocent IV had pressed al-Murtaḍā on the subject of safe places for the Christian population,[88] just a month later, he asked Bishop Lope, in the face of the caliph's persistent refusal to facilitate the presence in his land of his own mercenaries and of the Christian population as a whole, to turn instead to their evacuation, and, of course, to render void any compromise with the Moroccan sovereign.[89]

The military route remained open and perhaps, as we have seen, Fernando III could have taken some action. Death stalled his efforts, and the African project was passed on to his son, devoid of imperial whims. And yet the awareness of the possibility of an imperial project in Africa would not disappear completely in the following years. In fact, we know that the *Rey Sabio* himself, following the announcement of the Toledo Cortes of 1259 concerning the *fecho del Imperio*, sought advice from his vassal, Emir Muḥammad I of Granada, a man who had been very close to Fernando III and his policies. The Nasrid king responded that he should direct himself towards Africa rather than Germany, and that

---

84 Ibn ʿIdhārī, *Al-Bayan*, II: 199.
85 Ibn Abī Zarʿ, *Rawd al-qirtās*, II: 501–2.
86 The French translation of the text can be found in Tisserant and Wiet, "Une lettre de l'almohade Murtaḍā," 34–7.
87 Rodríguez García, *Ideología cruzada*, 113.
88 Quintana, *Inocencio IV*, no. 712.
89 Ibid., nos. 718–9.

with Granada's help, Alfonso could obtain a much greater and better empire to the south.[90] Yet this remained a vision that would not be articulated until many years later, when the *Poema de Alfonso XI* was to spell out the association of crusade leadership, empire and Africa:

Don Alfonso, rey d'España,
luego emperador será,
con gran poder de compaña
el Estrecho pasará.[91]

Works Cited

Primary Sources (Published)

Alfonso X el Sabio. *Setenario*. Ed. Kenneth H. Vanderford. Barcelona: Crítica, 1984.

Alberic of Trois-Fontaines. "*Chronica Alberici, monachi Trium fontium a monacho novi monasterii Hoiensis interpolata.*" In *Monumenta Germaniae Historica. Scriptores*, ed. P. Scheffer-Boichorst. Vol. 23. Hanover: 1874.

"*Annales Colonienses Maximi.*" In *Monumenta Germaniae Historica. Scriptores*, ed. Karl August Fredrich Pertz. Vol. 17. Hanover: 1861.

Charlo Brea, Luis, ed. *Chronica latina regum Castellae*. In *Chronica Hispana Saeculi XIII*, ed. Luis Charlo Brea, Juan Estévez Sola and Rocío Carande Herrero. Vol. 73 of *Corpus Christianorum: Continuatio medievalis*, 7–118. Turnhout: Brepols, 1997.

Domínguez Sánchez, Santiago. *Documentos de Gregorio IX (1227–1241) referentes a España*. León: Universidad de León, 2004.

Fernández Conde, Francisco Javier, Isabel Torrente Fernández, and Guadalupe de la Noval Menéndez. *El Monasterio de San Pelayo de Oviedo. Historia y Fuentes*, I. *Colección Diplomática (996–1325)*. Oviedo: Monasterio de San Pelayo, 1978.

Gambra, Andrés. *Alfonso VI. Cancillería, Curia e Imperio*, II. *Colección Diplomática*. León: Centro de Estudios e Investigación "San Isidoro," 1998.

González Jiménez, Manuel, ed. *Diplomatario Andaluz de Alfonso X*. Sevilla: Caja de Huelva y Sevilla, 1991.

González, Julio, ed. *Reinado y Diplomas de Fernando III*. 3 vols. Córdoba: Monte de Piedad y Caja de Ahorros, 1980–1986.

---

90 *muy mayor e meior imperio que aquél*: González Jiménez, *Diplomatario Andaluz de Alfonso X*, no. 286.
91 Victorio, *Poema de Alfonso Onceno*, 394. See Nussbaum, "El pensamiento político," 28 and fn. 34.

Herrero de la Fuente, Marta. *Colección diplomática del monasterio de Sahagún (857–1230), III (1073–1109)*. León: Centro de Estudios e Investigación "San Isidoro," 1988.

Huici Miranda, Ambrosio, trans. *Al-Hulal al Mawsiyya: crónica árabe de las dinastías almorávide, almohade y benimerín*. Tetuan: Editora Marroquí, 1951.

Huillard-Bréholles, Jean-Louis-Alphonse. *Historia Diplomatica Frederici Secundi, sive constitutiones, privilegia, manata, instrumenta...* Vol. 5, Part 1. Paris: Henricus Plon, 1857.

Ibn Abī Zarʿ. *Al-anīs al-muṭrib bi-rawḍ al-qirṭās fī akhbār mulūk al-Maghrib wa-taʾrīkh madīnat Fās*. Trans. Ambrosio Huici Miranda. 2 vols. Valencia: Textos Medievales, 1964.

Ibn ʿIdhārī al-Marrākushi. *Al-Bayan al-Mughrib fi ijtisar akhbar Muluk al-Andalus wa al-Maghrib*. Trans. Ambrosio Huici Miranda. 2 vols. Tetuan: Editora Marroquí, 1953–1954.

Jimeno, Roldán and Aitor Pescador. *Colección documental de Sancho Garcés III, el Mayor, rey de Pamplona (1004–1035)*. Pamplona: Nabarralde, 2003.

Jiménez de Rada, Rodrigo. *Historia de rebus Hispanie, sive Historia Gothica*. Ed. Juan Fernández Valverde. Vol. 72 of *Corpus Christianorum: Continuatio mediaeualis*. Turnhout: Brepols, 1987.

Lucas of Tuy. *Chronicon mundi*. Ed. Emma Falque Rey. Vol. 74 of *Corpus Christianorum: Continuatio mediaeualis*. Turnhout: Brepols, 2003.

MacDonald, Robert A. *Espéculo. Texto jurídico atribuido al Rey de Castilla Don Alfonso X, el Sabio. Edición, introducción y aparato crítico*. Madison: Hispanic Seminary of Medieval Studies, 1990.

Mansilla, Demetrio. *La documentación pontificia de Honorio III (1216–1227)*. Rome: Instituto Español de Historia Eclesiástica, 1965.

Mansilla, Demetrio. *La documentación pontificia hasta Inocencio III, 965–2016*. Rome: Instituto Español de Estudios Eclesiásticos, 1955.

Martínez Díez, Gonzalo. "La tradición manuscrita del Fuero de León y del Concilio de Coyanza." In *El Reino de León en la Alta Edad Media*, II. *Ordenamiento jurídico del Reino*, 117–188. León: Centro de Estudios e Investigación "San Isidoro," 1992.

Mas Latrie, M.L. de. *Traités de paix et de commerce et documents divers concernant les relations des chrétiens avec les árabes de l'Afrique septentrionale au Moyen Âge*. Paris: Librairie Droz, 1866.

Matthew Paris. *Chronica Majora*. Ed. Henry R. Luard. Vol. 5. London: Longman, 1880.

Primera crónica general de España. Ed. Ramón Menéndez Pidal et al. Madrid: Gredos, 1955.

Quintana Prieto, Augusto. *La documentación pontificia de Inocencio IV (1243–1254)*. Rome: Instituto Español de Historia Eclesiástica, 1987.

Rymer, T. *Foedera, conventiones, litterae et cuiuscumque generis acta inter reges Angliae et alios imperatores, reges, pontifices, principes vel communitates ab ineundo saeculo duodecimo*. London, 1704.

Sbaralea, Juan Jacinto. *Ad Bullarium Franciscanum*. Rome, 1759.
Tisserant, Eugène and Gaston Wiet. "Une lettre de l'almohade Murtaḍā au pape Innocent IV." *Hesperis* 6 (1926): 27–53.
Victorio, Juan, ed. *Poema de Alfonso Onceno*. Madrid: Cátedra, 1991.
Wading, Lukas. *Annales minorum...*, Rome, 1732.

Secondary Sources

Albarrán Iruela, Javier. "De la conversión y expulsión al mercenariado: la ideología en torno a los cristianos en las crónicas almohades." In *La Península Ibérica en tiempos de Las Navas de Tolosa*, ed. Carlos Estepa and María Antonia Carmona, 79–91. Madrid: Monografías de la Sociedad Española de Estudios Medievales, 2014.

Ayala Martínez, Carlos de. "De nuevo sobre la documentación de Honorio III y Castilla." In *Medieval Studies: In Honour of Peter Linehan*, ed. Francisco Hernández, Rocío Sánchez Ameijeiras and Emma Falque, 153–168. Florence: Sismel, 2018.

Ayala Martínez, Carlos de. *Directrices fundamentales de la política peninsular de Alfonso X (Relaciones castellano-aragonesas de 1252 a 1263)*. Madrid: Universidad Autónoma de Madrid, 1986.

Ayala Martínez, Carlos de. "Fernando I y la sacralización de la *reconquista*." *Anales de la Universidad de Alicante. Historia Medieval* 17 (2011): 67–115.

Ayala Martínez, Carlos de. "Fernando III: figura, significado y contexto en tiempo de cruzada." In *Fernando III, tiempo de cruzada*, ed. Carlos de Ayala Martínez and Martín Ríos Saloma, 17–91. Madrid-México: Sílex-UNAM, 2012.

Ayala Martínez, Carlos de. "La realeza en la cronística castellano-leonesa del siglo XIII: la imagen de Fernando III." In *Monarquía, crónicas, archivos y cancillerías en los reinos hispano-cristianos*, ed. Esteban Sarasa-Sánchez, 247–276. Zaragoza: Institución "Fernando el Católico," 2014.

Ayala Martínez, Carlos de. "Los inicios de la Orden de Calatrava y la monarquía castellana." In *Órdenes militares y construcción de la sociedad occidental. Cultura, religiosidad y desarrollo social de los espacios de frontera (siglos XII–XV)*, ed. Raquel Torres Jiménez and Francisco Ruiz Gómez, 223–266. Madrid: Sílex, 2016.

Ayala Martínez, Carlos de. "Obispos, guerra santa y cruzada en los reinos de León y Castilla (s. XII)." In *Cristianos y musulmanes en la Península Ibérica: la guerra, la frontera y la convivencia. XI Congreso de Estudios Medievales*, 219–256. León: Fundación Sánchez Albornoz, 2009.

Ayala Martínez, Carlos de. *Órdenes militares, monarquía y espiritualidad militar en los reinos de Castilla y León (siglos XII–XIII)*. Granada: Universidad de Granada, 2015.

Ayala Martínez, Carlos de. "Religiosidad Militar y Cancillería Regia: El discurso sobre la Guerra Santa en el Reinado de Alfonso VII (1135–1157)." In *Cister e as Ordens Militares na Idade Média. Guerra, Igreja e Vida Religiosa*, ed. Albuquerque Carreiras and Ayala Martínez, 47–72. Tomar: Studium Cistercium et Militarium Ordinum, 2015.

Bartolomé Bellón, Gabriel. "La *idea imperial* leonesa (ss. IX–XII)." *Ab Initio* 9 (2014): 61–117.

Barton, Simon. "Traitors to faith? Christian mercenaries in al-Andalus, c. 1100–1300." In *Medieval Spain. Culture, Conflict and Coexistence. Studies in Honour of Angus MacKay*, ed. Roger Collins and Anthony Goodman, 23–45. Basingstoke: Palgrave Macmillan, 2002.

Benaboud, Muhammad and Angus Mackay. "The authenticity of Alfonso VI's letter to Yûsuf b. Tâsufin." *Al-Andalus* 43 (1978): 233–237.

Carlyle, Robert and Alexander Carlyle. *A History of Mediaeval Political Theory in the West*. Vol. 2. Edinburgh: Blackwood, 1950.

Castellanos, Fr. Manuel P. *Apostolado seráfico en Marruecos, o sea Historia de las misiones franciscanas en aquel Imperio desde el siglo XIII a nuestros días*. Madrid: Librería de D. Gregorio del Amo, 1896.

Catalán, Diego. "Alfonso X no utilizó el *Toledano romanzado*," excerpt from "El Toledano romanzado y las Estorias del fecho de los godos del s. XV." In *Estudios dedicados a James Herriott*, ed. James Herriott, 9–102. Madison: University of Wisconsin, 1966.

Catalán, Diego. "El taller historiográfico alfonsí. Métodos y problemas en el trabajo compilatorio." *Romania* 84 (1963): 354–375.

Catalán, Diego. *La Estoria de España de Alfonso X. Creación y evolución*. Madrid: Fundación Ramón Menéndez Pidal – Universidad Autónoma de Madrid, 1992.

Cenival, Pierre de. "L'église chretienne de Marrakech au XIIIe siècle." *Hesperis* 7 (1927): 69–83.

Chodorow, Stanley. *Christian Political Theory and Church Politics in the Mid-Twelfth Century: the Ecclesiology of Gratian's "Decretum."* Berkeley: University of California Press, 1972.

Claverie, Pierre-Vincent. *Honorius III et l'Orient: Étude et publication de sources inédites des Archives Vaticanes (ASV)*. Leiden: Brill, 2013.

Colmenero López, Daniel. "La boda entre Fernando III el Santo y Beatriz de Suabia: motivos y perspectivas de una alianza matrimonial entre la Corona de Castilla y los Staufer." *Miscelánea Medieval Murciana* 34 (2010): 9–92.

Craddock, Jerry R. "El *Setenario*: última e inconclusa refundición alfonsina de la primera *Partida*." *Anuario de Historia del Derecho Español* 56 (1986): 441–466.

Diago Hernando, Máximo. "La monarquía castellana y los Staufer. Contactos políticos y diplomáticos en los siglos XII y XIII." *Espacio, Tiempo y Forma. H^a Medieval* 8 (1995): 51–83.

Estepa Díez, Carlos. *El reinado de Alfonso VI*. Madrid: Hullera Vasco-Leonesa, 1985.

Estepa Díez, Carlos. "El reino de Castilla y el imperio: de Alfonso VIII a Fernando III." In *La Península Ibérica en tiempos de Las Navas de Tolosa*, ed. Carlos Estepa and María Antonia Carmona, 237–264. Madrid: Monografías de la Sociedad Española de Estudios Medievales, 2014.

Fanning, Steven. "Bede, *Imperium* and the Bretwaldas." *Speculum* 66 (1991): 1–26.
Fernández Gallardo, Luis. "La *Crónica particular de San Fernando*: sobre los orígenes de la crónica real castellana, I. Aspectos formales." *Cahiers d'Études Hispaniques Médiévales* 32 (2009): 245–265.
Fernández Gallardo, Luis. "La *Crónica particular de San Fernando*: sobre los orígenes de la crónica real castellana, II. Los contenidos." *Cahiers d'Études Hispaniques Médiévales* 33 (2010): 215–246.
Fernández Gallardo, Luis. "La crónica real, ca. 1310–1490, Conflictividad y memoria colectiva." In *El conflicto en escenas. La pugna política como representación en la Castilla bajomedieval*, ed. José Manuel Nieto Soria, 281–322. Madrid: Sílex, 2010.
Fernández-Ordóñez, Inés. "La denotación de 'España' en la Edad Media. Perspectiva historiográfica (siglos VII–XIV)." In *Actas del IX Congreso Internacional de Historia de la Lengua Española (Cádiz, 2012)*, ed. Teresa Bastardín Candón and Manuel Rivas Zancarrón. Vol. 1, 49–106. Madrid: Iberoamericana, 2015.
Ferreiro Alemparte, Jaime. "España y Alemania en la Edad Media." *Boletín de la Real Academia de la Historia* 170 and 171 (1973–1974): 319–376 and 467–573.
Fierro, Maribel. "La religión." In *Historia de España*, VIII-2. *El retroceso territorial de al-Andalus. Almorávides y almohades. Siglos XI al XIII*, ed. Ramon Menéndez Pidal, 435–546. Madrid: Espasa-Calpe, 1997.
García Sanjuán, Alejandro. "Mercenarios cristianos al servicio de los musulmanes en el norte de África durante el siglo XIII." In *La Península Ibérica entre el Mediterráneo y el Atlántico. Siglos XIII–XV*, ed. M. González Jiménez and I. Montes Romero-Camacho, 435–447. Seville-Cádiz: Sociedad Española de Estudios Medievales, 2006.
Gil, Juan. "A apropiação da ideia de Império pelos reinos da Península Ibérica: Castela." *Penélope: revista de história e ciencias sociais* 15 (1995): 17–18.
Gómez Redondo, Fernando. *Historia de la prosa medieval castellana*, I. *La creación del discurso prosístico: el entramado cortesano*. Madrid: Cátedra, 1998.
Gómez Redondo, Fernando. *Historia de la prosa medieval castellana*, II. *El desarrollo de los géneros. La ficción caballeresca y el orden religioso*. Madrid: Cátedra, 1999.
Goñi Gaztambide, José. *Historia de la bula de cruzada en España*. Vitoria: Editorial del Seminario, 1958.
González Jiménez, Manuel. *Fernando III el Santo*. Seville: Fundación José Manuel Lara, 2006.
Goodman, Anthony. "Alfonso X and the English Crown." In *Alfonso X el Sabio, vida, obra y época*, ed. Manuel González Jiménez and Juan Carlos de Miguel Rodríguez, 39–54. Madrid: Sociedad Española de Estudios Medievales, 1989.
Gorosterratzu, Javier. *Don Rodrigo Jiménez de Rada, gran estadista, escritor y prelado*. Pamplona: Imp. y Lib. de viuda de T. Bescansa, 1925.
Isla Frez, Amancio. *Realezas hispánicas del año mil*. A Coruña: Seminario de Estudos Galegos, 1999.

Kedar, Benjamin Z. *Crusade and Mission: European Approaches toward the Muslims.* Princeton: Princeton University Press, 1988.

Ladero Quesada, Miguel Ángel. "Unidad y diversidad en la España medieval. En torno a las ideas de nación, patria y estado." In *Fundamentos medievales de los particularismos hispánicos. IX Congreso de Estudios Medievales*, 17–39. León: Fundación Sánchez-Albornoz, 2003.

Lomax, Derek. "La conquista de Andalucía a través de la historiografía europea de la época." In *Andalucía entre Oriente y Occidente (1236–1492). Actas del V Coloquio Internacional de Historia Medieval de Andalucía*, ed. Emilio Muñoz Cabrera, 37–49. Córdoba: Diputación Provincial, 1988.

López, Fr. Atanasio. *Obispos de África septentrional desde el siglo XIII.* Tánger: Instituto General Franco para la Investigación Hispano-Arabe, 1941.

Mackay, Angus and Muhammad Benaboud. "Alfonso VI of León and Castile, *al-Imbrtūr dhū-l-Millatayn*." *Bulletin of Hispanic Studies* 56 (1979): 95–102.

Mackay, Angus and Muhammad Benaboud. "Yet again Alfonso VI, 'the Emperor, Lord of [the Adherents of] the Two Faiths, the Most Excellent Ruler': A rejoinder to Norman Roth." *Bulletin of Hispanic Studies* 61 (1984): 171–181.

Martin, Georges. "De nuevo sobre la fecha del *Setenario.*" *e-Spania* 2 (2006). DOI: 10.4000/e-spania.381.

Menéndez Pidal, Ramón. *La España del Cid.* 2 vols. Madrid: Espasa-Calpe, 1969.

Mosquera Merino, María del Carmen. *La señoría de Ceuta en el siglo XIII (Historia política y económica).* Ceuta: Instituto de Estudios Ceutíes, 1994.

Nieto Soria, José Manuel. "La monarquía fundacional de Fernando III." In *Fernando III y su tiempo (1201–1252). VIII Congreso de Estudios Medievales*, 31–66. León: Fundación Sánchez Albornoz, 2003.

Nussbaum, Fernanda. "El pensamiento político en el *Poema de Alfonso XI*: La relación Monarquía-Iglesia." *Boletín Hispánico Helvético* 7 (2006): 5–44.

O'Callaghan, Joseph. *El Rey Sabio. El reinado de Alfonso X de Castilla.* Sevilla: Universidad de Sevilla, 1996.

O'Callaghan, Joseph. *Reconquest and Crusade in Medieval Spain.* Philadelphia: University of Pennsylvania, 2003.

Ochoa Sanz, Javier. *Vincentius Hispanus, canonista boloñés del siglo XIII.* Rome-Madrid: CSIC, 1960.

Post, Gaines. "*Blessed Lady Spain*: Vincentius Hispanus and Spanish National Imperialism in the Thirteenth Century." *Speculum* 29 (1954): 198–209.

Post, Gaines. *Studies in Medieval Legal Thought: Public Law and the State 1100–1322.* Princeton: Princeton University Press, 1964.

Robinson, I.S. *The Papacy, 1073–1198: Continuity and Innovation.* Cambridge: Cambridge University Press, 1990.

Rodríguez García, José Manuel. *Ideología cruzada en el siglo XIII. Una visión desde la Castilla de Alfonso X*. El Puerto de Santa María: Cátedra Alfonso X el Sabio-Universidad de Sevilla, 2014.

Rodríguez López, Ana. "El Reino de Castilla y el Imperio germánico en la primera mitad del siglo XIII. Fernando III y Federico II." In *Historia social, Pensamiento historiográfico y Edad Media. Homenaje al Prof. Abilio Barbero de Aguilera*, ed. María Isabel Loring García, 613–630. Madrid: Ediciones del Orto, 1997.

Sánchez Candeira, Alonso. *El "regnum-imperium" leonés hasta 1037*. Madrid: Escuela de Estudios Medievales, 1951.

Sayers, Jane. *Papal Government and England during the Pontificate of Honorius III (1216–1227)*. Cambridge: Cambridge University Press, 1984.

Sirantoine, Hélène. *Imperator Hispaniae. Les idéologies impériales dans le royaume de León (IXe–XIIe siècles)*. Madrid: Casa de Velázquez, 2012.

Smith, Damian. "The Iberian Legations of Cardinal Hyacinth Bobone." In *Pope Celestine III (1191–1198): Diplomat and Pastor*, ed. John Doran and Damian J. Smith, 81–111. Aldershot: Ashgate, 2008.

Tyerman, Christopher. *How to Plan a Crusade: Religious War in the High Middle Ages*. Pegasus Books: New York, 2017.

CHAPTER 2

The Man "Who Broke and Destroyed All of His Enemies": The Military Action of Fernando III

Francisco García Fitz

The epitaphs that Alfonso X ordered to be inscribed on the tomb of Fernando III in the cathedral of Seville, written in four languages – Latin, Castilian, Arabic and Hebrew – dwell on the personal virtues of the king of Castile-León: he was just, loyal, sincere, forthright, illustrious, wise, pious, patient, modest, a servant of God and champion of his friends, among other accolades.[1] It is reasonable to assume that these epithets represent the image of his father that Alfonso X wanted to consecrate to posterity. However, Alfonso X did not limit himself to expounding his father's unique virtues: he also capitalized on the perpetuity of the marble tomb to lay bare some of his political achievements, doubtless, those he considered to be the most relevant. Accordingly, it is especially noteworthy that, of the many political actions that he could have chosen to consecrate the memory and political legacy of his father, all of those chosen relate to his military activities. In each of the four versions of the epitaph there is a reminder of Fernando's conquest of Spain: *qui totam Hispaniam conquisivit* in the Latin; *el que conquisso toda España* in the Castilian text; and likewise in the Arabic and Hebrew.[2] Equally in all four it is pointed out that "he conquered the city of Seville," a pertinent point considering that Seville was the place of his burial. Significantly, the Latin version substitutes the idea of the city's "conquest" for that of seizing it from the hands of the pagans and restoring it to Christian worship. Also, in all four, Alfonso undertook to emphasize the fact that it was Fernando III "who broke and destroyed all of his enemies" or a very similar variant in the Latin text: *qui contrivit et exterminavit penitus hostium*

---

[1] This work was carried out in the context of the FFI2015-64765-P and HAR2016-74968-P research projects by the Ministry of Economy and Competitiveness and is part of the activities of Research Group HUM023 within the catalogue of Research Groups of the Regional Government of Extremadura, financed by ERDF funds. It was translated by Robert Taylor. These four epitaphs are reproduced and are translated in Nickson, "Remembering Fernando." For more on the epitaphs, see Castro, *La realidad histórica*, 31–2; Dodds, Menocal and Krasner, *The Arts of Intimacy*, 200–1, in this volume Boloix-Gallardo, Chp. 3.

[2] The Arabic states that "he conquered all of al-Andalus," and the Hebrew that "he conquered all of Spain."

suorum proterviam. Indeed, if we are to judge the historical significance of the reign of Fernando III according to the testimony bequeathed to us by his son, there is no doubt that his military endeavors, his role as a conquering king who prevailed over his enemies by force, stands out above any other aspect of his career, including, for instance, a political event as important as the unification of the kingdoms of Castile and León.

Aside from the undoubtedly well-informed opinion of Alfonso X, it is clear that the military action of Fernando III – particularly the wars he brought against his Muslim neighbors in al-Andalus – indisputably constitutes one of the primary leitmotifs of his political legacy. This was certainly the perception reflected in the works of contemporary chroniclers from elsewhere in the Latin West, notably, for example, in the writings of the English monk and chronicler from the abbey of St Alban's, Matthew Paris, who commented on the legacy of his "famous deeds and great conquests over the Muslims in Spain."[3] The chronicler also listed the scope of the conquests of the Castilian king as well as his titles and "wide-spread fame," to which he compared Edward I of England rather unfavorably.[4] Indeed, comparison of the military successes of Fernando III with those of his contemporaries, Sancho II of Portugal, Jaime I of Aragón, Louis IX of France, Frederick II of the Holy Roman Empire, and Edward I of England, led Derek Lomax to point out that "at a time when the crusading efforts of all the rest of Christendom hardly sufficed to maintain a foothold on the coast of the Holy Land, Fernando inflicted on medieval Islam its greatest defeat so far, and one equaled only by the Mongol sack of Baghdad ten years later."[5]

A look at the facts leaves no room for doubt concerning the success of Fernando's military action against Islam: in the twenty-eight years from 1224, when he embarked on his military activity on the southern borders of Castile, until his death in 1252, he had managed to annex the remains of the Islamic territory that still existed north of the Sierra Morena at the time of the death of Alfonso VIII, all of the Guadalquivir valley, including (as is well known) the foremost Andalusian cities of Jaén, Córdoba, and Seville, and the entire kingdom of Murcia. Finally, he completed the conquest of territory located between the Tagus and Guadiana rivers in Extremadura, which at the moment of death of Alfonso IX of León, had still remained under Muslim rule.

---

3 *Praeclara gesta sua et super infideles Hispaniae conquisitiones maximas*: Matthew Paris, *Chronica Majora*, v, 311. See also, Lomax, "La conquista de Andalucía," 37–50.
4 *Eisdem diebus dilitata est fama regis Hispaniae, sed non regis* [ie, of England], *cujus titulus in scriptis ipsius talis scribitur; Alfonsus* [Fernando III] *Dei gratia rex Castellae, Legionis, Galleciae, Toleti, Murciae, Cordubae, et Jehenni*: Matthew Paris, *Chronica Majora*, v, 399.
5 Lomax, *The Reconquest of Spain*, 156.

All this encompasses some 104,000 square kilometers, in other words, three times more than that conquered by Jaime I in the Balearic Islands and Valencia (28,247 km²), twenty times more than that conquered by the Portuguese kings in the Algarve (4,960 km²), slightly more than the inheritance he received from his father in León in 1230 (100,000 km²) and two thirds of what he had inherited from his mother in Castile in 1217 (150,000 km²). It should also be added that the most important of the Muslim states that survived his expansionist policy – the Nasrid Kingdom of Granada – was officially his vassal, as in all probability were other lesser kingdoms, such as the Kingdom of Niebla and the small villages that survived in the Guadalete valley following the conquest of Seville in 1248, and which were at least tributaries.[6]

In view of this, the famous phrase attributed to Fernando on his deathbed, addressed to his heir, reflected a palpable reality:

> I leave you Lord all the land on this side of the sea that the Moors won from King Roderick of Spain; all of it remains under your Lordship: one part conquered, the other part subject to tribute[7]

Clearly, it was Fernando's military endeavors that had made a political and territorial expansion on this scale possible.

1 The Rhetoric of Fernando III's Military Actions

Let us first turn to the nature and character of this military action. This study will start by clarifying, as far as possible, what Alfonso X himself wished to say by announcing on the epitaph at Seville that his father "broke and destroyed all of his enemies." Interpreted verbatim, the meaning is clear: he defeated and put an end to his enemies. In the Latin version of the epitaph, two other verbs are used which are even more forceful when describing the actions of Fernando III: *conterere* (that is, to destroy or grind,) and *exterminare* (that is, to crush, exterminate or eliminate), although these terms do not apply to the enemies themselves, as in the Castilian, Arabic and Hebrew versions, but rather to the evil or wickedness of these enemies.[8]

---

6   *Fernando III*, I: 287–395; see also Martínez Díez, *Fernando III*, 49–251, esp. 73–96, and 123–237; Rodríguez López, *Consolidación territorial*, 112–33; González Jiménez, *Fernando III*, 133–250.
7   *Señor te dexo de toda la tierra de la mar aca, que los moros del rey Rodrigo de Espanna ganado ouieron; et en tu sennorio finca toda: la vna conquerida, la otra tributada*: PCG, 772.
8   *contrivit et exterminavit penitus hostium suorum proterviam.*

This is not the only occasion on which Alfonso X turned to such an emphatic image to describe the military action of his father. In his wide-ranging encyclopedic work known as the *Setenario*, when explaining the meaning of the seven letters that spell the name FERNANDO, Alfonso repeats again that "the R shows that he was very robust in his will and in his actions to destroy the enemies of Faith and also the evildoers."⁹

This language refers us to a discourse within which the military action of Fernando is described in terms of an absolute, unequivocal confrontation with an enemy whose nature transcends the political plane and delves into the theological. The adversaries that have been vanquished are the enemies of the Faith, of God himself. They are infidels or pagans who at some stage disrupted and violated Christianity. As a consequence, the conquests are interpreted in terms that symbolize legitimate violence and the recovery of that which had belonged to Christianity.¹⁰ In the Latin version of the epitaph, this is precisely how Alfonso X presents the military endeavors of Fernando against Seville: he was "the one who seized from the pagans the city of Seville, the head and metropolis of all Spain, and returned it to the Christian cult."¹¹

Seizing from the pagans, returning to the Christians: such was the battle that his father had led, in the opinion of Alfonso X. This Alfonsine image ties in with that afforded by the many contemporary texts on Fernando III which formed the profile of what Carlos de Ayala defined as "a crusader king."¹² It also connects, in a very special way, with the discourse that the chancellor Juan of Osma attributes in the *Latin Chronicle of the Kings of Castile* to Fernando III when, in 1224, he gathered the court in Muñó to express his intent to wage war against Islam. The speech to which we refer is well-known to historians, but it is nonetheless worth recalling here because it presents a complete picture of the interpretation of Fernando's war against the Muslims of al-Andalus.¹³ According to Juan of Osma's account, Fernando III informed his royal court in 1224 that through Almighty God – or perhaps *by* Almighty God – the time had come for the king to serve the Lord Jesus Christ, for the honor and glory of his

---

9   *La R muestra que ffué muy rrezio en la voluntad e en ffecho para quebrantar los enemigos de la Ffe e otrossí los malffechores*: Alfonso X, *Setenario*, 8.
10 On this ideological rhetoric, see Tolan, "Las traducciones y la ideología de la Reconquista," 79–85.
11 *qui civitatem hispalensem, quae caput est, et metropolis totius Hispaniae de manibus eripuit paganorum, et cultui restituit christiano*: Castro, *La realidad histórica*, 31–2.
12 Ayala Martínez, "Fernando III," 17–9.
13 CLRC, 85–7; Echevarría, "Política respecto al musulmán," 383. See also in this volume Ayala Martínez, Chp. 1.

name, against the enemies of the Christian faith.¹⁴ The historical circumstances of the time, the king informed the assembly, revealed it thus: peace had been returned to the kingdom of Castile, while discord and enmities had arisen between the Moors. Divine providence had created favorable conditions for the king to enter the service of God, specifically, by fighting against the enemies of the Faith.

However, of the greatest significance – at least inasmuch as it concurs with the Latin content of the epitaph dedicated to him by his son – is the fact that he would not be alone in that fight; more specifically, Christ would be on the side of the Christians against their neighbors from the south. On the side of their adversaries, on the other hand, would be "the infidel, condemned apostate Muhammad."

> Behold, by Almighty God a time is revealed in which, unless I wish to feign cowardice and sloppiness, I can serve the Lord Jesus Christ against the enemies of the Christian faith, for who the kings reign, for the honor and glory of his name. The gates are open and the way is clear. Peace has been returned to us in our kingdom; discord and profound enmities sown among the Moors and disputes emerging afresh. Christ, God and man, on our side; on the side of the Moors, the infidel, condemned apostate Muhammad. What therefore remains?¹⁵

Both images – the Latin epitaph and the discourse reproduced by Juan of Osma – relate to a world view within which the king is merely an instrument of God's will in the context of a universal confrontation between two theologically constituted communities, one led by God and another by Muhammad: the *Civitas Dei* against the *Civitas Diaboli*, if we wish to apply Augustinian political logic.¹⁶ Thus, it is not a political or territorial war that Fernando III intends to embark on from the borders of his kingdom; instead, it is a conflict that transcends the earthly to become supernatural and absolute, namely that of Good against Evil.¹⁷

---

14 CLRC, 85–7.
15 *Ecce tempus reuelatur ab omnipotente Deo in quo, nisi tanquam pusillanimis et deses dissimulare uelim, domino Iesu Christo, per quem reges regnant, seruire possum contra inimicos fidei christiane ad honorem et gloriam nominis eius. Porta siquidem aperta est et uia manifesta. Pax nobis reddita est in regno nostro; discordia et capitales inimicicie inter Mauros, secte et rixe de nouo exhorte. Christus Deus et homo ex parte nostra; ex parte uero Maurorum infidelis et dampnatus apostata Mahometus. Quid ergo restat?* : CLRC, 62.
16 García Pelayo, "El Reino de Dios," 198–9.
17 García Fitz, "Conquista de Andalucía," 55–6.

The account of the war against Islam that arises from this principle is complex, but very coherent and, in addition to being present in many other passages of the *Latin Chronicle*, it is also found in various contemporary sources relating to Fernando III. As emphasized in Fernando's speech at Muñó, war against the Muslims is a service to God, and one that was undertaken, as Juan of Osma points out in his description of the conquest of Córdoba, "for the honor of the Christian faith."[18] Similarly, Lucas of Tuy, recounting the agreement between Alfonso IX of León and Fernando III of Castile, claims that "the kings of Spain fight for faith, and they conquer everywhere."[19]

And those who carry out this mission are not ordinary warriors, but rather soldiers of God. Fernando III was particularly so: he is literally regarded as *miles Christi* by the bishop of Osma.[20] This monarch had taken a solemn vow to Christ – he was *uoti compos* – which he was ready to fulfill; the *Latin Chronicle* tells us that "the Spirit of the Lord had erupted" within him; he was "guided by the Holy Spirit" and "his heart had been set on fire by Jesus Christ to go to the siege of Córdoba"; all in all, God was with him.[21] In the words of another contemporary, Archbishop Rodrigo Jiménez de Rada of Toledo, the Castilian monarch had offered "the first fruits of his military life" to Christ.[22] Therefore, it is clear that Juan of Osma considered that it was directly "the indignation of our Lord Jesus Christ and his power" that "oppressed such a large and strong mass of Muslims" in Córdoba; the warriors led by Fernando III were simply a tool of God.[23]

In light of this rhetorical backdrop, it becomes clear that, for King Fernando and his chroniclers, the exercise of war not only achieved the extension of political command over territory taken from an enemy people, but also extended the parameters of Christianity and the Christian faith, parameters which had been violated by Muslim conquest in the eighth century and which the victorious military activity of Fernando III was now able to restore: "by the virtue of our Lord Jesus Christ, Córdoba... which... since the time of the King of the Goths Don Rodrigo was held captive, was returned to the Christian faith thanks

---

18 *pro honore fidei christiana*: CLRC, 94.
19 *Pugnant Yspani reges pro fide et ubique uincunt*: CM, 334.
20 *miles Christi fortissimus rex Fernandus*: CLRC, 94.
21 *in quem Spiritus Domini irruerat*: CLRC, 69; *consilio Spiritus Sancti ductus*: Ibid., 96; *Dominus ego Iesu Christus... qui cor regis inflamauerat ad ueniendum Cordubam... Cum quo Deus erat*: Ibid., 97.
22 *milicie sue primicias uoluit Domino dedicare*: DrH, 292.
23 *quoniam indignatio Domini Iesu Christi et ipsius potencia tantam multitudine Maurorum et tam validam comprimebat*: CLRC, 93.

to the endeavor and bravery of King Fernando."²⁴ According to the Latin epitaph that Alfonso X had dedicated to him, that is exactly what Fernando III had done in Seville when he "restored it to the Christian faith."²⁵

Moreover, this interpretation concurred with the position of the papacy with regard to the military action of Fernando III on his southern borders. In response to the protests of certain Castilian bishops, led by the archbishop of Toledo, Rodrigo Jiménez de Rada, over the excesses committed by agents of the king against ecclesiastical privileges and revenue, in 1228 Pope Gregory IX reminded them that the king of Castile "fights for Christ, while challenging the traitorous nations, expands the dominion of the Bride of Christ and lays out the pavilions of the tabernacles, and the more the Christian religion spreads so does the Church"; consequently, he urged them, without detriment to ecclesiastical freedom, to prevent the king from "being compelled to abandon such a healthy, holy venture, for want of the desired subsidy."²⁶

In full accordance with this theologically all-encompassing vision of the war against the Muslims, Bishop and Chancellor Juan of Osma explains that having conquered Córdoba, as with so many other places, after proceeding to expel "the superstition or Mohammedan heresy" from the city's central mosque, "what was formerly a diabolical den was made a Church of Jesus Christ."²⁷ Once again, we are presented with the image of universal, theological confrontation and the king's "firm, irrevocable intention to destroy those cursed people."²⁸ Could there have been, faced with the supporters of Evil and enemies of God, any other option than their total destruction, such as Alfonso X enshrined on the epitaph of his father?

However, the analysis of the specific acts of war carried out by Fernando III throughout his career goes some way towards refuting, or at least offering a

---

24   *per uirtutem Domini nostri Iesu Christi Corduba... queque tanto tempore captiua tenebatur, scilicet a tempore Roderici, regis gotorum, redita est cultui christiano per laborem et strenuitatem domini nostri regis Ferrandi*: Ibid., 99.
25   *cultui restituit christiano*, Castro: *La realidad histórica*, 31–2.
26   *Rex Castelle illustris Christo militare probatur, dum impugnans perfidas nationes, dilatat locum tentorii sponse Christi et pelles tabernaculorum eius extendit. Et quanto in partibus illis latius propagatur religio chistiana, tanto generalis ecclesia et Toletana specialiter gratiora suscipiet incrementa... nec quod absit dictus Rex pro defectu sperati subsidii, rem tam salubrem, tam sanctam negligere compellatur*: 1228, December, 8. Archive of Toledo Cathedral, A.6.H.1.22b. See also Gorosterratzu, *Rodrigo Jiménez de Rada*, 257–8.
27   *preparantes, que neccesaria erant ad hoc, ut ecclesia fieret de mezquita, expulsa Mahometi superstitione uel spurcicia, santificauerunt locum per aspersionem aque cum salibus benedicte, et quod prius erat cubile diaboli facta ecclesia Iesu Christi*: CLRC, 100.
28   *Rex autem firmum gerens proponitum et irreuocabile destruere gentem illam maledictam*: Ibid., 69.

more nuanced handling of the radical, all-encompassing vision offered by the above testimonies. They doubtlessly contributed to the creation of a legitimizing discourse concerning the war against the Muslims on religious and legal grounds, to create a coherent universal ideology, and to invoke the image of a "crusader king." However, not only are they incongruent with the military practice of Fernando III, on the contrary, it seems that in many ways, they simplify and distort it.

2 The Political and Military Realities of Fernando III's Endeavors

If – beyond the propagandistic and ideological rhetoric outlined above – Fernando III came at some point to claim ownership over the program of actions implicit in it, there is nonetheless a great deal of evidence to suggest that political and military reality was constantly forcing him to regulate it and suspend it if necessary, at least provisionally.[29]

In fact, when Fernando III acceded to the Castilian throne in 1217, he counted on a long-standing tradition, a political inheritance from his ancestors, which dated back to at least the second half of the eleventh century, when a very similar vision of the war against Islam had been combined systematically with a political practice in which alliance, respect and even friendship with Muslim powers was on the agenda.[30] We cannot go into the details of these many precedents here, so for now it will suffice to recall a few examples, such as the political and military support of Alfonso VI for the final two Taifa kings of Toledo – al-Ma'mūn (r. 1042–75) and his grandson al-Qādir (r. 1075–85) – both against their external enemies and against their internal rivals; or the scheme by Alfonso VII to transform King Zafadola, not only into a figurehead of the Andalusi resistance against the Almoravid domination, but also into the political head of an al-Andalus joined in vassalage with the kingdom of Castile and León. Let us recall also the political and military collaboration of Alfonso VIII with Ibn Mardanīsh, the Wolf King of Murcia, against the establishment of the Almohads in al-Andalus.[31]

All of this points to a political project of great scope, which elsewhere I have referred to as the creation of "a submissive and tributary Muslim Spain," entailing the attachment of al-Andalus to Castile and León in terms akin to that of

---

29 Echevarría, "Política respecto al musulmán," 383–4. The contributions contained in this work complement those presented in Echevarría's study.
30 See García Fitz, *Relaciones políticas*; also Bronisch, *Reconquista y Guerra Santa*.
31 For more on these relationships, see García Fitz, *Relaciones políticas*.

vassalage, but which obviously also involved the upholding of Muslim society under the government of its own political leaders, with autonomous and autochthonous forms of government and administrative, fiscal or judicial structures, and respect for Islamic cultural and religious tradition and property.[32]

It goes without saying that the crystallization of a project of this nature required collaboration and mutual loyalty among the governmental elites of Castile and al-Andalus, but above all it had to be based on the survival of a certain *status quo* and the acceptance of the political, sociological and cultural reality of the "Other." It was, thus, far removed from any temptation for destruction or extermination, and indeed far from the theoretical, ideological and propagandistic formulations produced by the crusading language that we have previously remarked on.

Not only did Fernando III adhere to this inherited approach, he also did not delay in making a paradigm of this policy regarding Islam on the Peninsula. Here is not the place to review each one of his initiatives in chronological order, but we shall now present some of the mechanisms implemented to at least provide an overview. In any event, they had already been rehearsed when Fernando III came to power in 1217.

Perhaps the simplest – from a political or institutional perspective – was the acceptance of a truce, the end of armed hostilities, in exchange for the handing over of significant sums of money, sometimes supplemented by the surrender of territories. Indeed, this type of political agreement, which ultimately meant little more than the purchase of peace, came after a military assault or as a consequence of a realistic threat, with the weaker party attaining certain guarantees of peace, albeit in the short-term, that maintained the *status quo*, or prevented imminent destruction.

We encounter an example of this in 1227 when, having borne the brunt of the confrontation between the Almohads and the Castilians, the governor of Seville, Idris al-Ma'mūn, proclaimed himself caliph against his brother, 'Abd Allah al-'Adil, and was compelled to sign a truce with Fernando III to strengthen his position, which was also threatened by the emergence of a violent opposition led by Ibn Hūd. The cost of the truce amounted to a large sum of money and the pact was renewed in 1228 and again in 1229, on both occasions stipulating the payment of three hundred thousand maravedís. In this latter case, the caliph secured from Fernando III not only an extension of the truce,

---

32   *Una España musulmana sometida y tributaria*: García Fitz, "¿Una España musulmana?," 229.

but also direct military support which was significant for him to be able to impose his authority in North Africa.³³

With Almohad power now broken in the Peninsula, and the political map of al-Andalus fragmented in the wake of Ibn Hūd's thwarted attempts at unification, Ibn Hūd himself was forced, in 1233, to buy Fernando III's neutrality, paying 1,000 dinars a day in order to confront his two main rivals in the Peninsula – 'Abd Allah al-Bayāsī in Seville and Ibn al-Aḥmar in Arjona.³⁴ Two years later while he was attempting to take Niebla, where another local leader, Ibn Maḥfūẓ had seized power, Ibn Hūd was forced to buy not the neutrality of Fernando III, but the cessation of hostilities the latter had embarked upon against his territories in the upper Guadalquivir: 133,000 dinars for a truce lasting three years, which was accompanied by the abandonment by Ibn Hūd of two settlements in Jaén – Iznatoraf and San Esteban – which would soon pass into Castilian hands.³⁵

Considerably more complex and interesting are the political pacts made between Fernando III and certain Muslim leaders which – from the Castilian perspective – implied the submission to vassalage of the latter since they implicitly meant, on the Castilian side, the acceptance or maintenance of a Muslim state or a political core, which also benefitted from military protection against third parties. Throughout the career of Fernando III, two such examples are particularly outstanding: first, the early stages of the military intervention in the Guadalquivir valley between 1224 and 1226; and second, the events surrounding the conquest of Jaén in 1246.

The first of them offers us a truly revealing picture of the contrast between ideological message and political practice. We are already familiar with the radical, all-encompassing content of the speech that the chronicler Juan of Osma attributed to Fernando III at Muñó in 1224 and the commencement of hostilities against the Muslims subsequently, portrayed as a final confrontation of Christianity against Islam. Nevertheless, political reality offers us a substantially different account of the motivations and circumstances that led Fernando to take the initiative. Indeed, when Fernando solemnly proclaimed his intent to commence a war against al-Andalus, he was already fully aware of the division that had arisen amongst the Almohad leaders stemming from the death of al-Mustanṣir in January 1224, from which the immediate proclamation of two

---

33 Contemporary accounts of these events can be found in CLRC, 75; *Crónica de Veinte Reyes*, 303–4; Ibn 'Idhārī, *Al-Bayan*, I: 313; Ibn Khaldūn, *Historie*, II: 235; Ibn Abī Zar', *Rawḍ al-qirṭās*, 485–6; for further analysis, see García Fitz, *Relaciones políticas*, 172–6.
34 *Fernando III*, I: 319.
35 See Ibn Abī Zar', *Rawḍ al-qirṭās*, 527; *Anónimo de Madrid*, 157; Ibn 'Idhārī, *Al-Bayan*, II: 85; CLRC, 90; García Fitz, *Relaciones políticas*, 179–80.

caliphs arose – first ʿAbd al-Wahid I al-Makhlu, then al-ʿAdil – neither of whom, however, were recognized by all of the Almohad rulers of al-Andalus. One of these peninsular rulers, ʿAbd Allah al-Bayāsī, taking refuge in Baeza, would in turn proclaim himself caliph, giving rise to an armed conflict with his opponents.[36]

It is in this setting of internal conflict between the Almohad elites that the first campaign of Fernando occurred in the autumn of 1224. It is important to highlight, however, that according to the account offered by Juan of Osma, by the time Fernando set off towards the south, he had already reached a cooperative agreement with al-Bayāsī. As a result, if our chronicler the chancellor of Castile is right, and on this subject he shows himself to be very well informed, the first military intervention of Fernando III, which ended with the destruction of Quesada and the taking of a significant number of captives, aimed to consolidate the power of his Muslim ally – remember that al-Bayāsī was an Almohad ruler, previously the governor of Seville and Córdoba and recently proclaimed caliph – against his competitors for rule. The impassioned, almost eschatological crusading speech at Muñó took barely a few weeks to fade, although it is also possible that when it was pronounced – if it ever was – it was simply concealing or disguising political reality: the king of Castile had made a pact with one of the two Almohad caliphs and militarily defended his interests, meaning that he defended the political expression of Islam in al-Andalus and the Maghreb.

The agreement became official the following year. In summer 1225, Fernando again headed towards the border, and held a meeting with al-Bayāsī at Las Navas de Tolosa, where the latter and his sons became vassals of the king of Castile. Thenceforth and until the assassination of the Muslim leader in 1226, the Castilians who militarily intervened in al-Andalus did so in aid of one of the caliphs. Of course, their assistance did not come for free. In return, Fernando III would receive some settlements seized from the enemies of his vassal – Martos and Andújar – but he did not as a result of this cease to back the caliph. From barely commanding Baeza, thanks to military support from the Castilian monarch, al-Bayāsī came to control almost all of the Guadalquivir valley, including the city of Córdoba and the outskirts of Seville.[37]

It is still paradoxical that at the very same time – in September 1225 – when the territory of one of the Almohad caliphs was extending and consolidating thanks to Castilian military support, Honorius III would grant the crusaders who waged war in Castile the same indulgences as those who went to fight in

---

36   CLRC, 64–5.
37   García Fitz, *Relaciones políticas*, 164–70.

the Holy Land, and one month later urged the bishop of Palencia to donate his income from the *tercia,* originally destined for the construction of churches, towards the war against the Saracens, "for the confusion of the infidels... and for the glory and exaltation of the Christian name."[38]

The second example is well known; namely, the Treaty of Jaén, made in 1246 between Fernando III and the Nasrid Emir Muḥammad I (known before becoming emir as Ibn al-Aḥmar of Arjona).[39] The latter had already collaborated militarily with the king of Castile in 1236 during the conquest of Córdoba. Confronted with Ibn Hūd for control of al-Andalus, Muḥammad I had not hesitated to reach a military and political agreement with the Castilian king: in return for his military cooperation against Córdoba, not only did he benefit from a share of the *parias* (tributes) that Ibn Hūd ultimately had to pay, he was also able to extend his power to incorporate Granada. This agreement, which lasted until 1242, permitted the political consolidation of the Nasrid dynasty in the eastern part of Andalucía, to which it seems that Fernando himself must have acquiesced.[40]

At the end of 1242, this truce disintegrated. We do not know the motives or the origin of this fracture, but it is possible that it started in Granada, now strengthened with Tunisian economic support. The fact is that the new armed conflict ended in 1245 with the siege of Jaén. Castilian military pressure, which resulted in the conquest of the city, compelled Muḥammad I to restore the agreement with Fernando III. By virtue of this, Jaén passed into Castilian hands, the Nasrid emir promised to pay *parias* – 150,000 maravedís annually – and took center stage in a full-fledged pact of vassalage (at least according to the Christian sources). In return for staying in power in areas that he already controlled, he had to provide *consilium* – assistance to the courts – to his master, as well as military *auxilium*, which would manifest itself the following year in the contribution he provided during the siege of Seville.[41]

It is clear that the pact of Jaén gave Fernando III free reign to "break and destroy," to use the words from his epitaph, what remained of Islam in the lower Guadalquivir, particularly the city of Seville, but the fact remains that the agreement gave assurances of survival to his Muslim vassal, albeit subjugated and tributary. From this standpoint, those who have seen the "birth certificate" of the Nasrid emirate in the aforementioned pact are perhaps right: a birth

---

38   *pro confusione infidelium... et pro gloria et exaltatione nomini christiani*: Mansilla, *Honorio III*, 430–1, 440–1.
39   García Fitz, *Relaciones políticas*, 186–9. For more on the Treaty of Jaén, see in this volume Boloix-Gallardo, Chp. 3. See also García Sanjuan, "Consideraciones."
40   *CLRC*, 98–9.
41   *PCG*, 746; see in this volume Boloix-Gallardo, Chp. 3 for more on these events.

promoted and permitted by the "crusader king," about whom the propaganda confirmed his burning desire to do away with peninsular Islam.[42]

Lastly, from the perspective of the political practice and military action of Fernando III, the imposition of Castilian rule over the Muslims did not mean their destruction or extermination. On the contrary, it could be said that dominion over them ensured their survival. This was demonstrated, for instance, in all of the settlements situated in the countryside of Córdoba and Seville which, after being subjected to systematic military pressure in 1240–1, were forced to surrender to Fernando III, albeit in return for the establishment of capitulations whose terms are well known and involved the upkeep of the population, respect for their property, for their means of judicial and social organization, their taxation and their religion.[43] In all likelihood, these terms were witnessed again in certain settlements in the Guadalete valley following the conquest of Seville in 1248. On a larger scale, we encounter the same policy as a result of the incorporation of the kingdom of Murcia into the Castilian realm in 1244. From the negotiations held by the Infante Alfonso and the Muslim leaders of the region, the following was agreed: the imposition of Castilian sovereignty over Murcia; the surrender of income from the region, with the exception of that which would remain in the hands of the aforementioned leaders; the surrender of castles; and the settlement of Castilians in an area of the city of Murcia, in return for the upholding of the Murcian political elite, which, except in military matters, would continue to carry out governmental tasks over the population, also upholding their own customs and religion.[44]

Following the conquest of Seville in 1248 and until Fernando's death in 1252, we have no news of armed conflict between Christians and Muslims in Murcia, in the Guadalquivir valley nor in the Penibaetic Mountains. This means that the pacts established between Fernando III, the recognizable Islamic state powers – the Emir Muḥammad I in Granada and Ibn Maḥfūẓ in Niebla –, the local powers with limited autonomous jurisdiction (Murcia, for example), and the rural communities submitting to surrender in the Guadalquivir and Guadalete valleys, served their purpose: Islam persisted, the enemies of faith had not been completely broken or destroyed. Furthermore, the "crusader king" had in fact guaranteed their survival.

---

42 Ladero Quesada, *Granada*, 101.
43 *PCG*, 736; González Jiménez, "Mudéjares," 540–4; Echevarría, "Política respecto al musulmán," 405–7.
44 *PCG*, 741–2.

3   Conclusion

The ideological discourse that enveloped, justified, and legitimized the military action of Fernando III was clearly incompatible with a substantial proportion of his actions. Is it possible to explain this dichotomy, this apparent lack of harmony between the discourse and the fact? There are numerous possibilities for explanation, but here we will present the principal two.

Firstly, we could consider this to be a matter of pure political cynicism: saying one thing and doing another. Intentions are expressed through an incontestable account from the perspective of the dominant ideology and action is taken according to pragmatic political and military criteria. Furthermore, pronouncements are made that not only legitimize the action, but also serve to mobilize resources, both human and economic: we should recall the revenue derived from the crusading bulls or from the ecclesiastical *tercia*. However, the practical accomplishment of the will expressed in those terms is aligned with each specific context. Accordingly, a propagandistic and ideological message is kept intact, the validity of which does not necessarily need to be consistent with military actions or political decisions.

Nevertheless, however, we should also give credence to the idea that when we interpret the agreements, the truces, the military assistance, or the relationship of vassalage between Fernando III and any of his Muslim counterparts in terms of acceptance of the "Other" or the desire for its survival, we are confusing our perspective by attributing a definitive significance to the establishment of such capitulation treaties or the practice of vassalage. This loses sight of the fact that, even though they allowed the preservation of Islam, nearly all of the agreements reached were made at the cost of the payment of sums of money or in some cases the surrendering of territories which, in the medium- or long-term, created internal discontent and impoverished those bound by them. Furthermore, almost all of the agreements reached were made with the aim of aggravating internal divisions between Muslims or combining forces against other Muslim rulers who were not part of the pact, thus weakening the grip of Islamic polities within the Peninsula.

This was an old political practice. Alfonso VI had instigated it and had applied it whenever possible. It entailed the division of Muslim forces in order to weaken, to undermine, and finally, to conquer them. This could at times require, when necessary, the signing of temporary agreements and the upholding or even the provisional strengthening of individual Muslim polities within al-Andalus. However, it would always result in the heightening of conflicts between the Muslims or their conquest by Castile: thus al-Bayāsī is supported against the caliph al-Adil; the caliph al-Ma'mūn against Ibn Hūd; Ibn Hūd against Ibn Maḥfūẓ; Muḥammad I against Ibn Hūd or against the Sevillians. And in all cases, an economic, tributary or territorial price is demanded, or all three at once, in a policy designed to progressively wear down the adversary and strengthen the Castilian king's own hand.

The paths chosen varied, were at times indirect and included breaks or differing paces of implementation, but what did not change was the ultimate objective, which remained coherent with the ideological approach: to break the power of all of Fernando III's enemies. A suppressed and tributary Muslim "Spain" had no place in the project that arose from this ideology and, in the long-term, it also had no place in political reality, as determined by the military action of Fernando III. The bellicose rhetoric that Alfonso X emphasized in the epitaph of his father – the man who "broke and destroyed his enemies" – was perhaps not just an exercise in propaganda.

Works Cited

Primary Sources (Published)

Alfonso X. *Setenario*. Ed. Kenneth H. Vanderford. Barcelona: Grijalbo, 1984.

Anónimo de Madrid y Copenhague. Ed. A. Huici Miranda. Valencia: Anubar, 1917.

Charlo Brea, Luis, ed. *Chronica latina regum Castellae*. In *Chronica Hispana Saeculi XIII*, ed. Luis Charlo Brea, Juan Estévez Sola and Rocío Carande Herrero. Vol. 73 of *Corpus Christianorum: Continuatio medievalis*, 7–118. Turnhout: Brepols, 1997.

Crónica de Veinte Reyes. Ed. G. Martínez Díez, et al. Burgos: Ayuntamiento de Burgos, 1991.

González, Julio, ed. *Reinado y diplomas de Fernando III*, 3 vols. Córdoba: Monte de Piedad y Caja de Ahorros de Córdoba, 1983.

Ibn Abī Zarʿ. *Al-anīs al-muṭrib bi-rawḍ al-qirṭās fī akhbār mulūk al-Maghrib wa-taʾrīkh madīnat. Fās*. Trans. Ambrosio Huici Miranda. 2 vols. Valencia: Textos Medievales, 1964.

Ibn ʿIdhārī al-Marrākushi. *Al-Bayan al-Mughrib fi ijtisar akhbar Muluk al-Andalus wa al-Maghrib*. Trans. Ambrosio Huici Miranda. 2 vols. Tetuan: Editora Marroquí, 1953–1954.

Ibn Khaldūn. *Historie des Berbéres et des dynasties musulmanes de l'Afrique septentrionale*. Trans. Baron de Slane. Paris: P. Geuthner, 1925–6.

Jiménez de Rada, Rodrigo. *Historia de rebus Hispanie, sive Historia Gothica*. Ed. Juan Fernández Valverde. Vol. 72 of *Corpus Christianorum: Continuatio mediaeualis*. Turnhout: Brepols, 1987.

Lucas of Tuy. *Chronicon mundi*. Ed. Emma Falque Rey. Vol. 74 of *Corpus Christianorum: Continuatio mediaeualis*. Turnhout: Brepols, 2003.

Mansilla, Demetrio. *La documentación Pontificia de Honorio III (1216–1227)*. Rome: Instituto Español de Historia Eclesiástica, 1965.

Matthaei Parisiensis. *Chronica Majora*. Ed. Henry Richards Luard. 7 vols. London: Longmans, 1872–1884.

Primera crónica general de España. Ed. Ramón Menéndez Pidal et al. Madrid: Gredos, 1955.

Secondary Sources

Ayala Martínez, Carlos de. "Fernando III: figura, significado y contexto en tiempo de cruzada." In *Fernando III, tiempo de cruzada*, ed. Carlos de Ayala Martínez and Martín Ríos Saloma, 17–91. Madrid: Sílex, 2012.

Bronisch, Alexander. *Reconquista y guerra santa: la concepción de la guerra en la España cristiana desde los visigodos hasta comienzos del siglo XII*. Granada: University of Granada, 2006.

Castro, Américo. *La realidad histórica de España*. México: Porrúa, 1982.

Dodds, Jerrilynn D., María Rosa Menocal, and Abigail Krasner Balbale, ed. *The Arts of Intimacy: Christians, Jews and Muslims in the Making of Castilian Culture*. Yale: Yale University Press, 2008.

Echevarría, Ana. "La política respecto al musulmán sometido y las limitaciones prácticas de la cruzada en tiempos de Fernando III (1199–1252)." In *Fernando III, tiempo de cruzada*, ed. Carlos de Ayala Martínez and Martín Ríos Saloma, 383–413. Madrid: Sílex, 2012.

García Fitz, Francisco. "La conquista de Andalucía en la cronística castellana del siglo XIII: Las mentalidades historiográficas en los relatos de la conquista." In *Andalucía entre Oriente y Occidente (1236–1492). Actas del V Coloquio Internacional de Historia de Andalucía*, 51–61. Córdoba: Diputación Provincial, 1988.

García Fitz, Francisco. *Relaciones políticas y guerra. La experiencia castellano-leonesa frente al Islam. Siglos XI–XIII*. Seville: Universidad de Sevilla, 2002.

García Fitz, Francisco. "¿Una *España musulmana, sometida y tributaria*? La *España* que no fue." *Historia. Instituciones. Documentos* 31 (2004): 227–248.

García Pelayo, Manuel. "El Reino de Dios, arquetipo político. Estudios sobre las formas políticas de la Alta Edad Media." In *Los mitos políticos*, ed. Manuel García Pelayo. Alianza: Madrid, 1981.

García Sanjuan, Alejandro. "Consideraciones sobre el pacto de Jaén de 1246." In *Sevilla 1248. Actas del Congreso Internacional Conmemorativo del 750 aniversario de la Conquista de la Ciudad de Seville por Fernando III, Rey de Castilla y León*, ed. Manuel González Jiménez, 715–724. Madrid: Fundación Ramón Areces, 2000.

González Jiménez, Manuel. "Los mudéjares andaluces (ss. XIII–XV)." In *Andalucía entre Oriente y Occidente (1236–1492). Actas del V Coloquio Internacional de Historia de Andalucía*, ed. Emilio Cabrera Muñoz, 537–550. Córdoba: Diputación Provincial, 1988.

González Jiménez, Manuel. *Fernando III: El rey que marcó el destino de España*. Seville: Fundación José Manuel Lara, 2011.

Gorosterratzu, Javier. *Don Rodrigo Jiménez de Rada: Gran estadista, escritor y prelado*. Pamplona: Viuda de T. Bescansa, 1925.

Ladero Quesada, Miguel Ángel. *Granada. Historia de un país islámico (1232–1571)*. Madrid: Gredos, 1979.

Lomax, Derek. *The Reconquest of Spain*. New York: Longman, 1978.

Lomax, Derek. "La conquista de Andalucía a través de la historiografía europea de la época." In *Andalucía entre Oriente y Occidente (1236–1492). Actas del V Coloquio Internacional de Historia de Andalucía*, ed. Emilio Cabrera Muñoz, 37–50. Córdoba: Diputación Provincial, 1988.

Martínez Díez, Gonzalo. *Fernando III, 1217–1252*. Palencia: La Olmeda, 1993.

Nickson, Tom. "Remembering Fernando: Multilingualism in Medieval Iberia." In *Viewing Inscriptions in the Late Antique and Medieval World*, ed. Anthony Eastmond, 170–186. Cambridge: Cambridge University Press, 2015.

Rodríguez López, Ana. *La consolidación territorial de la monarquía feudal castellana. Expansión y fronteras durante el reinado de Fernando III*. Madrid: CSIC, 1994.

Tolan, John. "Las traducciones y la ideología de la reconquista: Marcos de Toledo." In *Musulmanes y cristianos en los siglos XII y XIII*, ed. Miquel Barceló and José Gázquez, 79–85. Bellaterra: Universitat Autonoma de Barcelona, 2005.

CHAPTER 3

Fernando III and Muḥammad I of Granada: A Time of Collaboration between Two "Incompatible Worlds"

Bárbara Boloix-Gallardo

1   Introduction

The first half of the thirteenth century saw substantial political, and above all, territorial change across the chessboard that comprised the medieval Iberian Peninsula.[1] The general crisis that had been visited upon al-Andalus following the resounding Almohad defeat at the battle of Las Navas de Tolosa or *al-ʿIqāb*, fought on the 14th of the Islamic month of *ṣafar* 609/July 16, 1212 CE, and the subsequent departure of the Caliph al-Maʾmūn in 625/1228 to the Maghrib – where the emergence of new local dynasties threatened the integrity of his domains, – turned al-Andalus into easy prey for the peninsular Christian kingdoms, above all, the crown of Castile.[2] Indeed, the *Estoria de España* recognizes that, after the aforementioned struggle, "the Moors were so broken that they never again raised their heads in Spain."[3] This episode inaugurated an era of uncertainty in al-Andalus, known as the third Taifa period. Several local leaders – Ibn Hūd al-Mutawwakil in Murcia (r. 625–635/1228–1238), Zayyān b. Mardanīsh in Valencia (r. 625–638/1228–1241) and, finally, Muḥammad I (previously known as Ibn al-Aḥmar) in Arjona (r. 629–671/1232–1273) – assumed the

---

1   I would like to express my gratitude to my colleague Damian Smith and to Edward Holt for having invited me to take part in the international conference on "San Fernando and his Age," which was celebrated at the campus of Saint Louis University in Madrid during October 6–7, 2017.
2   On this important battle for peninsular Christianity and its fatal consequences for the Almohad dynasty, see Huici Miranda, *Las grandes batallas de la Reconquista*, 217–327; Vara Thorbeck, *El lunes de las Navas*; Rosado Llamas and López Payer, *La Batalla de las Navas de Tolosa*, a study which analyzes this battle in depth from both the Muslim and the Christian perspectives; Cressier and Salvatierra, *Las Navas de Tolosa (1212–2012)*; Estepa Díez and Carmona Ruiz, *La Península Ibérica*.
3   *fueron los moros tan quebrantados que nunca después alzaron cabeza en España*: PCG, 689. The *Estoria de España* had the benefit of hindsight, being compiled over the late thirteenth and early fourteenth centuries; for more on this important source, see Catalán, *La "Estoria de España*,*"* and below, fn. 15.

military defense of the Andalusi territory, aiming to reunify it under their respective authorities. Although the Murcian ruler, Ibn Hūd al-Mutawwakil, succeeded at first in defending al-Andalus from the Christian kingdoms, creating an emirate that incorporated the most important Andalusi cities, nonetheless the military defeats that he suffered at the end of his life ultimately shook his authority and finally resulted in the widespread recognition of the authority of Muḥammad I. The power of the latter was consequently reinforced by the murder of Ibn Hūd in Almería in 635/1238 and the departure of Ibn Mardanīsh to Tunisia in 638/1241, making Muḥammad the principal leader of al-Andalus, an important part of which had recognized his power as ruler of the Nasrid Kingdom of Granada, a political entity that would survive, against all expectations, for two and a half centuries.[4]

An important part of the political arena of the Iberian Peninsula during the first half of the thirteenth century was, therefore, presided over by two principal sovereigns: Fernando III, king of Castile (and, from 1230, León), and Muḥammad I (629–671/1232–1273), the first emir and founder of the Nasrid Kingdom of Granada. One of the central policies of the Castilian king was the prosecution of war with al-Andalus, the so-called "Reconquista," to which end he undertook a series of conquests in the Muslim lands to the south of the Peninsula, and ultimately absorbed much of al-Andalus under Castilian control. However, despite both his ambition and the evident military success of Castile, Fernando III established a political relationship with Muḥammad I based on respect, and permitting the existence and indeed the development of the Nasrid emirate of Granada.

Throughout this chapter, the complex relationship between the crown of Castile and the Nasrid kingdom of Granada will be explored between the years 1232 and 1252, namely, from the proclamation of Muḥammad I as emir in Arjona (Jaén) to the death of Fernando III. Although we will pay attention to the information provided by medieval Christian sources, this analysis will primarily be approached "from right to left," that is to say, drawing closely on the Arabic sources composed in the Western Islamic domains of al-Andalus and the Maghrib, and rooted in Islamic political ideology.[5]

---

4   For a further explanation of this process, see Boloix-Gallardo, *De la Taifa de Arjona*, 17–40; and Boloix-Gallardo, *Ibn al-Aḥmar*, 77–9.

5   Because of this approach, the Islamic dates provided throughout this chapter are in both the Hegira and the Christian calendars in order to achieve a greater chronological accuracy.

2 From *thagr* to *furuntayra*: A New Concept of Border

The territorial regression of al-Andalus to the benefit of the Christian kingdoms was a consequence of one of the main features of the border: its mobility.[6] The supremacy of the Castilian defensive organization over that of the Muslim kingdoms in the thirteenth century became so evident that it found an echo in the Arabic terminology used to refer to the new Andalusi border situation.[7] On one hand, with the integration of Islamic lands into the kingdom of Castile, some of the classical terms related to Arabic territorial organization – such as that of *cora* or province – disappeared.[8] On the other, the Castilian military system ended up dominating and refashioning Andalusi concepts of border.[9] Thus, although the classical Arabic term *ṯagr* for the traditional idea of "border" was preserved in al-Andalus – and thus its derivatives like *ṯagrī* (border soldier) – several Castilian expressions permeated Arabic vocabulary, reflecting the weakness of the Andalusi military organization in comparison with the military superiority of the Christian kingdoms. Such was the case with the Castilian term *frontera* (border), literally adopted in several Arabic texts composed in the thirteenth century and reproduced as *furuntayra*, which was probably pronounced in Andalusi colloquial Arabic as *fruntīra*. This linguistic loan can be found in the popular Sufi work *Tuḥfat al-mughtarib* composed by Aḥmad al-Qashtālī (d. after 670/1271–1272), from Castril (Granada), which uses this term in one of its accounts to refer to Christian chieftains on the Andalusi border with Castile (*bi-l-fu[r]untayra*).[10] The archbishop of Toledo, Rodrigo Jiménez de Rada, writing in the 1240s, also employed the same term, *Frontaria*, to designate both the Islamic territories that had just been conquered by Castile, as well as to refer to areas of further military advancement in al-Andalus.[11] In the fourteenth century, the Tunisian historian Ibn Khaldūn (d. 808/1406)

---

6 For analysis of the linguistic transition from *ṯagr* to *furuntayra*, see Boloix-Gallardo, *De la Taifa de Arjona*, 46; Chalmeta Gendrón, "El concepto de *thagr*," 19, fn. 9.
7 Vidal Castro, "Frontera, genealogía y religion," 795, fn. 4.
8 According to the *Diccionario de Historia*, a "cora" (in Arabic, *kūra*) constituted a kind of territorial and administrative subdivision in al-Andalus, being equivalent to region or a district. It usually had its capital in an important city and was controlled by a governor (*wālī*). In general terms, the Andalusi "coras" corresponded geographically to the old Visigothic dioceses or counties.
9 See Torres Delgado, "El territorio y la economía," 507.
10 Granja Santamaría, "Geografía lírica," 71, no. 31; Spanish translation by Boloix-Gallardo, *Prodigios*, 151.
11 Jiménez de Rada, *Historia Arabum*, Chp. 47.

would likewise employ the same term with similar connotations in his celebrated work *Kitāb al-ʿibar*.[12]

3 The Official Establishment of the Castilian-Nasrid Border: The Treaty of Jaén or "the Great Peace"

Considering these changes in the Andalusi concept of border, it is important to investigate when and how the boundaries between the newly-formed Nasrid kingdom and Christian Castile were arranged within the Peninsula. In 1246, Fernando III established the *fruntīra* separating, and yet also communicating between, these two religious and political domains. The impetus of this process was the completion of the conquest of al-Andalus. Before 1246, Fernando III had tried to conquer Jaén several times, in 1225 and 1230.[13] However, 1246 would be a key year in the struggle between Castile and Granada, since, in this year, Jaén was finally taken by the Castilians, a fact that, paradoxically, also played a beneficial role in the establishment of the Nasrid Kingdom, thanks to the excellent management of emir Muḥammad I. In other words, the conquest of Jaén meant both the territorial consolidation of the kingdom of Granada and the normalization of its relationship with Castile.

The conquest of Jaén was quite unlike the previous Castilian blockades in al-Andalus. First of all, the political and military authority of Fernando III was stronger than before, since in 1230, he had just become king of León at the death of his father, Alfonso IX, resulting in a considerable increase in his military resources. Secondly, Castile already had conquered several important enclaves surrounding Jaén, as a result of which the city was practically besieged from a distance.[14] In fact, Jaén was so isolated that Muḥammad I was unable to send a convoy of food to combat the starvation that been inflicted on the city since 1245; both the *Crónica de Veinte Reyes* and the *Estoria de España*, the earliest Latin accounts of the conquest of Jaén, claim that Fernando III had heard about the dispatch of a convoy from Granada and ordered its interception.[15]

---

12   *Kitab al-ʿibar*, ed. Cairo, IV: 171, VII: 190, 193. Vidal Castro, "Frontera, genealogía y religion," 795, fn. 4.
13   On these attempts at conquest, see Martínez Díez, *Fernando III*, 160–2, 166; González Jiménez, *Fernando III*, 185–7; Boloix-Gallardo, *De la Taifa de Arjona*, 77–9; idem, *Ibn al-Ahmar*, 139.
14   Ballesteros, "La conquista de Jaén," 128.
15   *Crónica de Veinte Reyes*, 325–6; *PCG*, 744–5. These two closely related texts provide the earliest narrative Christian accounts of the conquest of Jaén, although it should be noted that both were produced in the late thirteenth or early fourteenth centuries and there has

As the siege of Jaén extended longer than expected, and the city was unable to resist it, Muḥammad considered that the best solution was surrender. Why surrender? The Nasrid emir knew that he could do nothing to save Jaén from Christian conquest but, at the same time, he needed a treaty to protect both his honor and the integrity of his young emirate. The result was the signing in 1246 of a twenty-year truce that constituted the cornerstone on which the kingdom of Granada was built.[16] Indeed, the historian Miguel Ángel Ladero Quesada has defined this treaty as the "birth certificate" of the emirate of Granada.[17]

Muḥammad I, evidently a master of political strategy, made the best decision possible as he declared himself a vassal of Castile, under terms more favorable than those achieved by the Muslim rulers of both Murcia and Niebla. With this strategy, he avoided Castilian military presence in his kingdom. The truce was, therefore, a masterful strategic move.

This Treaty of Jaén signified an important starting point in a long relationship of collaboration between Fernando III and Muḥammad I that entailed specific commitments for the Nasrid emir. Among the obligations that Fernando III imposed on Muḥammad I in the treaty were the following: (1) the immediate delivery of Jaén and its fortresses to the Crown of Castile with the subsequent evacuation of its inhabitants; (2) the payment of an annual tribute of 150 thousand maravedís (indeed, the tribute paid by the Nasrid Kingdom constituted the most significant income that the kingdom of Castile received); and (3) for the Nasrid emir to swear vassalage to the Castilian king in all his territories.

In exchange, Muḥammad I received official recognition of the border of his kingdom with Castile, drawn throughout the natural line of the Subbetic mountain range so that "the border was always well-defended and safe, and the Christians were owners of whatever they possessed."[18] This recognition allowed Muḥammad I to organize his emirate internally, as the Nasrid vizier Ibn al-Khaṭīb (d. 776/1375) himself recognized a century later: "He [Muḥammad I]

---

been considerable historiographical discussion over their exact provenance and relationship with the court of Alfonso X. See Catalán, La "Estoria de España"; Fernández Ordóñez, "La transmission textual"; Campa, "Crónica de veinte reyes." For more on the treatment of Fernando's wars after his death, see Ruiz-Gálvez Priego, "De reyes y de santos."

16 Unfortunately, we have no physical copy of the treaty, only partial descriptions in other sources, described below. See also García Sanjuan, "Consideraciones."
17 Ladero Quesada, Granada, 127; idem, "El Reino de Granada," 190.
18 *siempre después la frontera fue bien parada, segura, e los christianos que eran señores de lo que avian*: Crónica de Veinte Reyes, 327. On the border with Castile, see Vidal, "Historia política," 87.

negotiated the Great Peace (*al-silm al-kabīr*), his business prospered and he could equip himself with provisions."¹⁹

Some phenomena surrounding the signing of this truce warrant additional analysis. First, a curious change in both the concept and the practice of *jihād* took place in al-Andalus in the thirteenth century. As Abigail Balbale has suggested, throughout the third Taifa period, that is, between 1228 and 1238, conflict between Muslims increased, at the same time as this collaborative relationship developed between individual Muslim leaders and their Christian neighbors. Considering the rivalry that existed between the different local leaders, and especially between Ibn Hūd al-Mutawwakil of Murcia and Muḥammad I, as all of them aimed to reunify al-Andalus under their authorities, it became common to see both emirs fighting their own co-religionists and allying with the Castilians for their right to rule.²⁰ It is true that this phenomenon also occurred in previous Taifa periods of Andalusi history. However, it became much more evident in the "post-Navas" era (that is, post-1212), when the language of *jihād* became fundamental to the legitimization of the Andalusi dynasties, even as the weakness of al-Andalus made it necessary for local Muslim leaders to seek greater political and military support from the Christians.

Indeed Pièrre Guichard and Dominique Urvoy saw the alliances that proliferated across religious lines and the absence of unity among Andalusi Muslims as clear evidence of a lack of *jihād* ideology.²¹ At first glance, it seems contradictory that Muḥammad I presented himself before his subjects as a champion of the faith and made alliances with the Christian Castilians at the same time. Indeed, the inscription that decorated the grave of the first Nasrid emir and honored his memory illustrated him as "the hero" (*al-himām*) and the "keeper of the borders" (*ḍābiṭ al-thugūr*), recording that "he marched in front of a tumultuous army, before which shrank both the Arabs and the foreign peoples," and that "he always prepared against them [the enemies] a slender cavalry which drank from a well of blood."²² Despite these behavioral contradictions, and the paradoxical image that these testimonies aimed to project of Muḥammad I as a champion of peninsular Islam, the reality and the practice were quite different.

---

19   *Iḥāṭa*, II: 95; *Lamḥa*, 43, Spanish translation, 131.
20   Balbale, "*Jihād* as a Means of Political Legitimization," 88–92.
21   Guichard, *Al-Andalus*, 199; Urvoy, "Sur l'evolution de la notion de *gihad*," 335–7, 357.
22   For the Arabic version of this text, see Ibn al-Khaṭīb, *Iḥāṭa*: II, 100–1 and *Lamḥa*, 48–9. This inscription has been translated into Spanish by Lafuente Alcántara, *Inscripciones árabes de Granada*, 207–8; Lèvi-Provençal, *Inscriptions árabes d'Espagne*, 145–6, no. 161; Casciaro, *Historia de los Reyes de la Alhambra*, 139; and Boloix-Gallardo, "'Yo soy'," 39–40.

The accounts relating the signing of the Treaty of Jaén have been described by L.P. Harvey as revealing "a lack of communication between two incompatible worlds."[23] It is worthwhile to analyze the ways in which the Christian and the Islamic narratives of these events retrospectively reflected the establishment of this truce from very different perspectives. The first had to do with its denomination, which differs in both traditions, since it was referred to as "the Treaty of Jaén" by the Castilian chronicles while designated "the Great Peace" (al-silm al-kabīr) in the Arabic texts. Even more interesting is the difference of approach of both historiographies when reflecting the conditions of the pact, understood as a submission by the Christian chroniclers, and as a simple agreement by the Arabic historians. The Castilian historiography, exemplified in the *Crónica de Veinte Reyes* and the *Estoria de España*, our two earliest Christian sources for the events,[24] describes the situation in Jaén as follows:

> When *this king of Arjona, who was already called king of Granada*, saw King Fernando [III] going so firmly against Jaén, and fearing (…) that he would never leave until he took [the city], and seeing also that those [inhabitants] who were inside the city were suffering so greatly from hunger and were so defeated by all their miseries that they could not provide advice or encouragement to one another, and did not know what to do and could neither enter nor leave [the city]; and seeing also that he could not help them nor […] defend the city, *he decided to show respect for the king don Fernando, as well as to give him [Jaén] and to submit to him with both land and whatever he possessed* (…).[25]
>
> [*Then, the king of Granada] submitted directly to the power of the king don Fernando [III] and his favor, and, by kissing his hand, he became his vassal*, so that [the Castilian king] could do with him and his land what he wanted to do; later he [the king of Granada] handed over Jaén. The king don Fernando, full of mercy and all temperance when he saw how this

---

23   Harvey, *Islamic Spain*, 27–8; López de Coca Castañer, "El Reino de Granada," 316–7.
24   See Catalán, *La "Estoria de España"*; Fernández Ordóñez, "La transmisión textual"; Campa, "Crónica de veinte reyes."
25   *Mas leyendo este rey de Ariona, que se llamaua ya rey de Granada, tan afincadamente al rey don Fernando estar sobre Jahen, et temiendose –de lo que se tenie por çierto– que nunca ende se levantaría fasta que la tomase, et leyendo otrosi los de dentro estar tan aquexados de fanbre et tan afrontados de todas lazerias que se non sabien dar consejo nin confuerço vnos a otros nin se sabian ya que fazer nin podian ya entrar vno nin salir otro, et veyendo otrosi que el non los podia acorrer nin pudia aprovechar en ninguna cosa nin defender la uilla, acordose de traer pleitesía con el rey don Fernando et de la dar, et de se meter en su poder con la tierra et como quanto ouiese, ca non touo y otramiente guarda ninguna que podiese ayer contra el nin contra su poderio: Crónica de Veinte Reyes, 327*. Emphasis mine.

Moorish king came with great humility (...), without any malign ambition, which he never had (...), received him warmly and honored him. And [*Fernando III*] *did not want anything from him* [*the king of Granada*] *but to be his vassal with all his land* (...) and to pay him a certain tribute – 150,000 maravedís each year – , as well as to wage war and peace, and to attend the [Castilian] courts every year. Jaén, which he had already won, was surrendered later; and this was the agreement established between these two kings.[26]

However the Arabic sources offer a very different version of the facts.[27] Most explicit of them all is the chronicle *Al-Bayān al-mughrib* by the Maghrebi historian Ibn 'Idhārī (writing in the fourteenth century), who states that:

> *The Emir Abū 'Abd Allāh Muḥammad b. Yūsuf b. Naṣr made peace* (*ṣālaḥa*) *with the king of Castile* –may God exterminate him!– *regarding the territories of the Muslims who were under his authority*, his party, and his group for a period of twenty years. By this peace (*al-silm*), he [Muḥammad I] gave him [the Castilian king] the city of Jaén and the adjacent castles (*al-ḥuṣūn*) and fortresses (*al-ma'āqil*). All sensible Muslims left them, while others, the *Mudéjars*, inhabited them together with the

---

26 [*Entonces*] (...) *vinose* [*el emir Ibn al-Aḥmar*] *meter derechamiente en su poder del rey don Fernando et en la su merced, et besol la mano et tornose su vasallo en esta guisa, que feziese del et de su tierra lo que fazer quisiese; et entregol luego Jahen. Et el rey don Fernando, lleno de piadamiento et de toda mesura, leyendo en commo ese rey moro venia con grant humildad et tan paçiente a plazimiento de quanto el de la tierra et del quisiese fazer, nol forçando cobdicia maligna, la qual el nunca ouo, et guiandol mesuramiento et piadança natural, lo que siempre en el fue fallado contra quantos abedeçialmiente lo quisieron leuar, reçibiol muy bien et fizol mucha onra, et non quiso del otra cosa saluo que fincase por su vasallo con toda su tierra, et se la tosiese como se la ante tenie con todo su sennorio, et queldiese della tributo çierto: cada anno çient et çinquenta mill morauedis, et le feziese della gerra et paz, et le veniese cada anno a cortes; saluo Jahen que se tenie el ganada quel entrego el luego commo dicho es; et fue este el paramiento que entre estos reys ouo*: PCG, 746. Emphasis mine.

27 Among the different Arabic chronicles that reflect the signing of "the Great Peace" with the Castilian king Fernando III, are the following works: Ibn Abī Zar', *Rawḍ al-qirṭās*, 362, Spanish translation by Huici Miranda, II: 529, a source that incorrectly states that the conclusion of this pact took place in the Islamic year 644 (corresponding to 1246–1247 of the C.E.); Ibn 'Idhārī, *Al-Bayān al-mughrib, qism al-muwaḥḥidīn* (Volume of the Almohads), 367, Spanish translation by Huici Miranda, 162–3; Ibn Khaldūn, *Kitāb al-'ibar*, ed. Beirut, IV: 171, French translation by Gaudefroy-Demombynes, "Histoire des Banou l-Aḥmar," 324–5; Ibn al-Khaṭīb, *Iḥāṭa*, II: 95, 99, and *Lamḥa*, 43, 48, Spanish translation by Casciaro, 131, 137; al-Maqqarī, *Nafḥ al-ṭīb*, I: 448, English translation by de Gayangos, *History of Muhammedam dynasties in Spain*, II: 340–1.

Christians. Neither the people of Seville, nor the people of Jerez, entered this truce agreed that year, but they negotiated [a different treaty] of their own accord [paying] a sum of money per year until they gave them [the Castilians] their *qaṣba* and shared the city with them. Later [the Christians] expelled [the *mudéjars*] from it [the city] and hypocrisy took place between them, according to what will be mentioned, God willing.[28]

If we contrast both versions, we can see considerable divergences that should be highlighted for being sometimes contradictory and at other times complementary to each other. As Alejandro García Sanjuan has noticed, both historical discourses reflect different aspects of the same fact.[29] On one hand, the emblematic *Estoria de España* pays more attention to the oaths of vassalage undertaken by Muḥammad I, consisting of the mandatory payment of annual tributes (*parias*) and compulsory attendance at the Castilian court. On the other, the *Bayān* by Ibn ʿIdhārī stresses the forced surrender of Jaén and its attached fortresses as well as the unfair expulsion of the city's inhabitants.

The differences between these two narrative versions emphasize the political interests of each text. In the Castilian case, the account is very rich in detail as it aims to record the great triumph that the conquest of Jaén represented for the Crown of Castile. On the contrary, the Arabic sources are sparing with words, since the Muslim defeat and the subsequent vassalage of the Nasrids to Fernando III represented a humiliation that was not to be lavishly reflected upon. Indeed, Ibn al-Khaṭīb briefly refers to this historical episode and avoids giving a prolific explanation, justifying this by "not having enough time for that now."[30]

Attention should also be paid to the terminological differences between the two versions, which can be justified by the linguistic and political context of each. Andalusi polities employed specific terminology to express the idea of sovereignty and subordination, but not that of vassalage as such. The Castilian texts understood the terms of surrender (*capitulaciones*) of Jaén precisely in terms of the vassal-king relationship, reflected in the protocol by which Muḥammad I had to kiss the hand of Fernando III.[31] On the contrary, Arabic texts ignored these details and described the Treaty of Jaén according to their own concepts and terminology, using the Arabic term *silm* (which means "peace") as well as the verb *ṣālaḥa* and the Arabic root *ʿaqada* simultaneously,

---

28 *Qism al-muwaḥḥidīn*, 367, Spanish translation, II: 162–3. Emphasis mine.
29 García Sanjuan, "Consideraciones," 717.
30 *Iḥāṭa*, II: 95, 99; *Lamḥa*, 43, 48, Spanish translation, 131, 138.
31 *PCG*, 746.

expressions that involve both an act of conciliation, as well as a pact between two equal powers. Curiously, all of these semantic nuances are readily present in the version of the facts offered by the aforementioned Nasrid historian Ibn al-Khaṭīb:

> In the year 643 (1246), [the emir Muḥammad I] made peace (ṣalaḥa) with the tyrant [king] of the Christians [Fernando III] and agreed with him the peace ('aqada ma'a-hu al-silm) according to which Jaén was lost among its conditions (fī shurrūti-hi).[32]

Thanks to the anonymous chronicle *Ta'rīkh al-Andalus*, we can identify the enclaves that Muḥammad I was forced to surrender to Fernando III after signing the treaty:

> [Muḥammad I] Ibn al-Aḥmar gave the Christians the city of Jaén (*madīnat Jayyān*), Arjona (*Arjūna*), Porcuna (*Barshāna/Barshūna*), (*Mȳ?*), Vejer (*Al-Baḥīr/Al-Buḥayr*) and Alcalá de Guadaira (*qal'at Jābir*), agreeing with them a truce of twenty years.[33]

Once Fernando III took Jaén, he entered the city in great procession with all the clergy and headed towards its Grand Mosque, which was converted into a church and consecrated under the invocation of the Virgin Mary. Mass was celebrated, officiated by don Gutierrez, bishop of Córdoba. Subsequently, Fernando III erected a Christian fortress on the Arabic one, equipped with a church consecrated to Saint Catherine, also the dedicatee of the town's castle, both of which were conquered on that feast day.[34]

One of the first consequences of the conquest was the massive evacuation of the people of Jaén to allow the city to be populated by Christians. Before conquering the city, Fernando III had granted some of its properties to his nobles and also to institutions such as the Order of Santiago and the military commander of Segura, to whom the king donated houses belonging to a Rabi Zulema (Rabī' Sulaymān?) on February 28, 1246, as well as plot comprising a vineyard, orchard, mills, farmland and the towers of Mezquitiel (Mesquiteles) and Maquis with their surroundings.[35] The lamentations of the people of Jaén

---

32   *Iḥāṭa*, II: 99; *Lamḥa*, 48, Spanish translation, 137.
33   *Ta'rīkh al-Andalus*, 268. For the correct identification of some of these toponyms, see Martínez Enamorado, "Un país," 382.
34   PCG, 746–7.
35   González, "Las conquistas de Fernando III," 603.

are reflected in the short poem included by al-Ḥimyarī (d. 726/1325–1326) in his celebrated work *Al-Rawḍ al-miʿṭār* ("The perfumed garden") saying goodbye to the city:

> I say my goodbye to you, my Jaén,
> Dispersing my tears as pearls get dispersed.
> It is not, of course, that I want to separate myself from you.
> However, our time has been decided this way.[36]

The words reported to have been proclaimed by the preacher (*khaṭīb*) of the Grand Mosque of Jaén from the pulpit on that day were also emblematic: "Here is the last sermon (*khuṭba*) that will be delivered in Jaén."[37] From then onwards, the inhabitants started to leave their houses, heading towards other parts of al-Andalus (mainly Granada) or the rest of the *Dār al-Islām*. According to Ibn ʿIdhārī "all sensible Muslims left the city," and indeed, these must have been numerous, judging by the many references preserved in Andalusi biographical dictionaries.[38] Nor should we forget that the Muslim population had also been depleted by mortalities during the siege.

4   The Nasrid Commitments of *auxilium* and *consilium*

It is important to analyze the two main obligations to which the Nasrid emir was committed due to his vassalage to Fernando III: providing *auxilium* and *consilium* to the Castilian crown.[39] As a result of his duties of *auxilium*, the Nasrid emir was obliged to provide military assistance to the Castilian king whenever he needed it. By means of this obligation, Muḥammad I paradoxically contributed to the expansion of the Castilian kingdom at the expense of al-Andalus. Under Fernando III's rule, the kingdom of Castile-León underwent unprecedented territorial expansion, and the subsequent enrichment of its nobility, who obtained territories in recognition of their military collaboration.[40] On a theoretical level, the collaboration of Muslim troops was against the spirit of Islamic Law, which condemned military Muslim collaboration

---

36   Al-Ḥimyarī, *al-Rawḍ al-miʿtār*, 184, Spanish translation, 150.
37   Ibid.
38   *Bayān, qism al-muwaḥḥidīn*, 367, Spanish translation, II: 162.
39   For debate concerning *auxilium* and *consilium* within a feudo-vassilic system, see Rochwert-Zuili, "*Auxilium* et *consilium*," 1.
40   On the Reconquest, see García Fitz, "La Reconquista"; Ríos Saloma, *La Reconquista*; Peinado Santaella, *Guerra Santa, cruzada y yihād en Andalucía*.

with Christians against their own co-religionists as treason or even apostasy. However, L.P. Harvey goes further in his interpretation of Muḥammad's strategy, suggesting that the Nasrid emir not only sought to save his territories through the Treaty of Jaén, but also to become the supreme leader of al-Andalus, and therefore allowed the Christians (and especially Fernando III) to eliminate potential Muslim rivals for him, as a "game of uncertain outcome."[41] This "master move" was a consequence of the mutation of both the concept and the practice of *jihād* experienced in al-Andalus in the thirteenth century, as we have seen.

In the Islamic year 644/1246–1247, Muḥammad I showed the first sign of his promised military *auxilium* to Fernando III on the occasion of the Castilian conquest of Alcalá de Guadaira, which was followed by the capture of Carmona, Lora, Gerena, and Alcalá del Río, among other areas in the region around Seville.[42] However, this support would reach its zenith in 646/1248–1249 with the Nasrid participation in the Castilian conquest of Seville itself.[43] Apart from his obligations as a vassal of the Castilian king, Muḥammad I had other personal reasons for taking part in that conquest: to exact revenge on the Sevillians for having expelled him from their *qaṣba* in the year 631 /1234.

Fernando III considered Seville to be the "highest chapter of the royal crown of Andalusia," and therefore decided to attack it by land and sea, an amphibian strategy confirmed by Arabic sources (*barr^{an} wa-baḥr^{an}*).[44] We should not forget that Seville had been the capital of al-Andalus under the rule of the Almohad dynasty. For this purpose, the Castilian king deployed naval forces in the Cantabrian Sea, entrusting its leadership to Ramón Bonifaz, who, by mid-August of 1247, arranged a great fleet to block the mouth of the river Guadalquivir and to be anchored at the gates of Seville.[45] Meanwhile military reinforcements from Castile-León arrived from Córdoba to undertake the ground attack.

According to Ibn ʿIdhārī, in *jumādà* I of 645 (September 3–October 2, 1247) the first Castilian contingents to arrive in Seville, camped outside of the city. The siege was very long and intense and the city blockaded on several fronts.[46]

---

41 Harvey, *Islamic Spain*, 51. See above for a more in-depth discussion of the Treaty of Jaén.
42 *Crónica de veinte Reyes*, 328; PCG, 747–8.
43 On the siege and conquest of Islamic Seville, see González, "Las conquistas," 606–31.
44 *alto capítulo de coronamiento rreal del Andaluzía*: *Crónica de Veinte Reyes*, 329; PCG, 748. Ibn ʿIdhārī, *Bayān, qism al-muwaḥḥidīn*, 380, Spanish translation, II: 187.
45 González, "Las conquistas," 611; González Jiménez, *Alfonso X*, 34.
46 *Bayān, qism al-muwaḥḥidīn*, 380, Spanish translation, II: 187; González, "Las conquistas," 617–20.

Ibn 'Idhārī and other Arabic sources open a unique window onto the impact of the siege within the city:

> In this year [645/1247–1248] the siege escalated and the area around Seville was filled with them [the Christians]. [The Christians] made captive many of its inhabitants and took many of their children in their ships (...). [The Sevillians] shot stones with catapults. All provisions, numerous or scarce, were lacking, excepting what was available at the houses of some rich people who cared about this sort of thing, such as the *faqīh* and judge Ibn Manṣūr, who wished that the Christians should lift the siege from the city and ordered the people to combat and shoot arrows. However, the people [of Seville] were stunned due to this [situation]; they walked as if they were drunk although they were not, and lots of them died of hunger. Food [made of] flour and barley was lacking, and the people ate animal fur. A lot of common people and the regular army died.[47]

Given that they could not defend themselves, the Sevillians asked the Maghrebis for help, receiving maritime reinforces from Tangiers and Ceuta. However, the siege intensified in spring 1248 as also did the hunger and the isolation of the city, heightened by the destruction of the bridge of Triana, which prevented Muslim reinforcements from reaching the Aljarafe;[48] thereafter communications were reduced to boats or swimming.[49]

Feeling desperate, the Sevillians decided to write to the Almohad emir al-Sa'īd (r. 640–646/1242–1248), imploring his protection, Ibn 'Idhārī informs us, by the means of:

> notifications and letters which moved even the stones that heard them. They [the Sevillians] pleaded with them [the Almohads] for succor, encouraging them to conduct *jihād*. They explained their situation to them and how they were submerged into misfortune; but he [al-Sa'īd] (...) did not go out of his way as a result of their notifications and letters, nor felt sorry for their situation and what had happened to them.[50]

---

47 Ibn 'Idhārī, *Bayān, qism al-muwaḥḥidīn*, 380, Spanish translation, II: 188.
48 *Crónica de Veinte Reyes*, págs. 338–9; PCG, 760–1.
49 González, "Las conquistas," 622–3.
50 Ibn 'Idhārī, *Bayān, qism al-muwaḥḥidīn*, 384, Spanish translation, II: 188–9.

Although the people of Seville were besieged by land and sea and did not have the necessary strength to keep fighting nor the supplies to survive, the Muslim resistance at Triana was strong. Finally, when the Castilians had completely blockaded the city, the Sevillians decided to surrender.[51]

The Arabic texts confirm that in the year 646/1248–1249 Fernando III finally took Seville by surrender (*ṣulḥ*^{an}).[52] Al-Maqqarī specifies that the conquest of the city took place on Monday 5th of *shaʿbān* of 646 (November 23, 1248), a date that coincides with that offered by the Castilian sources, according to which Fernando III entered Seville on the day of Saint Clement.[53] The sorrow felt by the population has been perfectly illustrated in the biography of the celebrated grammarian Abū l-Ḥasan ʿAlī b. Jābir b. ʿAlī al-Lakhmī, nicknamed al-Dabbāj ("the brocade seller"), who was said to be terrified both by the ringing of bells and the silence in the absence of the call for prayer. He was said to be so afflicted that he died in the city only a few days after the conquest, on the 21st of *shaʿbān* (December 9, 1248).[54]

Once the terms of surrender or *capitulaciones* were established, the Sevillians were given a period of one month to sell their properties and whatever that they could not take with them. Following the deadline for these transactions – 27th of *ramaḍān* of that year (January 13, 1249), – they started to abandon the city, heading towards the other Mediterranean shore (*al-ʿudwa*), especially to Ceuta and the Almohad capital, Marrakesh, while others chose the Nasrid Kingdom of Granada as their destination.

Perhaps as a result of his obliged *auxilium* towards Fernando III, the first Nasrid emir also had to cede some enclaves of his kingdom to Castile at this time. Thanks to two anonymous chronicles, *Al-Dhakhīra al-saniyya* and the *Taʾrīkh al-Andalus*, we know that, in the final years of Fernando's rule, specifically "in the year 647 (1249–1250) Muḥammad I [gave the cities of] Alcaudete (*al-Qabdhāq*) and the castle of Sarīq (*ḥiṣn al-Sarīq*) to Alfonso."[55] The reference to the latter instead of to Fernando III may have been due to an error by both authors or, alternatively, to the real participation of Alfonso X in the political activity of his father concerning the Muslims of al-Andalus in his capacity as his heir.

---

51   *Crónica de Veinte Reyes*, 343; PCG, 766.
52   Ibn Abī Zarʿ, *Rawḍ al-qirṭās*, 362, Spanish translation, II: 529; Ibn ʿIdhārī, *Bayān, qism al-muwaḥḥidīn*, 384, Spanish translation, II: 188; al-Maqqarī, *Nafḥ al-ṭīb*, IV: 472.
53   *Nafḥ al-ṭīb*, IV: 472; *Crónica de Veinte Reyes*, 343; PCG, 767.
54   Al-Dhahabī, *Taʾrīj*, XIV: 552–3, no. 441; idem, *Siyar aʿlām al-nubalāʾ*, XXIII: 209–10, no. 125; Ibn al-Abbār, *Takmila*, III: 240, no. 603; Ibn al-Zubayr, *Ṣila*, IV: 142–3, no. 294; al-Suyūṭī, *Bughya*, II: 153, no. 1682.
55   *Al-Dhakhīra al-saniyya*, 77; *Taʾrīkh al-Andalus*, 268.

While the Arabic and Christian accounts reveal interesting details about the accomplishment of military *auxilium* by Muḥammad I, no information can be found, however, concerning the *consilium* (or "advice") that the founder of the Nasrid dynasty had to provide Fernando III in the internal affairs of his kingdom. In fact, the Nasrid emir does not appear to confirm any Castilian document issued between 1246 and 1252.[56] It was not until the reign of Fernando's son, Alfonso X, that Muḥammad I would sign official court documents such as privileges (*privilegios rodados*), together with other Muslim vassals of the kingdom.

However, we know that, shortly before the death of Fernando III, precisely in 649/1251–1252, an interesting Nasrid diplomatic visit to Seville took place. The figure responsible for this delegation was Abū Bakr Muḥammad b. Khaṭṭāb (d. 686/1287), a secretary of the Nasrid chancery, who arrived at the city on the morning of 5th of *rabīʿ* II of that year (June 27, 1251), staying there for a few days.[57] Although the main reason for this embassy to the former Almohad capital is not revealed in the account describing it, as we shall see, it is possible that it was a diplomatic mission. It is worthwhile to highlight that this delegation occurred only three years after the Christian conquest of the city. An interesting and telling document has survived that pertains to this delegation. A personal letter that was composed by Ibn Khaṭṭāb and addressed to his friends in Murcia some twelve days after his arrival in Seville (on 17th of *rabīʿ* II of 649/ July 9, 1251), offers a detailed description of the situation of the city and the changes that it had undergone in the process of its "Christianization":

> We arrived at Seville in the first part of the morning of Tuesday 5th of *rabīʿ* II [of 649] and the infante [Alfonso X] came out of the city by about two miles to receive us. [He] calmed us with the smiling face that he showed and his efforts so that our stay should be to our taste. We settled in tents on the city's outskirts, in a place known as "The Countryside" (*al-Qamb*), in which fountains flowed everywhere and the air and water was of much superior quality.
>
> [Infante Alfonso X] offered us to lodge in the houses [existing] inside the city. However we considered that it was better to stay in that place since it contributed to preserve the health, so we refused to settle in [the city] due to the intense heat, the dust that arose, and its brackish water.

---

56   López de Coca Castañer, "El Reino de Granada," 318.
57   For his biography, see Ḥassan El-Ghailani, *Edición*, 7–18; Boloix-Gallardo, "Ibn Jaṭṭāb," 712–8, at 710; al-Dhahabī, *Taʾrīj*, XV: 581, no. 414.

When the vigor of the breeze had calmed and the horses were released of their fatiguing load, I went out for a walk both outside and inside of the city; I stopped at its waters, and celebrated houses, and I gazed at its fast dappled flow. I followed the steps towards Triana at night observing its old buildings and its elegant minaret [the Giralda], which fill the eyes of he who observes them and leaves a clear path for reflections, even though I had not seen the city since the dishonor had over taken it and both elegance and illustrious lineage had forsaken it. As for its dwellings, you did not see anything but blurred ruins; regarding its wonders you did not perceive anything but a sullen face.

However if the person who contemplates [the city] has the ability to both appreciate how its original situation was and to give free rein to his imagination to repair what has been destroyed of its constructions, he will be able to visualize its beauty in his mind, which invites one to [make] licentious comments and console the sorrowful, were it not that the city has been submitted to the most gray-haired monk [Fernando III], who does not practice a religion other than a wine jar and only procures the company of the most lowly people.

In my opinion, I would describe it [Seville] as follows, saying: "Among the lands, [Seville] has the same dignity as does spring among the seasons of the year. And if my thoughts were not distracted [by different things] nor my mind occupied, I would praise it excessively and would not leave any of its places and ruins without being described."[58]

5   The Death of Fernando III

A final reflection of the loyalty paid by Muḥammad I to Fernando III was the Nasrid funeral honors held at the news of the death of the Castilian king on May 30, 1252. Both the *Crónica de Veinte Reyes* and the *Estoria de España* relates the reaction of the Nasrid emir as follows:

> When the *king of Granada, his vassal,* heard about the death of the king don Fernando [III], *he ordered for there to be weeping in all his kingdom*; and it was not astonishing that this be done, since [the Castilian king]

---

58   Ibn Khaṭṭāb, *Faṣl al-khiṭāb*, 184–6. A part of this epistle was reproduced by Ibn al-Khaṭīb, *Iḥāṭa*, II: 431–3 and translated from Arabic into Spanish by Granja Santamaría, "Geografía lírica," 93.

had both him and his kingdom protected and defended from all peoples.⁵⁹

These two sources also reveal that every year from 1252 onwards, Muḥammad I, as a sign of respect, used to send a hundred knights holding large white wax candles that were placed around the grave of King Fernando III to celebrate the anniversary of his death.⁶⁰

However, the relationship between the Castilian king and the Andalusi world found its final manifestation in the four inscriptions ornamenting Fernando's multilingual tomb in Seville cathedral, constructed in the decades immediately following the king's death and inscribed in Latin, Castilian, Arabic, and Hebrew.⁶¹ These inscriptions were brought to light for the first time by Henrique Flórez, who also provided transcriptions of them.⁶² He pointed out that both the Arabic and Hebrew inscriptions had remained hidden during "the lengthy period of five hundred and two years," until they were finally discovered and, consequently, studied and translated during the reign of King Fernando VI (1746–1759).⁶³ The four inscriptions are presented on two white marble tombstones of different dimensions, one displaying the Latin and Castilian texts and the other displaying the Arabic and Hebrew, and Flórez described them as follows:

---

59   *Quando el rey de Granada su vasallo sopo de la muerte del rey don Fernando su señor, mando fazer grandes llantos por todo su regno; et non era marauilla de lo fazer, ca tenie a el et a su reyno anparado et defendido de todas gentes*: PCG, 773–4. See also *Crónica de Veinte Reyes*, 348. Emphasis mine.
60   *Crónica de Alfonso X*, 27. Martínez Díez, *Fernando III*, 240.
61   For the dating of the tomb, see Nickson, "Remembering Fernando," 171–4.
62   These are to be found in Flórez, *Elogios del Santo Rey Don Fernando*, (5), (7), (11). The text is inserted between pages 8 and 9 of the aforementioned work. It should be noted that Flórez offers the translation of the Latin inscription as well as the interpretation of the Arabic and Hebrew legends into Spanish. The author also adds some linguistic and philological comments on the text of the first two engravings from his personal observations. These four epitaphs have been reproduced and are translated in Castro, *La realidad histórica*, 31–2, as well as in Dodds, Menocal and Krasner, *The Arts of Intimacy*, 200–1, and most recently, Nickson, "Remembering Fernando," 180–1.
63   *el dilatado espacio de quinientos y dos años*: Flórez, *Elogios*, (1) and (2). Flórez explains his intention in providing copies of the inscriptions and the delay that his task suffered due to the difficulty of reproducing a lettering that was alien to him. He was finally assisted by a scholar from Seville, called Livino Ignacio Leyrens, who reproduced the engravings for him with care and attention, conducting an accurate copy of the four legends in their original size. By way of colophon to his curious treatise, Henrique Flórez gives his own version of the date of death of King Fernando III, concluding that it took place on the May 30 –instead of on the 31st– according to the data provided by the four funeral steles.

The letters on these are embossed and gilded, perfectly conserved because of being in a well-preserved place. The rulings are marked by lines, or intermediary threads of the same stone... These two [the Hebrew and Arabic], (and the same is the case with the Latin and Castilian) which as we already said are placed together on the same stone, are separated from each other by a band of castles [for Castile] and lions [for León], which alternate from top to bottom between lion and castle.[64]

Flórez's transcriptions have been reproduced and translated on a number of occasions, most recently in the important study by Tom Nickson, whose revised translations present the text of the four epitaphs as follows:[65]

Latin:
Here lies the most illustrious king Ferrandus of Castile, and of Toledo, León, Galicia, Seville, Córdoba, Murcia, and Jaén, who conquered all *Hispania*, the most loyal, the most veracious, the most constant, the most just, the most energetic, the most tenacious, the most liberal, the most patient, the most pious, the most humble and the most effective in fear and in the service of God. He destroyed and utterly exterminated the impudence of his enemies. He raised up and exalted all who were his friends; he seized the city of Seville, capital and metropolis of all Spain, from the hands of the pagans and restored it to the Christian cult, and that is the city where he paid his debt to nature and passed to the Lord on the last day of May in the year of the Incarnation of the Lord, 1252.

Castilian:
Here lies the very honorable king don Ferrando, lord of Castile and of Toledo, of León, of Galicia, of Seville, of Córdoba, of Murcia, and of Jaén, he who conquered all *España*, the most loyal and the truest and most forthright and most courageous and most comely and most illustrious

---

64 *Las letras de unas y otras son de relieve, y doradas, con perfecta conservacion, à causa de estàr en sitio preservado. Los renglones se dividen unos de otros con lineas, ò filetes intermedios de la misma piedra, como veràs en las Estampas siguientes de la Hebrea, y la Arabiga. Estas dos (y lo mismo la Latina y Castellana) que digimos estar juntas en la misma piedra, se dividen una de otra, por medio de una orla de Castillos y Leones, que alternan de arriba à bajo en contraposicion del Leon al Castillo.* Ibid.

65 Nickson, 'Remembering Fernando,' 180–1, and see above, fn.63.

and most forbearing and most humble and he who most feared God, and he who most served Him, and he who broke and destroyed all his enemies and who exalted and honored all his friends, and conquered the city of Seville, which is the head of all Spain, and he died there on the last day of May in the *era* of 1290.

Arabic:
This is the tomb of the great king don Ferando, lord of Castile, Toledo, León, Galicia, Seville, Córdoba, Murcia, and Jaén, may God be pleased with him. Who ruled all al-Andalus, [who is] the most faithful, the most veracious, the most enduring, the most just, the most valiant, the most propitious, the most noble, the most forbearing, the most visionary, the greatest in modesty, most suitable to God and His greatest servant. He died (God had mercy on him) on the Friday night and God raised him. He ennobled and honored his loved ones and took possession of the city of Seville, which is the head of all al-Andalus, and in which he broke and destroyed all his enemies. [He] died on the twentieth of the month of Rabi' of the year 650 al-hijra.

Hebrew:
In this place is the tomb of the great king don Ferando
Lord of Castile, Toledo and León and Galicia and Seville
And Córdoba and Murcia and Jaén. May his soul [rest] in Paradise. He who
Conquered all Sefarad, the upright, righteous, the stronghold and tower,
The mighty, pious, humble, [a] God-fearing [man] who served Him all
His days. Who broke and destroyed all his enemies and raised up and honored all
His friends, and who conquered the city of Seville, which is
the head of all Sefarad and who died in it on Friday night
the twenty-second day of the month of Sivan in the year five
thousand and twelve since the Creation of the world.

The significance of the multi-lingual tomb of Fernando III remains a point of debate among scholars. Clearly, it would not be fair to assign this "quadrilingualism" simply to the king's relationship with Muḥammad I; after all, the tomb was erected decades after his death by his son, Alfonso X, nicknamed "the Wise." Alfonso's "love of knowledge" and cultivation of a multi-lingual court is well-known, as well as his sponsorship of translations from both Arabic and Hebrew, surely a crucial context for his design for Fernando's tomb.[66] Yet these epitaphs were also reflective of the legacy that Alfonso wished to create around his father's memory, a legacy built upon the conquest of al-Andalus and sustained relationships with the Arabic-speaking kingdoms of the Peninsula. As Tom Nickson has recently pointed out, the multi-lingual epitaphs had a symbolic value, "effacing dissent and staging a utopian vision of a multiconfessional society united in its recognition of crown and church."[67] This remarkable tomb thus enabled Alfonso X to shape the legacy of his father, who would go down in history as "glorious even in his own sepulchre for having been engraved in four languages as no other monarch had," and for having been commemorated by bringing together two supposedly incompatible worlds.[68]

Works Cited

Primary Sources (Published)

Al-Dhahabī. *Ta'rīj al-Islām wa-wafayāt al-mashāhir wa-l-a'lām*. Ed. Bashār 'Awwād b. Ma'rūf. Beirut: Dār al-Garb al-Islāmī, 2003, 50 vols.

Al-Dhahabī. *Siyar a'lām al-nubalā'*. Ed. Bashshār 'Awwād b. Ma'rūf and Muḥyī Halāl al-Sirḥān. Beirut: Mu'assasat al-Risāla, 1986, 25 vols.

Al-Maqqarī. *Nafḥ al-ṭīb fī-ghusn al-Andalus al-ratīb wa-dhikr wazīri-hā Lisān al-Dīn Ibn al-Khaṭīb*. Ed. Iḥsān 'Abbās. Beirut: Dār Ṣādir, 1968, 8 vols. English translation by Pascual de Gayangos, *History of Muhammedam dynasties in Spain*. London: Johnson Reprint, 1940, 2 vols.

Al-Qashtālī, Aḥmad. *Milagros de Abū Marwān al-Yuḥānisī*. Ed. Fernando de la Granja Santamaría. Madrid: Instituto Egipcio de Estudios Islámicos, 1974. Spanish translation by Bárbara Boloix Gallardo, *Prodigios del maestro sufí Abū Marwān al-Yuḥānisī de Almería*. Madrid: Mandala, 2010.

Al-Suyūṭī. *Bugyat al-wu'āt fī ṭabaqāt al-lugawiyyīn wa-l-nuḥḥāt*. Ed. Muḥammad Abū l-Faḍl Ibrāhīm. Cairo: Maṭba'at 'Īsā al-Bābī al-Halabī, 1964, 2 vols.

Crónica de Alfonso X. Ed. Manuel González Jiménez. Murcia: Real Academia de Alfonso X el Sabio, 1998.

---

66   Only two years after the death of his father, precisely in 1254, Alfonso X created two new centers of translation: the *Estudios e Escuelas Generales de latín é de arábigo* in Seville, and another similar institution in Murcia. Among the works that were translated under his patronage, are several books written in both Arabic and Hebrew languages, the contents of which were translated into Romance and not into Latin as had been customary in Toledo. González Jiménez, *Alfonso X*, 345.

67   Nickson, "Remembering Fernando," 179–80.

68   Flórez, *Elogios*, (3)–(4).

Crónica de Veinte Reyes. Transcribed by José Manuel Ruíz Asencio and Mauricio Herrero Jiménez. Introductory study by Gonzalo Martínez Díez, José Fradejas Lebrero and César Hernández Alonso. Burgos: Ayuntamiento, 1991.

Flórez, Henrique. *Elogios del Santo Rey Don Fernando, puestos en el sepulcro de Sevilla en hebreo y arábigo, hasta hoy no publicadas, con las inscripciones latina y castellana, dedicados al rey N. Señor*, en *España Sagrada. Teatro Geographico–Historico de la Iglesia de España. Origen, divisiones, y limites de todas sus Provincias, Antigüedad, Traslaciones y estado antiguo, y preferente de sus Sillas con varias Disertaciones críticas*. Madrid: Oficina de Antonio Marín, 1754.

Ibn al-Abbār. *Al-Takmila li-kitāb al-Ṣila*. Ed. ʿAbd al-Salām al-Harrās. Casablanca: Dār al-Maʿārif, 1990–1996, 4 vols.

Ibn Abī Zarʿ. *Al-Anis al-mutrib bi-Rawd al-qirtas fi ajbar muluk al-Magreb wa-tarij madinat Fas*. Ed. Abd al-Wahhab al-Mansur. Rabat: Al-Maṭbaʿa al-Mulkiyya, 1999. Spanish translation by Ambrosio Huici Miranda. Valencia: Anubar, 1964, 2 vols.

Ibn ʿIdhārī. *Al-Bayan al-mugrib fi ijtisar ajbar muluk al-Andalus wa-l-Magreb*. Ed. Muḥammad Ibrāhīm al-Kattānī, Muḥammad Zanaybar, Muḥammad b. Tāwit and ʿAbd al-Qādir Zamāma. Beirut-Casablanca: Dār al-Gharb al-Islāmī-Dār al-Thaqāfa, 1985, *volume of the Almohads (Qism al-muwahhidin)*. Spanish translation by Ambrosio Huici Miranda. Tetuán: Editora Marroquí, 1954.

Ibn Khaldūn. *Kitab al-ʿibar wa-dīwān al-mubtadaʾ wa-l-khabar*. Cairo: Bulaq, 1867, 7 vols.

Ibn Khaldūn. *Kitāb al-ʿibar wa-dīwān al-mubtadaʾ wa-l-khabar fi ayyām al-ʿarab wa-l-ʿajām wa-l-barbar*. Beirut: Muʾassasat al-ʿAlamī li-l-Maṭbūʿāt, 1971, 7 vols. French translation by Maurice Gaudefroy-Demombynes, "Histoire des Banou l-Aḥmar, rois de Grenade. Extraits du *Kitab al-ibar (Libro des Exemples)*." *Journal Asiatique* XII (1898): 309–340.

Ibn al-Khaṭīb. *Al-Iḥāṭa fī akhbār Gharnāta*. Ed. Muḥammad ʿAbd Allāh ʿInān. Cairo: Al-sharika al-Duwaliyya li-l-Ṭibāʿa, 2001, 4 vols.

Ibn al-Khaṭīb. *Al-Lamḥa al-badriyya fī l-dawla al-Naṣriyya*. Beirut: Dār al-Afāq al-Jadida, 1980. Spanish translation by José Mª Casciaro Ramírez and Emilio Molina López, *Historia de los Reyes de la Alhambra*. Granada: University of Granada Press, 2010.

Ibn Khaṭṭāb. *Faṣl al-khiṭāb fī tarsīl Abī Bakr Ibn Khaṭṭāb*. Ed. and study by Ḥasan el-Ghaylānī (unpublished Doctoral Dissertation supervised by Mª Jesús Viguera Molíns). Madrid: University Complutense of Madrid, 1994.

Ibn al-Zubayr. *Kitāb Ṣilat al-Ṣila*. Ed. Évariste Lévi-Provençal. Rabat: al-Maktaba al-Iqtiṣādiyya, 1938.

Jiménez de Rada, Rodrigo. *Historia Arabum*. Ed. Juan Fernández Valverde. Turnhout: Brepols, 1999.

Primera crónica general de España. Ed. Ramón Menéndez Pidal et al. Madrid: Gredos, 1955.

Taʾrīkh al-Andalus. Ed. ʿAbd al-Qādir Bubāya. Beirut: Dār al-Kutub al-ʿIlmiyya, 2009.

Secondary Sources

Balbale, Abigail Krasner. "*Jihād* as a Means of Political Legitimization in Thirteenth-Century Sharq al-Andalus." In *The Articulation of Power in Medieval Iberia and the Maghrib*, ed. Amira K. Bennison, 87–105. Oxford: Oxford University Press, 2014.

Boloix-Gallardo, Bárbara. *De la Taifa de Arjona al Reino nazarí de Granada (1232–1246). En torno a los orígenes de un Estado y de una dinastía*. Jaén: Instituto de Estudios Giennenses, 2006.

Boloix-Gallardo, Bárbara. "Ibn Jaṭṭāb, Abū Bakr Muḥammad." In *Biblioteca de Al-Andalus*, Ed. Jorge Lirola Delgado and José Miguel Puerta Vílchez, 712–718. Almería: Fundación Ibn Tufayl de Estudios Árabes, vol. 3, 2004.

Boloix-Gallardo, Bárbara. *Ibn al-Aḥmar. Vida y reinado del primer sultán de Granada (1195–1273)*. Granada: University of Granada Press – Patronato de la Alhambra y el Generalife, 2017.

Boloix-Gallardo, Bárbara. "'Yo soy el Yuhayna de sus noticias.' Ibn al-Jaṭīb historiador de la dinastía nazarí." In *Ibn al-Jaṭīb y su tiempo*, ed. Celia del Moral and Fernando Nicolás Velázquez Basanta, 17–41. Granada: University of Granada Press, 2012.

Castro, Américo. *La realidad histórica de España*. México: Porrúa, 1982.

Campa, Mariano de la. "Crónica de veinte reyes." *Revista de literatura medieval* 15, no. 1 (2003): 141–156.

Catalán, Diego. *La "Estoria de España" de Alfonso X. Creación y evolución*. Madrid: Fundación Ramón Menéndez Pidal – Universidad Autónoma de Madrid, 1992.

Chalmeta Gendrón, Pedro. "El concepto de *thagr*." In *La Marche supérieure d'al-Andalus et l'Ocident Chrétien. Actes recuellis et presentes par Philippe Senac*, 15–28. Madrid: Casa de Velázquez – University of Zaragoza, 1991.

Cressier, Patrice and Vicente Salvatierra, ed. *Las Navas de Tolosa (1212–2012). Miradas cruzadas*. Jaén: University of Jaén Press, 2014.

Dodds, Jerrilynn D., María Rosa Menocal, and Abigail Krasner Balbale, ed. *The Arts of Intimacy: Christians, Jews and Muslims in the Making of Castilian Culture*. Yale: Yale University Press, 2008.

Estepa Díez, Carlos and Mª Antonia Carmona Ruiz, ed. *La Península Ibérica en tiempos de las Navas de Tolosa*. Madrid: SEEM, 2014.

Fernández-Ordóñez, Inés. "La transmisión textual de la Estoria de España y de las principales Crónicas de ella derivadas." In *Alfonso X el Sabio y las Crónicas de España*, ed. Inés Fernández-Ordóñez, 219–260. Valladolid: Universidad de Valladolid, 2001.

García Fitz, Francisco. "La Reconquista y formación de la España medieval (de mediados del siglo XI a mediados del siglo XIII)." In *Historia militar de España*, ed. Miguel Ángel Ladero Quesada, Vol. 2, 142–216. Madrid: Ediciones del Laberinto – Ministerio de Defensa, 2010.

García Sanjuan, Alejandro. "Consideraciones sobre el pacto de Jaén de 1246." In *Sevilla 1248. Actas del Congreso Internacional Conmemorativo del 750 aniversario de la Conquista de la Ciudad de Seville por Fernando III, Rey de Castilla y León*, ed. Manuel González Jiménez, 715–24. Madrid: Fundación Ramón Areces, 2000.

González, Julio. "Las conquistas de Fernando III en Andalucía." *Hispania* 6 (1946): 515–631.

González Jiménez, Manuel. *Alfonso X (1252–1284)*. Burgos: La Olmeda, 1999.

González Jiménez, Manuel. *Alfonso X el Sabio*. Barcelona: Ariel, 2004.

González Jiménez, Manuel. *Fernando III el Santo. El Rey que marcó el destino de España*. Sevilla: Fundación José Manuel Lara, 2006.

Granja Santamaría, Fernando de la. "Geografía lírica de Andalucía musulmana." In *Historia de Andalucía*, ed. Antonio Domínguez Ortiz, Vol. 5, 81–96. Madrid: Editorial Planeta, 1981.

Guichard, Pièrre. *Al-Andalus frente a la conquista cristiana. Los musulmanes de Valencia (siglos XI–XIII)*. Madrid: Universitat de València, 2001.

Harvey, L.P. *Islamic Spain (1250 to 1500)*. Chicago: University Press, 1990.

Huici Miranda, Ambrosio. *Las grandes batallas de la Reconquista durante las invasiones africanas*. Preliminar study by Emilio Molina López and Vicente Carlos Navarro Oltra. Granada: Archivum, 2000.

Ladero Quesada, Miguel Ángel. "El Reino de Granada y la Corona de Castilla en la Baja Edad Media." In *Historia del Reino de Granada. Vol. 1: De los orígenes a la época mudéjar (hasta 1502)*, ed. Rafael Peinado Santaella and José Enrique López de Coca Castañer, 189–210. Granada: University of Granada Press – El Legado Andalusí, 2000.

Ladero Quesada, Miguel Ángel. *Granada. Historia de un país islámico (1232–1571)*. Madrid: Gredos, 1989.

Lafuente Alcántara, Emilio. *Inscripciones árabes de Granada*. Granada: University of Granada Press, 2000.

Lévi-Provençal, Évariste. *Inscriptions árabes d'Espagne*. Leiden – Paris: E.J. Brill – E. Larose, 1931.

López de Coca Castañer, José Enrique. "El Reino de Granada: ¿un vasallo musulmán?" In *Actas del IX Congreso de Estudios Medievales "Fundamentos medievales de los particularismos hispánicos,"* ed. José Enrique López de Coca Castañer, 313–46. León: Fundación Sánchez Albornoz, 2005.

Martínez Díez, Gonzalo. *Fernando III. 1217–1252*. Palencia: La Olmeda, 1993.

Martínez Enamorado, Virgilio. "Un *país que reporta todo tipo de bienes*. Sobre el sentido histórico de la cora de Sidonia." *RAMPAS* 10 (2008): 375–398.

Nickson, Tom. "Remembering Fernando: Multilingualism in Medieval Iberia." In *Viewing Inscriptions in the Late Antique and Medieval World*, ed. Anthony Eastmond, 170–186. Cambridge: Cambridge University Press, 2015.

Peinado Santaella, Rafael G. *Guerra Santa, cruzada y yihād en Andalucía (siglos XIII–XV)*. Granada: University of Granada Press, 2017.

Ríos Saloma, Martín. *La Reconquista: Una construcción historiográfica (siglos XVI–XIX)*. Madrid: Marcial Pons, 2011.

Rochwert-Zuili, Patricia. "*Auxilium* et *consilium* dans la *Chronica regum Castellae*." *E-Spania* 2 (2006). http://journals.openedition.org/e-spania/281. doi: 10.4000/e-spania.281.

Rosado Llamas, Mª Dolores and Manuel Gabriel López Payer. *La Batalla de las Navas de Tolosa. Historia y mito*. Jaén: Caja Rural, 2001.

Ruiz-Gálvez Priego, Estrella. "'De reyes y de santos': San Fernando, de las crónicas de la edad media a las hagiografías del siglo XVII: permanencia y adaptación de una imagen." In *Homenaje a Henri Guerreiro: La hagiografía entre historia y literatura en la España de la Edad Media y el Siglo de Oro*, ed. Marc Vitse, 1015–31. Madrid: Vervuert, 2005.

Urvoy, Dominique. "Sur l'evolution de la notion de gihad dans l'Espagne musulman." *Mélanges de la Casa de Velázquez* 9 (1973): 335–371.

Vara Thorbeck, Carlos. *El lunes de las Navas*. Jaén: University of Jaén Press, 1999.

Vidal Castro, Francisco. "Frontera, genealogía y religión en la gestación y nacimiento del Reino Nazarí de Granada. En torno a Ibn al-Aḥmar." In *Actas del III Estudios de Frontera. Convivencia, Defensa y Comunicación en la Frontera*, 793–810. Jaén: Diputación Provincial, 2000.

Viguera Molíns, Mª Jesús, ed. *El Reino nazarí de Granada. Política e Instituciones. Espacio y economía*. Vol. VIII/3 of the *Historia de España* coordinated by Ramón Menéndez Pidal. Madrid: Espasa Calpe, 2000.

CHAPTER 4

In exercitu loco eius pontificalia exercet: Warrior Clerics in the Era of Fernando III

Kyle C. Lincoln

In the *Song of Roland*, Archbishop Turpin is a cleric apart. Around the hundredth verse of the text, Turpin commits a daring deed that fits so neatly into the expectations of *chansons des gestes* that it is easily missed: "Archbishop Turpin slew Siglorel/ The wizard, who erst had been in hell/ By Jupiter thither in magic led."[1] Although his actions garnered praise from Roland and nods of approval from his confreres, what is most remarkable about Turpin's portrayal is how it compares to another famous adventuring prelate. Jerónimo, companion of Rodrigo Díaz de Vivar, had a similar experience in battle alongside el Cid, although his opponents were not wizards but an innumerable number of Muslim troops.[2] In the early thirteenth century, Archbishop Rodrigo Jiménez de Rada of Toledo portrayed himself in the same light, inspiring the royal counter charge at Las Navas in his account of the battle known as *Hic moriamur*, a scene that was also depicted above the archbishop's tomb at Santa María de Huerta.[3] While they were real historical figures, these portrayals in literature were not the product of some overactive imagination or a portrait of a cleric that courtly audiences *wished* they had, but were instead the kind of cleric they rode into battle alongside. If the age of Charlemagne and El Cid knew such clerics, it is hardly surprising that their royal and aristocratic descendants expected that their own clerical colleagues should behave any differently.

I have argued elsewhere that the clergy of medieval Castile were inclined to do just that: take up arms when their bellicosity fitted within the contemporary legal framework of "just war."[4] Of course, while this is not a new point – Peter Linehan noted it in 1993 – renewing the debate on and documenting

---

1 Hagan, *The Song of Roland*, 123.
2 Garci-Gómez, *Cantar de mío Cid*, 67, ll. 1288–91.
3 In the *De rebus Hispaniae*, Rodrigo narrates the events: *DrH*, 272. Alvira's discussion of the scene and the fresco appear in his volume on the campaign of Las Navas: Alvira, *Las Navas*, 430–3. Alvira also discussed an early liturgical version of the episode, embedded in a larger celebration of the feast of the "Triumph of the Cross," as part of the eleventh *lectio*: Alvira, "Antes de *De rebus Hispaniae*."
4 Lincoln, "Beating Swords into Croziers."

cases of warrior-clerics has lasting significance for our understanding of the permeable intellectual and cultural boundaries between the laity and clergy in medieval Christendom.[5] First, it suggests that the normative images of prelates projected by papal reformers as *boni pastores* was only part of the picture; clerics could be different things on different occasions, and could rise to the challenges of their day in a variety of fashions. Second, in the wake of monographs by Craig Nakashian and Lawrence Duggan, the renewal of this debate suggests that a more extensive study of warrior clerics in medieval Europe – undertaken by specialists working on a variety of periods and regions – may yet reveal a more complex understanding of who these warrior clerics were or how they fulfilled the duties of their office.[6] In this study, I wish to do just that, focusing on the reign of Fernando III and the bellicose actions of the senior clergy under his sovereignty. In studying the *locus pontificali* – the place of the bishop on the front line – we are of course focusing on one of several roles that the bishops of Fernando III took upon themselves in war: their spiritual support of Fernando through the preaching of crusade and the ceremonial consecration of conquered lands is well known and has benefitted from ample scholarship elsewhere.[7] Instead, this study will explore the direct military involvement of the bishops of Fernando III, their place in war when they themselves took up arms, in order to trace their activities in the light of the expanding scholarly context of militarily-active prelates in the medieval Latin West.

First, though, the contextual evidence linking the legal status of arms-bearing clergy in Iberia to the wider framework established in Christendom beyond the Pyrenees bears repeating. Duggan has already noted that the legal restraints around clerical arms-bearing were relaxed during the pontificate of Alexander III in murder/manslaughter cases within canon law. Effectively, self-defense clauses – *vim vi repellere* – imported from Roman Law made any action of force taken by clerics in defense of a just cause, itself linked with ideas of just war, licit in legal terms, if not necessarily within a theological framework.[8] Gratian's *Decretum* included these clauses, but also made clear that prelates were allowed to bear arms, provided they were doing so to defend

---

5 Linehan, *History and the Historians*, 604.
6 Duggan, *Armsbearing and the Clergy*, 119–20; Nakashian, *Warrior Churchmen of Medieval England*, 215–40. I am grateful to Prof. Nakashian for providing me with an advanced text of his work while I was in the early stages of preparing this study.
7 See especially, Pick, *Conflict and Coexistence*; Ayala Martínez, "Honorio III, la cruzada y la Península Ibérica"; Ayala Martínez, "Fernando III y la Cruzada Hispánica"; García Fitz, *Castilla y León frente al Islam*; O'Callaghan, *Reconquest and Crusade*, 185–93; Smith, "Las Navas and the Restoration of Spain," 39–4; and Lomax, *The Reconquest of Spain*.
8 Duggan, *Armsbearing and the Clergy*, 225–6.

themselves in actions that fell within the framework of just war.⁹ Moreover, there is specific evidence that clergy in Castile were participating in military campaigns, at least in Toledo under the archiepiscopate of Archbishop Rodrigo Jiménez de Rada (abp. 1209–47). In a 1226 letter that I have edited elsewhere, Honorius III instructed Archbishop Rodrigo Jiménez de Rada that Toledan clerics who went with the armies in campaigns *contra Sarracenos* should have the use of their benefices and should have their goods protected; the language of the text was quite similar to other crusading privileges.¹⁰

Evidence from the municipal *fueros* that governed the towns of Fernando's kingdom suggests that chaplains went with the Castilian armies and were well-rewarded.¹¹ In the *Fuero* of Cuenca, chaplains that journeyed with the army received a slave as their base pay from among the spoils of war.¹² The code issued by Bishop Ramón II de Minerva in 1180 for the city of Palencia includes an extensive (and grammatically torturous) discussion about which wars townsfolk were permitted to fight in, and it is hard to read earlier papal correspondence concerning the bishop's lust for military derring-do as anything other than his incentive here.¹³ Ostensibly, clerics in Castile were accustomed to violence, and the examples from the reign of Alfonso VIII show both a legal and cultural framework within which clerical arms-bearing was not only allowed but encouraged, provided such action was on behalf of king and country. Even though these earliest pieces of evidence date to the reign of Fernando III's grandfather, the sources pertaining to Alfonso VIII's bishops demonstrate that they played a key role in the affairs of the kingdom, including in the military operations led by the crown.¹⁴ What remains to be seen, however, is whether any of the clerics – and the bishops are by far the most visible in the sources – of Fernando's kingdoms took advantage of these precedents to build up their own spiritual treasures by risking their earthly bodies on the battle field in the *negotium Christi*.

There are a number of campaigns in which we can trace the involvement of bishops in the military affairs of Fernando III. During his reign as king of Castile (r. 1217–52) and of León (r. 1230–52), Fernando led numerous military

---

9   Gratian, *Decretrum Gratiani. First Recension*, C.23, q. 8, esp. d.p.c. 28.
10 Lincoln, "Beating Swords into Croziers," 103.
11 Powers, *Society Organized for War*, 178–9.
12 Powers, *The Code of Cuenca*, 165.
13 Abajo Martín, *Documentación de Palencia*, 176. On the papal mischaracterizations of Ramón de Minerva, and his usefulness as a warrior cleric: Lincoln, "*Mihi pro fidelitate militabat*," 33–40; Lincoln, "Beating Swords into Croziers."
14 Estepa Díez, "La Monarquía castellana"; García Fitz, "Las huestes de Fernando III"; García Fitz, *Castilla y León, frente al Islam*; Ayala Martínez, "Los obispos de Alfonso VIII."

actions against his political opponents, both Christian and Muslim, although his campaigns against Andalusian powers are better studied and remembered.[15] There are a handful of campaigns in which we can detect clerical involvement or leadership, but the evidence is varied and the cases require individual attention. The conclusion of this study will also consider why, in an age of growing momentum for Fernando's Andalusian conquests, clerics begin to recede into the background.

The earliest definitive evidence from Fernando's reign for military actions conducted by the high clergy comes from an entry in the *Anales Toledanos*, a compendium of annalistic historical entries that exists in several iterations in the Toledan archives. The entry in question, dated to AD 1221, notes that:

> The archbishop Don Rodrigo of Toledo made Crusade, and he was helped by more than 200,000 foot- and horsemen, and he entered the land of the Moors from the part of Aragón on the day of Saint Mathew the Evangelist, and he took three castles, Sierra, Serresuela, and Mira. Afterward he besieged Requena on the day of St. Michael and they fought with catapults and with launchers, and with the *delibra*, and they pulled down towers and *azitaras* and they were not able to take it, and more than two thousand Christians died, and they returned on St. Martin's day. The Era 1257.[16]

The towns mentioned in the text lie on the modern road from Cuenca toward Valencia, which validates the notation that the campaign was in territory that lay on the Aragonese side of the border established by the 1179 Treaty of Cazola, in which Alfonso VIII of Castile and Alfonso II of Aragón divided their putative future conquests of al-Andalus along a shared border.[17] Although the

---

15 The impact and vocabulary of a plural monarchy in Castile was described recently by Bianchini, and by her coining denotes not only the familial aspects of monarchy but those affiliated in the work of the monarch as part of a larger constellation of authority, which would, of course, include bishops: Bianchini, *The Queen's Hand*, 3–4.

16 *El arzobispo D. Rodrigo de Toledo fizo Cruzada, e ayuntó entre peones e Caballeros mas de ducentas veces mil, e entró a tierra de Moros de part de Aragon dia de S. Matheus Evangelista, e prisó tres Castiellos, Sierra, e Serresuela, e Mira. Después cercó a Requena dia de S. Miguel, e lidiaronla con almajanequis e con algarradas e con delibra e derrivaron torres e azitaras e non la pudieron prender, e murieron y mas de dos mil Christianos e tornaronse el dia de S. Martin, Era MCCLVII*: Porres-Cleto, *Anales Toledanos*, 195.

17 On the terms of the treaty of Cazola and its lasting impact as a defining feature of the internal borders between the Kingdoms of Castile and Aragón, see: Linehan, *History and the Historians*, 287–8; O'Callaghan, *Reconquest and Crusade*, 56; Martínez Díez, *Alfonso VIII*, 190–1; Ladero Quesada, *La formación medieval de España*, 321.

head-count of the forces led by Rodrigo are an excellent example of the problems of medieval crowd-counting, the loss of two thousand Christian soldiers may represent either a total of one-percent losses from the troops marshalled by Rodrigo or an actual count of those left on the battlefield. Of course, the attribution of the army to Rodrigo indicates that he was its leader, and certainly responsible for its muster, but we know little about whether he directed the military maneuvers himself or if an *adalid* from Toledo was in his party.[18] The presence of so many siege weapons suggests that the forces were considerable, and may have even made use of military engineers similar to those employed by Jaime I of Aragón in his campaigns in Valencia.[19] The cost of these materials would have required substantial financial resources and manpower, suggesting that Rodrigo may have played a role similar to that of Arnau Amalric during the Albigensian Crusade.[20] As the leader of the force, it seems likely, too, that many of his cathedral canons and tenants would have been deeply invested in the military actions undertaken by the archbishop and would have had to support their own participation in the campaigns.

Given the losses on the field in the campaigns of 1221 and the role played by clergy in the campaign, the possibility of canons and clergy being captured in battle must have taken on even greater gravity for the canons of Toledo. In this context, it is not surprising that Rodrigo sought papal clarification on whether his canons were allowed to enjoy the use of their benefices in military contexts – which he apparently did before October 1226, when he received a response from Pope Honorius III (now conserved in the Toledo Cathedral's archive).[21] The *narratio* of this letter notes specifically that Rodrigo had inquired if they were to receive the fruits of their positions when "they went personally in the Christian army against the Moors."[22] Two points in this line from the rescript stand out as being particularly pertinent. First, the canons (both those with full and those with partial prebends) are described as going personally, rather than those forces supported by the incomes of the clergy or serving in their stead. Second, the pointed reference to a specifically religious,

---

18 Local charters from the period do not list the *adalid* as a confirmatory, but there were several who must have served in that position.
19 James of Aragón, *The Book of Deeds*, trans. Smith and Buffery, 158.
20 On Arnau Amalric in the Albigensian Crusade, see: Alvira, "El 'venerable' Arnaldo Amalrico"; Kienzle, *Cistercians, Heresy, and Crusade in Languedoc*, 152–61; Marvin, *The Occitan War*, 40–3, 52–4; Pegg, *A Most Holy War*, 69–71, 86–9; Moore, *The War on Heresy*, 242–53, especially 247–8 and 252–3; Ames, *Medieval Heresies*, 209–10.
21 ACT C.11.C.1.7. See the text of this privilege, cited above, in my article: Lincoln, "Beating Swords into Croziers," 103.
22 *personaliter vadunt in xristiano exercitu contra mauros*: Ibid., 103.

perhaps even crusading, context for the combat suggests that, while Castilian clerics had ridden into battle against Leonese and Navarrese forces in the previous half century, Rodrigo was careful to frame the question in starkly religious terms (thus, being likely more appealing to papal ears). The papal reply not only granted canons the use of their benefices, but further stipulated "those who were absent [from their benefices] for such a favorable cause should be held in esteem," suggesting that the papacy not only condoned clerical participation in military action, but was effectively encouraging it.[23] Of course, the brevity of the privilege, likely based on the brevity of Rodrigo's own original question, circumscribed exactly what role the canons played, although the presence of *portionarios* – who were not full canons and were usually figures outside the full protections of canon law – suggests that the clergy were not merely chaplains in the camps but *caballeros en campo*.

By far the most well-known episcopal campaign from Fernando's reign is the conquest of Quesada by Archbishop Rodrigo Jiménez de Rada in 1234.[24] The conquest of Quesada, 80 km east of Jaén and 50 km southeast of Baeza, represented an important step in the larger move by the Castilian crown to take this region, and to shore up the eastern frontier of the territory held by the former emir of Baeza, al-Bayāsī.[25] As one of the largest landholders in the third Taifa period, al-Bayāsī's death in 1226 left a major vacuum, and Fernando's expansion was a careful follow-up to earlier successes.[26] Understandably, there were also parallel developments in the royal efforts to incorporate the former kingdom of Baeza into Fernando's kingdom. Prior to the campaign itself, Fernando III granted Rodrigo the lordship of Quesada, ostensibly to relieve Rodrigo's episcopal fisc of some of the financial burdens of Fernando's campaigns and to reward the archbishop's faithful support.[27]

While Rodrigo's conquest of Quesada and its *alfoz* is better known, Bishop Domingo of Plasencia also took part in his own conquest of the city of Trujillo in 1232.[28] Two geographical items deserve a note here. First, Trujillo's position

---

23 *qui absunt ex tam favorabiili causa presentia debeat merito reputari*: Ibid.
24 Interestingly, in his whole volume on wars between Castile-León and Muslim powers in al-Andalus, only the Quesada campaign of 1234 is mentioned by García Fitz, although his focus was much wider than the goals of this present study: García Fitz, *Castilla y León frente al Islam*, 122.
25 González, *Repartamiento de Sevilla*, I: 35–6. For more on al-Bayāsī, see in this volume García Fitz, Chp. 2.
26 Ayala Martínez, "Fernando III y la Cruzada Hispánica," 39–40.
27 This privilege is ACT X.9.E.1.2. This initiative is described by Torija Rodríguez: Torija Rodríguez, "De la conquista de Toledo," 74.
28 For the evidence for this campaign, see *DrH*, 46–50; Porres-Cleto, *Los Anales Toledanos*, 201.

80 km south of Plasencia made it an obvious annexation for the bishops of that city, but it was also some 50 km south of the important fortifications at Monfrague. Second, Trujillo was also 45 km east of Cáceres, then only in its third or fourth year of Castilian-Leonese control, having been taken by Fernando's father, Alfonso IX of León, in 1229 after several abortive attempts by the Leonese kings.[29] This particular region of Extremadura was, as Carlos de Ayala has shown, mostly held by the military orders and their clients, whose close connections to the Castilian crown likely exacerbated the financial needs of the bishops of Plasencia.[30] Moreover, the city of Plasencia and the diocese centered on it was intended, from the very start, to be a launching pad for raids deeper into Extremadura. Its creation from one of the archdeaconates of the diocese of Ávila (whose walls, fortified cathedral and adventuring townsfolk are the stuff of *chansons de gestes* in their own right) suggests an intentionally militarized episcopal program from the earliest moments of Plasencia's existence.[31] We know remarkably little about the early career of Bishop Domingo, owing in large part to the total loss of any archival material from Plasencia before the 1220s. What is quite clear is the quality of Domingo's participation in the campaign, about which we are informed in Rodrigo's narration of events in the archbishop's historical magnum opus *De rebus Hispanie*.[32] As just the second bishop of Plasencia, we may suspect that much of Domingo's episcopate was informed by the context of his colleagues' actions rather than by any nascent Plasencian traditions of clerical action. If Julio González is correct in speculating that Domingo was a former abbot of the royal monastery at Valladolid (who was previously also a royal notary), then his connection to the crown would have been quite near indeed, and as Sam Conedera has demonstrated, the connection between the crown and the military orders at the time of Alfonso VIII was especially close toward the latter years of his reign.[33] However, the heavy influence of the military orders in the region of Plasencia suggests that arms-bearing clergy were held in high regard, much like Archbishop Rodrigo's canons were when they ventured *in xristiano exercitu*.

---

29 García Fitz, *Castilla y León frente al Islam*, 298.
30 Ayala Martínez, *Las Ordenes Militares*, 590, 635, 727. See also: Ladero Quesada, *La Formación medieval de España*, 222.
31 On the foundation of Plasencia from territory formerly pertaining to Ávila, see Palacios Martín, "Alfonso VIII." On the fortifications of Ávila, see Gutiérrez Robledo, "Las murallas de Ávila."
32 Domingo's election suggests that he was capable, but local archival documents do not provide any deeper background: Serrano, "Las Elecciones episcopales."
33 *Alfonso VIII*, 1: 471–2; Conedera, "A Wall and a Shield."

In his narration of the Trujillo campaign, Archbishop Rodrigo notes:

> in this expedition, the Toledan Pontiff Rodrigo was not present, for he remained at Guadalajara fatigued by the height of a fever which he barely survived, but sent instead with the army his own chaplain, a venerable man, Bishop Domingo of Plasencia, who took his pontifical place (*locus pontificali*) in the army.[34]

Domingo of Plasencia appears in an additional description of the campaign. The *Anales Toledanos* noted in their vernacular version of the episode nothing about Rodrigo's fever, but did report "the Brothers of the [Military] Orders and the bishop of Plasencia took Trujillo on the day of the Conversion of Saint Paul in January, the Era 1270" [ie, AD 1232].[35] The connection between the conquest of Trujillo in 1232 and the bishop of Plasencia is clear both in the *De rebus* and in the *Anales Toledanos*. What makes this narrative so interesting is that the local Toledan record seems to suggest that the campaign was fought on behalf of Plasencia from the beginning, rather than regarding Trujillo as a Toledan prize won by Bishop Domingo simply by virtue of his health.

There are two plausible readings here, both of which deserve fuller iteration. In one version, we might conjecture that Archbishop Rodrigo was excusing his absence from a campaign that was politically important for the whole of the kingdom, but not for him personally.[36] In doing so, he was able to focus on the fact that the work was still accomplished, but that someone with whom he had close ties and a special bond took the action. Creating a proxy that was close to his own heart allowed Rodrigo to insert himself emotionally within the narrative without having been able to be there personally. In another interpretation, Rodrigo was aggrandizing his own *expected* role in the campaign, even though he had no intention of taking up his *locus pontificali*. In this iteration, then, the focus should rest on why Rodrigo would create a false space for his participation in a campaign that served his interests only tangentially. That narrative space allowed him to demonstrate that his pontifical place was important enough to deserve comment, even if it was never a practiced enterprise within the conquest machine. Employing either explanation underlines

---

34 *in hac expedicione non interfuit Rodericus pontifex Toleanus, qui Guadalfaiarie remanserat febris acumine fatigatus, ubi finis periculum vix evasit; set misit cum exercitu Dominicum capellanum suum, virum venerabilem, episcopus Placentinensem qui in exercitu locus eius pontificalis exerceret*: DrH, 46–50.

35 Porres-Cleto, *Los Anales Toledanos*, 201.

36 Trujillo had been the site of a spinoff order from the Leonese military order of San Julian de Pereira in the 1180s and 1190s, but was captured by the Almohads after the defeat at Alarcos in 1195. Conedera, "A Wall and a Shield," 105–6.

the importance of the position of the archbishops of Toledo, but even this gets ahead of the real clerical agent in the episode: Bishop Domingo of Plasencia.

It is entirely reasonable to raise the question of what place the bishop of Plasencia actually took in the battle lines at Trujillo. In the murals of the battle of Las Navas de Tolosa, such as the ones that adorn the space above Rodrigo Jiménez de Rada's wall-tomb at Santa María de Huerta or a similar mural at Santa María la Real de Las Huelgas in Burgos, Archbishop Rodrigo is depicted as unarmed and bearing a crozier, advising the king from the third line of the battle, as the archbishop's own narration relates.[37] If the advisory role that appears in both the later frescoes and the contemporary chronicles was the *locus pontificali* mentioned by Rodrigo, then Domingo was unlikely to be bearing arms in the melee but it is generally accepted that he died soon after the battle which suggests he was wounded and defended himself with mixed success.[38] Despite the many occasions on which clerical and ecclesiastical discipline played a role, the *Siete Partidas* – admittedly, a much later codification of law during the times of Alfonso X – made no mention of such a place or the role of clerics in the armies, even though, as Simon Barton has recently suggested, the text does describe military leadership on a number of occasions and in significant detail.[39] If the *locus pontificali* was more than a rhetorical flourish, it is rather difficult to pin down, but the relative infrequency of pitched battles requires that we consider a series of alternative possibilities.

In his famous narration of the battle of Las Navas, Rodrigo Jiménez de Rada identified the rightful episcopal place as being in the third line of battle, and at the right hand of the king. Fortunately for participants but unfortunately for scholars desirous of extensive narratives, most medieval military actions were not pitched battles. Instead, sieges appear to have been the norm, and it is very difficult, without narrative or (exceptionally fortunate) archaeological detail to determine the location and command structure of a siege camp.[40] In light of this observation, then, we must consider the location for clerics in battle, based on the available sources. We know that many musters carried a standard, and in some cases, these were imbued with overtly religious significance.

---

37   These images are reproduced in Alvira's volume on Las Navas: Alvira, *Las Navas*, 287, 431, 433.
38   González Cuesta, "Sobre el episcopologio de Plasencia," 359.
39   *Siete Partidas*, 2.22. Simon Barton suggested this passage and examined its importance in an unpublished paper presented in Stockholm in 2015. He sent me a copy of this paper, but it was still unpublished at the time of his tragic and much-too-early passing.
40   The example of the siege of Seville, where the camps' locations are discernible demonstrates how infrequently these kinds of details are extant: García Fitz, *Castilla y León frente al Islam*, 452.

The example of the sacralization of the French oriflamme or the banner of Mary carried by the Toledans at Las Navas suggests that a process of reifying, on the battlefield, a communally constructed identity was in full force.[41] We might imagine, too, that figures like the Toledan canon Diego Pascual who bore the standard – all the way to the caliph's tent, according to his archbishop – were more common than we might imagine, since clergy below the episcopal rank are infrequently mentioned in chronicles but were far more numerous.[42]

The *Repartamiento de Sevilla* – a series of donations of territories by the court of Fernando III of the newly-conquered territories of Seville between 1246–8 – should preserve fragments of evidence regarding clerical participation in the wars of Fernando III. Problematically, the many grants to the bishops and archbishops of Fernando's kingdom say much more about the quantity of land that was available at the king's disposition than the quality of service by clerics that prompted those donations.[43] One clarification from the archives of Segovia notes that Fernando III granted donations in Seville to Bishop Ramón of Segovia – soon-to-be elevated to the archiepiscopate of Seville – "on behalf of the many services which [the bishop] did for [him]."[44] It is difficult to parse exactly what those *servicios* were in the context of the donation, but in a traditionalist sense, the word has a context of military service-at-arms.[45] The fact that Fernando made such donations in the aftermath of the conquest in gratitude to the participants gives further credence to this suggestion. Even beyond these tentative identifications of Bishop Ramón of Segovia as a participant-turned – recipient in the history of the conquest of Seville, the evidence is only a speculative link, and cannot support direct identification of Ramón as a leader of forces or *ballestero* in the lines given the circumstantial nature of the evidence.

---

41   On the *oriflamme* and its liturgical and historical significance for French kings, see Gaposchkin, "From Pilgrimage to Crusade," 53–4. For Rodrigo's description of the banner of Santa María carried at Las Navas: *DrH*, 273.

42   In most instances, Castilian and Leonese chapters had at least 60 canons and, where the practice was tolerated, many more "portionary" canons who subdivided a single prebend. Thus, we might imagine that characters like Diego Pascual were more frequently active in military campaigns than we suppose, and Diego's election to the archiepiscopate after Rodrigo Jiménez de Rada's death suggests that his colleagues had no qualms about his participation in wars: Alvira, *Las Navas*, 438.

43   González, *Repartimiento de Sevilla*, I:281–2, II:28–9.

44   Villar García, *Documentación de Segovia*, 248–9; Colmenares, *Historia de Segovia*, XXI: 15.

45   Although this is the tertiary definition offered by Niermeyer et al., the primary and secondary definitions are so generalized that, for specific and iterative usages, "servitium" *qua* "vassalité, la condition d'un vassal" suggests the military service owed by vassals to lords: Niermeyer, *Mediae Latinitatis Lexicon Minus*, s.v. "servitium."

The military participation of Domingo of Plasencia, Rodrigo Jiménez de Rada, and seemingly of Ramón of Segovia constitutes the sum of the evidence of active military engagement by the bishops of Fernando III that we have been able to ascertain, as afforded to us by the sources for his reign. It is a tally that would seem to suggest a somewhat more limited deployment of senior clergy in warrior roles under Fernando than under his grandfather, Alfonso VIII.[46] However, the *locus pontificali* did not always involve the physical presence of the bishop on the military frontline, and in some instances, a vacant see could be just as valuable to the Castilian king as an occupied one. For the remainder of this study, we shall examine the changing place of the military bishop under Fernando III in two ways: firstly, the "professionalization" of war, that is, the increasing reliance of the Castilian king on mercenary troops, and not on the personal dynamism of individual prelates, and secondly, the ways in which Fernando relied upon the Church of Castile as a valuable, and often crucial, source of funds, something that did not always coincide with the best interests of the episcopacy and which led, at times, to the absence of the bishop altogether, not only from the military frontline but from the diocesan see itself.

In describing the nature of caudillos, the *Siete Partidas*, whose sentiments are likely to echo those of the period of Fernando III, employs only aristocratic terms for leaders – *duque, conde*, and those appointed by the hand of the emperor, in days of old – but not clerical figures.[47] The earlier *Fuero juzgo*, a text widely dated to the mid- thirteenth century, located the powers of war-making in the *señor*, and made no mention of clerical participation, focusing its attention on slaves of the *señor* and their activities in a campaign.[48] The more extensive commentaries on war-making extant in earlier local fueros circumscribe exactly *who* would be leading campaigns. At the diocesan see of Cuenca, clerics were nearly absent in the *Fuero*, save as chaplains; the *adalid* of the town, presumably a laymen, has a variety of roles but none of these were *de jure* incompatible with a canon serving in that post.[49] The *Fuero* of Belinchón notes that the townsfolk were required to support the military service in which the archbishop participated and to render to the archiepiscopal fisc a share of the spoil that is noticeably similar to those rendered to the leader of an expedition.[50] It is likely that these late twelfth- and early thirteenth-century codes

---

46   For a discussion of the military involvement of bishops under Alfonso VIII, see Lincoln, "Beating Swords into Croziers," 83–103; Lincoln, "Mihi pro fidelitate militabat."
47   *Siete Partidas*, 2.2.11
48   *Fuero juzgo*, VIII.1.vii–viii.
49   Powers, *Code of Cuenca*, 165–6.
50   Rivera Recio, *La Iglesia de Toledo*, II: 102–6.

were ambiguous about who was leading the forces on campaign precisely because their contemporary reality presented an ambiguous sample: clergy, like Martín López de Pisuerga, or nobles, like Diego López de Haro, were leading armies with comparable success.[51] Indeed, as armies were becoming more professionalized and employed more heavily armed men in the late twelfth and early thirteenth centuries, some flexibility about who led those armies may have been included by necessity.[52] If later law-codes prevented the participation of clerics, this may suggest that their participation was thus less necessary, or perhaps less desirable. These explanations fit with commentaries about war-making in the period from other legal sources, like canon law.

Military affairs had fallen within the purview of larger canon law tracts since at least the Peace and Truce of God Movements in the late tenth and early eleventh centuries, and these two phenomena are often linked to the development of crusading.[53] Given the impact that conciliar gatherings had on the canon law that governed the Latin Church, the evidence of canon legal restrictions on clerical violence deserves attention here. At the Third Lateran Council, the twenty-seventh canon named a number of mercenary companies that were subject to papal disapproval and the provision of an indulgence for two years' penance suggests that Alexander III's curia understood them to have play a significant military role.[54] The Fourth Lateran Council went further to note that clerics in major orders were forbidden from commanding or directing mercenary companies or crossbowmen.[55] If these canons were reflective of contemporary practice, it suggests that military engagement was becoming increasingly professionalized, a fact which fits generally with the shift toward the *passagium particulare* phenomenon in crusading, favoring professionalized crusading armies and musters from military orders.[56] This

---

51 On the military activities of Archbishop Martín López de Pisuerga, see Lincoln, "Beating Swords into Croziers," 91–5. For the life and career of Diego López (II) de Haro, see Baury, "Diego Lopez 'le Bon'."

52 For the scholarship on mercenaries and professional armies in the twelfth and thirteenth centuries, along with the increased resources they required, see below, fn. 57. On the increasing professionalization of armies generally, the important links between the Plantagenets and Fernando III's grandfather makes Hosler's work on Henry II invaluable. Hosler, *Henry II*, 103–25.

53 An examination of this trend is offered in Flori, "L'Église et la Guerre Sainte."

54 Tanner, *Decrees of the Ecumenical Councils*, 224–5.

55 Tanner, *Decrees of the Ecumenical Councils*, 244.

56 The focused nature of smaller crusading forces was a part of the early crusading movement, although the vocabulary took much longer to develop. On this tension in the sources: Jotischky, *Crusading and the Crusader States*, 246–8; Riley-Smith, *The Oxford History of the Crusades*, 46–8; Bird, Peters, and Powell, *Crusade and Christendom*, 16–8.

increasing professionalization, of course, required greater economic support for these campaigns from the faithful, and would have necessitated increased financial contributions from non-combatants. It seems likely that clerical participation in wars fell out of favor as military service became more professionalized. As a result, clerics transitioned to a role as fundraisers and administrators, likely in direct proportion to the increased professionalization of the armies of crusaders.[57]

Financial inventories of Castilian and Leonese dioceses begin to appear more frequently from the early 1210s. Increasing focus on finance suggests that *something* was draining the resources of chapters, but whether it was the costs of the campaigns to the south or the increasing strain of supporting canons in chapters (or both) is not directly available in the sources. What *is* detectable are the efforts by Fernando – and more than a few of his supporters – to secure financial contributions from the resources of the Church.[58] A few particularly acute instances demonstrate this phenomenon. The first is the case of a few heretics whose properties were confiscated in Palencia, and the second was the prolonged vacancy of the see of Segovia.

A pair of papal epistles from the curia of Gregory IX concerning a prolonged incident in Palencia relates the cases of two heretics in the city and the confiscation of their properties by Fernando III. The first letter, sent to Fernando III, dates to March 12, 1236 and required that the king should turn back over to the bishop of Palencia those goods which Fernando's *merino* and *mayordomo* had seized as a result of the former owners being convicted of heresy.[59] In the first

---

57 The increasing scale of taxation to cover military salaries, beginning under Alfonso VIII and continuing into the reign of Sancho IV has been examined by Estepa Díez, and we should not overlook the fact that paying a stipend necessarily cultivated increased professionalism in the soldiers: Estepa Díez, "War and Taxation." 216–23. Lower has noticed the rising use of Christian mercenaries in the thirteenth century drawn from the warriors of Iberia, suggesting that this professionalization was already in progress: Lower, "The Papacy and Christian Mercenaries of Thirteenth-Century North Africa," 604–13, esp. 604 n. 8. The phenomenon of the "routiers" as mercenary forces predates the period under study here, and the prevalence of their use in the Plantagenet world. Boussard, "Les mercenaires au XIIe siècle." It may have inspired similar trends given the geographical proximity and the important political connections between the Plantagenets and Castile in the period. Gerrard has noted a number of occasions where clerics hired and directed mercenaries. Gerrard, "The Military Activities of Bishops." The prohibitions against hiring mercenary forces at Third Lateran (canon 27) and Fourth Lateran (18), and especially against clerics commanding those same forces, demonstrates that the issue had come to the attention of Rome, suggesting that it was either notorious or widespread: Tanner, *Decrees*, 1:224–5; 1:244.

58 Linehan's treatment is still the standard: Linehan, *Spanish Church and the Papacy*, 110–51.

59 Domínguez Sánchez, *Gregorio IX*, no. 539.

letter, Fernando was reminded that the goods confiscated were officially the property of Tello Téllez de Meneses, the bishop, and were owed to him, lest Fernando and his men be subject to excommunication for their transgression. The second letter is dated to August 10, 1236 and concerns the treatment of several reformed heretics from that diocese, after they had repented and sought reacceptance into Christian society.[60] Gregory describes the process by which King Fernando III had confiscated the properties of the accused heretics, the means by which their guilt had been determined, and the mercy which ought to be offered to them. Unfortunately, the letter does not mention the charges assessed or the ways in which the accusations were brought. The epistle does however note the importance of the concerned parties' rights to due process and the validity of the royal edict – at least with regard to the penalty, should the charges hold up. By the terms of a 1213 inventory of the diocesan fisc of Palencia, the annual income of Bishop Tello and his church came to more than 100,000 maravedís, which might suggest that the properties that Fernando's *merino* and *mayordomo* had confiscated were of substantial value to merit a formal protest.[61] Unfortunately, the only details regarding the heretics mention neither which heresy they were accused of or who they were, both facts which Fernando's men would have known. Further, there were no reference to which goods or properties were seized, only that the seized properties were in the hamlet of Cea in southern Galicia.

Canon law instructed kings that vacancies in clerical appointments of more than six months were forbidden and that bishops elect were allowed to take possession of their episcopal resources.[62] As a result, the extended absence of Master Bernardo of Segovia – who, according to papal correspondence was prevented from taking hold of his diocese from 1226 to 1228 – suggests that the revenues of the diocese were much sought after by Fernando III.[63] It is possible that part of this development was influenced by the governorship of Rodrigo Jiménez de Rada during the mental infirmity of bishop Gerardo, whose madness had provoked an uproar at a synod in Guadalajara in 1216.[64] Archbishop Rodrigo served as a governor in Gerardo's stead for several years, and

---

60   Domínguez Sánchez, *Gregorio IX*, no. 580.
61   Abajo Martín, *Documentación de Palencia*, 256–63.
62   Tanner, *Decrees of the Ecumenical Councils*, 246.
63   Villar García, *Documentación de Segovia*, 182–3. Diego de Colmenares narrates Bernardo's struggles in a manner that accords with the extant cathedral documents: Colmenares, *Historia de Segovia*, XXI: 1–4. Linehan describes Fernando's actions in this period as "pillaging" the dioceses of Calahorra and Segovia: Linehan, *Spanish Church and the Papacy*, 11, 139–40.
64   García y García, *Historia del Concilio*, 112–32.

would have been able to use the episcopal resources of Segovia for his own devices.[65] Given his record of supporting campaigns against the Almohads and partisanship on behalf of the Castilian monarchy, it seems likely that at least some of those funds found their way into the anti-Almohad offensive.[66] In fact, Gregory IX commissioned a panel of judges-delegate to discover whether Gerardo's infirmity had allowed some to nefariously profit, and, if some parties had, to restore to Segovia the properties and privileges wrongfully alienated.[67] In the aftermath of his death, Gerardo's successor, Bernardo, was left unconfirmed from nearly a decade.[68] In some instances (and especially if the clerics in question were not the most bellicose), then, it may well be that episcopal vacancies had some use for the purposes of the assault on al-Andalus. Too many vacancies had created political problems for Fernando's Plantagenet great-grandfather and his great-uncles, but a few could provide much-needed resources.[69] If even one-tenth of the revenues of Segovia, reported in the inventories drawn up in the 1250s by Cardinal Gil Torres as being more than 11,000 maravedís annually, were funneled to Fernando's war efforts, that total would have exceeded 1100 maravedís, enough to pay the costly Las Navas stipends of some 412 knights or 1650 sergeants.[70] The revenues, then, of a diocese could lend considerable support to the forces mustered by the Crown, but doing so would have required undertaking something of a political risk. Of course, the exploitation of episcopal vacancies was hardly an innovation by the Castilian king, but nevertheless, they provided a simple means of boosting royal income, and at a time when Fernando was waging war to the south, the income for a vacant diocese such as that of Segovia would have been extremely useful.

Even if there are questions about whether or not a bishop was more useful on the battlefield or in (or indeed vacant from) his chapter, the increasing participation of the aristocracy and the curia of the infante Alfonso in campaigns

---

65   The governorship was thoughtfully addressed by García y García: García y García, *Historia del Concilio*, 112–32.
     For the records of Rodrigo's governorship: Villar García, *Documentación de Segovia*, 164–8.
66   On Rodrigo as clerical crusading supporter *par excellance*: Gómez, "Alfonso VIII"; Ayala Martínez, *Ibn Tumart*, 1–42.
67   Villar García, *Documentación de Segovia*, 188–9.
68   Linehan, "Segovia: a 'Frontier' Diocese in the Thirteenth Century," 487–90.
69   Peltzer, "Henry II and the Norman Bishops"; Turner, "Richard Lionheart and English Episcopal Elections"; Packard, "King John and the Norman Church."
70   Villar García, *Documentación de Segovia*, 216–40. Rodrigo reports their wages as 20 *sueldos* per knight and 5 per footman: *DrH*, 263.

against al-Andalus made episcopal arms-bearing less necessary.[71] Certainly, other investigations may reveal a resurgence in clerical arms-bearing in the civil wars at the end of the thirteenth century and during the fourteenth century. However, the diminution of clerics fighting battles during the reign of Fernando III suggests that, when Fernando had a still comparatively weak grasp on his kingdom, prelates *in proelio* were needed early on, but not once the young monarch had gained a firmer footing. Clerics did participate in Fernando's wars, but their presence was muted somewhat by changing circumstances and there would be no great Las Navas scene, with a latter-day Rodrigo goading a new Alfonso VIII into a dangerous counter-charge. New realities dictated a different approach, but one that brought the Church, curiously enough, more closely into alignment with the reformers of a previous age than was perhaps intended. If only briefly, there was a *locus pontificali* in the armies of Fernando, and it was occupied by fewer and fewer clerics as the years wore on.

Works Cited

Primary Sources (Published)

Abajo Martín, Teresa, ed. *Documentación de la Catedral de Palencia*. Palencia: Garrido Garrido, 1986.

Colmenares, Diego. *Historia de la insigne ciudad de Segovia y compendio de las historias de Castilla*. Segovia: Academia de Historia y Arte de San Quirce, 1982.

Domínguez Sánchez, Santiago. *Documentos de Gregorio IX (1227–1241) referentes a España*. León: Universidad de León, 2004.

Garci-Gómez, Miguel ed. *Cantar de mío Cid*. Madrid: CUPSA Editorial, 1977.

González, Julio. *Repartimiento de Sevilla*. Madrid: CSIC, 1951.

González, Julio. *El reino de Castilla en la época de Alfonso VIII*. 3 vols. Madrid: CSIC, 1960.

Gratian. *Decretrum Gratiani. First Recension*. Ed. Winroth et al. https://sites.google.com/a/yale.edu/decretumgratiani/ (accessed March 28, 2019).

Hagan, John, trans. *The Song of Roland*. New York: C.K. Paul and Company, 1880.

Jiménez de Rada, Rodrigo. *Historia de rebus Hispanie, sive Historia Gothica*. Ed. Juan Fernández Valverde. Vol. 72 of *Corpus Christianorum: Continuatio mediaeualis*. Turnhout: Brepols, 1987.

Porres-Cleto, Julio Porres. *Anales Toledanos*. Toledo: Instituto Provincial de Investigaciones y Estudios Toledanos, 1993.

---

71 For a fuller treatment of the relationship between Alfonso X and his prelates, see Ayala Martínez, "La politica eclesiástica de Alfonso X," esp. 56–8, 95–105.

Powers, James. *The Code of Cuenca: Municipal Law on the Twelfth-Century Castilian Frontier*. Philadelphia: University of Pennsylvania Press, 2000.

Real Academia de España. *Fuero Juzgo*. Madrid: Ibarra, 1815.

Real Academia de la Historia. *Las Siete Partidas del Rey Don Alfonso el Sabio*. Madrid: Imprenta Real, 1807.

Smith, Damian and Helena Buffery, ed. *The Book of Deeds of James I of Aragon: a translation of the medieval Catalan Llibre dels Fets*. Aldershot: Ashgate, 2003.

Tanner, Norman. *Decrees of the Ecumenical Councils*. Washington, DC: Georgetown University Press, 1990.

Villar García, Luis-Miguel. *Documentación medieval de la Catedral de Segovia*. Salamanca: Ediciones Universidad de Salamanca, 1990.

Secondary Sources

Alvira, Martín. "El 'venerable' Arnaldo Amalrico (h. 1196–1225): idea y realidad de un cisterciense entre dos Cruzadas." *Hispania Sacra* 48 (1996): 569–591.

Alvira, Martín. *Las Navas de Tolosa 1212: idea, liturgia y memoria de la batalla*. Madrid: Sílex, 2013.

Alvira, Martín. "Antes de *De rebus Hispaniae*. La primera versión de la batalla de Las Navas de Tolosa de Rodrigo Jiménez de Rada." *e-Spania* 25 (2016). doi: https://doi.org/10.4000/e-spania.26168.

Ames, Christine Caldwell. *Medieval Heresies: Christianity, Judaism, and Islam*. New York: Cambridge University Press, 2015.

Ayala Martínez, Carlos de. *Las Ordenes Militares en la Edad Media*. Madrid: Arco Libros, 1998.

Ayala Martínez, Carlos de. "Fernando III y la Cruzada Hispánica." *Bulletin of Spanish and Portuguese Historical Studies* 42, no. 1 (2017): 23–45. doi: https://doi.org/10.26431/0739-182X.1247.

Ayala Martínez, Carlos de. *Ibn Tumart, el Arzobispo Jiménez de Rada, y la "Cuestion sobre Dios."* Madrid: Ediciones de La Ergástula, 2018.

Ayala Martínez, Carlos de. "Los obispos de Alfonso VIII." In *Carreiras eclesiásticas no Ocidente Cristão: séc. XII–XIV*, 151–186. Lisbon: Universidade Católica Portuguesa, Centro de Estudos de História Religiosa, 2007.

Ayala Martínez, Carlos de. "La política eclesiástica de Alfonso X: El rey y sus obispos." *Alcanate: Revista de Estudios Alfonsies* 9 (2014/15): 41–106.

Ayala Martínez, Carlos de. "Honorio III, la cruzada y la Península Ibérica." In *Hombres de religión y guerra. Cruzada y guerra santa en la Edad Media península (siglos x–xv)*, ed. Carlos de Ayala Martínez and J. Santiago Palacios Ontalva, 419–465. Madrid: Sílex, 2018.

Baury, Ghislain. "Diego López 'Le Bon,' Diego López 'Le Mauvais.' Comment s'est construite la mémoire d'un magnat du règne d'Alphonse VIII de Castille." *Berceo* 144 (2003): 37–92.

Bianchini, Janna. *The Queen's Hand: Power and Authority in the Reign of Berenguela of Castile*. Philadelphia: University of Pennsylvania Press, 2012.

Bird, Jessalynn, Edward Peters, and James M. Powell. *Crusade and Christendom: Annotated Documents in Translation from Innocent III to the Fall of Acre, 1187–1291*. Philadelphia: University of Pennsylvania Press, 2013.

Boussard, Jean. "Les mercenaires au XIIe siècle : Henri II Plantegenet et les origines de l'armée de métier." *Bibliothèque de l'École des chartes* 106, no. 2 (1946): 189–224.

Conedera, Sam Zeno, S.J. "A Wall and a Shield: Alfonso VIII and the Military Orders." In *King Alfonso VIII: Government, Family, and War*, ed. Miguel Gómez, Kyle C. Lincoln, and Damian J. Smith, 102–117. New York: Fordham University Press, 2019.

Duggan, Lawrence. *Armsbearing and the Clergy in the History and Canon Law of Western Christianity*. New York: Boydell, 2013.

Estepa Díez, Carlos. "La Monarquía castellana en los siglos XIII–XIV. Algunas consideraciones." *Edad Media. Revista de historia* 8 (2007): 79–98.

Estepa Díez, Carlos. "War and Taxation. The Soldadas from the Reign of Alfonso VIII of Castile to the 13th Century." *Imago Temporis: Medium Aevum* 25, no. 9 (2015): 211–223.

Flori, Jean. "L'Église et la Guerre Sainte: de la 'Paix de Dieu' a la 'croisade'." *Annales. Histoire, Science Sociales* 47, no. 2 (1992): 453–466.

Gaposchkin, Cecilia. "From Pilgrimage to Crusade: The Liturgy of Departure, 1095–1300." *Speculum* 88, no. 1 (2013): 44–91.

Gerrard, Daniel M.G. "The Military Activities of Bishops, Abbots and other Clergy in England c.900–1200." PhD thesis, University of Glasgow, 2011.

García Fitz, Francisco. *Castilla y León frente al Islam: Estrategias de expansión y tácticas militares (siglos XI–XIII)*. Sevilla: Universidad de Sevilla, 2005.

García Fitz, Francisco. "Las huestes de Fernando III." *Archivo hispalense* 77, no. 234–236 (1994): 157–189.

García y García, Antonio. *Historia del Concilio IV Lateranense de 1215*. Salamanca: Centro de estudios orientales y ecuménicos "Juan XXIII," 2005.

Gómez, Miguel Dolan. "Alfonso VIII and the Battle of Las Navas de Tolosa." In *King Alfonso VIII of Castile: Government, Family, and War*, ed. Damian J. Smith, Miguel D. Gómez, and Kyle C. Lincoln, 143–171. New York: Fordham University Press, 2019.

González Cuesta, Fernando. "Sobre el episcopologio de Plasencia." *Hispania Sacra* 47 (1995): 347–376.

Gutiérrez Robledo, José Luis. "Las murallas de Ávila." In *Historia de Ávila*, ed. Ángel Barrios García, 2 vols., 479–517. Ávila: Diputación de Ávila, Institución Gran Duque de Alba, 1998.

Hosler, John. *Henry II: A Medieval Soldier at War, 1147–1189*. Leiden: Brill, 2007.

Jotischky, Andrew. *Crusading and the Crusader States*. New York: Taylor & Francis, 2014.

Kienzle, Beverly Mayne. *Cistercians, Heresy, and Crusade in Languedoc, 1145–1229: Preaching in the Lord's Vineyard*. Rochester, NY: Boydell and Brewer, 2001.

Ladero Quesada, Miguel Ángel. *La formación medieval de España: territorios, regiones, reinos*. Madrid: Alianza Editorial, 2014.

Lincoln, Kyle C. "Beating Swords into Croziers: warrior bishops in the kingdom of Castile, c.1158–1214." *Journal of Medieval History* 44 (2018): 83–103.

Lincoln, Kyle C. "*Mihi pro fidelitate militabat*: cruzada, Guerra santa y Guerra justa contra cristanos durante el reino de Alfonso VIII de Castilla según las fuentes episcopales." In *Hombres de religión y guerra. Cruzada y guerra santa en la Edad Media península (siglos x-xv)*, ed. Carlos de Ayala Martínez and J. Santiago Palacios Ontalva, 29–49. Madrid: Sílex, 2018.

Linehan, Peter. *History and Historian of Medieval Spain*. Oxford: Oxford University Press, 1993.

Linehan, Peter. "Segovia: a 'Frontier' Diocese in the Thirteenth Century." *The English Historical Review* 96, no. 380 (1981): 481–508.

Lomax, Derek. *The Reconquest of Spain*. London: Longman, 1978.

Lower, Michael. "The Papacy and Christian Mercenaries of Thirteenth-Century North Africa." *Speculum* 89, no. 3 (2014): 601–631.

Martínez Díez, Gonzalo. *Alfonso VIII, rey de Castilla y Toledo*. Burgos: Editorial la Olmeda, 1995.

Marvin, Lawrence. *The Occitan War: a Military and Political History of the Albigensian Crusade*. New York: Cambridge University Press, 2008.

Moore, R.I. *The War on Heresy*. Cambridge, MA: Harvard University Press, 2012.

Nakashian, Craig. *Warrior Churchmen of Medieval England, 1000–1250*. New York: Boydell, 2016.

Niermeyer, Jean. *Mediae Latinitatis Lexicon Minus*. Leiden: Brill, 1976.

O'Callaghan, Joseph. *Reconquest and Crusade in Medieval Spain*. Philadelphia: University of Pennsylvania, 2003.

Packard, Sidney R. "King John and the Norman Church." *The Harvard Theological Review* 15, no. 1 (1922): 15–40.

Palacios Martín, Bonifacio. "Alfonso VIII y su Politica de frontera en Extremadura: La creación de la diócesis de Plasencia." *En la España Medieval* 15 (1982): 77–96.

Pegg, Mark. *A Most Holy War: the Albigensian Crusade and the Battle for Christendom*. New York: Oxford University Press, 2008.

Peltzer, Jörg. "Henry II and the Norman Bishops." *The English Historical Review* 119, no. 484 (2004): 1202–1229.

Pick, Lucy K. *Conflict and Coexistence: Archbishop Rodrigo and the Muslims and Jews of Medieval Spain*. Ann Arbor: University of Michigan Press, 2004.

Powers, James. *A Society Organized for War: The Iberian Municipal Militias in the Central Middle Ages*. Berkeley: University of California Press, 1988.

Riley-Smith, Jonathan. *The Oxford History of the Crusades*. Oxford: Oxford University Press, 2002.

Rivera Recio, Juan. *La Iglesia de Toledo en el siglo XII*. 2 vols. Rome: Iglesia Nacional Española, 1966–1976.

Serrano, Lora. "Las Elecciones episcopales de la diócesis de Plasencia durante la edad media." *Historia Instituciones Documentos* 36 (2009): 259–260.

Smith, Damian. "Las Navas and the restoration of Spain." *Journal of Medieval Iberian Studies* 4, no. 1 (2012): 39–43.

Torija Rodríguez, Enrique. "De la conquista de Toledo al Adelantamiento de Cazorla. La batalla de las Navas de Tolosa como punto de inflexión en la política de cruzada de los arzobispos de Toledo." In *Las Navas de Tolosa 1212–2012: miradas cruzadas*, ed. Patrice Cressier and Vicente Salvatierra Cuenca, 69–76. Jaén: Universidad de Jaén, 2014.

Turner, Ralph. "Richard Lionheart and English Episcopal Elections." *Albion: A Quarterly Journal Concerned with British Studies* 29, no. 1 (1997): 1–13.

CHAPTER 5

Dilecta consanguinea mea: Fernando III's Donation to a Nun of Fontevraud

Martín Alvira

This is the story of a strange and surprisingly interesting document.[1] It is the *vidimus* made in 1250 by the Breton Bishop Stephen of Dol of a donation of one hundred maravedís a year from the toll of Burgos, originally issued by King Fernando III in Toledo on March 31, 1220 to a relative, Alix of Blois, a nun of the abbey of Fontevraud (Figure 5.1).

1   An Unknown Document

This parchment has remained unpublished and, as far as we know, totally unknown for several reasons. The original and other copies are not preserved among the documents of the monastery of Fontevraud deposited in the Archives départementales de Maine-et-Loire (Angers).[2] It is not mentioned in the mutilated and recently edited *Grand Cartulaire ou Pancarte de l'abbaye de Fontevraud* (1115–1206).[3] Nor is it cited in the *Inventaire des titres du Thrésor de*

---

1 I am very grateful to Stefano M. Cingolani, Eduard Juncosa, Anna Gudayol, Arnaud Baudin, Martin Aurell, Michael Jones, and Lindy Grant for reading the initial draft of this work and their helpful comments. I also want to thank the kind help received from Christophe Gazon, Santiago Domínguez, Frédéric Morvan, Charles Garcia, and Nicholas Vincent. To Damian J. Smith, Michael Jones, Edward Holt and Teresa Witcombe I owe the correction of this text in good English. Naturally, any error or omission is my responsibility. This work is part of the research project *Confrontatio. Violencia religiosa en la Edad Media peninsular: guerra, discurso apologético y relato historiográfico (ss. X–XV)*, funded by the Agencia Estatal de Investigación, Ministerio de Economía y Competitividad–Gobierno de España (reference: HAR2016-74968–P).
2 AdM-L, Fonds de Fontevraud, https://www.archives49.fr/histoire-de-lanjou/pages-choisies/le-tresor-de-labbaye-de-fontevraud/ (accessed June 6, 2017). There is a repertoire of the documents in 101 H 1 to 437 by Jacques Levron in 1954, and a more precise inventory of the records relating to the priories (102 H 1 to 246 H 3) drawn up in the 1960s by Robert Favreau, director of the Archives. I would like to thank Christophe Gazon for helping me to consult these documents.
3 BnF (Paris), ms. nouvelles acquisitions latines 2414 (136 f.); AdM-L, 101 H 225 (9 f.); *Grand cartulaire* (2000, 2005).

FIGURE 5.1   *Vidimus* (1250, January 5) of the donation of Fernando III to the nun Alix of Blois (1220, March 31. Toledo). Biblioteca de Catalunya (Barcelona), Parchments, no. 343, reg. 15196 (*recto*)
PHOTO REPRINTED WITH KIND PERMISSION OF THE BIBLIOTECA DE CATALUNYA, BARCELONA

Fontevraud by Dom Jean Lardier, archivist and historian of the Order in the mid-seventeenth century.[4] Lardier also wrote several genealogical biographies of the abbesses from which our document is likewise omitted.[5] Neither is it referred to in the source traditionally relied upon by historians of Fontevraud, a seventeenth-century cartulary preserved in the Bibliothèque nationale de France. This cartulary includes a section dedicated to Spain with facsimile copies of several Castilian documents whose originals are preserved in Angers. Among them is the well-known donation to the monastery of a hundred maravedís promised by the rulers of Castile, Alfonso VIII and Leonor Plantagenet, at the time of their wedding, granted in June 1190.[6] Also, an exemption from the payment of taxes (*pechos*) conceded by King Enrique I of Castile in September

---

[4] He did not use the Spanish sources, only noting that there was a sack containing documents from Fontevraud in Spain. Lardier, *Inventaire*, VI: 612; Touchard, *Domaines espagnols*, 8.

[5] "Traité des personnes illustres de l'Ordre de Fontevraud, tant abbesses et religieuses que fondatrices et bien-factrices," in Lardier, *Saincte Famille*, 223–708.

[6] *Chartularium*, I: 297–314, at 299, 304–5 (Burgos, 30.06.1190); French translation 18th c., AdM-L, 240 H 1, no. 1; reg. Touchard, *Domaines espagnols*, 135–6, ap. 4, no. 1–2; *Alfonso VIII*, 551 and I: 191–2, 509–10; *Fernando III*, I: 491, 495, fn. 173.

1215 in Tejar, Moslares and Albunes.[7] There are also copies of two documents of Fernando III: a facsimile of the confirmation of this exemption, granted in October 1217;[8] and the copy of a letter dated to the year 1230, and addressed to the Jews of Burgos, assigning them payment of the rent granted to Fontevraud by Alfonso VIII in 1190.[9] The oldest of the Fontevraud census books, dated to c. 1225–50, mentions an income of one hundred maravedís from Burgos to be paid at Easter.[10] The notice does not offer any more information, so it does not seem to be the donation to Alix of Blois, but rather the donation of Alfonso VIII confirmed by Fernando III in 1230. Nor have we found any trace of our document in Castilian documentary repertoires, nor in any bibliography concerning the reign of Fernando III or Fontevraud Abbey. An explanation for the absence of scholarship on this donation is the fact that the charter is preserved in Barcelona, in the Biblioteca de Catalunya (BC), a place where a historian of Fernando III might not think of going in search of new sources.[11] The document is part of the collection of scrolls and manuscripts donated by the famous Catalan sculptor Frederic Marès in the 1980s. Since 2012, it has been digitized on the website of the Biblioteca de Catalunya.[12] My colleague and good friend Stefano M. Cingolani coincidentally found it here when he was looking for medieval documents to transcribe with his son Camillo for palaeography practice, and I would like to thank him sincerely for giving it to me.

The characteristics of the *vidimus* of 1250 and the original of 1220 do not raise any doubts about the authenticity of the parchment or the texts.[13] The list of those confirming and the witnesses both coincide with slight variations in other documents granted by Fernando III before and after March 31, 1220.[14] The copy made by the scribe of the bishop of Dol is very good, containing only two small errors. In the first column, after the name of Bishop Tello Téllez de

---

7   Ibid., 308–9 (Valladolid, 22.09.1215); French transl. 18th c., AdM-L, 240 H 1, no. 4 (1); Touchard, *Domaines espagnols*, 113–5, ap. 2, no. 2; *Alfonso VIII*, III: no. 1033; *Trésor des chartes*, no. 18.
8   Ibid., 312–3 (Valladolid, 13.10.1217); French translation 18th c., AdM-L, 240 H 1, no. 4 (2); *Fernando III*, III: no. 447; reg. Touchard, *Domaines espagnols*, 116, ap. 2, no. 3.
9   Ibid., 298 (Toledo, 1.05.1230); French transl. 18th c., AdM-L, 240 H 1, no. 2; reg. Touchard, *Domaines espagnols*, 137, ap. 4, no. 3; *Fernando III*, III: no. 475.
10 *In Hyspania apud Burgos centum marbotinos ad Pascha*: AdM-L, 101 H 95, no. 1: *Censif de l'abbaye de Fontevraud*; Bienvenu, "Recettes," 42; *Trésor des chartes*, 41, no. 25.
11 The importance of the diplomatic sources preserved in the archives of Barcelona for the history of Castile has been noted by Cingolani, "El Archivo de la Corona de Aragón" (2016).
12 BC, Parchments, no. 343, reg. 15196, Memòria Digital de Catalunya, http://mdc.cbuc.cat/cdm/ref/collection/pergamiBC/id/35502 (Toledo, 6.01.1250); Mundó, *Catàleg*, 33, P 13 (Dol, 6.01.1250 [1251]).
13 See Figure 5.1 and Edition.
14 *Fernando III*, II: nos. 110–2, 849, 113, 136.

Meneses, he wrote *Placentinus* (from Plasencia) instead of *Palentinus* (from Palencia). In the second column, he converted the very Iberian name of *Suerius* (Suero) into the more familiar form of *Severius*. The dating clause of the original Castilian version includes an important element: the well-known reminder of the chivalric investiture ceremony of Fernando III at the abbey of Las Huelgas (November 27, 1219) and of his marriage three days later (November 30) to Beatriz of Swabia:

> Truly it was at that same time that I, the aforesaid king, F[ernando], in the royal monastery of St Mary at Burgos, girded myself by my own hand with the belt of knighthood, and three days later, I solemnly married lady B[eatriz], daughter of Philip, formerly king of the Romans.[15]

The donation to Alix of Blois should be added to the other twenty-seven documents granted between December 1219 and September 1220 that include this chancellery formula.[16] We will see later how the marriage of Fernando III may lie behind the origin of the donation, but first, let us turn to the identification of the beneficiary.

2 A Nun and Abbess of Fontevraud

The name of the nun Alix of Blois (also called Adèle of Champagne) is found in the Fontevraud documents with numerous orthographic variants.[17] According to the necrology of the abbey, she was the daughter of Count Thibaut of Blois and descendant of the kings of France and England.[18] She was one of the granddaughters of Louis VII and Eleanor of Aquitaine. They had two daughters together: Mary (1145–98) and Alix (Alice, Aélis or Aélith) of France (1151–c. 1198), both of whom were married to the counts of Blois-Champagne.[19] Alix,

---

15   *eo uidelicet tempore quo ego, prefatus rex F*[errandus]*, in monasterio Sancte Marie Regalis de Burgis manu propria cingulo milicie me accinxi et tercia die post dominam B*[eatricem]*, Philippi quondam Regis Romanorum filiam, duxi sollempniter in uxorem*. See Edition.

16   Studied, among others, by Sirantoine, "La cancillería regia," 182–3; Holt, "*In eo tempore*," 11–6 (accessed February 3, 2018).

17   *A., Alix, Aliz, Aelizia, Adelicia, Adelitia, Adilidis, Adilis, Aalidi, Aalidis, Alaydis, Aylidis, Aylis, Haeliz...*

18   *nobilissimi Theobaldi Comitis Blesensium filia, ex utroque latere Francorum Anglorumque Regum, et spectabilium genere procreata*: "Extrait du Grand Nécrologe," 4–5; "Epitaphia et elogia abbatissarum," 5–6, at 5; "Migravit de Fontevraud," 122–3.

19   Evergates, "Louis VII," 113–4.

the younger daughter and considered the least known of the five daughters of Eleanor of Aquitaine,[20] married Count Thibaut V of Blois and Chartres (c. 1127–91).[21] From this marriage seven children were born, with the youngest of them being named, once again, Alix, the woman who would go on to become abbess of Fontevraud and to be known as Alix of Blois.[22] Her kinship with Fernando III comes, on the Plantagenet side, from Eleanor of Aquitaine, grandmother of Alix and great-grandmother of Fernando, and, on the Capetian side, from Blanche of Castile, wife of King Louis VIII and mother of Louis IX, cousin and nephew respectively of Alix of Blois, and aunt of Fernando III.

The obituary of Alix of Blois tells us that she entered the monastery in her youth and as a virgin, persevering until becoming abbess.[23] The notice includes many compliments about both her government[24] and her character.[25] Alix of Blois is also remembered in the necrology entries of her relatives: her father, Thibaut V of Blois,[26] her nephew, Thibaut VI,[27] her sister, Marguerite,[28] her

---

20   Labande, "Les filles," 104–5, at 104. Also Dupré, "Les comtesses," 224–6; Labande, "Pour une image," 191; Brown, "Eleanor of Aquitaine," 8–9, 11–2, 16; Shadis and Berman, "A taste," 182, 192, 201, n. 22; Flori, *Aliénor d'Aquitaine*, 80–2; Turner, *Eleanor of Aquitaine*, 97–8, 107, 273; Bowie, *The Daughters*, 129; Rodríguez, *La estirpe*, 36.
21   Gouget and Le Hête, *Les comtes de Blois*, 102–4.
22   Her brothers were Thibaut (c. 1165–d. 1182), Henri (mentioned 1182–d. young), Louis I (c. 1171–1205), Count of Blois and Chartres (1191–1205), father of Thibaut VI (1205–18); Marguerite (c. 1170–1230), Countess of Blois and Chartres since the death of her nephew Thibaut VI (1218–30); Isabelle or Élisabeth (c. 1175/1180–c. 1248), Countess of Chartres; and Philippe (mentioned 1189–1202, d. young), Ibid., 103, 105–6; Shadis and Berman, "A taste," 194–5; Baudin, *Emblématique*, 545 (Tableau généalogique no. 3).
23   *virgo Deo sacrata ... que dum in primo juventutis sue flore nostre Religionis assumens habitum*: "Extrait du Grand Nécrologe," 4–5; "Epitaphia et elogia abbatissarum," 5; "Migravit de Fontevraud," 122–3, at 122.
24   *Magna sunt et inenarrabilia sunt eius beneficia que nobis et multis Ecclesie nostre cenobiis studuit misericorditer impertiri*: "Epitaphia et elogia abbatissarum," 5–6; "Migravit de Fontevraud," 122–3.
25   *creuit ergo ... etate et sapientia ... de matre facta est filia obediens et humiliter et deuote*: "Epitaphia et elogia abbatissarum," 5–6; "Migravit de Fontevraud," 122–3.
26   *Theobaldus junior, comes Ble[sen]sis, pater precordialissime domine et matris nostre Adilidis, abbatisse nostre, specialis amice*: "Nécrologe de Fontevraud (cotté B, 1ᵉ finestre)," 89.
27   *Theobaldus junior, comes Blesensis et Claremontis, nepos domine Adelidis, karissime domine nostre*: Ibid., 94.
28   *Domina Margareta, excellentissima comitissa Burgundie atque Blesensis regali genere orta soror Domina Adelidis, dulcissime matris nostre ac precordialis amice*: "Migravit de Fontevraud," 118. Also "Migravit ou Nécrologe de Fontevraud (1 fenestre, cotté D)," 161; "Obituaire du Prieuré de Fontaines," 191 C (*comitissa Blesensis, soror domine Adelidis, abbatissa Fontis Evraldi*). Her epitaph in Pavillon, *Robert d'Arbrissel*, 592, no. 101.

sister, Isabelle,[29] and her many nephews and nieces, namely Hughes of Amboise (who died very young), Marguerite, daughter of the Count of Burgundy, Count Jean of Blois, the nun Petronilla, Countess Mathilde of Chartres and Soissons, who was *domina* of Amboise and also benefactress of the monastery, and Adelaide of Burgundy.[30] She was thus an abbess of exceptional pedigree.

3 Alix of Blois and Adelaide of Brittany: A History of Confusion

The list of abbesses of Fontevraud established in the seventeenth century placed the government of Alix of Blois between 1209 and 1218. There is another prioress and abbess of the same name, Adelaide, Adèle or Alix of Brittany, also related to Queen Eleanor of Aquitaine, whose rule has been placed later, between 1228 and 1242–44 (Table 5.1).[31] The possible confusion between both abbesses was signalled by Dom Lardier, but unfortunately his work remained unpublished in the archive of Fontevraud.[32]

In the middle of the nineteenth century, the French historian Léopold Delisle argued, mainly from his reading of the *Chartularium* of Fontevraud, that the list of abbesses published by the authors of the *Gallia Christiana* was not correct, since Adelaide of Brittany was abbess before Alix of Blois. The key fact, unnoticed by the authors of the *Gallia Christiana*, was a document already handled by Dom Lardier in which our nun is mentioned as abbess in 1229.[33]

---

29 *Domina Helisabeth, venerabilis Carnotensis comitissa regum sanguine procreata, illustris Theobaldi comitis Blesis filia, soror Domine Adilidis quondam abbatisse Fontis Ebraldi domine et amice nostre*: Ibid., 127; "Epitaphia et elogia benefactorum," 57.

30 *Hugo, puer domine Anbarie* [Anbacie], *nepos domine Adilidis, karissime domine nostre*: "Nécrologe de Fontevraud (cotté B, 1ᵉ finestre)," 91; *Margarite ... comitis Burgundie filia, neptis Domine Adelidis de Blesis, karissime matris nostre et domine*: Ibid., 95; *Johannes, comes Blesensium, nepos domini Adilidis de Blesis, karissime matris et abbatisse nostre*: Ibid.; *Petronilla, sacrata Deo ... neptis domine Adelidis de Blesis, karissime domine et amice nostre*: Ibid., 96; *Domina Matildis, venerabilis comitissa Carnotensis, Suessionensis et domina Ambazie ... neptis Domine Adilidis de Blesis, karissime matris nostre et Domine, que dum in mundo uiueret nos corde sincero diligebat et ad nos visitandi gratia sepius ueniebat et ad exemplum precordialissime matertere sue inter nos quasi socia erat, et de bona et amabili societate sua nos omnes consolabatur*: "Epitaphia et elogia benefactorum," 57; "Migravit de Fontevraud," 114; *Domina Adilidis quondam Burgundie venerabilis Comitissa ... Domine Adilidis Blesensis neptis Karissima*: Ibid., 132–3.

31 Nicquet, *Histoire*, 434–5 (9th abbess), 438–42 (12th abbess); *Gallia Christiana*, 2: 1.321–2, 1.329 (8th and 10th abbess).

32 Lardier, *Saincte Famille*, 420–1, 444–5. Lardier himself confused both once, considering Alix of Blois the ninth abbess, idem, *Table générale*, 296v (*Alix IX abbesse de Font-Evraud*).

33 *Anno Domini M CC XXIX, cum domina A. de Blesis, abbatissa Fontis Ebraldi*: *Chartularium*, 1: 69; Delisle, "Mémoire," 518–22. Also Lardier, *Saincte Famille*, 444.

The archivist of Anjou, Paul Marchegay, in a study published in 1858, confirmed that Léopold Delisle was right to correct the traditional list of abbesses.[34] Other authors belonging to the Fontevrist order, such as Henri Touchard, were aware of this correction.[35]

Surprisingly, however, Delisle's correction was not taken into full consideration. In fact, the study published in 1873–74 by Abbot Édouard, taken up in 1913 by the canonical *Histoire de l'Ordre de Fontevrault*, compounded the confusion between Adelaide of Brittany and Alix of Blois in the official historiography of the Fontevrist order.[36] The error therefore recurs in the work of later authors.[37] It was repeated in 1980 and 1986 by the leading modern specialist in the history of Fontevraud;[38] in 1992, by the catalogue of a major exhibition held in Paris;[39] in 1993, by a specialist on the papal documentation of Fontevraud;[40] and in 2003, by a historian of the counts of Champagne.[41] The error can also be

TABLE 5.1   List of Abbesses of Fontevraud

9. *Alix of Blois (1209–18)*	9. Adelaide or Alix of Brittany (1207–16)
10. Bertha (1218–28) – donation of Fernando III (1220)	10. Bertha (1217–27) – donation of Fernando III (1220)
11. Adelaide or Alix of Brittany (1228–44)	11. *Alix of Blois (1228–43)*
12. Mabille de la Ferté (1244–65) – *vidimus* of the donation of Fernando III (1250)	12. Mabille de la Ferté (1244–65) – *vidimus* of the donation of Fernando III (1250)

---

34   Marchegay, "Chartes," 337.
35   Touchard, *Domaines espagnols*, 111, 117.
36   Édouard, *Fontevrault*, 1: 238, 247–50 (9th: Alix of Champagne, 1209–18), 255–8 (11th: Adèle of Brittany, 1228–44); *Histoire de l'Ordre*, 2: 82, 85, 93–9 (9th: Alix or Adèle of Champagne or of Blois, 1209–18), 104–10 (11th: Adèle of Brittany, 1228–44). See also Malifaud, *L'Abbaye de Fontevraud*, 28; Parrot, *Mémorial*, 4, 129–30.
37   Boase, "*Fontevrault*," 6.
38   Bienvenu, *Les premiers temps*, 2: 606, 608, 609 ("Alix de Blois, 1210–1218"); Bienvenu, "Aliénor d'Aquitaine," 25 ("la future abbesse Alix, 1210–1218, fille d'Alix de Blois"). Unlike previously: idem, "Recettes," 10 (11th abbess: Adèle of Champagne, 1228–44).
39   *Trésor des chartes*, 35 (9th: Alix of Blois or of Champagne, 1209–18; 11th: Alix or Adèle of Brittany, 1228–44).
40   Salette, "Fontevraud et la papauté," 72.
41   *Littere Baronum*, doc. 103.

seen on the panel which greets visitors at the entrance of the abbey.[42] Today, the Archives nationales de France (Paris) and the Archives départementales de l'Aube (Troyes) conserve an abbatial seal of Alix of Blois, dated to 1235, but catalogued as belonging to Abbess Adelaide of Brittany (Figure 5.3).[43]

Hence, the unknown donation of Fernando III to Alix of Blois obliges us, in a totally unexpected way, to remember forgotten studies and gather scattered data, and to establish (or better re-establish) the following in relation to the history of the abbesses of Fontevraud.

4   Adelaide of Brittany (Abbess of Fontevraud 1207–1216)

Let us first address the identity of Adelaide or Alix of Brittany. Although cited briefly by historians of Brittany and the Plantagenets, no one writing after Dom Lardier (as far as we know) has drawn on all of the available sources in order to better understand her history.[44] The obituaries of Fontevraud affirm that *Adelidis de Britannia* was the daughter of the Count of Brittany, Eudes II (d. c. 1180), Viscount of Porhoët.[45] Indeed, Adelaide came from the Breton high aristocracy, since her mother was Bertha of Cornouaille, Duchess of Brittany (d. 1158–63), daughter of Duke Conan III (d. 1148) and mother of Conan IV (d. 1171).[46] Viscount Eudes II of Porhoët was one of the greatest opponents of King Henry II of England in his struggle to impose Plantagenet hegemony in Brittany.[47] Despite being the guardian of the young Conan IV, Eudes tried to usurp Conan's

---

42 *Abbesses de Fontevraud* (9. Alix of Champagne, 1209–18; 11. Adèle or Alix of Brittany, 1228–44). I would like to thank Julien Bertreux (Abbaye de Fontevraud, Médiation-patrimoine) for his help regarding this panel. The same mistake is visible on a website dedicated to the history of Fontevraud, *Dictionnaire* (accessed February 26, 2018).

43 AdA, 42 Fi 200 (the document in 27 H: priory of Foissy or 4 H abbey of Larrivour); AN (Paris), sc/Ch 2813–2813bis and sc/D 9205–9205bis. See Douët d'Arcq, *Collection*, 3: 152, no. 9205 ("Fontevrault : Adèle de Bretagne, abbesse de"); Coulon, *Inventaire*, 7 ("Fontevraud : Adèle de Bretagne, abbesse de," c. 1235); Baudin, *Collection*, 152–3 ("Adèle de Bretagne, abbesse de Fontevraud, 1228–1244 [1235]"). I am grateful to Arnaud Baudin for his kind help in relation to this seal.

44 In a brief and very genealogical biography, Lardier, *Saincte Famille*, 419–29 (9th abbess).

45 *Hec comitis Britanniae filia*: "Epitaphia et elogia abbatissarum," 6; "Migravit de Fontevraud," 124; "Nécrologe de Fontevraud (cotté B, 1e finestre)," 105; "Extrait du Grand Nécrologe," 5–6, at 5; "Martyrologe ou Migravit de Fontevraud," xxxiii (9. *abbatissa*); Morice, *Mémoires*, 1: 845.

46 Lardier, *Saincte Famille*, 419; Morvan, "Les règlements," Annexe 17 : Généalogie des Porhoët; idem, *Les Chevaliers bretons*, 282.

47 La Borderie, *Histoire de Bretagne*, 3: 269–79; Warren, *Henry II*, 74–6, 563–4; Chédeville and Tonnerre, *La Bretagne féodale*, 72, 83–95; Everard, *Brittany and the Angevins*, 34–75; Morin, *Trégor, Goëlo, Penthièvre*, 138–49; Morvan, *Les Chevaliers bretons*, 48–51, 64–5.

accession to power in Brittany, leading the latter to ally with the Angevin monarch. It was then that Eudes adopted the title of "Count of Brittany." By 1164–67, Eudes had been defeated by Henry II and was required to deliver one of his daughters as a hostage to the English king. Everything indicates that this daughter was Adelaide or Alix of Porhoët, the future prioress and abbess of Fontevraud.[48] We know this from a letter by John of Salisbury reporting a meeting at La Ferté-Bernard in July 1168 between the kings of England and France, at which *Eudo Britonum comes* was present. There, he bitterly reproached Henry II for having committed adultery and incest, leaving his daughter pregnant, who had been a virgin and had been given as a guarantee of peace, since the Angevin monarch and Bertha of Brittany, wife of Eudes, were relatives.[49]

Historians have noted this accusation, although considering it impossible to separate the facts from the malicious rumours concerning this and other love affairs attributed to Henry II.[50] The important thing for our purposes is that the delivery as a hostage of Adelaide of Porhoët coincides with the entries in the necrology of Fontevraud, which state that Abbess Adelaide of Brittany was "from the time of her early youth brought up honourably in the court of the King and Queen of England."[51]

The same source reports that Adelaide joined Fontevraud when she was thirty years old, perhaps in 1188–91,[52] becoming prioress of the abbey probably from 1191.[53] Let us note that the Queen Eleanor of Aquitaine's retirement to Fontevraud from 1194 coincides with the time when Adelaide of Brittany was prioress.[54] One of the most frequently cited documents in modern discussions is a donation by Eleanor, made around the year 1199, of an annual rent of ten Poitevin pounds on the island of Oléron "to our dear *alumpna* Alix, prioress of

---

48 Everard, *Brittany and the Angevins*, 45–6; Vincent, "The Court of Henry II," 331, no 5.

49 *sed Eudo specialiter deplorauit quod filiam eius uirginem, quam illi pacis obsidem dederat, impraegnauit ut proditor, ut adulter, ut incestus; rex enim et uxor Eudonis de duabus sororibus nati sunt*: *Letters of John of Salisbury*, II: no. 279. Also Charles, *Histoire*, 36.

50 Warren, *Henry II*, 119, 611–2; Flori, *Richard Coeur de Lion*, 52, 88–9, 149–50; idem, *Aliénor d'Aquitaine*, 171–3.

51 *a primoevo juventutis sue tempore in aula regis Anglorum et regine venerabiliter educata*, "Epitaphia et elogia abbatissarum," 6; "Migravit de Fontevraud," 124; "Extrait du Grand Nécrologe," 5–6; Lardier, *Saincte Famille*, 420; Morice, *Mémoires*, 845.

52 Her mother Bertha died c. 1158–63.

53 *Chartularium*, I: 153 (1191: *Adilidis, priorissa*), 173 (1192: *Adilis, priorissa*), 121 (1194: *Adilis, Fontis Ebraldi priorissa*), 108–9 (1201: *A. prioriza*). Also Ibid., 106–7 (undated: *Aalit, priorissa*), 181 (undated: *priorissa Aaladis*); AdM-L, 132 H 1, no. 4 and 158 H 1, no. 6 (12th Century).

54 Martindale, "Eleanor of Aquitaine: The Last Years," 139; Brown, "Eleanor of Aquitaine," 89; Favreau, "Aliénor d'Aquitaine," 43; Hivergneaux, "Aliénor et l'Aquitaine," 68.

FIGURE 5.2   Seal of Adelaide of Brittany, Abbess of Fontevraud (1210): SIGILLUM ADILIDIS, [ABBATISSE BEA]TE MARIE FONTIS [EBRALDI]. AD Maine-et-Loire (Angers) 240 H 1, no. 3
© ARCHIVES DÉPARTEMENTALES DE MAINE-ET-LOIRE (PHOTO: MARTÍN ALVIRA)

Fontevraud."[55] This status of *alumpna* (pupil) fits perfectly with a childhood spent at the court of Henry II and Eleanor as confirmed by the obituary of Fontevraud. This donation of 1199 could be related to the journey that the queen made to Rouen to care for her daughter Joan, then pregnant by Count Raymond VI of Toulouse. In the copy of Joan's will, the prioress of Fontevraud is mentioned, and it appears that Joan was subsequently received into the order and her body moved to the abbey to be buried.[56]

---

55 *dilecte alumpne nostre Alize, priorisse Fontis Ebraldi*, AdM-L, 193 H 1, no. 4 (Poitiers, [1199]); fot. Favreau, "Aliénor d'Aquitaine," 45; Lardier, *Saincte Famille*, 420; *Chartularium*, 1: 467; Marchegay, "Chartes," 338; Round, *Calendar*, 394, no. 1.108; Bienvenu, "Aliénor d'Aquitaine," 25; Martindale, "Eleanor of Aquitaine," 18. Confusion here between Alix of Blois and Alix of Brittany in Boase, "Fontevrault," 6; Turner, *Eleanor of Aquitaine*, 288.

56 AdM-L, 101 H 55, no. 10 (1199); English transl. Round, *Calendar*, no. 1.105 (contains errors: "prior" instead of "prioress"); "Migravit de Fontevraud," 120–1; Pavillon, *Robert d'Arbrissel*, 588, no. 96; Édouard, *Fontevrault*, 2: 114.

Adelaide of Brittany was abbess between 1207 and 1216.⁵⁷ She administered her position "wisely and kindly" in both spiritual and material matters, according to her obituary.⁵⁸ During her rule she secured Innocent III's reinforcement of abbatial authority, prohibiting appeals against the decisions of the abbess and authorizing her to correct excesses in clothing or other goods of the brothers and sisters. The Pope also extended his protection to Fontevraud and confirmed property received from the Duke of Burgundy.⁵⁹ Abbess Adelaide died after falling ill at the end of October, probably in 1220.⁶⁰ She was succeeded by Abbess Bertha of Lorraine, formerly the prioress.⁶¹

5   Alix of Blois (Abbess of Fontevraud 1228–1244)

Alix's only known biography is the unpublished and strictly genealogical work of Dom Lardier.⁶² The obituary of Fontevraud states that Alix of Blois became abbess when she was forty years old (c. 1227–28), so she must have been born around 1187–88.⁶³ The first known reference to her is in 1189, when she was in the company of her brother Louis, then count of Blois, and of their older sisters Marguerite and Isabelle. She is mentioned again in 1191, 1193, 1194, and 1196.⁶⁴ She appears as a nun of Fontevraud in a letter from her brother Louis, written in March 1197, so she must have been about ten years old when she entered the monastery, as the necrology states.⁶⁵ In Fontevraud she lived with her aunt

---

57   *Chartularium*, I: 62 (1207), 205, 334 (1208), 78, 83, 97 (1209), 180, 199, 299, 340 (1210), 42, 109 (1211), 156, 389 (1212), 98 (1214), 345 (1216); Delisle, "Mémoire," 519.
58   *sagaciter et benigne*, "Epitaphia et elogia abbatissarum," 6; "Migravit de Fontevraud," 124; "Extrait du Grand Nécrologe," 6; Morice, *Mémoires*, 845.
59   AdM-L, 101 H 1, no. 19 (Lateran, 7.02.1208), 21 (Lateran, 1.02.1212); Salette, "Fontevraud et la papauté," 85, 72. Another letter of 1208 in Pavillon, *Robert d'Arbrissel*, 621–2, no. 232.
60   Morice, *Mémoires*, 845; "Migravit de Fontevraud," 124; "Nécrologe de Fontevraud (cotté B, 1ᵉ finestre)," 105; "Extrait du Grand Nécrologe," 5; "Migravit ou Obituaire de Saint-Lazare (cotté C)," 157; "Migravit ou Nécrologe de Fontevraud (1 fenestre, cotté D)," 163; "Anniversaires de Fontevraud," 142; "Obituaire du Prieuré de Fontaines," 193 C (1216); "Obituaire du Prieuré de Collinances," 203 A (1216).
61   Lardier, *Saincte Famille*, 429–42 (10th abbess); "Migravit de Fontevraud," 115.
62   Lardier, *Saincte Famille*, 443–62 (11th abbess). Also "Martyrologe ou Migravit de Fontevraud," xxxii (*XI abbatissa*).
63   *Que quidem circiter annos 40 habens, abbacie nostre et nostri regiminis onus assumens*: "Migravit de Fontevraud," 122; "Extrait du Grand Nécrologe," 5.
64   *Cartulaire de Sainte-Euverte d'Orléans*, 552–3 (1189); *Cartulaire de Bourgmoyen*, f. 18v, 22r, 24v (1189); Bernier, *Histoire de Blois*, "Preuves," xix (1189); *Chartularium*, I: 198 (1191, 1193); Delisle, "Mémoire," 521 (1194); Bernier, *Histoire de Blois*, "Preuves," xxvi-xxvii (1196).
65   *karissima mater mea Adelicia, Blesensis comitissa dedit Adelicie, filie sue, sorori mee, Fontis Ebraudi moniali*: AdM-L, 101 H 55, no. 6 (03.1197); *Chartularium*, I: 360; Delisle, "Mémoire," 521; "Migravit de Fontevraud," 122; "Extrait du Grand Nécrologe," 4.

Marguerite of Blois, sister of Count Thibaut V and a nun, possibly counting on the frequent presence of her grandmother Queen Eleanor of Aquitaine.[66] Alix could, perhaps, be the same as the Alix who received an annuity of six marks in the will of Countess Joan Plantagenet.[67] It has been said that Eleanor's granddaughter was in Rouen when her aunt Joan died, but that is probably a confusion with the prioress of Fontevraud.[68] It is certain that, in around 1199, she received from her grandmother an annual income of ten pounds from the island of Oléron, a rent that on her death was to pass to the abbey. In this well-known document, the queen addresses her as "our dear granddaughter Alix, daughter of Alix our beloved daughter of blessed memory, once countess of Blois."[69] This memory of Alix of France, mother of Alix of Blois, is interesting, since it is often stated that Eleanor of Aquitaine probably did not have contact with her daughters after her separation from Louis VII, since the daughters were legally in the hands of their father.[70] As Léopold Delisle already observed, the nun Alix disappears from the family documents of the counts of Blois in 1200 and 1201, although not so in 1202, since she was mentioned in May of that year in a donation from her brother Louis.[71] The other notices found date from her years as abbess.[72]

The extant documents, to which those traditionally attributed by mistake to Adelaide of Brittany must be added, confirm the importance of her

---

66   *Chartularium*, I: 439–40; "Migravit de Fontevraud," 116 (Adèle of Blois, Queen of France); Delisle, "Mémoire," 521; Turner, *Eleanor of Aquitaine*, 277; Baudin, *Emblématique*, 543 (Tableau généalogique no. 1–2).

67   *domine Agathe et domine Aelicie, sancti monialibus Fontis Ebraudi*, AdM-L, 101 H 55, no. 10 (1199); English transl. Round, *Calendar*, no. 1.105. Also Jasperse, "Matilda, Leonor and Joanna," 542, n. 85 (accessed February 21, 2018); Salette, "Fontevraud et la papauté," 72 (AdM-L, 101 H 1, no. 34–5: Perugia, 26.05.1252).

68   Turner, *Eleanor of Aquitaine*, 278. The "Obituaire du Prieuré de Fontaines" reports the death of a *domina Ala, reverendissima monacha, olim ducissa, karissima et benefactrix ecclesie Fontis Ebraldi* (191 C) not identified.

69   *dilecte nepti nostre Aelizie, filie felicis memorie Aelizie, quondam comitisse Blessensis, karissime filie nostre*, AdM-L, 193 H 1, no. 5; phot. Hivergneaux, "Aliénor et l'Aquitaine," 67; *Chartularium*, I: 466; Marchegay, "Chartes," 340–1; Bienvenu, "Aliénor d'Aquitaine," 25; Martindale, "Eleanor of Aquitaine," 18; Favreau, "Aliénor d'Aquitaine," 43.

70   Turner, "Eleanor of Aquitaine and her Children," 323; DeAragon, "Wife, Widow, and Mother," 102; Flori, *Aliénor d'Aquitaine*, 81, 350; Turner, *Eleanor of Aquitaine*, 107; Bowie, *The Daughters*, 7, n. 13; Rodríguez, *La estirpe*, 226.

71   *Adelicie, karissime sorori mee, moniale Fontis Ebraudi*, *Chartularium*, II: 437–8, at 437.

72   Ibid., I: 130 (07.1228), 369–70 (1228); Delisle, "Mémoire," 521–2.

FIGURE 5.3 Great seal of Alix of Blois, Abbess of Fontevraud (1235): [SIGILLUM] ADILIDIS, ABBATISSE BE[ATE] MARIE FONTIS E[BRALDI]. AD Aube (Troyes), 42 Fi 200; AN (Paris), sc/Ch 2813 -2813bis and sc/D 9205 -9205bis
© DÉPARTEMENT DE L'AUBE, NOËL MAZIÈRES. PHOTO REPRINTED BY KIND PERMISSION OF THE ARCHIVES DÉPARTEMENTALES DE L'AUBE, TROYES

government.[73] Her concern for the internal life of the abbey can be observed in the measures adopted in relation to food and clothing, as well as in the promulgation of statutes confirmed by Pope Innocent IV in 1252 at the request of Abbess Mabille de la Ferté, who was the prioress when Alix was abbess.[74] She was also an energetic defender of the rights of the abbey, as shown by the orders of

---

73 *Chartularium*, I: 69–70 (1229: in the margin: *A. de Blois, abbesse*); AdM-L, 138 H 3, no. 18 (03.1229), 201 H 1, no. 6 (1229–30); *Chartularium*, I: 370 (05.1236); Pavillon, *Robert d'Arbrissel*, 622, no. 233 (05.1237); *Chartularium*, I: 162 (11.1238), 319 (1238); AdM-L, 193 H 1, no. 17 (1238); *Cartulaire de l'abbaye de Lagny*, f. 116v-117r (02.1240); *Cartulaire de Champagne*, f. 390; *Chartularium*, I: 439 (01.1242), 411 (1243). Also Delisle, "Mémoire," 519.
74 *Chartularium*, I: 439 (01.1242); Delisle, "Mémoire," 522; AdM-L, 101 H 1, no. 36 (Perugia, 11.06.1252); *Chartularium*, II: 227; Salette, "Fontevraud et la papauté," 86.

Henry III of England to pay the rents granted by Queen Eleanor of Aquitaine, including those which Alix herself had received.[75] Her relationship with Rome is recorded in several letters from Gregory IX and Innocent IV, including a 1240 confirmation of the donations of the Duke of Burgundy.[76] The praise that can be read in her very extensive obituary confirms the benefits she had sought for the Order[77] and the memory that she left as "our most pious and most sweet mother and lord."[78]

Alix of Blois left the position of abbess in around 1243 for unknown reasons.[79] She died a few years later on October 11;[80] Dom Lardier dated her death to c. 1247.[81] The editors of the obituary of the priory of Collinances delayed it to after 1249.[82] Following indirect references, Léopold Delisle claimed that she was still living in 1250 and perhaps in 1252, dying as late as 1266.[83] However, a letter from Countess Mathilde of Chartres alludes to the death of her maternal aunt in June 1249:

> I granted perpetual alms to the church of Blessed Mary of Fontevraud ... [to the sum of] 20 pounds ... after the death of my most beloved maternal aunt, lady Alix of Blois, at Chartres, from the 60 pounds which I gave to her during her life.[84]

In August 1250, her successor Abbess Mabille de la Ferté collected the rents received by Alix of Blois from her relatives (her grandmother Eleanor of Aquitaine, her brother Louis of Blois, her niece Mathilde of Chartres, her second

---

75   AdM-L, 193 H 1, no. 13–6 (1234), 22 (1235), 18 (1246), 19 (1252). Also Delisle, "Mémoire," 522.
76   *Chartularium*, II: 185 (1234), 187–8 (1239), 189, 191 (1241); AdM-L, 101 H 1, no. 26–7 (Lateran, 29.04.1240), 193, 195 (1243), 197, 199 (1244), 201, 203–6 (1245), also perhaps 173–4 (s.d.); Delisle, "Mémoire," 522; Salette, "Fontevraud et la papauté," 72.
77   *magna sunt et inenarrabilia sunt eius beneficia que nobis et multis Ecclesie nostre cenobiis studuit misericorditer impertiri*: "Migravit de Fontevraud," 122–3.
78   *piissima et dulcissima mater nostra et domina*: "Migravit de Fontevraud," 122–3.
79   Delisle, "Mémoire," 522. Also see Tunc, "De l'élection," 208.
80   "Epitaphia et elogia abbatissarum," 7; "Migravit de Fontevraud," 123; "Nécrologe de Fontevraud (cotté B, 1ᵉ finestre)," 104; "Migravit ou Obituaire de Saint-Lazare (cotté C)," 156; "Migravit ou Nécrologe de Fontevraud (I fenestre, cotté D)," 163; "Anniversaires de Fontevraud," 143 (*Adelaïdis de Blois*); "Martirologe de *Fontanis*," in Pavillon, *Robert d'Arbrissel*, 581, no. 86.
81   "Epitaphia et elogia abbatissarum," 5.
82   "Obituaire du Prieuré de Collinances," 202 E ("post ann. 1249").
83   *Chartularium*, 1: 179, 279–80 and 2: 227; Delisle, "Mémoire," 522. Gouget and Le Hête, *Les comtes de Blois*, 104, are of the same opinion.
84   *ego dedi in perpetuam elemosinam Ecclesie Beate Marie Fontis Ebraldi ... 20 libras ... post decessum karissime matertere mee domine Aalidis Blesensis, apud Carnotum, de 60 libris quas eidem dedi ad vitam suam*: *Chartularium*, 1: 198–9.

nephew Louis IX, and her cousin Richard of Cornwall), an income that passed on her death to Fontevraud.[85]

On the back of this parchment, which Léopold Delisle did not consult, it is expressly indicated in the same hand that the abbess had already died.[86] The date of this collection of rents (1250) coincides with that of the *vidimus* of the donation of Fernando III. According to Dom Lardier's *Inventaire*, in 1250 Abbess Mabille was also interested in a donation to Alix of Blois from Eleanor of Provence, Queen of England.[87]

Thus, by June 1249, Alix of Blois was dead, and her successor at Fontevraud, Abbess Mabille de la Ferté had set out in an attempt to recover the income of her predecessor. It was to this end that, in January 1250, she requested from Bishop Stephen of Dol a copy of the donation by Fernando III of the one hundred maravedís from the toll of Burgos, granted to Fernando's Castilian relative, Alix, in 1220.

6   Why Bishop Stephen of Dol?

The relationship between the abbey of Fontevraud and the Breton aristocracy and Church is well-known.[88] The founder of the order of Fontevraud, Robert d'Arbrissel, was originally from Brittany, and his first *Vita* was composed around 1118 by Bishop Baldric of Dol (1117–30).[89] This bishopric possessed churches and estates in Brittany, Normandy, and Flanders. The bishops had been engaged in a long struggle with the archbishopric of Tours for the right to be a metropolitan diocese, a conflict related to the French kings' desire to extend their influence over the Breton Church. Finally, Popes Eugenius III (1146)

---

85 *Nos autem huic ipsius immo divine pre provisioni benigniter annuentes, volumus et concedimus quod predicti redditus in usus pulmenti conventus ut domus est convertantur perpetuo per manum ipsius Aalidis quamdiu vixerit. Post mortem vero ipsius per manum monialis alicuius quam domina abbatissa futura pro tempore et conventus ad hos duxerint eligendam*: AdM-L, 242 H 1, no. 28; *Chartularium*, 1: 279–80 (partial transc.); Delisle, "Mémoire," 522 (only on the partial transcription of the cartulary).

86 *Carta super emptionibus bone memorie deffuncte Aalidis quondam abbatisse Fontis Ebraldi*: AdM-L, 242 H 1, no. 28 (*verso*).

87 Lardier, *Inventaire*, 6: 605. In 1259, the Abbess requested a report on the status of the priory of Vega, AdM-L, 239 H 1, no. 3, ed. Touchard, *Domaines espagnols*, 93–101, ap. 1, no. 7. See *infra*.

88 There is some news of the Duke John I (1237–86), AdM-L, 158 H 1; *Chartularium*, 1: 114–5; Lemeillat, *Actes de Jean I*^{er}, no. 62 (06.1253), 133 (05.1270).

89 See *Robert d'Arbrissel*, ed. and trans. Bruce L. Venarde.

and Innocent III (1199) decreed Dol's dependence on Tours, as the metropolitan see of all Brittany.[90] The author of our *vidimus* is Bishop Stephen I (1244–65), a figure about whom very little is known.[91] One of his actions was the promulgation in 1265 of a detailed set of statutes concerning the behaviour of the canons of Dol and how they were to perform the divine office.[92] Unfortunately, we have not been able to discover why Bishop Stephen was asked to produce a *vidimus* of the donation of Fernando III. It might be explained by his relationship with Fontevraud, with Abbess Mabille de la Ferté,[93] or with Alix of Blois herself.[94] Nor we should rule out a possible relationship between Stephen of Dol and Blanche of Castile, because another *vidimus* is conserved in Angers, also from 1250, of a letter from Queen Blanche relating to the will of Count Raymond VII of Toulouse, who died in 1249 and who was buried at Fontevraud.[95]

7 The Destination of the *vidimus*

In order to claim the payment of the hundred maravedís from the toll of Burgos donated to Alix of Blois, Bishop Stephen of Dol sent the *vidimus* to the Castilian-Leonese court. We know that most of the concessions of Fernando III to ecclesiastical institutions were exemptions from the payment of tolls and *montazgo*, although donations of rents due from tolls were not frequent during his reign.[96] We have found no trace of the *vidimus* in the royal archives, nor amongst the documents conserved by the Council of Burgos.[97] We still have to

---

90 Morice, *Mémoires*, 598–600; Amiot, *Dol de Bretagne*, 25–32.
91 *Stephanus Dei gratia Dolensis episcopus, in territorio Britannico*. Brief reviews of his life in Duine, *La métropole de Bretagne*, 166–7, no. 42; Amiot, *Dol de Bretagne*, 83.
92 Lobineau, *Histoire de Bretagne*, 2: 1.614; Morice, *Mémoires*, 994–5. Other documents in AdC-A, H 69 A 7; Geslin de Bourgogne and Barthélemy, *Anciens évêchés de Bretagne*, IV: 116, no. clv (1244); Morice, *Mémoires*, 931 (1247), 946–7 (1250), 993–4 (1264). I wish to thank Frédéric Morvan for his kind help in relation to this topic.
93 She was possibly related to Hugues de la Ferté, the trouvère in the entourage of Pierre Mauclerc, Duke of Brittany. On the lords of La Ferté-Bernard, see Charles, *Histoire*, 44–58, at 53. On Abbess Mabille, see Lardier, *Saincte Famille*, 463–79 (12th abbess); "Migravit de Fontevraud," 123.
94 Several *vidimus* of charters the Counts of Blois made by the bishops of Rennes Jean I Gicquel (1253) and Maurice de Trézéguidy (1273) are preserved, AdM-L, 122 H 1, no. 3, 12 (1253), 6 (1273).
95 AdM-L, 101 H 55, no. 24 (4 and also 2–3).
96 *Fernando III*, I: 480–90; Rodríguez, "La política eclesiástica," 13.
97 González, *Colección diplomática*; Estepa, et al., *Burgos en la Edad Media*; Bonachía, "Historiografía sobre Burgos."

inspect the documents relating to the six priories of the Order of Fontevraud in Spain, studied by Henri Touchard in an unpublished work.[98] These priories include Santa María de la Vega del Cea in Valladolid (henceforth referred to as the Monasterio de Vega), and Santa María de la Vega de Oviedo, in Asturias, both in the kingdom of León,[99] and the monastery of Peramán (Zaragoza) in Aragón.[100] Those of the kingdom of Castile – namely, Tejar, Moslares (de la Vega), and Albunes, all three in Saldaña (Palencia) – have their origin in a donation by King Alfonso VIII in 1208 to the abbess Adelaide of Brittany,[101] confirmed and enlarged in 1215 by King Enrique I in a document already cited.[102] In December 1210, Abbess Adelaide delivered *domos nostras de Hypania, videlicet de Teillart, de Molaires et Album* with their belongings to chaplain Peter,[103] surely the same *Petrus de Hyspania*, chaplain and sacristan of the houses of Tejar, Moslares and Albunes, who wrote to Abbess Alix of Blois in 1232 and who was remembered for his efforts in the necrology of Fontevraud.[104]

On the reverse side of our *vidimus* there is an old annotation: *Fuente Uraldo, Cajón 2° San Christobal, Leg. 1°, Letra A, Núm. 5°* (Figure 5.4). The first and most important priory of Fontevraud in Spain, the Monasterio de Vega, was originally a sanctuary dedicated to Saint Christopher and Saint Andrew.[105] Some documents from its archive bear the same annotation *Cajón San Christobal*.[106] Others have a direct relationship with France, including a *translatum* made by

---

98   Édouard, *Fontevrault*, II: 349–50; Bienvenu, "Recettes," 5, 16, 18, 42, 70, 74; Bienvenu, *Les premiers temps*, II: 326–33; *Trésor des chartes*, 24; and especially Touchard, *Domaines espagnols* (1942).
99   In 1181, unsuccessful efforts were made to establish another in Zamora. See Garcia, "Un prieuré fontevriste" (forthcoming). I would like to thank the author for allowing me to consult his unpublished work.
100 See Barlés, "Monasterios femeninos olvidados," 135–8.
101 Serrano, *Cartulario de Monasterio de Vega*, 29: no. 38 (*Libro de los Vicarios* of Monasterio de Vega, f. 56); *Alfonso VIII*, I: 509, no. 873.
102 *Chartularium*, I: 308–9 (Valladolid, 22.09.1215); French transl. 18th c., AdM-L, 240 H 1, no. 4 (1); Touchard, *Domaines espagnols*, ap. 2, no. 2, 113–5; *Alfonso VIII*, III: no. 1033; *Trésor des chartes*, no. 18.
103 AdM-L, 240 H 1, no. 3; *Chartularium*, I: 299–300; Touchard, *Domaines espagnols*, 111–2, ap. 2, no. 1.
104 AdM-L, 240 H 1, no. 5; *Chartularium*, I: 300 (in the margin: *Adèle de Bretagne*); Touchard, *Domaines espagnols*, 117–8, ap. 2, no. 4; "Nécrologe de Fontevraud (cotté B, 1ᵉ finestre)," 103.
105 Serrano, *Cartulario*, viii-ix; Domínguez, "El monasterio de Vega," 17–9, 26–46; idem, "Oficios y artesanos," 37–8.
106 Domínguez, *Colección documental*, no. 11 (17.04.1070); BC, Parchements, no. 343, reg. 15191 (Palencia, 4.01.1139), no. 343, reg. 15215 (Lateran, 9.12.1302). I would like to thank Santiago Domínguez for kindly confirming this point.

FIGURE 5.4 *Vidimus* (1250, January 5) of the donation of Fernando III to the nun Alix of Blois (1220, March 31. Toledo). Biblioteca de Catalunya (Barcelona), Parchments, no. 343, reg. 15196 (*verso*)
PHOTO REPRINTED WITH KIND PERMISSION OF THE BIBLIOTECA DE CATALUNYA, BARCELONA

a clerical notary from the diocese of Dol,[107] and, even more important, a *vidimus* ordered by the archbishop of Tours at the request of the Abbess Mabille de la Ferté.[108]

The archive of the Monasterio de Vega suffered in the Napoleonic Wars, as well as from Mendizábal's program of *desamortización*, and, finally, the extinction of the community in 1958, leaving its documents scattered in several archives. Some went to Catalonia, to the abbey of Montserrat.[109] An interesting

---

107 Ibid., no. 124 (Anagni, 29.06.1260, *translatum* 4.08.1336 by Jean Pagani, clerk of the diocese of Dol and apostolic notary in Tours, at the request of Eleanor of Brittany, abbess of Fontevraud, and authorized by the officer of the Court of Tours).

108 Ibid., no. 84 (Lateran, 20.06.1260, *vidimus* s.d.). The archbishop of Tours was not Geoffroy de la Lande (1207–1208), but Geoffroy Marcel (1245–1250), contemporary of the Abbess Mabille de la Ferté. Other documents related to France are: no. 35 (13.12.1129), 80 (Burgos, 30.06.1190). In Angers, three documents of the priory of Vega dating to this abbess are conserved, AdM-L, 239 H 1, no. 3 (1259), 4 (1255), 5 (1256).

109 Domínguez, *Colección*, 91–103; idem, "El monasterio de Vega," 20–2, 46–50; idem, "Oficios y artesanos," 37, 39–40.

set of eight documents from the monastery (five still unpublished, two registered, and only one edited) ended up in the private collection of the sculptor Frederic Marès i Deulovol and are today preserved in the Biblioteca de Catalunya.[110] We do not know how he got them. Some of his charters and manuscripts were inherited from his father, the bookseller and collector Pere Marès Oriol (d. 1915), whom the sculptor remembered as an "man sensitive to the good book, document, signature, engraving, coin, etc." and well connected with important historians of the time, such as Marcelino Menéndez y Pelayo and Ramón Menéndez Pidal, who came to him in search of sources to document their own work.[111] Our charter is endorsed with the *ex libris* of the "*Biblioteca Pere Marés Oriol*" (Figure 5.4), so it would have been acquired before 1915 by the father of the sculptor. However, three of the eight medieval documents from the Monasterio de Vega in the "Marès Collection" come from the same *Cajón San Christobal*,[112] and only two (the one of Alix of Blois and one of King Fernando I of León) carry the *ex libris* of his father.[113] There are, then, two possibilities: Pere Marès obtained this document before 1915, or his son, Frederic Marès, obtained it after 1958, a time when he acquired many artworks and books from religious orders.[114] In the case of the latter, the acquisition could have been "aged" by adding the *ex libris* of his father, a practice that is verified in the case of one of the manuscripts of his collection donated to the Biblioteca de Catalunya.[115] However, *a priori*, the first hypothesis seems the most probable.

---

110 BC, Parchements, no. 309, reg. 15190 (Monasterio de Vega, 13.06.[1055–1060]) [unpublished], no. 343, reg. 15191 (Palencia, 4.01.1139) [unpublished]; no. 343, reg. 15196 (6.01.1250) [unpublished], no. 343, reg. 15215 (Lateran, 9.12.1302) [unpublished], no. 343, reg. 15230 (1176) [ed. Domínguez, *Colección*, no. 76], no. 343, reg. 15245 (04.1231) [reg. Domínguez, *Colección*, no. 108], Calaixera C-10 (GF), reg. 15282 (10.07.1317) [unpublished]. See Mundó, *Catàleg*, xvi, 32 (P 7), 32–3 (P 8), 33 (P 13), 37 (P 32), 39 (P 47), 41 (P 62), 46 (P 99). There is another document not picked up by Mundó in his catalog: no. 343, reg. 15222 (Monasterio de Vega, 11.02.1091) [reg. incomplete Domínguez, *Colección*, no. 21 (15.02.1091)].
111 *hombre sensible al buen libro, documento, autógrafo, grabado, moneda, etc*: Marès, *El mundo fascinante*, 23, 25. Also Vayreda, "Frederic Marès," 5–6, 8; Mundó, *Catàleg*, xix–xxi.
112 BC, Perg. no. 343, reg. 15191 (Palencia, 4.01.1139), no. 343, reg. 15196 (6.01.1250), no. 343, reg. 15215 (Lateran, 9.12.1302).
113 BC, Parchements, no. 309, reg. 15190 (Monasterio de Vega, 13.06.[1055–1060]), no. 343, reg. 15196 (6.01.1250). Several manuscripts of the BC bear the *ex libris* of Pere Marès: mss. 3173 (s. XV), 3218 (s. XVI), 3222, 3224 (s. XVII), 3226 (ss. XVII–XVIII), 3227, 3228, 3217 (s. XVIII), 3231 (ss. XVIII–XIX).
114 Vayreda, "Frederic Marès," 12.
115 Santanach, "Perduts, amagats i retrobats," 110–4; idem, "Manuscrits lul·lians," 95–101. I thank Anna Gudayol (BC, Secció de Manuscrits) for her kind help in relation to the "Marès Collection."

Thus, after the death of Alix of Blois, sometime before June 1249, the Abbess Mabille de la Ferté asked Bishop Stephen of Dol to copy the donation made by Fernando III to her predecessor, and to send it to the Monasterio de Vega to claim the payment and, eventually, take charge of its collection. However, since it was a donation for life (that is, the life of the recipient), and bore no indication that, upon the death of Alix, it should pass to Fontevraud, as was the case in donations by Eleanor of Aquitaine and other relatives recorded in the document preserved in August 1250, this claim was null and void. It was surely for this same reason that a copy of the donation was not kept in the archive of Fontevraud, and nor was it included among the *recettes* of the abbey, nor later copied into the cartulary.[116]

8 The Donation of Fernando III and the Journey of Beatriz of Swabia: A Hypothesis

At this point we must ask a key question: why did Fernando III donate a hundred maravedís to Alix of Blois in March 1220? Unfortunately, lack of data prevents us from giving a convincing answer, but in its place, we may at least advance a reasonable hypothesis.

The date of the donation suggests that its origin has to do with the marriage of King Fernando III and, more specifically, with the journey to Castile of Beatriz of Swabia. In January 1220, the king rewarded the prior of San Zoilo de Carrión for traveling to Germany in search of his future wife. And in June 1221, Bishop Maurice of Burgos, head of the Spanish embassy, was rewarded for the same reason.[117] The donation to Alix of Blois dates between these two grants.

Much has been written about the idea and intention of the marriage of Fernando III to Beatriz, and, following the testimony of the Castilian chroniclers closest to the king, it is presumed to have been arranged at the initiative of his mother, Queen Berenguela.[118] At the same time, we know that the Spanish

---

116 The *Censif de l'abbaye de Fontevraud* provides information on some forty benefactors of the abbey, including the Kings of France and England, but not those of Castile, Bienvenu, "Recettes," 21. On other donors of the Order see Béchet, *Le « réseau » de bienfaiteurs* (2006).
117 *Fernando III*, II: nos. 100, 136.
118 CLRC, 58–9; *DrH*, 290–1. See Serrano, *Don Mauricio, obispo de Burgos*, 42–4; Martínez, *Fernando III*, 55–6; Diago, "La monarquía castellana," 63–7, at 64–6; Shadis, "Berenguela of Castile," 337–8, 340; Rodríguez, "El reino de Castilla," 614–5; González, *Fernando III el Santo*, 62–5, 76; Shadis, "Berenguela of Castile," 104–10; Colmenero, "La boda," 9–92; Bianchini, *The Queen's Hand*, 145–8; Martínez, *Berenguela la Grande*, 561–73; Estepa, "El reino de Castilla," 252–62.

embassy stopped in Paris when it was traveling back with Beatriz of Swabia. There, the future bride was received by Philip Augustus, king of France, uncle of Alix of Blois, and father-in-law of Blanche of Castile, who was sister of Berenguela and aunt of Fernando III.[119] Julio González raised the possible influence of Blanche in negotiating the marriage with Beatriz of Swabia, with the intention of strengthening the alliance between Philip Augustus and Frederick II.[120] According to Miriam Shadis, this would have involved an exchange of letters between Queen Berenguela and Blanche, as well as the active involvement of the latter in the French court, something which would have been difficult during the lifetime of Philip Augustus, for which reason Shadis does not believe that González's hypothesis is "the simplest explanation, nor the most probable."[121] However, contacts between Berenguela and Blanche are well attested, and recently H. Salvador Martínez has once again pointed out the probable influence of the future queen of France in the marriage negotiations of Fernando III.[122] So, even if she were not in a position to take this initiative of her own accord, it seems probable that Blanche could have played some role in Fernando's marriage to Beatriz because of her Iberian connections.

To all of this we must add the existence in the abbey of Fontevraud of an "obituarial memory" of the Castilian royal family that goes beyond the well-known records of Alfonso VIII and Leonor Plantagenet.[123] This institutional memory also commemorates Queen Berenguela, who died during the lifetime of Alix of Blois. It does so by highlighting her familial relationship with Blanche of Castile:

> Lady Berenguela, noble queen of Castile and Toledo, most honorable descendent of Richard King of England, and sister of the lady Blanche, most excellent queen of France, and our own most dear beloved, departed

---

119 *Et cum Parisius aduenissent, rex Francorum Philipus nomine, qui tunc Galiis presidebat, eam honeste recepit per terram suam honorifice dans ducatum, et ad regnum Castelle felici itinere peruenerunt*: DrH, 290–1.

120 *Fernando III*, I: 96–9, at 97. As she also intervened later in the marriage of Fernando with Jeanne de Ponthieu. Ibid., 114.

121 Shadis, "Berenguela of Castile," 337–8; idem, *Berenguela of Castile*, 104–10.

122 Martínez, *Berenguela la Grande*, 561–5. Also Hernández, "La corte de Fernando III," 106–8; Bianchini, *The Queen's Hand*, 186; Grant, *Blanche of Castile*, 164–6.

123 *VI. idus Octob. Aldefonsus venerabilis rex Castelle et benefactor Ecclesie nostre*: "Nécrologe de Fontevraud (cotté B, 1ᵉ finestre)," 104; *III. nonas Nov. Domina Alienores, regina Castelle et Tholeti, filia domini regis Henrici Anglie, optima benefactrix Ecclesie nostre*: Ibid., 105; "Epitaphia et elogia benefactorum," 49; "Migravit ou Obituaire de Saint-Lazare (cotté C)," 156, 157; "Martirologe de *Fontanis*," in Pavillon, *Robert d'Arbrissel*, 580–1.

from this world, on behalf of whose soul let us pray to the Lord Jesus Christ.[124]

We are also aware of Blanche of Castile's relations with Fontevraud Abbey, where she lived for a short time in 1200 during her journey from Castile to Normandy in the company of Queen Eleanor of Aquitaine. This personal experience, the powerful influence of her grandmother and the awareness of her Angevin past explain the donations of Blanche to Fontevraud (a thousand pounds in her will),[125] the great praise heaped upon her in the necrologies of the Fontevrist Order, and the memory that she left in the abbey as "supporter and benefactor above all to our mother church of Fontevraud."[126] As Lindy Grant has observed, Blanche of Castile's support for Fontevraud may also be explained by the fact that the abbess, Alix of Blois, was her relative.[127] In fact, the two women had very similar family ties with both the Plantagenet and the Capetian dynasties. The most extensive obituary of Blanche of Castile explicitly links her protection of the Order with her kinship with Alix of Blois, using the same words as the donation of Fernando III:

> The lady Blanche of sweet and excellent memory has departed from the world, most excellent queen of France, mother of the illustrious king Louis of France and daughter of the lord Alfonso, King of Spain, and Eleanor his wife, she [i.e., Blanche] who, amongst other rulers and governors of the world, in nobility and goodness and discretion, shone like Lucifer amongst the stars, planting abbeys and churches, supporting the poor, consoling the oppressed, embracing all religious persons in the heart of her charity; yet especially protecting us, among the other daughters of

---

124 *Migravit de hoc mundo domina Berengeria, nobilis Regina Castilie et Toleti, neptis illustrissima Richardi Regis Anglie et soror domine Candide, excellentissime Regine Francie et karissime dilecte nostre, pro cuius anima exoremus dominum Jhesum Christum*: "Epitaphia et elogia benefactorum," 53; "Migravit de Fontevraud," 126; "Nécrologe de Fontevraud (cotté B, 1ᵉ finestre)," 105; *2° nonas nov. Domina Berengeria, Regina Castelle et Tholeti, soror D. Blanche, Francorum Regine*: "Migravit de Fontaines," 167; "Obituaire du Prieuré de Fontaines," 193 D; *Migravit a seculo pie memorie domina Berengeria, regina Castille et Toleti, soror domine Blanche, Francorum regine*: "Migravit ou Obituaire de Saint-Lazare (cotté C)," 157.

125 *extremo vite sue termino mille libras nobis legavit*: "Epitaphia et elogia benefactorum," 49–50, at 49; "Migravit de Fontevraud," 125; Delisle, "Mémoire," 522; Grant, *Blanche of Castile*, 207.

126 *maxime matris nostre ecclesie Fontis Ebraldi adjutrix et benefactrix*: "Obituaire du Prieuré de Fontaines," 193 F.

127 Grant, *Blanche of Castile*, 207.

mother Church, in memory of her relative, our venerable mother lady A[lix] of Blois.[128]

The same notice reports that Blanche donated five hundred pounds to the abbey.[129] Through a document of Alix of Blois we know that Blanche made this donation alongside her son, Louis IX, before January 1242.[130] Léopold Delisle believed that the abbess and the queen had met in 1241 at an audience held in Poitiers in Louis IX's chamber and in the presence of Countess Isabelle of Chartres, sister of Alix.[131] However, the letter from a royal officer at La Rochelle reporting this audience was sent to Queen Blanche, indicating that the queen present on that occasion was not her, but Margaret of Provence, wife of Louis IX.[132] Fontevrist tradition suggests that Abbess Alix of Blois used Blanche's important donations in the construction of a wonderful chapel named the *Grande-Claverie*, founded in 1228.[133] In fact, however, the five hundred pounds received before 1242 served to sustain a lawsuit with the bishop of Poitiers, as indicated in the collection of rents ordered by Abbess Mabille de la Ferté in August 1250.[134]

Returning to Beatriz of Swabia's journey, neither Castilian nor French sources report the itinerary of the embassy sent by Fernando III to Germany. Luciano Serrano suggested that the emissaries entered France through Gascony and arrived in Swabia through Alsace.[135] However, most authorities agree that the lack of data makes it impossible to reconstruct the path followed by the

---

128   *Migravit a seculo dulcis et felicis memorie domina Candida, excellentisima Francie Regina, illustris Ludovici Regis Francie mater et domini Aldefonsi, Regis Hispanie, et Alienoris eius sponse filia, que inter alias mundum regentes et gubernantes nobilitate discretione et bonitate quasi Lucifer inter astra refulsit, abbatias et ecclesias plantando, pauperibus erogando, oppressos consolando, cunctas personas religiosas caritatis visceribus amplectans. Nos autem inter ceteras matris Ecclesie filias specialius protegendo memorie venerabilis matri nostre domine A[dilidis] Blesensi, consanguinee sue*: "Epitaphia et elogia benefactorum," at 49; "Migravit de Fontevraud," 125; Grant, *Blanche of Castile*, 207, 380, n. 37. See also "Nécrologe de Fontevraud (cotté B, 1ᵉ finestre)," 106; "Migravit ou Nécrologe de Fontevraud (1 fenestre, cotté D)," 164; "Migravit de Fontaines," 168; Pavillon, *Robert d'Arbrissel*, 564.

129   Ibid.; Delisle, "Mémoire," 522.
130   *Chartularium*, I: 439 (01.1242).
131   *Sedebat rex, ex una parte lecti, et regina cum comitissa Karnotensi et sorore sua abbatissa, ex altera*: Delisle, "Mémoire," 522, 525–7, at 526.
132   Grant, *Blanche of Castile*, 125–6, 176, 357, fn. 114.
133   Édouard, *Fontevrault*, 2: 352, n. 1.
134   AdM-L, 242 H 1, no. 28 (08.1250). Also Marchegay, "Chartes," 333.
135   Serrano, *Don Mauricio*, 44–6, at 45.

Castilian envoys.[136] The only detail is in manuscript Q of the *Crónica Geral de Espanha de 1344*, a Castilian version of 1434, derived from Portuguese text of 1400, which incorporates a passage on the difficulties of the Castilian delegation on its way through France. In this text, it is said that the princess had to disguise herself as a squire so as not to be recognized.[137] A simple glance at the map shows that the natural path from Paris to Castile passes by Fontevraud, which suggests that Beatriz of Swabia and her companions might have stopped on the way to Poitiers and Angoulême. A precedent for this has already been mentioned: the stay of Blanche of Castile in Fontevraud with her grandmother Eleanor of Aquitaine in 1200 after she travelled from Castile to Normandy to marry Prince Louis of France.[138] It can be added that Beatriz of Swabia and her entourage, after leaving Paris, had to cross the county of Blois, ruled after the death of Count Thibaut VI in 1218 by Marguerite, the eldest sister of the nun Alix.

There is one last important clue: three necrologies of Fontevraud record the death of Beatriz of Swabia.[139] The wife of Fernando III died in 1235, when Alix of Blois was already abbess, and the only document of the King of Castile known in the Fontevraud archive (the letter sent to the Jews of Burgos in 1230) does not mention her. Without other donations to the monastery or further mentions of her name in other documents, why remember Beatriz of Swabia in the necrologies of Fontevraud? Perhaps because of the memory left by her sojourn at the abbey on the way to Castile?

Hence, the hypothetical origin of the donation of Fernando III could be the possible assistance provided by the nun Alix of Blois to the Castilian delegation and to Beatriz of Swabia, at the request of Blanche of Castile, during Beatriz's journey from Paris to Castile through the county of Blois and at the abbey of Fontevraud. We must recognize, however, an important objection to this hypothesis: in almost all the documents of Ferdinand III made between

---

136 Hernández, "La corte de Fernando III," 110–1, 130; Colmenero, "La boda," 16–9; Bianchini, *The Queen's Hand*, 146–7; Witcombe, "Building Heaven on Earth," 54–5.

137 *E quando fueron en Françia vinieron muy escusadamente por non ser conosçidos, en tanto que la donzella vino en tajo de escudero fasta que salieron del su señorío*: *Crónica General de España de 1344*, ms. Q (1434), f. 182r; Rodríguez, "El reino de Castilla," 615, n. 4. On this source see *Crónica Geral de Espanha de 1344*, ed. Lindley Cintra, 1: dxxiii, dxxxii–dxl; *Crónica de 1344*, ed. Catalán and Andrés, xv–xxi, at xvi–ii, lxxvii–iii.

138 Turner, "The Role of Eleanor," 89; Grant, *Blanche of Castile*, 29–31, 207.

139 *uxor excellentissimi et laudabilissimi viri Ferrandi regis Castelle et Toleti, neptis Federici Imperator Allemannie*: "Nécrologe de Fontevraud (cotté B, 1ᵉ finestre)," 105; "Migravit ou Obituaire de Saint-Lazare (cotté C)," 157; "Martirologe de *Fontanis*," in Pavillon, *Robert d'Arbrissel*, 581. Also Lardier, *Saincte Famille*, 454.

December 12, 1219 and April 11, 1220, "his wife Queen Beatriz" is mentioned,[140] yet she is absent from the donation to Alix of Blois, where only his mother, Queen Berenguela, is cited.

The study of the donation of Fernando III to his relative Alix of Blois in March 1220, a document largely ignored until now, has allowed us to review the list of abbesses of Fontevraud, restoring corrections which had already been made in the nineteenth century but then subsequently forgotten. We have also been able to specify more precisely the origin of Abbess Adelaide of Brittany. The donation as such must be framed within the scope of the familial relations of Fernando III in the context of his marriage to Beatriz of Swabia and, quite possibly, the journey that his future wife made through France to reach Castile. At the root of the donation lay the familial and political links between the royal house of Castile and other great European royal and aristocratic families (the Plantagenets, the Capetians and the Counts of Blois), links that hinged on the movement of individuals in the same political circles (Blanche of Castile and Alix of Blois), all the more so when their mutual interests were at stake: in our case, those of Fernando III, his mother Berenguela, his aunt Blanche, and his relative, Alix of Blois.

9   Edition

1220, March 31. Toledo

Fernando III, King of Castile and Toledo, with the approval of his mother, Queen Berenguela, donates a hundred maravedís from the toll of Burgos to his relative Alix, daughter of Count Thibaut of Blois and nun at Fontevraud Abbey.

A. (Original, parchment) Lost.
B. *Vidimus* dated 1250, 5 January, Wednesday, by Bishop Stephen of Dol after *A*. Parchment. 220 x 305 mm. Good condition. Letters patent, sealed through turn-up on a double tag. *Signo rodado* in black imitating that of Fernando III's documents. Remains of pendant wax seal with parchment strip. French gothic script. Biblioteca de Catalunya (Barcelona), Parchments, no. 343, reg. 15196. Online since 2012: Memòria Digital de Catalunya, Pergamins de la Biblioteca de Catalunya, http://mdc.cbuc.cat/cdm/ref/collection/pergamiBC/id/35502 (1250 January 6. Privilege. Toledo).

---

140 *cum uxore mea domina Beatrice regina*: *Fernando III*, II: nos. 93–5, 99–103, 105–13; Ibid., III: 849.

Ind.: Anscari M. Mundó, *Catàleg del Museu del Llibre Frederic Marès. Biblioteca de Catalunya*, Barcelona, Biblioteca de Catalunya, 1994, 33, P 13 (1250 [1251] January 6. Dol).[141]

[*Christogram*] Uniuersis Christi fidelibus ad quos presens scriptum peruenerit, Stephanus, Dei gratia Dolensis episcopus, in territorio Britannico, salutem in uero salutari. Noueritis nos cartam domini Ferrandi, /² Dei gratia illustris regis Castelle et Toleti, non abolitam non cancellatam nec in aliqua parte sui uiciatam, diligenter inspexisse et legisse ibi uerba hic inferius annotata: /³

Modernis ac posteris presentibus innotescat quod ego FERRANDUS, Dei gratia Rex Castelle et Toleti, ex assensu et beneplacito domine Beren/⁴garie regine, genitricis mee, facio cartam donationis, concessionis, confirmationis et stabilitatis uobis domine Aliz, dilecte consanguinee /⁵ mee, filie T[*heobaldi*], comitis Blesensis, moniali Fontis Ebraldi diebus omnibus uite uestre irreuocabiliter ualituram. Dono itaque uobis centum morabetinos in porta/⁶tico meo de Burgis percipiendos pacifice annuatim, precipiens portagiariis quod in tota uita uestra homini uestro presentis pagine portitori mediante /⁷ Quadragesima annis singulis illos soluant. Siquis uero hanc cartam infringere seu diminuere in aliquo presumperit, iram Dei Omnipotentis plenarie incurrat et cum /⁸ Juda Domini proditore penas sustineat infernales, et regie parti mille aureos incauto persoluat et dampnum ei super hoc illatum restituat dupplicatum. Facta carta apud /⁹ Toletum, ultima die Marciis, Era Mª.CCª.Lª octaua, Anno regni mei tercio, eo uidelicet tempore quo ego, prefatus rex F[*errandus*], in monasterio Sancte Marie Regalis de Burgis /¹⁰ manu propria cingulo milicie me accinxi et tercia die post dominam B[*eatricem*], Philippi quondam Regis Romanorum filiam, duxi sollempniter in uxorem. Et ego sepedictus rex F[*errandus*], /¹¹ regnans in Castella et Toleto, hanc cartam quam fieri iussi, manu propria roboro et confirmo.

Rodericus, Toletane sedis archiepiscopus, Hyspaniarum primas, confirmat.

[*1st Column*] Mauricius, Burgensis episcopus, confirmat. / Tellius, Placentinus [*Palentinus*] episcopus, confirmat. / Geraldus, Secobiensis episcopus, confirmat. / Rodericus, Segontinensis episcopus, confirmat. / Garsias, Conchensis episcopus, confirmat. / Melendus, Oxomensis episcopus, confirmat. / Dominicus, Abulensis episcopus, confirmat. / Dominicus, Placentinus episcopus, confirmat. / Johannes, domini regis cancellarius, abbas Vallisoleti, confirmat. /

---

141 The date of January 5, 1250 is probably correct, since it fell on Wednesday that year, but the Bretons often used Easter-style dates and, if so, in 1251, the Wednesday before Epiphany would be January 4. I would like to thank Michael Jones for his kind help regarding this issue.

[*Signo rodado:* SIGNUM FERRANDI REGIS CASTELLE]
[*Around the "signo rodado":* Goncaluus Roderici, maiordomus curie regis, confirmat. Didaci de Faro, alferiz domini Regis, confirmat]
[*2nd Column*] Rodericus Didaci confirmat. / Aluarus Petri confirmat. / Aluarus Didaci confirmat. / Alfonsus Tellii confirmat. / Rodericus Roderici confirmat. / Johannes Gonçalui confirmat. / Seuerius [*Suerius*] Tellii confirmat. / Garsias Ferrandi, maiordomus Regine domine Ber[*engarie*], confirmat. / Gonçaluus Petri, maior merinus in Castellam, confirmat. /

Egidius iussu iamdicti cancellarii scripsit. /

Nos uero ad maiorem premissorum certitudinem presenti scripto sigillum nostrum apponi fecimus. Actum die mercurii ante Epiphaniam Domini, anno gratie M°.CC°. Quinquagesimo.

Works Cited

Primary Sources
Unpublished

Archives départementales de Côtes-d'Armor, Saint-Brieuc (AdC-A)

    H 69 A 7: *Abbaye de Beauport, Bréhat*

Archives départementales de l'Aube, Troyes (AdA)

    42 Fi 200: *Sceau d'Adèle de Bretagne, abbesse de Fontevraud*

Archives départementales de Maine-et-Loire, Angers (AdM-L)

    1 Mi 74: Jean Lardier, *La Saincte Famille de Font-Evraud*, 3 vols., 1648–1650 (only vol. III)

    "Martyrologe ou Migravit de Fontevraud." xiii–xl

    "Epitaphia et elogia abbatissarum." 1–34

    "Epitaphia et elogia benefactorum." 39–77

    "Traité des personnes illustres de l'Ordre de Fontevraud, tant abbesses et religieuses que fondatrices et bien-factrices." 223–708

    101 H 1–437: Abbaye de Fontevraud

    101 H 55: Dons des rois de France, ducs, comtes, évêques, etc. (XIIe–1737)

    101 H 95, no. 1: *Censif de l'abbaye de Fontevraud*

    101 H 153–159: Jean Lardier, *Inventaire des titres du Thrésor de Fontevraud*, 7 vols., 1646–58

    101 H 160/1: Jean Lardier, *Thrésor de l'Ordre de Fontevraud*, 3 vols., 1649 (only vol. I)

    101 H 160/2: Jean Lardier, *Table générale de toutes les sciences*, 1653

    101 H 225: *Grand Cartulaire de Fontevraud* (9 f.)

    102 H 1–246 H 3: Prieurés et domaines de l'abbaye de Fontevraud

    122 H 1: Domaine de Bray (v. 1180–1315)

132 H 1: Titres de donations – Chemillé (1124–1250)
138 H 3: Domaine de Danzay (1229–1739)
158 H 1: Les Îles de Vert (1138–1572)
193 H 1: L'Île d'Oléron (1199–1403)
201 H 1: Domaine des Ponts-de-Cé (XIIe s.–1767)
239 H 1: Prieurés de Veiga (1125–1480)
240 H 1: Domaine de Teijar, Moslares, Albunes (1190–1480)
242 H 1: Angleterre. Dons, confirmations (1129–1480)

Archives nationales de France, Paris (AN)
    Sc/Ch 2813–2813bis and Sc/D 9205–9205bis: *Sceau d'Adèle de Bretagne, abbesse de Fontevraud*

Biblioteca de Catalunya, Barcelona (BC)
    Pergamins, Memòria Digital de Catalunya, http://mdc.cbuc.cat/cdm/search/collection/pergamiBC

Biblioteca Nacional de España, Madrid (BNE)
    Crónica General de España de 1344, ms. 10815

Biblioteca Vaticana, Rome (BV)
    Cartulaire de Bourgmoyen, ms. Ott. lat. 2966, f. 18r–31v

Bibliothèque nationale de France, Paris (BnF)
    Cartulaire de Champagne, ms. lat. 5993 A
    Cartulaire de Lagny, ms. lat. 9902
    Cartulaire de Sainte-Euverte d'Orléans, ms. lat. 10089 (transl. 18th c)
    Chartularium monasterii Fontis-Ebraldi, 2 t., ms. lat. 5480 (17th c.)
    "Extrait du Grand Nécrologe de Fontevraud." 1: 1–11
    "Nécrologe de Fontevraud (cotté B, 1e finestre)." 2: 89–108
    "Migravit de Fontevraud." 2: 109–141
    "Anniversaires de Fontevraud." 2: 142–143
    "Migravit ou Obituaire de Saint-Lazare (cotté C)." 2: 149–157
    "Migravit ou Nécrologe de Fontevraud (I fenestre, cotté D)." 2: 158–164
    "Migravit de Fontaines." 2: 165–168
    Grand Cartulaire de Fontevraud, ms. nouvelles acquisitions latines 2414 (136 f.)

Published

Actes de Jean Ier Duc de Bretagne (1237–1286), ed. Marjolaine Lémeillat. Rennes: Presses Universitaires de Rennes – Société d'histoire et d'archélogie de Bretagne, 2014.

Charlo Brea, Luis, ed. *Chronica latina regum Castellae*. In *Chronica Hispana Saeculi XIII*, ed. Luis Charlo Brea, Juan Estévez Sola and Rocío Carande Herrero. Vol. 73 of *Corpus Christianorum: Continuatio medievalis*, 7–118. Turnhout: Brepols, 1997.

Crónica de 1344 que ordenó el Conde de Barcelos don Pedro Alfonso, ed. Diego Catalán and María Soledad de Andrés. Madrid: Universidad Complutense de Madrid – Seminario Menéndez Pidal, 1970.

Crónica Geral de Espanha de 1344, 4 t., ed. Luís Filipe Lindley Cintra. Lisbon: Imprensa Nacional-Casa da Moeda-Academia Portuguesa da História, 1951–90.

González, Julio, ed. *Reinado y diplomas de Fernando III*, 3 vols. Córdoba: Monte de Piedad y Caja de Ahorros de Córdoba, 1983.

Grand cartulaire de Fontevraud (Pancarta et cartularium abbatissae et ordinis Fontis Ebraudi), ed. Jean Marc Bienvenu (with Robert Favreau and Georges Pon), 2 vols. Poitiers: Société des antiquaires de l'Ouest, 2000 and 2005.

Jiménez de Rada, Rodrigo. *Historia de rebus Hispanie, sive Historia Gothica*. Ed. Juan Fernández Valverde. Vol. 72 of *Corpus Christianorum: Continuatio mediaeualis*. Turnhout: Brepols, 1987.

Letters of John of Salisbury. Volume 2: The Later Letters (1163–1180), ed. and transl. William J. Millor and Christopher N.L. Brooke. Oxford: Clarendon Press, 1979.

Littere Baronum. The Earliest Cartulary of the Counts of Champagne, ed. Theodore Evergates. Toronto: University of Toronto Press, 2003.

"Obituaire du Prieuré de Collinances." In *Obituares de la province de Sens, Tome IV: Diocèses de Meaux et Troyes*, dir. Auguste Lognon, 201–203. Paris: Imprimérie Nationale, 1923.

"Obituaire du Prieuré de Fontaines." In *Obituares de la province de Sens, Tome IV: Diocèses de Meaux et Troyes*, dir. Auguste Lognon, 17–194. Paris: Imprimérie Nationale, 1923.

Robert d'Arbrissel: A Medieval Religion Life, ed. and trans. Bruce L. Venarde. Washington: The Catholic University of America Press, 2003.

Secondary Sources

Amiot, Patrick. *Dol de Bretagne d'hier à aujourd'hui. Tome III : Regard sur son histoire à travers son évêché*. Dinan: Presses bretonnes, 1990.

Barlés, Elena. "Monasterios femeninos olvidados, 2: Peramán y Santa María la Real." In *Comarca de Ribera Alta de Ebro*, ed. Mónica Vázquez and Miguel Hermoso, 135–140. Zaragoza: Diputación General de Aragón, 2005.

Bernier, Jean. *Histoire de Blois*. Paris: F. Muguet, 1682.

Baudin, Arnaud. *Collection de sceaux détachés. Catalogue analytique*, dir. Nicolas Dohrmann. Troyes: Archives départementales de l'Aube, 2011.

Baudin, Arnaud. *Emblématique et pouvoir en Champagne. Les sceaux des comtes de Champagne et de leur entourage (fin XIe–début XIVe siècle)*. Langres: D. Guéniot, 2012.

Béchet. Gaëlle. *Le « réseau » de bienfaiteurs de Fontevraud au XIIᵉ siècle*, Mémoire prépa-thèse de Master II, dir. Noël-Yves Tonnerre and Bruno Lemesle, Université d'Angers, 2006 (AdM-L, BIB 12721).

Bianchini, Janna. *The Queen's Hand: Power and Authority in the Reign of Berenguela of Castile*. Philadelphia: University of Pennsylvania Press, 2012.

Bienvenu, Jean-Marc. "Le plus ancien état des recettes de l'abbaye de Fontevraud : second quart du XIIIᵉ siècle." *Cahiers d'études médiévales de l'Université de Rouen* 1 (1979): 9–86.

Bienvenu, Jean-Marc. *Les premiers temps de Fontevraud (1109–1189), naissance et évolution d'un Ordre religieux*. 6 t., Thèse de Doctorat d'État, Université de la Sorbonne, 1980 (AdM-L, BIB 11072/1–6).

Bienvenu, Jean-Marc. "Aliénor d'Aquitaine et Fontevraud." *Cahiers de civilisation médiévale* 29, no. 113 (1986): 15–27.

Boase, Thomas S.R. "Fontevrault and the Plantagenets." *Journal of the British Archaeological Association* 3rd series, 34 (1971): 1–10.

Bonachía, Juan Antonio. "Historiografía sobre Burgos en la Edad Media: estado de la cuestión." In *Introducción a la historia de Burgos en la Edad Media. I. Jornadas Burgalesas de Historia (Burgos 23–26 de abril de 1989)*, 69–122. Burgos: Asociación Provincial de Libreros, 1990.

Bowie, Colette. *The Daughters of Henry II and Eleanor of Aquitaine*. Turnhout: Brepols, 2014.

Brown, Elisabeth A.R. "Eleanor of Aquitaine's reconsidered: the woman and her seasons." In *Eleanor of Aquitaine: Lord and Lady*, ed. Bonnie Wheeler and John C. Parsons, 1–54. New York: Palgrave Macmillan, 2002.

Charles, Léopold. *Histoire de La Ferté-Bernard. Seigneurs, administration municipale, église, monuments, hommes illustres*. Mamers-Le Mans: G. Fleury et A. Dangin-Pellechat, 1877.

Chédeville, André and Tonnerre, Noël-Yves. *La Bretagne féodale, XIᵉ–XIIIᵉ siècle*. Rennes: Ouest-France, 1987.

Cingolani, Stefano M. "Desde el otro lado. El Archivo de la Corona de Aragón y la historia de la Corona de Castilla" (lecture, Universidad Complutense de Madrid, December 2, 2016).

Colmenero, Daniel. "La boda entre Fernando III el Santo y Beatriz de Suabia: motivos y perspectivas de una alianza matrimonial entre la Corona de Castilla y los Staufer." *Miscelánea Medieval Murciana* 34 (2010): 9–92.

Coulon, Auguste. *Inventaire des Sceaux de Champagne. Table des noms de personnes et de lieux complétée et corrigée par Jean-Marc Roger*. Paris: Centre historique des Archives Nationales, 2003.

DeAragon, RáGena C. "Wife, Widow, and Mother: Some Comparisons between Eleanor of Aquitaine and Noblewomen of the Anglo-Norman and Angevin World." In

Eleanor of Aquitaine: Lord and Lady, ed. Bonnie Wheeler and John C. Parsons, 97–113. New York: Palgrave Macmillan, 2002.

Delisle, Léopold. "Mémoire sur une lettre à la reine Blanche." *Bibliothèque de l'École des Chartes* 17, no. 1 (1857): 513–555.

Diago, Máximo. "La monarquía castellana y los Staufer. Contactos políticos y diplomáticos en los siglos XII y XIII." *Espacio, Tiempo y Forma, Serie III, Historia Medieval* 8 (1995): 51–83.

Dictionnaire de l'ordre monastique de Fontevraud, https://Dictionnaireordremonastiquedefontevraud.Wordpress.Com/Lordre-Monastique-De-Fontevraud/.

Domínguez, Santiago. *Colección documental medieval de los monasterios de San Claudio de León, Monasterio de Vega y San Pedro de las Dueñas*. León: Centro de Estudios e Investigación "San Isidoro," 2001.

Domínguez, Santiago. "El monasterio de Vega: de los orígenes alto medievales a la Edad Moderna." In *Fundadores, fundaciones y espacios de vida conventual. Nuevas aportaciones al monacato femenino*, coord. María Isabel Viforcos and María Dolores Campos, 17–50. León: Universidad de León, 2005.

Domínguez, Santiago. "Oficios y artesanos medievales en el monasterio leonés de Vega." *Hispania Sacra* 65, Extra 2 (2013): 33–57.

Douët d'Arcq, Louis-Claude. *Collection de sceaux des Archives de l'Empire*. 3 t. Paris: H. Plon, 1868.

Duine, François. *La métropole de Bretagne. Chronique de Dol, composée au XIe siècle, et catalogues des dignitaires jusqu'à la Révolution*. Paris: H. Champion, 1916.

Dupré, Alexandre. "Les comtesses de Chartres et de Blois. Étude historique." *Mémoires de la société archéologique d'Eure-et-Loir* 5 (1872): 198–236.

Édouard (pseud. Abbot Armand Biron). *Fontevrault et ses monuments ou histoire de cette abbaye depuis sa fondation jusqu'à sa suppression (1100–1793)*, 2 t. Paris – Marseille: Aubry – Victor Boy, 1873–1874.

Estepa, Carlos. "El reino de Castilla y el Imperio: de Alfonso VIII a Fernando III." In *La Península Ibérica en tiempos de Las Navas de Tolosa*, ed. Carlos Estepa and María Antonia Carmona, 252–259. Madrid: Sociedad Española de Estudios Medievales, 2014.

Estepa, Carlos, Bonachía, Juan Antonio, Ruiz, Teófilo F., and Casado, Hilario. *Burgos en la Edad Media*. Valladolid: Junta de Castilla y León, 1984.

Everard, Judith A. *Brittany and the Angevins. Province and Empire, 1158–1203*. Cambridge: Cambridge University Press, 2000.

Evergates, Theodore. "Louis VII and the Counts of Champagne." In *The Second Crusade and the Cistercians*, ed. Michael Gervers, 109–117. New York: St Martin's Press, 1992.

Favreau, Robert. "Aliénor d'Aquitaine et Fontevraud." *Revue 303. Arts, Recherches et Créations* 81 (2004: *Aliénor d'Aquitaine*, dir. M. Aurell): 41–45.

Flori, Jean. *Richard Coeur de Lion, le roi chevalier*. Paris: Payot, 1999.

Flori, Jean. *Aliénor d'Aquitaine. La reine insoumise*. Paris: Payot, 2004.

Gallia Christiana in provincias ecclesiasticas distributa, Vol. 2. Paris: Ex Typographia Regia, 1720.

Garcia, Charles. "Un prieuré fontevriste frustré dans l'Espagne du XIIe siècle: Gema del Vino." *Fontevraud et ses prieurés*. Poitiers: CESCM (outcome).

Geslin de Bourgogne, Jules Henri, and Barthélemy, Anatole Jean Baptiste Antoine de. *Anciens évêchés de Bretagne. T. IV : Diocèse de Saint-Brieuc*. Paris – Saint-Brieuc: A.L. Herold – Guyon Frères, 1864.

González, Emiliano. *Colección diplomática del Concejo de Burgos (884–1369)*. Burgos: Ayuntamiento, 1984.

González, Julio. *El reino de Castilla en la época de Alfonso VIII*. 3 vols. Madrid: CSIC, 1960.

González, Manuel. *Fernando III el Santo. El rey que marcó el destino de España*. Seville: Fundación José Manuel Lara, 2006.

Gouget, Jean, and Le Hête, Thierry. *Les comtes de Blois et de Champagne et leur descendance agnatique. Généalogie et histoire d'une dynastie féodale, X^e–XVIIe siècle*. La Bonneville-sur-Iton: T. Le Hête, 2004.

Grant, Lindy. *Blanche of Castile, Queen of France: Power, Religion and Culture in the Thirteenth Century*. New Haven: Yale University Press, 2016.

Hernández, Francisco Javier. "La corte de Fernando III y la casa real de Francia: documentos, crónicas, monumentos." In *Fernando III y su tiempo (1201–1252). VIII Congreso de Estudios Medievales (León, 1–4 de octubre de 2001)*, 103–156. Ávila: Fundación Sánchez-Albornoz, 2003.

Histoire de l'Ordre de Fontevrault (1100–1908) par les religieuses de Sainte-Marie de Fontevrault de Boulaur (Gers) exilées à Vera de Navarra (Espagne), 2: *Les trente-six abbesses qui ont gouverné l'Ordre de Fontevrault (1115–1792)*, 2 t. Auch: Imprimérie de L. Cocharaux, 1913.

Hivergneaux, Martine. "Aliénor et l'Aquitaine : le pouvoir à l'épreuve des chartes (1137–1204)." *Revue 303. Arts, Recherches et Créations* 81 (2004: *Aliénor d'Aquitaine*, dir. M. Aurell), 65–69.

Holt, Edward L. "*In eo tempore*: The Circulation of News and Reputation in the Charters of Fernando III." *Bulletin for Spanish and Portuguese Historical Studies* 42, no. 1 (2017): 3–22. doi: https://doi.org/10.26431/0739-182X.1253.

Jasperse, Jitske. "Matilda, Leonor and Joanna: the Plantagenet sisters and the display of dynastic connections through material culture." *Journal of Medieval History* 43, no. 5 (2017): 523–547.

Labande, Edmond-René. "Pour une image véridique d'Aliénor d'Aquitaine." *Bulletin de la Société des Antiquaires de l'Ouest* 4e série, 2 (1952): 175–234.

Labande, Edmond-René. "Les filles d'Aliénor d'Aquitaine : étude comparative." *Cahiers de civilisation médiévale* 29, no. 113 (1986): 101–112.

La Borderie, Arthur de la Moyne de. *Histoire de Bretagne. Tome 3 : 995–1364*. Rennes-Paris: J. Plihon et L. Hervé-A. Picard, 1899.

Lobineau, Guy-Alexis. *Histoire de Bretagne*. Paris: François Muguet, 1707.

Malifaud, G. *L'Abbaye de Fontevraud : notice historique et archéologique*. Angers: J. Bouserez, 1868 (first ed. 1866).

Marchegay, Paul. "Chartes de Fontevraud concernant l'Aunis et La Rochelle." *Bibliothèque de l'École des chartes* 19 (1858): 132–170 and 321–347. Reprinted in Idem, *Notices et pièces historiques. L'Anjou, l'Aunis et la Saintonge, la Bretagne et le Poitou*, 201–265. Angers-Niort: Lachèse, Belleuvre et Dolbeau-P. Clouzot, 1872.

Marès Deulovol, Frederic. *El mundo fascinante del coleccionismo y de las antigüedades: memoria de la vida de un coleccionista*. Barcelona: Museo Frederic Marés, 2000.

Martindale, Jane. "Eleanor of Aquitaine." In *Richard Coeur de Lion in History and Myth*, ed. Janet Nelson, 17–50. London: King's College, 1992.

Martindale, Jane. "Eleanor of Aquitaine: The Last Years." In *King John: New Interpretations*, ed. Stephen D. Church, 137–164. Woodbridge: Boydell & Brewer, 1999.

Martínez, Andrés, *El Monasterio de Santa María de la Vega. Colección diplomática*. Oviedo: Idea, 1991.

Martínez, Gonzalo. *Fernando III, 1217–1252*. Palencia: Diputación-La Olmeda, 1993.

Morice, Hyacinthe. *Mémoires pour servir des preuves à l'histoire ecclésiastique et civile de Bretagne*. Vol. I, Paris: Charles Osmont, 1742 (reimpr. Farnborough, Hants, 1968).

Morin, Stephane. *Trégor, Goëlo, Penthièvre. Le pouvoir des Comtes de Bretagne du XIe au XIIIe siècle*. Rennes: Presses universitaires de Rennes-Société d'Émulation des Côtes d'Armor, 2010.

Morvan, Frédéric. "Les règlements des conflits de succession dans la noblesse bretonne au XIIIe siècle." *Annales de Bretagne et des Pays de l'Ouest* 116, no. 2 (2009): 7–53.

Morvan, Frédéric. *Les Chevaliers bretons. Entre Plantagenêts et Capétiens, du milieu XIIe au milieu XIIIe siècle*. Spézet: Coop Breizh, 2014.

Mundó, Anscari M. *Catàleg del Museu del Llibre Frederic Marès. Biblioteca de Catalunya*. Barcelona: Biblioteca de Catalunya, 1994.

Nicquet, Honorat. *Histoire de l'Ordre de Fontevrault, contenant la vie et les merveilles de la Sainteté de Robert d'Arbrissel et l'histoire chronologique des abbesses*. Paris: Michel Soly, 1642.

Parrot, Armand. *Mémorial des abbesses de Fontevraud issues de la maison royale, accompagné de notes historiques et archéologiques*. Paris: Imprimérie Lachèse et Dolbeau, 1880.

Pavillon, Baltazar. *La vie du bienheureux Robert d'Arbrissel*. Saumur-Paris: F. Ernou-F. Coustelier, 1666.

Rodríguez, Ana. "La política eclesiástica de la monarquía castellano-leonesa durante el reinado de Fernando III (1217–1252)." *Hispania* 48, no. 168 (1988): 7–48.

Rodríguez, Ana. "El reino de Castilla y el Imperio Germánico en la primera mitad del siglo XIII. Fernando III y Federico II." In *Historia social, pensamiento historiográfico y Edad Media. Homenaje al Prof. Abilio Barbero de Aguilera*, coord. María Isabel Loring García, 613–630. Madrid: Ediciones del Orto, 1997.

Rodríguez, Ana. *La estirpe de Leonor de Aquitania. Mujeres y poder en los siglos XII y XIII*. Barcelona: Crítica, 2014.

Round, J. Horace. *Calendar of documents preserved in France illustrative of the history of Great Britain and Ireland. Volume 1, 918–1206*. London: H.M. Stationery Office, 1899.

Salette, Madeleine. "Fontevraud et la papauté d'après les actes pontificaux du Trésor des chartes de Fontevraud (Analyse des 109 actes conservés aux AD de Maine-et-Loire)." *Fontevraud: histoire-archéologie. Comité d'histoire fontevriste* 2 (1993): 67–96.

Salvador Martínez, H. *Berenguela la Grande y su época (1180–1246)*. Madrid: Polifemo, 2012.

Santanach, Joan. "Perduts, amagats i retrobats. Història de dos manuscrits de la *Doctrina pueril*." *Els Marges* 68 (2000): 106–117.

Santanach, Joan. "Manuscrits lul·lians de la Biblioteca de Catalunya. Testimonis de la *Doctrina pueril* (mss. 3187, 481 i 700)." *Studia Lulliana* 44 (2004): 95–107.

Serrano, Luciano. *Don Mauricio, obispo de Burgos y fundador de su catedral*. Madrid: Junta para Ampliación de Estudios e Investigaciones Científicas – Escuela Española en Roma, 1922.

Serrano, Luciano. *Cartulario de Monasterio de Vega con documentos de San Pelayo y Vega de Oviedo*. Madrid-Burgos: Junta para Ampliación de Estudios e Investigaciones Científicas-Centro de Estudios Históricos-Aldecoa, 1927.

Shadis, Miriam. "Berenguela of Castile's Political Motherhood: The Management of Sexuality, Marriage, and Succession." In *Medieval Mothering*, ed. John C. Parsons and Bonnie Wheeler, 335–358. London: Routledge, 1996.

Shadis, Miriam. *Berenguela of Castile (1180–1246) and Political Women in the High Middle Ages*. New York: Palgrave Macmillan, 2009.

Shadis, Miriam and Berman, Constance Hoffmann. "A taste of the feast: reconsidering Eleanor of Aquitaine's female descendants." In *Eleanor of Aquitaine: Lord and Lady*, ed. Bonnie Wheeler and John C. Parsons, 177–211. New York: Palgrave Macmillan, 2002.

Sirantoine, Hélène. "La cancillería regia en época de Fernando III: ideología, discurso y práctica." In *Fernando III, tiempo de cruzada*, ed. Carlos de Ayala and Martín Ríos, 175–203. Madrid: Sílex, 2012.

Touchard, Henri. *Étude sur les domaines espagnols de l'abbaye de Fontevraud au Moyen Age*, Mémoire pour le diplôme d'études supérieures, Université d'Angers, 1942 (AdM-L, BIB 1612bis).

Trésor des chartes de l'Abbaye royale de Fontevraud. Paris: Ministère de la culture et de la communication, 1992.

Tunc, Suzanne. "De l'élection des abbesses de Fontevraud à leur nomination par le roi." *Annales de Bretagne et des pays de l'Ouest* 99, no. 3 (1992): 205–213.

Turner, Ralph V. "Eleanor of Aquitaine and her Children: An Inquiry into Medieval Family Attachment." *Journal of Medieval History* 14, no. 4 (1988): 321–335.

Turner, Ralph V. "The Role of Eleanor in the Governments of Her Sons Richard and John." In *King John: New Interpretations*, ed. Stephen D. Church, 77–95. Woodbridge: Boydell & Brewer, 1999.

Turner, Ralph V. *Eleanor of Aquitaine: Queen of France, Queen of England*. New Haven: Yale University Press, 2009.

Vayreda, Montserrat. "Frederic Marès, notes biogràfiques." In *La Vida i l'obra de Frederic Marès i Deulovol*, 3–20. Figueres: Arts gràfiques Trayter, 1993.

Vincent, Nicholas. "The Court of Henry II." In *Henry II: New Interpretations*, ed. Christopher Harper-Bill and Nicholas Vincent, 278–334. Woodbridge: Boydell, 2007.

Warren, Wilfred L. *Henry II*. London: Eyre Methuen, 1973.

Witcombe, Teresa. "Building Heaven on Earth: Bishop Maurice and the *novam fabricam* of Burgos cathedral." *Bulletin for Spanish and Portuguese Historical Studies* 42, no. 1 (2017): 46–60. doi: https://doi.org/10.26431/0739-182X.1252.

CHAPTER 6

Laudes regiae: Liturgy and Royal Power in Thirteenth-century Castile-León

Edward L. Holt

In 1217, having been hurried away from the court of his father (King Alfonso IX of León) at Toro, the soon-to-be Fernando III arrived in Valladolid.[1] Here, according to the *Latin Chronicle of the Kings of Castile*, he was

> acclaimed by all in a great shout: "Long live the king!" Then with great joy everyone went to the church of Saint Mary; there, giving thanks to God, all who were present, both the magnates and the people of the cities and other towns, kissed the hand of lord King Fernando in homage.[2]

Rituals, such as those of coronation or acclamation, demonstrate an articulation of power by the king and a chance for the negotiation of his position

---

1 I would like to thank the *Casa de Velazquez*, Hill Museum and Manuscript Library, Saint Louis University History Department and the Saint Louis University Center for Medieval and Renaissance Studies for providing funding to complete this research. I would also like to thank Dr. Sergio Vidal Álvarez of the *Museo Arqueológico Nacional* for access to a manuscript otherwise locked behind exhibition glass. Finally, I would like to thank Damian Smith, Richard Allington, and Teresa Witcombe for their comments on drafts of this text.

2 *Clamatum est ab omnibus clamore valido: Viva rex. Exinde cum ingenti leticia venerunt omnes ad ecclesiam Sancte Marie, et ibidem Deo gratias. Agentes, fecerunt omagium manuale omnes qui aderant, tam magnates quam populi civitatum et aliarum villarum, regidomino Fernando*: CLRC, 79. See *DrH*, 286: *Et ibidem omnes ei fecerunt hominium et fidelitatem regi debitam iuraverunt ... Omnibus aprobantibus ad ecclesiam sancta Marie ducitur et ibidem ad regni solium sublimatur anno etatis sue XVIII, clero et populo decantantibus: Te Deum laudamus, te Dominum confitemur.* See *PCG*, 714: *Et este rey don Fernando de quien dixiemos, alabando a todos este fecho tan alto de su madre, alço las manos et bendixo a Dios por ello; et tomaronle luego dalli los obispos et la otra clerezia et los altos omnes de Castiella et de Estremadura, et aduxieronle del mercado a la eglesia de Sancta Maria. Et fue esto en el xviii anno de su edad del rey don Fernando. Et allí estando en la eglesia de Sancta Maria cantando toda la clerezia* Te Deum laudamus *con don Fernando su rey nuevo, et el pueblo todo alabando a Dios et rogandol et pidiendol merçed que les diesse en el buen rey; et pues quel otorgaron por su rey yl reçibieron por su sennor, allí en aquel logar mismo en Sancta Maria de Valladolit, fizieronle todos omenage, et yuraronle quel guardasen bien et lealmientre la lealtat que es devida a rey. Et fue aducho de cabo dalli al palaçio real, con onrra de rey.*

relative to his future subjects. Paradoxically, while a great deal of scholarship focuses on power dynamics at the moment of coronation, ultimately a coronation is just that: a singular moment, and a fleeting one in the context of a long reign such as that of Fernando's.[3] Since these displays of the king's majesty happen so infrequently, they have a limited ability to influence ordinary political behavior, as the ceremony falls short of providing a sustained presence of the king, one that dictates a vision of loyalty whether or not the king is physically present.[4] Instead, one must look elsewhere, namely, to regular and repetitive public liturgies, in order to appreciate the means through which understandings of authority could be made habitual and the construction of the king's authority ubiquitous.

Scholars have traditionally considered such displays of regal majesty to have been rare in medieval Castile-León. Teófilo Ruiz argues that "from 1135 on, the Castilian and Spanish rulers consciously rejected the traditional emblems of power and authority in use elsewhere in the medieval west."[5] Instead, Ruiz argues that the exercise of power resided in martial prowess, and ceremonies, such as the one described above surrounding the accession of the king, reflected this pattern.[6] Since their lands were conquered from Muslim enemies, there was no need to create sacral trappings to justify rule; it was justified on the battlefield.

The four main chronicle accounts concerning the accession of Fernando III all portray the secular hallmarks outlined by Ruiz.[7] In no case do we encounter any parallels to the French ceremonies of anointment and coronation. It was a fact that did not escape the notice of medieval contemporaries from beyond the Peninsula, as the thirteenth-century Welsh churchman Gerald of Wales noted that "in modern times Spanish kings were neither crowned nor anointed

---

3   Kantorowicz, *Laudes regiae*; Tellenbach, *Römischer und christlicher*, 349–71; Jackson, *Vive le roi!*; Aurell, "Self-Coronations of Iberian Kings"; Maravall, *Estudios de historia del pensamiento Español*; Ruiz, "Unsacred Monarchy"; Serrano Coll, "Art as a Means of Legitimization"; Nieto Soria, *Fundamentos ideológicos del poder real*; Linehan, "Frontier Kingship."
4   Koziol, *Begging Pardon and Favor*, 298–9. Of course, one way that the royal chancelleries "extended" the value of such moments was through the use of dating clauses in royal charters. See Holt, "*In eo tempore*."
5   Ruiz, "Unsacred Monarchy," 110.
6   Ibid., 116. Ruiz isolates several components that demarcate the acclamation and ritual surrounding the installation of a new king: emphasis on martial ability; ensuring heredity in succession; succession by election; knighting; royal arms; raising of the standards of Castile; exchange of oaths between people and monarch; presenting a royal horse that could be ridden only by the king; kissing of the king's hand.
7   *CM*, 332; *DrH*, 286; *PCG*, 714; *CLRC*, 78.

anywhere."[8] While the bishops were participants, it was their secular influence rather than their spiritual conveyance of power that played a preeminent role.[9] Furthermore, the king himself was not crowned but rather "elevated" to the position of ruler.[10] Such imagery was underscored by the use of secular ceremonies of homage and fealty, which negotiated the respective positions of royal, ecclesiastical and noble power.[11] The Castilian monarchy, at least as constructed by chronicle evidence, was built on military success, hereditary right and the deployment of the trope of election.

However, this is not to say that there were no religious elements. As we saw in the account of Fernando's accession, these sacral and secular elements coexisted within the text of the chronicle. As such, rather than a duality between sacralization or secularization, perhaps it is better to consider the range of possible options at the hand of the monarch and considered by his subjects in the negotiation of his election and succession. In other words, the monarch could choose the symbols necessary to support his authority. This approach, in the words of Jaume Aurell, "avoids the excessive polarization (sacralization vs secularization) into which the history of symbolic meaning in medieval Iberian monarchies is prone."[12] But more importantly, it recognizes that the secular was not the only option available to Castilian monarchs, for they could select sacred practices and transpose them into the secular sphere.

Returning to the moment of accession, tucked in between the secular acts of acclamation and homage is the deployment of sacred and religious support of the king. The singing of the *Te Deum*, requesting God's mercy for the king, and using the church in Valladolid hint at what may have been obvious religious ceremony. Perhaps, liturgical acts were so woven into the rhythm of everyday life that the chronicler did not need to mention what the contemporary audience already took for granted. However, these liturgical moments are critical to understanding the ways in which a construction of the king's image

---

8   *Hispaniae principes, qui nec coronari tamen consueverant nec inungi, onos quidem et sanctos fuissa fama praedicit*: Gerald of Wales, "De instructione principis," VIII: 138. Peter Linehan points out that this reference was in support of the similar circumstances of the Scottish monarchs and that both dynasties were "none the worse for it." Linehan, *History and Historians*, 390.

9   Linehan notes that "their function was essentially decorative." Linehan, *History and Historians*, 393.

10 Linehan, *History and Historians*, 393.

11 Valdés Fernández, "Reyes y obispos," 42; Grassotti, *Las instituciones feudo-vasalláticas*, I: 208–10; Linehan, *History and Historians*, 393. See also Nieto Soria, "La monarquía fundacional de Fernando III," 52–8.

12 Aurell, "Self-Coronations," 175.

was projected to a wider audience. It was only through the regular and repetitive public liturgy that understandings of authority could be made habitual.[13]

This article will examine two moments of habitual liturgical performance: those for the living monarch contained in the *Missa pro rege* (Mass in Favor of the King) and those for deceased monarchs contained within necrology and obituary entries. It will argue that these ceremonies, far more than the rites of accession, provided a sustained and ever-present construction of the monarch's regal image. Furthermore, they served as a means to laud a ruler and a way for the populace to express loyalty to a particular vision of power.

1   *Missa pro rege*

The *Missa pro rege* (Mass in Favor of the King) is a votive mass, performed for special purposes or on special occasions. Under investigation in the pages that follow are twelve liturgical documents in which the *Missa pro rege* can be found, comprising nearly all of the extant thirteenth-century Castilian-Leonese liturgical texts which contain an example of the mass.[14] Of these, the majority have been dated to the thirteenth century and the remainder consist either of earlier compositions in use during the thirteenth century or a later copy of a thirteenth-century tradition. The sacramentaries and missals discussed here represent a variety of ecclesiastical institutions within five different dioceses. All originate from the Carolingian precedent of the *Missa cotidiana pro rege*.

The historical study of the *Missa pro rege* has to this point largely been concentrated around the emergence of this liturgical form at the nexus of liturgy and society within the Carolingian dynasty. The genre of votive masses stemmed from Roman imperial ideas that began to be Christianized in late Roman political thought.[15] Yitzhak Hen notes that the Merovingian liturgy stressed the warlike aspects of kingship. The textual dialogue from these two strands of political ideology resulted in prayers that expressed a general concern for the well-being of the kingdom, anchored both in tradition and within a complex network of patronage, endowments and liturgical practice.[16] And even though the original

---

13 Garipzanov, *Symbolic Language*, 52.
14 Burgos, AC Burgos, ms. 23; Burgo de Osma, Archivo Capitular, cod. 165; Chicago, Newberry Library, Case Vault, ms. 69; León, AC León, ms. 27; León, San Isidro de León, codex 5; Madrid, BNE, ms. 20324; Madrid, BNE, ms. Vitr 20-8; Madrid, Escorial, ms. I.II.8; Toledo, BCT 37-27; Toledo, BCT 37-18; Segovia, AC Segovia, ms. 356; Seville, AC Seville, ms. Vitr BB 149-11.
15 Tellenbach, *Römischer*. See also Hen, *Royal Patronage*; Garrison, "Missa pro principe."
16 Hen, *Royal Patronage*, 41.

prayers were constructed for a Roman Christian imperial context, the language gradually permutated to reflect the new historical realities of a *gens Francorum*.

From the outset, within the Carolingian empire the patronage of liturgy functioned as a tool of political machinery. Through the prayers on behalf of the king and kingdom, Charlemagne "disseminated political messages of consensus, solidarity, peace and victory to his subjects, and through these prayers, the king made his presence felt throughout the kingdom."[17] Personal invocations – the prayers of each subject – invested that subject in the work of the kingdom and bestowed on them a personal responsibility for the welfare of not only the king but also the kingdom.[18] For the Carolingians, the construction and deployment of liturgy was not a passive action, based on conservative traditions. Liturgy, and in particular that used for the political purposes of the king, was an active process whereby the mass and message were shaped differently depending on the context.[19]

Within thirteenth-century Castile and León, masses in favor of the king, contained within sacramentaries and missals, uniformly descended from two strands of the above-mentioned Carolingian form of the *Missa cotidiana pro rege*.[20] It should be noted however that they are generally rubricated under the heading *Missa pro rege* or simply *pro rege*. This particular liturgical form was disseminated by the successive waves of French clerics that arrived in the Iberian Peninsula during the late eleventh-century transition from the Hispanic (sometimes referred to as Mozarabic) traditions to those promoted by the papacy.[21] Ramón Gonzálvez Ruiz highlights the strong influence that first the Cluniacs, then the Cistercians, and finally various groups of canon regulars exerted on the Peninsula and, in particular, the see of Toledo.[22] Although liturgical

---

17 Hen, *Royal Patronage*, 93.
18 Ibid.
19 Garipzanov argues for two contexts. The *Missa pro rege* operated as a centerpiece of Carolingian authority. As a royal mass, it was intended to be at the centerpiece of public performances of the liturgy of authority. Meanwhile, the *Missa cotidiana pro rege* may have been intended for more private performance within Carolingian monasteries. Thus the first served as a sign of authority, whereas the second instead functioned as a sign of proximity to the ruler (and thus symbolic of importance of their position and their devotion). Garipzanov, *Symbolic Language*, 402.
20 Authored by Benedict of Aniane in his supplement to the *Hadrianum*, a text which is said to have been sent to the Carolingians by Pope Hadrian I at the behest of Charlemagne.
21 See Montenegro Valentín, "La alianza"; Walker, *Views of transition*; Reilly, *Santiago, Saint-Denis and Saint Peter*; Rubio Sadia, *Las órdenes religiosas*.
22 Gonzalvéz Ruiz, *Hombres y libros*, 66. On the Cluniac presence in the Iberian Peninsula, see also Henriet, "Cluny and Spain before Alfonso VI."

TABLE 6.1 Comparison of Castilian *Missa Pro Rege* Prayers

Missa cotidiana pro rege	Variant
Quasumus, omnipotens deus, ut famulus tuus (rex noster), qui tua miseratione suscepit regni gubernacula, virtutum etiam omnium percipiat incrementa , quibus decenter ornatus, et vitiorum monstra devitare et ad te, qui via, veritas et vita es, gratiosus valeat pervenire.[a]	Quasumus, omnipotens deus, ut famulus tuus (rex noster), qui tua miseratione suscepit regni gubernacula, virtutum etiam omnium percipiat incrementa, quibus decenter ornatus, et vitiorum monstra devitare *et hostes superare* et ad te, qui via, veritas et vita es, gratiosus valeat pervenire.[b]

a *Corpus Orationum*, 4880a.
b Ibid.

texts pertaining to the Hispanic rite continued to be held in sacristies, they no longer served as the model for future sacramentaries by the twelfth century, and from this time on, liturgy in Castile and León was based on exemplars brought over the Pyrenees, in particular by the canon regulars.[23]

We find in the sacramentaries and missals of thirteenth-century Castile and León two variants of this *Missa pro rege*, with the principle difference stemming from a twelfth-century addition to the collect. Table 6.1 is a comparison of the two forms with my emphasis on the difference between the two texts.

In the variation, the phrase *et hostes superare* is inserted. This addition can be traced to a family of manuscripts that originate within the Premonstratensian tradition.[24] Originally founded by Norbert of Xanten near Laon in 1120, this order adhered to the rule of St. Augustine. As canon regulars, their life of poverty also included pastoral work and it is in this function that their uses and customs crossed the Pyrenees and penetrated Iberian dioceses, including that of Toledo.[25] According to Norbert Backmund, it was Alfonso VII (r. 1126–57) and Alfonso VIII (r. 1158–1214) who enabled the propagation of the Premonstratensians in Castile in the first half of the twelfth century.[26] Consequently, the oldest sacramentaries in Castile containing the Roman Rite, such as the

---

23 Gonzalvéz Ruiz, *Hombres y libros*, 80.
24 Ibid.
25 Gonzalvéz Ruiz, *Hombres y libros*, 67.
26 Backmund, "La orden premonstratense," 58–9. He also noted that, curiously, the order did not make as strong a presence in León. Ibid. That is not to say that Premonstratensians were absent from the Kingdom of León. For example, see Fita, "Los premonstratenses en Ciudad Rodrigo."

eleventh-century Sacramentary of Sahagún, proceed from the older Carolingian tradition.[27] The inclusion of the phrase cannot be uniformly found in the sacramentaries and missals of Castile. However, the phrase *et hostes superare* is included not only in the sacramentaries and missals of institutions that held Prémontré as their mother house such as San Vincente de Sierra, located outside of Toledo, but also in liturgical manuscripts of the cathedral of Toledo, and the Cistercian monastery of Las Huelgas, and a later unknown Carthusian foundation.[28]

The inclusion (or not) of the variation on the text of the *Missa pro rege* indicates a degree of liturgical flexibility, and more significantly, what appears to be a notable degree of uniformity of choice by the prelates of Castile-León for this particular mass form, as all of the manuscripts under investigation employ this particular prayer. In the selection of the mass in favor the king, prelates were therefore able to select a mass that matched their "horizon of expectations" of what a king should be held responsible for as well as what the congregation's responsibility was.[29] In this case, they selected a mass which focused on the king's responsibility to advance the recovery of Christendom through the defeat of enemies. In so doing, it mirrored (and provided spiritual support for) the royal military objectives and language of Castilian kings, and in particular, Fernando III.[30]

This liturgical selection is particularly interesting as this was not the only mass available to the prelates of Iberia. A comparison with other thirteenth-century liturgical works from the neighboring polities in the Iberian Peninsula offer a diversity of options. For example, within the cathedral of Tortosa, the mass utilized for the king derives from the Gregorian sacramentary's rite of the

---

27 Madrid, BNE, ms. Vitr 20–8. Janini and Serrano, *Manuscritos litúrgicos*, 248–51.
28 For instance, Toledo, BCT ms. 37–18; Toledo, BCT ms. 37–27; Madrid, BNE, ms. 20324; Chicago, Newberry Library, Case Vault ms. 69.
29 Garipzanov, *Symbolic Language*, 62.
30 For more on the language of monarchs, especially as produced by their chanceries, see Holt, "*In eo tempore*"; Arias Guillén, "Algun fecho"; Sirantoine, "La guerra"; Sirantoine, "La cancillería"; Ostos Salcedo, "La cancillería de Fernando III"; Ostos Salcedo and Pardo Rodríguez, "Signo y símbolo"; Laffón Álvarez, "Arenga Hispana"; Sanz Fuentes, "Cancillería y cultura." While the Roman liturgical tradition in Castile exhibited a uniformity of the rite in favor of the king, the continuation of the Hispanic tradition presents a caveat. After the conquest of Toledo in 1085, while many areas under royal pressure converted to the Roman Rite, six parishes were allowed to continue to use the Hispanic Rite. Ecker, "How to Administer a Conquered City," 58; Pick, Conflict and Coexistence, 201; Javier Hernández, "Los que parecían árabes," 55. Consequently, there existed in the articulation of power from certain pulpits the possibility of an additional means to articulate a vision of kingship, one that contained within it strains of the Visigothic past. See in particular the edited votive mass in Janini, *Liber ordinum episcopal*, 234–7.

Missa pro principe.³¹ On the other side of the Iberian Peninsula, located within the National Archives of Portugal are two thirteenth-century missals previously housed in the Alcobaça Monastery. Although entitled *Missa pro rege*, the votive mass in the first missal originates from an earlier imperial mass, *Missa pro imperatore* or *Missa pro rege vel imperatore*.³² Written around 960 for the coronation of the Holy Roman Emperor Otto I, this intercessory mass includes much more warlike language, not only praying for victory but providing strength to the king in war.³³ In the full mass, it references early Israelite military leaders such as Joseph and Gideon, further underscoring the desire of divine support in military endeavors.³⁴ The other Portuguese missal, also from the thirteenth century, only includes the *Missa pro rege vel imperatore*.³⁵

As such, when Iberian ecclesiastics offered their prayers in support of a monarch, they were able to select from a range of possibilities. Prayer encapsulates the aspirations of the supplicant. The same can be said of the masses in favor the king. Within the Castilian context, the uniform liturgy, at least as prescribed within the studied manuscripts, offers such a view into the vision of the ruler projected to the wider public by the Castilian-Leonese Church.

While these liturgical documents provide a prescriptive account of the prayers that should be said, they do not often provide a corresponding descriptive record concerning actual performances of the prayer. The chronicles written in thirteenth-century Castile-León do not specify the use of this votive mass; however, they do note the celebration of special masses at major milestones in the reign of Fernando III, for which the *Missa pro rege* would be one of several suitable options. Although the chronicles are vague as to the performance of a mass during the rituals of Fernando's acclamation at Valladolid in 1217, they are more explicit about the celebration of a mass at other key moments in Fernando's career. For instance, on the occasion of the knighting of King Fernando immediately before his marriage in 1219, Bishop Maurice of Burgos celebrated a mass at the royal monastery of Las Huelgas, and afterwards blessed the arms that the king removed from the altar there, as we are informed by the *Latin Chronicle of the Kings of Castile*.³⁶ There are numerous reports of masses being conducted after moments of conquest, as part of the cleansing

---

31   Tortosa, AC Tortosa, codex 13, f. 129r-v. For more on the *Missa pro principe*, see Garrison, "The Missa pro principe." Garrison points to the mass as part of a Gallician tradition, with origins in Bavaria.
32   Lisbon, Biblioteca Nacional de Portugal, Codices Alcobacence, CLXV/255, f. 188r-v.
33   *Corpus Orationum*, 2177. Bachrach, *Warfare in Tenth-Century Germany*, 188.
34   Bachrach, *Warfare in Tenth-Century Germany*, 188.
35   Lisbon, Biblioteca Nacional de Portugal, Codices Alcobacence 252, f. 229v.
36   CLRC, 83; PCG, 718-9.

and rededication of mosques.[37] Finally a mass was also conducted as part of the penitential rituals that Fernando III participated in as he neared death.[38]

The most explicit description of the use of the *Missa pro rege* can be located in a marginal annotation from the thirteenth-century sacramentary of Osma. Written above the rubrication for the *Missa pro rege* is a separate ritual to be added when the king is present.[39] Thus, this votive mass also held the symbolic significance of being performed when in the presence of the king, bringing together the person of the king and the rest of the congregation within the same liturgical performance.

However, the mass does not need to be performed in the presence of the monarch. Its performance provides an opportunity to pray for God's protection over the king and the kingdom. The ritualistic invocation of the king's name serves to create a separate spatial dimension of royal ubiquity so that the king could be made ritually present even in his physical absence.[40] Thus, it fosters a regular interface of the monarchical image with ecclesiastics and the wider public (as many would not regularly have physical access to the king).[41] Nor was this mass merely propaganda; rather it should be viewed as part of the ecclesiastical negotiation of power with the monarch.[42] For kings, the liturgy provided a means of strengthening links with their subjects and harnessing their prayers in his support, especially in time of crisis.[43] Additionally, Ildar Garipzanov stresses the need to take seriously the liturgy as a tool to guide, even correct, the king.[44] The selection of which mass was to be performed provides a window into the concerns of society and the needs of the monarch. As such, the *Missa pro rege* serves as a sort of "mirror of princes" presenting a vision of kingship. This construct, when celebrated in the presence of the king himself, thus serves to either elevate the monarch or offer a rebuke.

Returning to the text of the *Missa pro rege,* having established the precedents for the mass and potential occasions for its celebration, we must ask: what was the image of the ruler that was projected to wider society by the Castilian-Leonese Church? Each votive mass includes a set of prayers known as the "proper." These non-scriptural portions of the collect, sacra and post

---

[37] CLRC, 94, 116–7; *DrH*, 299; PCG, 733, 746–7, 767.
[38] PCG, 772.
[39] Burgo de Osma, AC Burgo de Osma, cod. 165, f. 84r; Janini, "Notas," 153.
[40] Costa Gomes, "Invoking the name of the king," 229–30.
[41] Garipzanov, *Symbolic Language*, 55.
[42] Garipzanov, *Symbolic Language*, 50.
[43] McCormick, *Eternal Victory*, 358.
[44] Garipzanov, *Symbolic Language*, 50. This is especially the case for when the king is present to hear the mass.

complendum individuate the office to provide a unique set of prayers for specific situations. These three pieces complement each other to form a homogenous unit which contains within it the vision of the officiant. However, these triple sets of prayers are not necessarily unique. In the case of the triple set for the *Missa pro rege*, this proper is the same as that used for the rites *ad ordinandum regum*. Thus in its performance, it recreates the liturgical accession of the king.

The collect of the *Missa cotidiana pro rege* reads:

> We pray, o Omnipotent God, that your servant, our king, who through your mercy undertook the government of the kingdom, may also experience a growth of all virtues, by which he is adorned gracefully, and may gratuitously avoid the monsters of sins, conquer enemies, and come to you who is the way, the truth and the life.[45]

The prayer is a clear expression of political theology. The first line delineates a chain of power; the king is placed as the mediator between God, for whom he is a servant, and the supplicants, for whom he is the lord. Moreover the end of the prayer evokes a Christ-centric model of kingship, citing John 14:6 – "Jesus answered 'I am the way, and the truth, and the life'" – according to which the king should mimic the actions of Christ. The choice of the word *gubernacula* has a literal meaning of government. However, it also has a more figurative sense of the helm of the "ship of state," a reference to the metaphor employed by Plato in his *Republic* and used in discussions of medieval kingship in the Middle Ages.[46] Ultimately, it presents two visions of the role of the king. The first is the moral head of the body of Christ (ie, as head of the Church). Through the avoidance of sin, the king preserves the polity against judgements that should arise as the result of sin. In doing so, this liturgy roots good kingship within the individual sanctity and personal virtue of the king, common tropes that governed understandings of pre-scholastic rulership.[47] Cecilia Gaposchkin argues that this vision underscores the medieval theory that power was a response to the fall and the maintenance of an imperfect society.[48] This Augustinian

---

45   *Quasumus, omnipotens deus, ut famulus tuus (rex noster), qui tua miseratione suscepit regni gubernacula, virtutum etiam omnium percipiat incrementa, quibus decenter ornatus, et vitiorum monstra devitare et hostes superare et ad te, qui via, veritas et vita es, gratiosus valeat pervenire*: Corpus Orationum, 4880a. Translation by Garipzanov, *Symbolic Language*, 334–5.
46   For instance, see Aquinas, *De regno*, 3.
47   Gaposchkin, "Talking about Kingship," 139–49.
48   Gaposchkin, "Talking about Kingship," 139.

response provided the framework for what Jacques Krynen has labeled the "ethical-religious interpretation of royalty" and the trope of kingship characterized by the personal sanctity of the ruler that would persist throughout the remainder of the Middle Ages.[49]

Secondly, the invocation that the king should "conquer enemies" invokes the martial tradition of the Castilian monarchy. Although other masses provide a more clearly defined physical enemy, here the enemy is couched in the context of sin.[50] Thus, within the *oratio*, prelates provide a moral rejoinder to the king, and charge him to protect the kingdom from sin and enemies, all working within a religious context, one in which they have spiritual authority.

Following from the collect is the sacra:

> O Lord, we pray that you sanctify our offered gifts so that they may become for us the body and blood of your only son and by your largess, may be of benefit in everything to your king for maintaining spiritual and bodily health and for fulfilling the assigned office.[51]

Here at the moment of epiclesis, the transfiguration of the sacraments, the officiant blesses the bread and wine. In addition, he connects the physical welfare of the kingdom with the spiritual and bodily health of the person of the sovereign. By participating in the Eucharist, even if everyone does not partake of the elements, the community contributes to the work of the polity and thus garners the blessings of the Lord.

Finally, the third part of the proper is the post complendum:

> Lord, may this beneficial prayer protect your servant N. from all dangers, insofar as he may maintain the tranquility of ecclesiastical peace and arrive at the eternal inheritance after the descent of time.[52]

---

49 Krynen, *L'Empire du roi*, 33. See also Wallace-Hadrill, "The *Via Regia*."
50 This dualism between visible and invisible enemies often arrives in the context of military contest and crusade, both of which fall under the purview of Castilian monarchs. See for example see the November 24, 1217 letter of Honorius III: *Adversus hostes visibiles invisibilibus armis ... dimicare veteribus exemplis instruimur*.
51 *Munera quaesumus domine oblata sanctifica ut et nobis unigenta tui corpus et sanguis fiat et illis regi ad obtinendam anime corporisque salutem et peragendum iniunctum officium te largiente usquequaque proficia*: *Corpus Orationum*, 3413b. Translation by Garipzanov, *Symbolic Language*, 334–5.
52 *Hec domine oratio salutaris famulum tuum, N, ab omnibus tueatur adversis quatenus ecclesiastice pacis obtineat tranquillitatem et post istius temporis de cursus ad eternem perveniat*

Here again is the placement of the king as a servant of God, defining him within a spiritual realm. And once again the supplicants participate in the work of the kingdom by explicitly creating a transaction by their prayers for the preservation of the monarch. However, these prayers are conditioned on the continued maintenance of ecclesiastical peace. Thus, in the broader liturgical context of the mass, in the midst of praising the king, the ecclesiastical hierarchies introduce a reminder of their own agenda and needs with regard to the role of the monarch. This acts as a check on the authority of the monarch, who gains the spiritual support of the kingdom only through fulfilling the qualities outlined by the clergy.

Beyond the proper, there are the choices of scriptural readings within the mass. The votive *Missa pro rege*, a manuscript which contains a list of gospel selections to accompany various votive masses, lists Luke 22:28–30:

> You are those who have stayed with me in my trials, and I assign to you, as my Father assigned to me, a kingdom, that you may eat and drink at my table in my kingdom and sit on thrones judging the twelve tribes of Israel.[53]

Within this choice, the prelates literally demonstrate the spiritual inheritance from Christ. Moreover, allegorical exegesis denotes the place of the king as ruler by the grace of God and provides the additional role of the monarch as judge.

As a final note on the text of the mass and its relationship to performance, there is the aforementioned marginal annotation over the sacramentary of Osma. Here, the *Missa pro rege* is situated within a larger religious reception of the king within a church service. The sacramentary includes the following directions for the officiant of the service:

> Ad recipiendam regem dicatur. R. *Tua est potencia* V. *Domine salvum fac regem.* Ps. *Exaudi.* Aliud V. *Deus iudicum tuum regi da.* Ps. *Et iusti.*[54]

---

hereditatem: *Corpus Orationum*, 2793. Translation by Garipzanov, *Symbolic Language*, 334–5.

53   NSRV Luke 22:28–30; selection found in an eleventh-century German missal (Chicago, Newberry Library, Case Vault ms. 4, f. 123v). Curiously BCT ms. 35–18, a more native Iberian text which contains an epistolary for votive masses, does not include one for *Missa pro rege*.

54   Burgo de Osma, Archivo Capitular, cod. 165, f. 84r; Janini, "Notas," 153.

Here the use of Psalms 19:9 and Psalms 72:1 provide two additional invocations to God to protect the monarch.⁵⁵ Furthermore, the choral response of *Tua est potencia* serves to elide the figures of God, the celestial monarch, and the earthly manifestation of this power in the king. The use of these Psalms creates an ideal vision about what a monarch is to be; on hearing hymns or other prayers concerning the role of the Lord as king, individual supplicants are then primed to desire the same qualities in their own ruler.

The *Missa pro rege* serves as a means to understand cultural conceptions of medieval kingship. As opposed to brief moments of encounter with a vision of kingship located in actions with a minimal audience, the *Missa pro rege* provided a means for a greater distribution of the message of kingship. And unlike the coronation ritual, for which the monarchy took the organizational lead, within this liturgical context, the clergy took the initiative.

2   Anniversaries of Death in Necrologies and Obituaries

When discussing the funerary practices of monarchs, it is customary to refer to their eulogies, often found in chronicles, or to their funerary architecture and sepulchers. When it comes to the study of Fernando III, we are fortunate in having both the long eulogy that serves almost as an *ars moriendi* within the *Estoria de España*, and Fernando III's elaborate sepulcher in the cathedral of Seville.⁵⁶

But beyond these sources, the memory of kings was also inscribed in liturgy. Emerging sometime during the ninth century as a means to remember and commemorate the anniversaries of death, liturgical records of the dead can be classified into two basic types: necrologies and obituaries. The necrology is a list of the dead written in the margin of a calendar or a martyrology in order to be read in the context of choral prayer.⁵⁷ The obituary was also a list of deceased and likewise often written in margins, but served a more administrative purpose to remind the ecclesiastical community of the dead and to prompt the performance of the attendant works of mercy which accompanied the anniversary, as well as the collection of incomes related to this.⁵⁸ In terms of the dates for which these notes are written, the necrology respects as much as

---

55   NSRV Psalms 19:9, "O Lord, save the king: and hear us in the day that we shall call upon thee"; NSRV Psalms 72:1, "Give the king Your judgements, O God, and thy righteousness unto the king's son."

56   For the eulogy, see *PCG*, 772. On the sepulcher, see Nickson, "Remembering Fernando," and in this volume, García Fitz, Chp. 2 and Boloix-Gallardo, Chp. 3.

57   Genicot, *Typologie*, 35.

58   Genicot, *Typologie*, 35; Binski, *Medieval Death*, 32–3.

possible the actual date of death, whereas for the obituary, the correct date is often of secondary importance as the rites to be performed may not coincide with the date of death.[59]

While these texts originated with two distinct purposes, their similar organizational scheme makes them difficult to distinguish, and in many smaller communities, necrologies and obituaries became interchangeable. In terms of the performance of the texts, the readings mainly occur during the gathering of the community at the office of prime, although it is not unusual to be heard during one of the smaller hours and in certain communities outside of the framework of office, either during refectory or chapter.[60] With respect to the language, the typical format often includes the word *obiit* followed by the name of the individual, status and then a place of precision.

A reading of these liturgical sources surrounding death affords us an insight into the complex negotiation of power between royal patrons and ecclesiastical sites of memory. Of all of the manuscripts, due to its place as the site of burial for thirty-two royal figures, the texts of the Cistercian monastery of Las Huelgas provide some of the richest sources of information for the period in question.[61] In what follows, we will focus on the construction of royal power within and around the royal anniversaries of death primarily from the Cistercian monastery of Las Huelgas, although points of comparison will be drawn between similar texts in other Iberian religious institutions.

Memory was preserved above all by the infantas who had taken the veil at Las Huelgas.[62] The martyrology includes a note informing us that in the year of infanta Berenguela's enclosure (1241), and "through the prayers and through the requests of the most religious infanta lady Berenguela," a number of altars were dedicated at the monastery, especially noting that of Alfonso VIII, those of the other kings and those of the infantas.[63] Amancio Rodríguez López has

---

59   Genicot, *Typologie*, 36.
60   Ibid., 35–7.
61   MAN 1962/73/3. See Janini, *Manuscritos litúrgicos*, 182; Revilla, "Un códice latino"; Catalunya, "The Royal Customary," 156–9. Janini and Serrano note the calendar of a missal for Las Huelgas additionally includes anniversaries for Alfonso VIII, Leonor, and Louis IX (Janini y Serrano, *Manuscritos litúrgicos*, 198–9; Madrid, BNE, ms. 20324, f. v-xi). Finally, not discussed here but of relevance is a manuscript known as the musical codex of Las Huelgas, which contains three *plancti* dedicated to monarchs (Sancho III, Alfonso VIII, and Fernando III). Angles, *El Códex Musical*. Raquel Alonso Álvarez argues that these songs were performed as part of procession through the royal sepulchers of Las Huelgas, thus connecting the sacral, aural, and physical spaces together in a ritualized performance (idem, "La memoria de Alfonso VIIII").
62   For more on the infantas, see in this volume Bianchini, Chp. 7.
63   *hoc totum factum sunt ad preces et pro mandatum religiosissimae dompne infantissae Berengarie*: MAN 1962/73/3, f. 8.

commented upon the efforts made by the family of the founders, both infantas Constanza and Berenguela, to ensure the diligent commemoration of their souls, and, for example, upon the death of her grandmother, Queen Berenguela of Castile, in 1246, the infanta Berenguela, her namesake, acquired an indulgence of forty days for all who visited her sepulcher.[64] In 1253, the same infanta Berenguela gained a broader concession of an indulgence of ten days for anyone who confessed at the tomb of a buried king, queen, or infanta on whose anniversary it was.[65]

The royal names that populate the margins of this late thirteenth-century necrology are principally patrons, either noted for their role in the foundation or rebuilding of the monastery, as well as their immediate family.[66] The text recognizes Alfonso VIII as well as "Leonor ... the most serene wife of the Alfonso, both of whom were founders of this monastery."[67] The supreme importance of the status of the royal founder in these texts is highlighted by the genealogical tag highlighting descent from the most immediate royal male patron. Thus, while Enrique I is referred to as the son of Alfonso, king of Castile, and Sancho IV as the son of Alfonso, king of Castile and León, the entry for neither Alfonso VIII nor Fernando III (the respective heads of two familial generations of patronage) reference their genealogy.[68] The only exception to this appears to be Beatriz of Swabia, who is referred to as not only the wife of Fernando III but also the daughter of "Philip, Emperor of the Romans," no doubt a point of pride for the monastery that they housed not one but four royal lines (two of which were imperial).[69]

The necropolis of Las Huelgas and the related necrology do not perpetuate an unbroken royal lineage. They instead ensure prayers for those individuals who have provided support to the monastery throughout their lifetimes, as

---

64   Rodríguez López, *El Real Monasterio*, 141.
65   Rodríguez López, *El Real Monasterio*, 141.
66   Catalunya provides information pertaining to the provenance of the manuscript, compiled between 1271 and 1276. Catalunya, "The Royal Customary," 154–5.
67   *Obiit alinor ... uxor serenissimum regis Castelle aldefonsi qui fuerunt fundatores huius cenobi*: MAN 1962/73/3, f. 160, f. 175.
68   See respectively Ibid., f. 95v, f. 71v, f. 160, f. 91v.
69   *philipi romanorum imperatis*: Ibid., f. 177r. For more on the cultural currency of the name of Beatriz of Swabia, see Benito-Vessels, *Lenguaje*. One could also make the argument that Beatriz represents an additional royal line of Byzantine emperors through her descent from Isaac II Angelos; however, that association is not present in the necrology in question. We also need to include the Plantagenet ancestry of their founder, Leonor, a fact further underscored by the inclusion of an anniversary for "the king, Henry the great, of England, the second." MAN 1962/73/3, f. 112: *Rex Henricus maior de Anglie secundus*.

well as for their families.⁷⁰ Further evidence for this can be found in the martyrology of Las Huelgas, in a prayer commemorating patrons connected with the monastery.⁷¹ The end of this prayer specifically commemorates the king Alfonso VIII and his venerable wife, who founded the monastery, as well as the most serene Fernando and his wife Beatriz.⁷² Following these words, around half a folio is left blank, before the sentence is completed with the phrase "and all other benefactors of our order."⁷³ Already commemorating two royal households, this space indicates an interrupted desire to commemorate additional future benefactors and their families. Although Las Huelgas is often considered as a royal necropolis and a symbol of royal power, the memory preserved by the necrology of Las Huelgas is one that hinges around the relationship between monastery and patron, and the foundation of a burial site for Alfonso VIII himself and all of his family. And perhaps this was Fernando's intention as well, as he buried his first wife there, alongside his uncle, King Enrique I, and is also recorded in the necrologies of the monastery as a benefactor, although, of course, Fernando himself would be buried in Seville cathedral in 1252 by his son, Alfonso X.⁷⁴

Beyond the function of founder, we shall now turn to the ways in which the kings and queens of Castile were commemorated and exalted in the necrologies. Within the Las Huelgas manuscript, the superlatives "most serene" (*serenissimi*) and "most distinguished" (*illustrissimi*) are the favored words used to describe deceased kings, markers of respect that highlight the dignity of the monarch. Female rulers are accorded a different marker of rule. Both Beatriz and Berenguela are noted as "most noble and venerable" (*nobilissima et venerabilis*), while Berenguela gains the additional marker of rule as "powerful" (*potens*).⁷⁵

The other commonly used descriptor enhances the religious image of the deceased. Due to the concern of these institutions for spiritual welfare, it should come as no surprise that the obituary annotations stress their spiritual and religious status. This was accomplished primarily through referring to religious works, such as the foundation of Las Huelgas, or describing the devotion

---

70   For a list of royal burials at Las Huelgas, see Arco y Garay, 95–6. See also Gómez Bárcena, "El Panteón Real," 51–72.
71   MAN 1962/73/3, f. 21.
72   MAN 1962/73/3, f. 21v.
73   *et aliorum benefactorum ordinis nostri*: MAN 1962/73/3, f. 21v.
74   Beatriz's body would be removed from Las Huelgas and taken to join Fernando in Seville in 1279. Arco y Garay, 106–10.
75   Beatriz (MAN 1962/73/3, f. 177); Berenguela (MAN 1962/73/3, f. 176v).

of the deceased to the propagation of the Christian faith more broadly. Fernando alone is lauded as "most devout," indicating at an early stage the development outside of the Alfonsine scriptorium of the proto-cult of Fernando III.[76] Indeed, as we shall see, his religiosity seems to feature more prominently in the Las Huelgas necrology than his military accomplishments.

Even though the liturgical purpose of the necrologies was to serve as a vehicle for prayer for the individual in the afterlife, nonetheless the texts often contained more earthly references. The most common was to exalt the military role of the monarch. The Las Huelgas manuscript describes the military victories of two kings: Alfonso VIII and Sancho IV.[77] It is very curious that Fernando III's military exploits are not given similar treatment, especially given the fact that it was for his deeds of conquest that Fernando III was eulogized elsewhere.[78] However, this fact becomes less odd when it is remembered that Fernando III was not buried in Las Huelgas. The military conquests of Alfonso VIII and Sancho IV could be remembered by virtue of the fact that listing of them did not detract from the status of the monastery. However, to mention Fernando's conquests would highlight his burial in Seville. Consequently, the omission of the territorial recovery of Fernando III stands in stark contrast to the standard eulogy of the king and represents a local interest to remember its founder, whose family and first wife were buried there without also recognizing the inconvenient fact that Alfonso X ultimately had his father buried elsewhere.

While the military conquests of Fernando are not mentioned in the Las Huelgas text, there are several mentions of Fernando and his military conquests in other necrological records produced beyond the scriptorium of Las Huelgas.[79] Two obituaries can be found in the cathedral archive of Calahorra,

---

76   *Obiit domnus ferdinandus devotissimus rex castelle y legionis*: MAN 1962/73/3, f. 91v.
77   Alfonso VIII: *Obiit illustrissimus Allefonsus rex Castelle, hedificator monasterii Sancte Marie Regalis, qui potentissimum regem marrochitanum campestri prelio superavit in loco qui dicitur Las nava de Tolosa.* MAN 1962/73/3, f. 160. Sancho IV: *Obiit triumphator magnificus, belliger invictus illustrissimus, memoria dingus, deo devotus, Rex Sancius, cuius marte sensit Africa, cuius levitatem desideravit Gallia, cuius genus astiny Portugaliam, cuius zelus comprehensit Aragoniam, nobilis Ilifonsi regis Castelle et Legionis filius.* MAN 1962/73/3, f. 71v.
78   This is especially true given the composition date of c. 1271–1276 and, as Catalunya suggests, its connection to the Alfonsine scriptorium, Catalunya, "The Royal Customary," 155. For a eulogy of Fernando III, see *PCG*, 773. See also the *planto* of the Galician Pero da Ponte, which proclaims how Fernando "conquered from sea to sea (*conquis de mar a mar*)." *Fernando III*, I: 80.
79   *Obiit domnus ferdinandus devotissimus rex castelle y legionis*: MAN 1962/73/3, f. 91v.

in manuscripts dating from the thirteenth and fifteen centuries.[80] Curiously, references to the conquest of Seville, found in the earlier of the two texts, disappears from the later manuscript, although this can largely be attributed to the fluidity of genre between the two obituaries, as the thirteenth-century copy also embodied details characteristic of a chronicle.[81] The more salient trend among the records of military conquest in the entries concerning Fernando III is an increased role that military conquest played in liturgical remembrance. In an obituary produced in the cathedral of León, there is a record of the creation of a mass by Alfonso X in memory of his parents, commemorating the conquest of Córdoba, Jaén, and Seville.[82] Alfonso X played a pivotal role in the construction of the image of his father and thus the corresponding notices of these conquests found in the description of Alfonso's donation for this mass mirror this royal policy encoded into the liturgical text. An obituary entry within the thirteenth-century *Libro de Regla* for the cathedral of Oviedo also mentions the conquest of Córdoba, Seville, Jaén and Murcia.[83] Interestingly though, it is not simply a record of conquest but rather includes the pious comment that the lands were restored to the Christian faith. Moreover, this particular entry is dated to the 1290s and thus provides early evidence for the more widespread devotion being attached to Fernando III.[84] The mid fourteenth-century obituary from Burgos, provides a similar entry that mentions the work accomplished on behalf of Christianity, although combining all of Fernando's conquered territories within a reference to "all of Andalusia."[85] A thirteenth-century obituary from Toledo does not explicitly mention the conquests of Fernando III, but instead provides evidence of his military victories by adding the same reference to his conquest of "all of Andalusia" among his royal titles.[86] Consequently, while the markers of description generally focus on more devout superlatives, over the centuries, military markers crept into the descriptions of Fernando III. With the growing status of his cult, perhaps these terms

---

80 Rodríguez de Lama, "Cronica-obituario de Calahorra"; Ubieto Arteta, *Un obituario calahorrano*.
81 *Obiit Ferdinandus Rex Castelle qui cepit Siviliam*: Rodríguez de Lama, "Cronica-obituario de Calahorra," 98; *Obiit domnus Ferrandus, illustrissimus rex Castelle*: Ubieto Arteta, *Un obituario calahorrano*, 48.
82 Herrero Jiménez, *Colección*, 371.
83 *Ipso die obiit illustrissimus rex Fernandus Castelle, Legionis et Toleti, per quem dominus Cordubam, Sibiliam et Iahen, Murciam christiane fidei subiugavit*: Rodríguez Villar, *Libro de Regla*, 274.
84 Ibid.
85 *Obiit inclitus rex Fernandus, qui totam Andaluziam divino cultui subiugavit*: Serna Serna, *Los obituarios*, 430.
86 *toti andalucia*: BCT 39–25, f. 36v.

marked him out as different from the monarchs recorded in the obituaries and provided further proof of his pious recovery of territory, one of the principle reasons for his growing saintly status.

An examination of necrologies and obituaries provides a new source of evidence for understanding how ecclesiastical hierarchies envisioned a deceased monarch. They display both a communal remembrance of the individual in question, and a conscious choice about who was to be remembered, reflecting the relative importance that the community granted them as well as the values of that community. Study of necrological texts also represents a counter narrative to the more normative projection of the eulogies contained within chronicles. Death was not simply a matter of burial and negotiation of space for the individual, but also the negotiation of memory within a larger pattern of liturgy that conditioned everyday life in the Middle Ages.

3   Conclusion

Although there are numerous other examples, the preceding pages have discussed two of the liturgical forms that played a role in the construction of the image of the monarch in medieval Iberia. From missals, we have looked at the votive mass in favor of the king, known as the *Missa pro rege*. From necrologies and obituaries, we have examined the marginal annotations that recognize and commemorate individual patrons. In both of these liturgical forms, a vision of kingship arises from negotiations between the Church of Castile-León and royal court. Whereas the Castilian monarch normally took the lead in the propagation of the royal image at the moment of accession, in these liturgies we see the reversal, with the clergy taking the lead in negotiating the royal image. Through reading the often-ignored liturgical evidence, we can recover a definition of kingship that resonates within a broader cultural context, one that extends beyond court chroniclers and scholastic treatises.

These forms of liturgical representation were not simply a means to impose an image of kingship from the top down. By being involved in the spiritual welfare of the king, the public – that is, the supplicants at the mass – were themselves participating in the work of the kingdom and helping to shape the future of the realm through prayer for the king. Active participation in the liturgy served the dual purposes of supporting the work of the kingdom in the legitimization of the monarch and the demonstration of loyalty by the populace, through a liturgical lineage encoded with imperial aspirations. And above all, it made the figure of the king ubiquitous throughout the realm, even if he himself was not always capable of being present.

Works Cited

Primary Sources
Unpublished

Archivo Catedralico de Burgos, Burgos (AC Burgos)
- ms. 23

Archivo Catedralico Burgo de Osma, Burgo de Osma (AC Burgo de Osma)
- cod. 165

Chicago, Newberry Library, Case Vault
- ms. 4
- ms. 69

Archivo Catedralico León, León (AC León)
- ms. 27

San Isidro de León, León
- codex 5

Biblioteca Nacional de Portugal, Codices Alcobacence, Lisbon
- cod. 252
- cod. 255

Biblioteca Nacional de España, Madrid (BNE)
- ms. 20324
- ms. Vitr 20-8

Escorial, Madrid
- ms. I.II.8

Museo Arqueológico Nacional, Madrid (MAN)
- 1962/73/3

Biblioteca Capitular de Toledo, Toledo (BCT)
- ms. 35-18
- ms. 37-18
- ms. 37-27
- ms. 39-25

Archivo Catedralico de Tortosa, Tortosa (AC Tortosa)
- codex 13

Archivo Catedralico de Segovia, Segovia (AC Segovia)
- ms. 356

Archivo Catedralico de Seville, Seville (AC Seville)
- ms. Vitr BB 149-11

Published

Angles, Higinio. *El Códex Musical de las Huelgas*. Barcelona: Institut d'Estudis Catalans, 1931.

Aquinas, Thomas. *De regno ad regem Cypri (On Kingship to the King of Cyprus)*. Trans. Gerald Phelan. Toronto: Pontifical Institute, 1949.

Charlo Brea, Luis, ed. *Chronica latina regum Castellae*. In *Chronica Hispana Saeculi XIII*, ed. Luis Charlo Brea, Juan Estévez Sola and Rocío Carande Herrero. Vol. 73 of *Corpus Christianorum: Continuatio medievalis*, 7–118. Turnhout: Brepols, 1997.

Gerald of Wales. "De instructione principis." In *Giraldi Cambrensis opera*, ed. G.F. Warer, 8 vols. Cambridge: Cambridge University Press, 1891.

González, Julio, ed. *Reinado y diplomas de Fernando III*, 3 vols. Córdoba: Monte de Piedad y Caja de Ahorros de Córdoba, 1980–1986.

Herrero Jiménez, Mauricio. *Colección documental del archivo de la catedral de León: obituarios medievales*. León: Centro de Estudios e Investigación "San Isidoro," 1994.

Honorius III. *Honorii iii ... opera omnia quae exstant*. Medii ævi bibl. patristica ser. 1. Vol. 2. Paris: Bibliothèque Ecclésiastique, 1879.

Janini, José. *Liber ordinum episcopal: cod. Silos Arch. Monástico 4*. Silos: Abadía de Silos, 1991.

Jiménez de Rada, Rodrigo. *Historia de rebus Hispanie, sive Historia Gothica*. Ed. Juan Fernández Valverde. Vol. 72 of *Corpus Christianorum: Continuatio mediaeualis*. Turnhout: Brepols, 1987.

Lucas of Tuy. *Chronicon mundi*. Ed. Emma Falque Rey. Vol. 74 of *Corpus Christianorum: Continuatio mediaeualis*. Turnhout: Brepols, 2003.

Moeller, Edmond and Jean-Marie Clément, eds. *Corpus Orationum*. 14 vols. *Corpus Christianorum series latina* 160. Turnhout: Brepols, 1992.

Primera crónica general de España. Ed. Ramón Menéndez Pidal et al. Madrid: Gredos, 1955.

Ramon Revilla, "Un códice latino de Burgos," *Anuario del Cuerpo facultativo de Archiveros, Bibliotecarios y Arqueólogos* 1 (1934): 211–221.

Rodríguez de Lama, Ildefonso. "Crónica-obituario de Calahorra." *Berceo* 97 (1979): 87–120.

Rodríguez Villar, Víctor Manuel. *Libro de Regla del Cabildo (Kalendas I): estudio y edición del manuscrito numero 43 de la Catedral de Oviedo*. Oviedo: Real Instituto de Estudios Asturianos, 2001.

Serna Serna, Sonia. *Los obituarios de la Catedral de Burgos*. León: Centro de Estudios e Investigación "San Isidoro," 2008.

Ubieto Arteta, Agustin. *Un obituario calahorrano del siglo XV*. Logroño: Diputación Provincial, 1976.

Secondary Sources

Alonso Álvarez, Raquel. "La memoria de Alfonso VIIII de Castilla en Las Huelgas de Burgos: arquitectura y liturgia funeraria." In *1212: un año, un reinado, un tiempo de despegue*, ed. Esther López Ojeda, 349–376. Logroño: Instituto de Estudios Riojanos, 2013.

Arco y Garay, Ricardo del. *Sepulcros de la casa real de Castilla.* Madrid: CSIC, 1954.

Arias Guillén, Fernando. "Algun fecho señalado que sea a honra del rey: royal privileges and the construction of royal memory in Castile (c. 1158–1350)." *Journal of Medieval Iberian Studies* 11, no. 1 (2019): 40–58.

Aurell, Jaume. "The Self-Coronations of Iberian Kings: A Crooked Line." *Imago Temporis, Medium Aevum* 8 (2014): 151–175.

Bachrach, David. *Warfare in Tenth-Century Germany.* New York: Boydell & Brewer, 2014.

Backmund, Norbert. "La orden premonstratense en España." *Hispania Sacra* 35 (1983): 57–85.

Benito-Vessels, Carmen. *Lenguaje y valor en la literatura medieval española.* Newark: Juan de la Cuesta – Hispanic Monographs, 2014.

Binski, Paul. *Medieval Death: Ritual and Representation.* Ithaca: Cornell University Press, 1996.

Catalunya, David. "The Customary of the Royal Convent of Las Huelgas of Burgos: Female Liturgy, Female Scribes." *Medievalia* 20, no. 1 (2017): 91–160.

Costa Gomes, Rita. "Invoking the name of the king: context and meaning in late medieval Portugal." In *Political Theology in Medieval and Early Modern Europe: Discourses, Rites and Representations*, ed. Monserrat Herrero, Jaume Aurell, and Angela C. Miceli Stout, 229–244. Turnhout: Brepols, 2017.

Ecker, Heather. "How to Administer a Conquered City in al-Andalus: Mosques, Parish Churches and Parishes." In *Under the Influence: Questioning the Comparative in Medieval Castile*, ed. Cynthia Robinson and Leyla Rouhi, 45–66. Leiden: Brill, 2005.

Fita, Fidel. "Los premonstratenses en Ciudad Rodrigo: datos inéditos." *BRAH* 62 (1913): 468–480.

Gaposchkin, Cecilia. "Talking about Kingship when Preaching about Saint Louis." In *Preaching and Political Society*, ed. Franco Morenzoni, 135–172. Turnhout: Brepols, 2013.

Garipzanov, Ildar. *The Symbolic Language of Authority in the Carolingian World (c. 751–877).* Leiden: Brill, 2008.

Garrison, Mary. "The Missa pro principe in the Bobbio Missal." In *Bobbio Missal: Liturgy and Religious Culture in Merovingian Gaul*, ed. Yitzhak Hen and Rob Meens, 187–205. Cambridge: Cambridge University Press, 2009.

Genicot, Léopold. *Typologie des sources du Moyen Age Occidental.* Turnhout: Brepols, 1972.

Gómez Bárcena, María Jesús. "El Panteón Real de las Huelgas de Burgos." In *Vestiduras Ricas: el Monasterio de las Huelgas y su época, 1170–1340*, 51–72. Madrid: Patrimonio Nacional, 2005.

Gonzalvéz Ruiz, Ramón. *Hombres y libros de Toledo (1086–1300).* Madrid: Fundación Ramón Areces, 1997.

Grassotti, Hilda. *Las instituciones feudo-vasalláticas en León y Castilla*, 2 vols. Spoleto: Centro italiano di studi sull'alto Medioevo, 1969.

Hen, Yitzhak. *The Royal Patronage of Liturgy in Frankish Gaul: to the Death of Charles the Bald, 877*. Woodbridge: Boydell & Brewer, 2001.

Henriet, Patrick. "Cluny and Spain before Alfonso VI: remarks and propositions." *Journal of Medieval Iberian Studies* 9, no. 2 (2017): 206–219.

Hernández, Francisco J. "Los que parecían árabes." *Revista de Occidente* 224 (2000): 51–65.

Holt, Edward L. "*In eo tempore*: The Circulation of News and Reputation in the Charters of Fernando III." *Bulletin for Spanish and Portuguese Historical Studies* 42, no. 1 (2017): 3–22. doi: https://doi.org/10.26431/0739-182X.1253.

Jackson, Richard. *Vive le roi! A History of the French Coronation from Charles V to Charles X*. Chapel Hill: University of North Carolina Press, 1984.

Janini, José. *Manuscritos litúrgicos de las bibliotecas de España*. 2 vols. Burgos: Ediciones Aldecoa, 1977–1980.

Janini, José. "Notas sobre libros litúrgicos hispánicos." *Hispania Sacra* 14, no. 27 (1961): 145–154.

Janini, José and José Serrano. *Manuscritos litúrgicos de la Biblioteca Nacional*. Madrid: Dirección General de Archivos y Bibliotecas, 1969.

Kantorowicz, Ernst. *Laudes Regiae: A Study in Liturgical Acclamations and Mediaeval Ruler Worship*. Berkeley: University of California Press, 1946.

Koziol, Geoffrey. *Begging Pardon and Favor: Ritual and Political Order in Early Medieval France*. Ithaca: Cornell University Press, 1992.

Krynen, Jacques. *L'Empire du roi: idées et croyances politiques en France XIIIe–XVe siecle*. Paris: Gallimard, 1993.

Laffón Álvarez, Luisa. "Arenga Hispana: una aproximación a los preámbulos documentales de la edad media." *Historia. Instituciones. Documentos* 16 (1989): 133–232.

Linehan, Peter. "Frontier Kingship: Castile, 1250–1350." In *La Royauté Sacrée Dans Le Monde Chrétien Colloque De Royaumont, Mars 1989*, ed. Alain Boureau and Claudio Sergio Ingerflom, 71–79. Paris: Éd. de l'École des Hautes études en sciences sociales, 1992.

Linehan, Peter. *History and the Historians of Medieval Spain*. Oxford: Clarendon Press, 1993.

Maravall, José Antonio. *Estudios de historia del pensamiento Español*. Madrid: Ediciones Cultura Hispánica, 1967.

McCormick, Michael. *Eternal Victory: Triumphal Rulership in Late Antiquity, Byzantium and the Early Medieval West*. Cambridge: Cambridge University Press, 1999.

Montenegro Valentín, Julia. "Algunas consideraciones sobre los orígenes del merino mayor." *Anuario de historia del derecho español* 67 (1997): 1093–1108.

Nickson, Tom. "Remembering Fernando: Multi-lingual inscriptions in medieval Iberia." In *Viewing Inscriptions in the Late Antique and Medieval World*, ed. Antony Eastmond, 170–186. Cambridge: Cambridge University Press, 2015.

Nieto Soria, José Manuel. *Fundamentos ideológicos del poder real en Castilla (siglos XIII–XVI)*. Madrid: EUDEMA, 1988.

Nieto Soria, José Manuel. "La monarquía fundacional de Fernando III." In *Fernando III y su tiempo (1201–1252): VIII Congreso de Estudios Medievales*, 31–66. León: Fundación Sánchez Albornoz, 2003.

Ostos Salcedo, Pilar. "La cancillería de Fernando III, rey de Castilla (1217–1230): una aproximación." *Archivo hispalense* 77, no. 234–236 (1994): 59–70.

Ostos Salcedo, Pilar and María Luisa Pardo Rodríguez. "Signo y símbolo en privilegio rodado." In *Sevilla, ciudad de privilegios: escritura y poder a través del privilegio rodado*, ed. Mercedes Borrero Fernández, et al., 15–47. Seville: Universidad de Sevilla, 1995.

Pick, Lucy. *Conflict and Coexistence: Archbishop Rodrigo and the Muslims and Jews of Medieval Spain*. Ann Arbor: University of Michigan, 2004.

Reilly, Bernard. *Santiago, Saint-Denis and Saint Peter: The Reception of Roman Liturgy in León-Castile in 1080*. New York: Fordham University Press, 1985.

Rodríguez López, Amancio. *El Real Monasterio de las Huelgas de Burgos y el Hospital de Rey*. Burgos: Centro Católica, 1907.

Rubio Sadia, Juan Pablo. *Las órdenes religiosas y la introducción del Rito Romano en la Iglesia de Toledo: una aportación desde de las fuentes litúrgicas*. Toledo: Instituto Teológico San Ildefonso, 2004.

Ruiz, Teófilo. "Unsacred Monarchy: The Kings of Castile in the Late Middle Ages." In *Rites of Power: Symbolism, Ritual, and Politics since the Middle Ages*, ed. Sean Wilentz, 109–144. Philadelphia: University of Pennsylvania Press, 1985.

Sanz Fuentes, María Josefa. "Cancillería y cultura: los preámbulos en la documentación de Alfonso VIII." In *II Curso de Cultura Medieval: Aguilar de Campóo, 1–6 octubre, 1990, Seminario: Alfonso VIII y su época*, ed. Jaime Nuño González, 387–392. Madrid: Centro de Estudios del Roma, 1992.

Serrano Coll, Marta. "Art as a Means of Legitimization in the Kingdom of Aragon: Coronation Problems and Their Artistic Echos during the Reigns of James I and Peter IV." *IKON* 5 (2012): 161–172.

Sirantoine, Hélène. "La cancillería regia en época de Fernando III: ideología, discurso, y práctica." In *Fernando III: tiempo de cruzada*, ed. Carlos de Ayala Martínez and Martín Ríos Saloma, 175–203, Madrid: Sílex, 2012.

Sirantoine, Hélène. "La guerra contra los musulmanes en los diplomas castellanoleoneses (siglo XI-1126)." In *Orígenes y desarrollo de la Guerra Santa en la Península Ibérica: palabras e imágenes para una legitimación (siglos X–XIV)*, ed. Carlos de Ayala

Martínez, Patrick Henriet and J. Santiago Palacios Ontalva, 51–65. Madrid: Casa de Velázquez, 2016.

Tellenbach, Gerd. *Römischer und christlicher Reichsgedanke in der Liturgie des frühen Mittelalters.* Heidelberg: C. Winter, 1934.

Valdés Fernández, Manuel. "Reyes y obispos en las ceremonias de coronación real en el reino de León y en la corona de Castilla y León." In *Reyes y prelados: la creación artística en los reinos de León y Castilla (1050–1500)*, ed. Dolores Teijeira, Victoria Herráez and Concepción Cosmen, 17–44. Madrid: Sílex, 2014.

Walker, Rose. *Views of Transition: Liturgy and Illumination in Medieval Spain.* London: The British Library, 1998.

Wallace-Hadrill, J.M. "The *Via Regia* of the Carolingian Age." In *Trends in Medieval Political Thought*, ed. Beryl Smalley, 22–41. Oxford: Blackwell, 1965.

CHAPTER 7

"At the Command of the Infantas": Royal Women at Las Huelgas in the Thirteenth Century

Janna Bianchini

Fifteen years ago, Rose Walker offered the intriguing argument that the foundation of a royal Cistercian abbey at Las Huelgas in Burgos had been inspired by the royally founded and patronized monastery (later canonry) at San Isidoro in the city of León. She pointed out that Las Huelgas and San Isidoro were both located in the capitals of their respective kingdoms; they both served as dynastic pantheons for the royal family; and, perhaps most importantly, they were both under the lordship of royal women.[1] The double house of SS. Pelayo and Isidoro had been a key part of the so-called Infantazgo, an amorphous group of royal properties held by sisters and daughters of the reigning monarch.[2] Like many other Infantazgo properties, San Isidoro was a monastic foundation; like Las Huelgas, too, it had been a feminine institution, at least until 1148, when its Benedictine nuns were moved to Santa María de Carbajal and replaced by Augustinian canons. San Isidoro had been part of the dominion of a succession of royal women, or infantas – most famously, the daughters of Fernando I of León-Castile, Urraca Fernández (c. 1033–c. 1103) and Elvira Fernández (c. 1038–1101), and the daughter of Queen Urraca of León-Castile, Sancha Raimúndez (c. 1095–1159). Similarly, not long after its foundation, Las Huelgas began receiving royal daughters as nuns, and some of these infantas subsequently emerged in the authoritative role of "Lady of Las Huelgas."[3]

Walker argued that the foundation of Las Huelgas, as a conscious imitation or continuation of the legacy of SS. Pelayo and Isidoro, was part of a project of

---

1 Walker, "Leonor of England."
2 There is a substantial and growing body of scholarship on the Infantazgo. Most significantly, see Martin, "Fuentes de potestad"; idem, "Hacia una clarificación del infantazgo"; idem, *Queen as King*; Pick, *Her Father's Daughter*; Bianchini, "The Infantazgo in the Reign of Alfonso VIII"; Cavero, "Sancha Raimúndez"; Henriet, "Infantes, *Infantaticum*"; idem, "Deo votas"; Cayrol Bernardo, "On *Infantas, Domnae,* and *Deo Votae*"; idem, "El monasterio de San Pelayo de Oviedo"; Martin, "Le testament d'Elvire"; Reglero de la Fuente, "*Omnia totius regni sui monasteria*"; Viñayo González, "Reinas e Infantas de León."
3 Gayoso, "The Lady of Las Huelgas."

dynastic identity.[4] The king and queen who founded Las Huelgas were among the earliest rulers of the independent kingdom of Castile.[5] Castile had been a county, albeit a largely autonomous one, until its Count Fernando married the inheriting queen Sancha of León in circa 1037 and united the realms as Fernando I of León-Castile.[6] Upon his death, Fernando partitioned his realm among his sons and made his eldest, Sancho II (r. 1065–1072), king of an independent Castile. But within seven years, Sancho II had reunified his parents' kingdom, at the expense of his two younger brothers. When Sancho II died at the siege of Zamora in 1072, the reunified realm was claimed in its entirety by one of those brothers, now Alfonso VI of León-Castile (r. 1065–1109). Thereafter León-Castile remained a single kingdom for three generations, until King Alfonso VII partitioned it between *his* two sons in 1157. The new king of Castile, Sancho III, reigned only a year before dying, leaving Castile to his infant son, now Alfonso VIII of Castile (r. 1158–1214).

At his accession, then, Alfonso VIII was only the third monarch to bear the title "king of Castile," rather than "king of León and Castile." Moreover, his two predecessors had only reigned for a total of eight years, with an eighty-five-year interval between them. It was largely left to Alfonso VIII, in the course of his own fifty-six-year reign, to forge an identity for Castile as an independent kingdom, distinct from the older kingdom of León but still heir to its ancient legacies. Part of this project was the foundation of Las Huelgas and its deliberate association with the old Leonese-Castilian Infantazgo.[7]

While acknowledging the value of Walker's insight, Carlos Reglero de la Fuente has raised necessary cautions about a too-facile connection between the royal women of Las Huelgas and the *dominae* of the Infantazgo.[8] He observes, for example, that the royal women associated with Las Huelgas were nuns, while the *dominae* of the Infantazgo were not. He also points out the nearly century-long lapse between the death of Sancha Raimúndez, the last twelfth-century ruler of the Infantazgo, and the emergence of the "Lady of Las Huelgas" with Berenguela Fernández in the thirteenth. Finally, he notes that while the Leonese-Castilian Infantazgo included many different monastic foundations, the "Lady of Las Huelgas" had sway over only one.[9] However, I believe these discrepancies can be explained if we think of Las Huelgas as a reincarnation of the Infantazgo rather than a continuation of it. In this chapter I

---

4 Walker, "Leonor of England," 367–8.
5 Shadis, *Berenguela of Castile*, 39–40.
6 Pick, *Her Father's Daughter*, 76–7.
7 Walker, "Leonor of England," 368.
8 Reglero de la Fuente, "Las 'señoras' de las Huelgas de Burgos," 46–8.
9 Reglero de la Fuente, "Las 'señoras' de las Huelgas de Burgos," 46–8.

will argue that Alfonso VIII did in fact intend Las Huelgas to serve as a gendered link to the dynastic legacy of León-Castile. But the establishment of infantas as *dominae* of the monastery happened primarily in the reign of Fernando III of Castile and his mother Berenguela. Their promotion of Las Huelgas as a version of the Infantazgo, *mutatis mutandis*, signifies the enduring value of royal women's sanctity in thirteenth-century Castile and León.

1 Alfonso VIII and Castilian Dynastic Legitimacy

Alfonso VIII and his wife, Leonor of England, founded Las Huelgas in 1187.[10] Whether or not it was intended from the beginning to be a royal burial site, it *was* intended to be a royal residence as well as a monastery.[11] The monarchs built a palace beside the convent – an echo of practice in Leonese royal monasteries, including in the Infantazgo from its earliest origins, beginning with San Salvador de Palat del Rey and continuing up through SS. Pelayo and Isidoro de León.[12]

Alfonso and Leonor also endowed Las Huelgas with lands that belonged to the Castilian territories of the Infantazgo. The Castilian Infantazgo had previously been centered on two monasteries, SS. Cosmas y Damián de Covarrubias and San Salvador de Oña.[13] Without transferring either community to Las Huelgas's spiritual or temporal authority, the monarchs did concede some properties formerly possessed by Covarrubias (in Estépar and Belbimbre) and Oña (in San Felices) to their new foundation.[14] Walker suggests that these concessions may have been symbolic, representing a translation of the Infantazgo tradition into a novel, specifically Castilian form.[15]

It should be noted that over a decade earlier, in 1175, Alfonso VIII had given Covarrubias, "with all the rights and heritable properties that belong or once belonged to that monastery," to the cathedral of Toledo. He acted to expiate an unspecified "injury" and "violation" that he had committed against the cathedral.[16] If he had been considering the project of reviving the Castilian Infantazgo, this was perhaps ill-advised; the only Infantazgo properties that Castile

---

10 Shadis, *Berenguela of Castile*, 39–40.
11 Walker, "Leonor of England," 366–7.
12 Walker, "Leonor of England," 357, 361; Martin, "Sobre mujeres y tumbas," 9.
13 García Calles, *Doña Sancha*, 111–2; Henriet, "*Deo votas*," 192–3.
14 Lizoain Garrido, *Las Huelgas de Burgos (1116–1230)*, no. 11. Cayrol Bernardo, "On *Infantas, Domnae*, and *Deo Votae*," 138; Baury, *Les religieuses de Castille*, 46.
15 Walker, "Leonor of England," 361.
16 Serrano, *Cartulario del Infantado de Covarrubias*, no. 24.

could reasonably claim were at Covarrubias, Oña, and in the Tierra de Campos, the borderland between Castile and León, which in 1175 was securely in the grip of Fernando II of León.[17] However, the choice of gift may have lain with the archbishop and cathedral chapter of Toledo, as the offended parties. And having surrendered the crown's rights to Covarrubias, which lies less than 35 km from Burgos, the monarchs may have found it all the more desirable to build a new monastery for their purposes in that city.

In 1175 Alfonso VIII, however well supplied with Infantazgo lands he might be, nevertheless faced a real dearth of royal women to inhabit them. He had no sisters, and he and Leonor had not yet had children.[18] His only surviving and legitimately-born aunts were the queens of Navarre and Aragón-Cataluña, and Infantazgo lands were not traditionally granted to married women living outside the kingdom.[19] Even if he had been inclined to bestow Infantazgo property on a Leonese infanta, rather than a Castilian one, he could not have found one: his uncle, Fernando II of León, had no daughters. Instead, Alfonso VIII had granted certain Infantazgo-linked lands to his wife, Leonor, as part of her arras, or dower.[20] But Leonor was a queen-consort, not a Castilian infanta. Any serious attempt to revive the Infantazgo would have to wait until Alfonso VIII had daughters of his own.

By the time Las Huelgas was founded, in 1187, Alfonso VIII had two, Berenguela and Urraca. They acted jointly with their father and mother to issue the

---

17 Alfonso VIII reclaimed the Infantazgo de Campos from Fernando II in 1181: *Alfonso VIII*, II: no. 363.
18 Leonor was still only about fourteen.
19 We know, for example, that infantas who held Infantazgo properties while young ceased to control them once they had married abroad. This is the case for Elvira Alfonso II (c. 1100–1135), a daughter of King Alfonso VI, who held the monastery of San Pelayo de León as a girl. After marrying King Roger II of Sicily in 1117, she no longer appears in possession of Leonese-Castilian properties. See Martin, "Fuentes de potestad," 120; Fernández Catón, *Colección documental del archivo de la Catedral de León*, V: nos. 1349, 1351. Similarly, King Alfonso VII's daughter Urraca Alfonso, though entrusted in childhood to his powerful sister Sancha Raimúndez, received vast Infantazgo lands only after she returned to León-Castile as a widow, following the death of her husband, King García Ramírez of Navarre. See Fernández Conde, "La reina Urraca."

The only (and glaring) exception to this trend would seem to be another daughter of Alfonso VII, Sancha Alfonso II. In 1165, while she was married to King Sancho VI of Navarre, her brother Fernando II of León purportedly gave her "all the Infantazgo in my entire kingdom": Henriet, "*Deo votas*," 202–3. I suspect strongly, however, that this document is interpolated or forged, based both on its internal characteristics and on the circumstances under which the earliest extant copy was created. Bianchini, "The Infantazgo in the Reign of Alfonso VIII," 60–4, 67.

20 Rodríguez López, "Dotes y arras," 274–6; Shadis, *Berenguela of Castile*, 25–31.

diploma that endowed the monastery. Berenguela was about seven years old, Urraca only about one. But between them had come another brother and sister, Sancho and Sancha. Although neither of these two had survived early childhood, the four births suggested that the couple were likely to produce more children. With two living infantas and a reasonable hope of a male heir in the future, Alfonso VIII and Leonor were in a position to start building a dominion that one of their daughters might eventually rule. Indeed, this may have been part of the reason for founding Las Huelgas in 1187, and not earlier.

Lucy K. Pick has explained the spiritual and cultural benefits that accrued to the royal family from consecrating its daughters to God and establishing them within the kingdom.[21] For Alfonso VIII, such benefits could only be enhanced by the link they provided between his young kingdom and the dynastic traditions of the Leonese crown.[22] His desire to highlight Castile's status as a continuation, not merely a cadet branch, of the imperial Leonese dynasty is evident even in the names of his children. All of them harkened back either to the pre-partition monarchy, or to Queen Leonor's natal family, the Plantagenets, whose prominence on the Latin European stage was its own proof of Castile's prestige. The eldest, Berenguela, was named for Berenguela of Barcelona, the first wife of Alfonso VII of León-Castile, and Alfonso VIII's paternal grandmother. Sancho, the infante who died in early childhood, was named both for Alfonso VIII's own father and for Sancho II, the first king of an independent Castile. Sancha, who also died young, shared her name with several Leonese-Castilian infantas, but owed it ultimately to Queen Sancha of León, whose marriage to Fernando I of Castile had created the crown of León-Castile. Urraca, the next daughter, received a dynastic name that recalled not only Queen Urraca of León-Castile (r. 1109–1126), who had inherited the crown from her father, but also one of the most powerful *dominae* of the Infantazgo, Urraca Fernández, daughter of Fernando I. Urraca's younger sister Blanca (Blanche) was the namesake of Alfonso VIII's own mother, Blanca of Navarre; Blanca had been descended from Sancho III *el Mayor* of Pamplona, who ruled most of Christian Iberia in the early eleventh century. Alfonso VIII's first surviving son, Fernando, was named not for the king's Leonese uncle and rival but for Fernando I of León-Castile. The next two daughters were named Mafalda and Leonor – the first in honor of her maternal great-grandmother, Empress Matilda of England, and the second for both her mother and her maternal grandmother, Eleanor of Aquitaine. The youngest daughter was Constanza, a

---

21 Pick, *Her Father's Daughter*.
22 On the "great symbolic value" of infantas' properties to royal legitimation in both Castile and León, see Rodríguez López, "Stratégies matrimoniales," 176–7.

name brought into the dynasty by Constance of Burgundy, wife of Alfonso VI of León-Castile, and carried forward by a daughter of Alfonso VII. The youngest son, born when Leonor of England was in her mid-forties, was Enrique, after his maternal grandfather, Henry II.[23] It is perhaps significant that none of their known children received the name Alfonso.[24] Although Alfonso was obviously a well-established dynastic name, contemporaries might have understood it as an allusion only to Alfonso VIII himself, rather than to his royal forebears as well. By contrast, his contemporaries Fernando II and Alfonso IX of León both had sons who shared their names.

It was, of course, traditional to give one's children dynastic names, particularly the names of one's own parents. Alfonso VIII and Leonor did this, but not in the typical sequence. A king would usually name his firstborn son after his father, which Alfonso VIII did; he might also name his firstborn daughter after either his mother or his wife's, which Alfonso VIII emphatically did not.[25] His mother's namesake, Blanca, was his fourth known daughter. Her elder sisters were Berenguela, Sancha, and Urraca – all names that carried more dynastic significance than Blanca's. Since the monarchs had no surviving son until after Blanca, their older daughters' names had to do the legitimating work that might otherwise be done through sons, and which Alfonso VIII evidently considered of the highest importance. Even when the couple did begin to use Plantagenet names for their children, they chose the name of Leonor's imperial grandmother first, and that of her mother second. Dynastic prestige took precedence over honoring immediate family.

The royal family frequented Burgos, and must often have resided at Las Huelgas. In 1197 the abbess sold property in Peñafiel to one of Leonor of England's officers, don Esteban. The queen herself witnessed the transaction, along with her oldest daughter, Berenguela, whom the document titles infanta and who therefore was not yet married.[26] Similarly, in 1207 an agreement between Las Huelgas and a married couple, Pedro Franco and doña Lambra,

---

23   On the dynastic significance of these names, see Shadis, "'Happier in Daughters than in Sons,'" 84–5.
24   The name could have been given to an unknown son who died in infancy, though there is no evidence for this. However, having given a name to a child who died – or even, in fact, to one who lived – did not exclude that name as an option for future children, as attested by Alfonso VIII's two aunts Sancha, born of the two marriages of Alfonso VII.
25   Fernando II and Alfonso IX of León both named their eldest sons after their fathers. Fernando II had no known daughters, but Alfonso IX named the daughters of his first marriage after his wife's parents, and the firstborn daughter of his second marriage after his wife's mother.
26   Lizoain Garrido, *Las Huelgas de Burgos (1116–1230)*, no. 43. She married Alfonso IX of León later that year.

was witnessed by Queen Leonor, Berenguela (who had returned to Castile following the dissolution of her marriage to the king of León), and Urraca, Berenguela's next-oldest sister, who was not yet married. Also present was Berenguela's elder son, Infante Fernando, then about six years old.[27]

Scholars have sometimes taken these documents to mean that the Castilian infantas generally lived at Las Huelgas.[28] If so, their interventions in the abbey's affairs were very rare. However, there is too little evidence to conclude that Las Huelgas was their permanent residence. They are visible at the royal court at least as often as they are at the abbey.[29]

At some point, Alfonso VIII's seventh daughter, Constanza Alfonso II (c. 1199–1243), does seem to have taken up permanent residence at Las Huelgas.[30] The thirteenth-century chronicler Lucas of Tuy, her contemporary, reports that Constanza, "taking up the habit of a nun, consecrated her virginity to the Lord."[31] He uses the same language, "taking up the habit of a nun," to describe the career of her niece, also named Constanza, who also is attested in other sources as having become a nun; it seems clear, therefore, that Constanza II did indeed enter religious life.[32] This cannot be taken for granted; traditionally, the *dominae* of the Leonese-Castilian Infantazgo had not been nuns.[33] Many of them were considered "dedicated to God" (*deo votae*), but they exercised secular power vigorously and were subject to no greater ecclesiastical authority than their lay relations. Others were not religiously consecrated; some infantas held Infantazgo properties prior to marriage, and some held them even *while* married.[34] For a royal *domina* to have taken vows was unprecedented; no Leonese-Castilian infanta had ever become a nun before.[35] But in Iberia as elsewhere, the thirteenth-century Church was less tolerant of women leading lives of piety outside the cloister than it had been one or two centuries earlier. Baury argues that by the 1220s, the Castilian crown had grown less vigorous in protecting the independence of its royal monasteries, especially Las Huelgas;

---

27 Lizoain Garrido, *Las Huelgas de Burgos (1116–1230)*, no. 92.
28 Shadis, "'Happier in Daughters than in Sons,'" 92–4. See also Gayoso, "The Lady of Las Huelgas," 102–3; Sánchez Ameijeiras, "Eventful Life," 493.
29 See, e.g., *DrH*, 277, 280.
30 Many infantas have the same name and patronym, so sequential numbers are essential to clarity. My numbering begins from the family of Fernando I and Queen Sancha. Constanza Alfonso I (c. 1138–1160) was a daughter of Alfonso VII, and a queen of France.
31 *monachilem suscipiens habitum uirginitatem suam Domino consecrauit*: *CM*, 321.
32 *habitum monachilem suscepit*: *CM*, 326.
33 Henriet, "*Deo votas*," 198.
34 Martin, "Fuentes de potestad," 100; Bianchini, "Daughters, wives, widows, lords," 14–21.
35 Pick, *Her Father's Daughter*, 62–5.

perhaps it was similarly less committed to the formal independence of such monasteries' *dominae*.[36]

Constanza II co-issued a privilege for the monastery of Santa María de Tórtoles with her parents and all of her siblings in Burgos in 1199, though she must have been little more than an infant.[37] But she is not named in the 1207 agreement between Las Huelgas, Pedro Franco, and doña Lambra that was witnessed by her mother, her sisters Berenguela and Urraca, and her nephew Fernando.[38] After that, she is absent from the documentation until 1222, when she appears only indirectly: several individuals sell property in El Embid and Buniel to an agent of Las Huelgas, who is identified as don Fernando, "the infantas' chaplain."[39] Not many infantas could have been at Las Huelgas in 1222. One of them was certainly Constanza II herself. Another was her niece Constanza Alfonso III.[40]

Constanza Alfonso III (c. 1199–1242) was a daughter of Queen Berenguela from her marriage to King Alfonso IX of León.[41] She came to Las Huelgas sometime after her mother returned to Castile in 1204, though she was almost certainly not intended for monastic life at first.[42] Even though her parents had been forced to separate on grounds of consanguinity, the Castilian and Leonese crowns were still laboring to preserve the peace agreement that had been founded on their marriage. Under the terms of that agreement, Constanza III's brother Fernando was to succeed their father as king of León; Constanza III herself, as one of Fernando's two living sisters, stood to become the means of a potentially valuable marriage alliance abroad for either her brother or her father.

According to Rodrigo Jiménez de Rada, the archbishop of Toledo, Constanza III took monastic vows; he says she "was a nun in the monastery of Burgos [Las Huelgas]."[43] However, there is no documentary trace of Constanza III at Las Huelgas (or elsewhere, for that matter) before the indirect reference to "the

---

36 Baury, *Les religieuses de Castille*, 175–6.
37 *Alfonso VIII*, III: no. 674.
38 Lizoain Garrido, *Las Huelgas de Burgos (1116–1230)*, no. 92.
39 *capellano de las infantes*: Lizoain Garrido, *Las Huelgas de Burgos (1116–1230)*, nos. 180–2.
40 It is also possible that "the infantas" included Constanza III's younger sister, Berenguela Alfonso, born c. 1204 and not yet married.
41 The two Constanzas were almost exactly the same age. However, since Constanza II belonged to an older generation of the royal family, my sequence follows that generational order.
42 It was quite common for elite girls to be educated in Iberian Cistercian abbeys even if they were ultimately destined for marriage: Baury, *Les religieuses de Castille*, 82.
43 *fuit in Burgensi monasterio monialis*: DrH, 247.

infantas" in the 1222 charters cited above. In other words, neither infanta was clearly associated with the royal monastery until well after Alfonso VIII's death. If Alfonso VIII had dreamed of creating a new Infantazgo with Las Huelgas at its heart, then its association with at least one infanta was indispensable. But the fact that neither Constanza's presence at Las Huelgas is recorded before 1222 raises interesting questions.

Was it, in fact, Alfonso VIII's intention to bestow one of his daughters there? Had he done so before he died? Constanza II would have been thirteen or fourteen years old at her father's death, old enough both to exercise authority at Las Huelgas and to take vows there. It may be suggestive that she is not said to have been present when Alfonso VIII died, though her sisters Berenguela and Leonor were;[44] all of Alfonso VIII's other daughters were either already deceased or married abroad at the time. Perhaps Constanza's obligations at Las Huelgas prevented her from traveling with or to the court as Berenguela and Leonor did.[45] But if Alfonso VIII and Leonor had indeed planned to establish Constanza II at Las Huelgas, it must be acknowledged that they were in no evident haste. Constanza II was their seventh daughter (though only the sixth to survive to adulthood). In the heyday of the Infantazgo, monarchs had been much readier to designate their daughters as its *dominae*. Fernando I and Queen Sancha had made both their daughters *dominae* of the Infantazgo. Their reigns lasted through most of the lifetime of their brother, Alfonso VI, who broke with tradition by marrying his several daughters off instead of assigning them to the Infantazgo.[46] After his sisters died, Alfonso VI's daughter Queen Urraca took over most of the Infantazgo. Urraca, in turn, had placed *her* only daughter, Sancha Raimúndez, in the care of her powerful aunts from an early age, apparently with an eye to making her the Infantazgo's next *domina*. As Urraca's only legitimately born daughter, Sancha Raimúndez might have made a significant marriage, but she remained the unwed and immensely powerful *domina* of the Infantazgo throughout her own brother's reign. To be sure, the pressure of creating alliances to strengthen their young kingdom must have been a compelling reason for Alfonso VIII and Leonor to marry their older daughters off. Still, the fact remains that Constanza II cannot be conclusively associated with Las Huelgas until long after her parents had died.

---

44 *DrH*, 280.
45 Fernando III's daughter Berenguela Fernández likewise failed to attend his deathbed, precisely – according to the *Estoria de España*, as edited by Menéndez Pidal – because she was a nun at Las Huelgas: *PCG*, 772.
46 Pick, *Her Father's Daughter*, 228–9.

It is also significant that the very first documentary indication of an infanta in power at Las Huelgas, in 1222, mentions more than one woman. Why had Constanza III also been established at Las Huelgas, and why then?

Constanza III represented a valuable potential marital alliance with the kingdom of León, so long as the king of León was her father or brother. However, in 1217, rather unexpectedly, her mother inherited the throne of Castile. Queen Berenguela made her son Fernando her co-ruler, and the much-tried peace between Castile and León broke down completely.[47] Berenguela's former husband, Alfonso IX of León, had previously agreed to make Fernando his own heir. But now that Fernando was the king of Castile, his inheritance in León would mean the reunification of the two kingdoms. Alfonso IX promptly disinherited Fernando in favor of the children of his earlier marriage.

Now that Fernando was no longer likely to be king of León, Constanza III could not become the means of a marriage alliance with that kingdom. She was, however, still the sister of the king of Castile, and thus a highly eligible bride. And since she and her younger sister Berenguela were both of marriageable age in 1217, and Fernando III would have no daughters of his own for over ten more years, ceding Constanza III to Las Huelgas was a fairly daring dynastic move.[48] But it was, again, in step with eleventh- and twelfth-century royal practice regarding the Infantazgo.

In 1222, both Constanzas were in their early twenties. Either of them could have made her profession at Las Huelgas well before this, but there is no clear evidence that they did so. Was the formal association between Las Huelgas and the Infantas Constanza the product not of Alfonso VIII's planning, but of Fernando III's? If so, then this expansion of Las Huelgas's ties to the royal family – and to its women in particular – should be seen all the more clearly in the light of dynastic competition with León, waged partly by reclaiming the Infantazgo tradition. And a great deal of the protagonism in that effort must be ascribed to Queen Berenguela; in addition to taking the principal role in determining the careers of her other female relatives, she had her own close ties to Las Huelgas and indeed chose to be buried there, alongside her siblings and her parents.[49]

---

47   See Bianchini, *The Queen's Hand*, 104–39.
48   Daring, but not entirely reckless; Queen Berenguela still had a daughter and a younger sister available for political matches, and indeed made one for each of them during the 1220s.
49   For the roles of Leonese-Castilian royal women in both determining marriage strategies and governing domains within their kingdoms, see Rodríguez López, "Stratégies matrimoniales."

Regardless of how Alfonso VIII had envisioned the link between Las Huelgas and the Infantazgo, it was not until the reign of Berenguela and Fernando III that that link was fully realized. Constanza III was almost certainly established at Las Huelgas after 1217; before that, her father would have had too keen an interest in her political destiny to allow her to enter a Castilian monastery. Indeed, the very fact that Constanza was a daughter of the king of León was a gesture of dominance by the Castilian crown: a Leonese infanta would step into the spiritual and temporal power of a religiously consecrated royal woman, but the charisma and authority she thus acquired would be at the service of the Castilian crown.[50] However once Alfonso IX broke off the troubled Leonese-Castilian alliance in 1217 and disinherited Fernando III, he lost whatever control he had had over Constanza III's career. She had no future in León as the mere half-sister of its next monarch; her destiny lay where her mother and brother ruled, in Castile.

It also stands to reason that Berenguela and Fernando III would make their bid to recreate the Infantazgo in the years between 1217 and 1222. Their reign was new and not entirely secure. A series of noble rebellions erupted during those five years; indeed, they were ongoing until precisely 1222.[51] Reclaiming the sacral status of the Infantazgo by installing not one but two royal women at Las Huelgas – women from different generations of the dynasty, at that – was a powerful statement of legitimation.

Once Constanza II and Constanza III do appear at Las Huelgas, they take on prominent roles. In 1227, doña Urraca Díaz and her son don Guillén Pérez donated property in Villarmentero de Campos "to the monastery of Las Huelgas de Burgos and to the infantas and to the abbess."[52] In July 1230, another charter records a sale of land to "you, the abbess of Santa María la Real [Las Huelgas] and to the whole convent and to the infantas."[53] These charters repeatedly acknowledge the infantas as both profoundly linked to Las Huelgas and yet distinct from its community of nuns – i.e., deliberately set apart from *el monesterio* or *todo el conuente*. In spite of their own religious vows, their royal status is what defines them here.

The infantas' distinctive status was not merely rhetorical; they held a separate kind of authority as well. In December 1230, a different charter describes a

---

50   Pick, *Her Father's Daughter*, 17, 62.
51   Bianchini, *The Queen's Hand*, 153–9.
52   *al monesterio de las Olgas de Burgos e a las infantes e a la abadessa*: Lizoain Garrido, *Las Huelgas de Burgos (1116–1230)*, no. 208.
53   *uos, abadessa de Sancta Maria la Real, e a todo el conuente e a las ifantes*: Lizoain Garrido, *Las Huelgas de Burgos (1116–1230)*, no. 251.

sale as made principally to the infantas, who are addressed directly. Fernando Pardo sells part of his inheritance "to you, infantas, and to the whole convent of the royal monastery of Santa María de Burgos."[54] The infantas act as the monastery's principal representative here, in place of the abbess, who is not mentioned. There was, in fact, no abbess at this moment; Sancha García is last named as abbess in November 1230, and thereafter the prioress, Inés Laínez, acted as abbess until 1231 or 1232. However, an exchange of properties on November 23, 1230 was made with "you, doña Inés, prioress of the monastery of Santa María la Real de Burgos, and with the convent of this same monastery."[55] In other words, Inés Laínez had stepped into the role of acting abbess – and had completed a transaction without the infantas' intervention – before Fernando Pardo's sale in December. His invocation of the infantas and the convent cannot, therefore, simply be ascribed to the lack of an abbess. Their authority is foregrounded here, albeit for reasons difficult to interpret from the extant documentation.

Perhaps the most significant attestation of the infantas' status at Las Huelgas, however, comes in a charter from 1229. María Vélez, a daughter of one don Vela de Carrión, donates a *solar* in Villarmentero de Campos for the souls of her parents and other relatives. She grants the property not to Las Huelgas's abbess or its convent, but *al monesterio de las ifantes* [sic] *de Burgos* – "to the monastery of the infantas in Burgos."[56] In a Leonese-Castilian context where the memory of the Infantazgo remained keen, calling Las Huelgas "the infantas' monastery" points to the crown's success at establishing a link between the royal monastery, its thirteenth-century *dominae*, and the ancient tradition of royal women ruling religious houses.[57]

It appears, then, that the crown's efforts to create a new version of the Infantazgo in Las Huelgas did not begin in earnest until the 1220s. If Alfonso VIII and Leonor had had such a project in mind, they made few efforts to complete it; although they certainly intended Las Huelgas as a royal monastery and pantheon to rival San Isidoro de León, and although they were intensely concerned

---

54   *a uos, ynfantes, e a todo el conuento del monesterio real de Sancta Maria de Burgos*: Lizoain Garrido, *Las Huelgas de Burgos (1116–1230)*, no. 254.

55   *uobis, domna Ygnes, priora del monasterio de Sancta Maria la Real de Burgos, e con el conuento daqueste mismo monasterio*: Lizoain Garrido, *Las Huelgas de Burgos (1116–1230)*, no. 253; see also Ibid., no. 252.

56   Lizoain Garrido, *Las Huelgas de Burgos (1116–1230)*, no. 233.

57   For the survival of the Infantazgo in early thirteenth-century memory, see Bianchini, "The Infantazgo in the Reign of Alfonso VIII." Reglero de la Fuente sees the wording as legal politesse, meant to foreground the authority of the monastic institution while still acknowledging the infantas' power, but it carries deeper historical resonances as well: Reglero de la Fuente, "Las 'señoras' de las Huelgas de Burgos," 14.

with establishing their young kingdom's legitimacy, they did not attempt to establish a royal daughter as *domina* of their new foundation.[58] That task was assumed instead by Queen Berenguela and Fernando III, who had even more urgent reasons to assert Castile's superior claim to Leonese-Castilian dynastic tradition, due to their complicated rivalry with the crown of León.

But Fernando III's later reign saw further evolution of the relationship between Las Huelgas and its infantas, after one of his own daughters took vows there. Despite scholarly attention to these developments, what has gone largely unremarked is that they occurred in the context of the reunification of the Castilian and Leonese crowns – in other words, at a point when dynastic competition no longer served a purpose, and when the traditional Leonese domains of the Infantazgo were newly at the Castilian monarch's disposal. Yet Las Huelgas retained its primacy as a sacral space for the royal family – above all for its women.

2 The Infantas of Las Huelgas under Fernando III

Alfonso IX of León died in September 1230. Berenguela and Fernando III rushed at once to secure the loyalty of León's towns and bishops, in the face of a strong rival claim from the Infantas Sancha and Dulce, the daughters of Alfonso IX's first marriage and his designated heirs.[59] It was not until mid-December that Fernando III was able to negotiate a settlement with his half-sisters.[60]

But the unification of the kingdoms had no immediate impact on his sister's and aunt's roles at Las Huelgas. If anything, Constanza II and Constanza III were far more active and prominent during the 1230s than they had been during the 1220s. One of the most assertive statements of the infantas' authority comes in a charter from 1232:

> This is a record of how, in 1232, Infanta doña Constanza ordered her chaplain, don Fernando, to write down all the heritable property of the monastery of Las Huelgas de Burgos, which was built by her father, King don Alfonso, and her mother, Queen doña Leonor.[61]

---

58 Walker, "Leonor of England," 359, 361.
59 Bianchini, *The Queen's Hand*, 192–207.
60 *Fernando III*, II: no. 270.
61 *Esta es remenbrança quemo, de M CC e LXX annos, mando la infanta dompna Costantia ha de don Ferrando, so capellan, escriuir todo el heredamiento del monesterio de Las Hvelgas de Burgos, que hedifico so padre el rey don Alfonso he su madre la reyna dompna Alyonor:*

This is the work of Constanza II, as the reference to her parents makes clear. The list that follows is a descriptive survey of the monastery's lands and rents, including such details as the yield of cultivated lands and the number of workers employed in each vineyard. To commission such a survey is itself a lordly act, not something a nun would ordinarily undertake. But the survey itself also reveals Constanza II's protagonism in managing the monastery's landed wealth. Among Las Huelgas's mills in Burgos, don Fernando (who appears here specifically as *her* chaplain, rather than as the chaplain of more than one infanta as he did in 1222) lists a house near the gate of the monastery "that the infanta ordered to be renovated," and another house "that Infanta Constanza ordered to be built in the orchard," with two millwheels.[62] These improvements to Las Huelgas's property were evidently made on land the abbey already owned, not ceded to the nuns after the cited projects were complete. Constanza II therefore had considerable authority to manage and develop Las Huelgas's endowment.

The same year, Constanza II, probably alongside Constanza III, helped Las Huelgas come to terms with a powerful family of Castilian nobles. The brothers Rodrigo Rodríguez and Gonzalo Rodríguez Girón had claimed ownership of various properties (*solares*) in the Tierra de Campos that, according to Las Huelgas, belonged to the abbey. "At the request of the infantas," the abbess, and the convent, the Girón brothers ceded their claim to a long list of *solares* in Villarmentero de Campos, Revenga de Campos, Villalonga, and Villovieco.[63] Las Huelgas's royal *dominae* were able to intervene with high-ranking magnates on the convent's behalf. Perhaps not coincidentally, the Tierra de Campos had been home to Infantazgo properties as well, both before and after the partition of Castile and León. And the Girón brothers were close allies of the crown's most powerful royal woman, Queen Berenguela – who was also, not incidentally, *domina* of much of what remained of the Infantazgo de Campos. This intercession links the infantas and Las Huelgas both to a region significant to

---

Lizoain Garrido, *Las Huelgas de Burgos (1231–1262)*, no. 269. The year is in the Spanish era, which is 38 years ahead of *anno Domini*.

62 *que mando renovar la infant ... que mando façer la infant dona Constantia ena huerta*: Lizoain Garrido, *Las Huelgas de Burgos (1231–1262)*, no. 269. It's unclear from the language whether Constanza had the house or the gate renovated. A later entry about orchards lists one within the monastery's gates which contains "the mills that the infanta ordered to be built," but this may refer to the house with two millwheels already mentioned. Ibid.

63 Lizoain Garrido, *Las Huelgas de Burgos (1231–1262)*, no. 270. Rodríguez illuminates the connections between Burgos, the Tierra de Campos, and León-Castile's royal women: Rodríguez López, "Stratégies matrimoniales," 169–81.

the Infantazgo and to a noble family known to have patronage ties to the female side of the dynasty.[64]

In 1233, a series of charters reveals a patronage relationship between the infantas themselves and an elite couple from the city of Burgos. In March that year, don Guiralt Aymeric granted a charter of arras (i.e., dower) to his new wife, doña María Raimúndez.[65] The arras provided that if doña María predeceased her husband, he was to inherit her moveable goods, except for one thousand maravedís, which don Guiralt would have to spend as doña María instructed. If doña María had failed to give instructions, then the decision of how to spend the money would go to "Infanta doña Constanza, daughter of King don Alfonso." If don Guiralt failed to bestow the money appropriately within thirty days of his wife's death, he would pay a penalty of three thousand maravedís to Infanta Constanza.[66]

On the same day, don Guiralt gave certain houses in the city of Burgos to Las Huelgas, though he retained usufruct of them for life. He acted alone in this charter, and specified that these were the houses in which he currently resided.[67] The following day, doña María joined him in giving his share of some additional houses to Las Huelgas – construed here specifically as the abbess, the infantas, and the whole convent.[68] However, that April, the abbess of Las Huelgas, "with the pleasure and consent of the infantas" and the convent, gave (concedimus) doña María Raimúndez life usufruct of these same houses, should she outlive her husband. The description of the houses' locations makes clear that they are the ones granted in the two March diplomas.[69] The fact that don Guiralt and doña María identified "the infantas" among the recipients of their gift, rather than just the abbess and the convent, indicates some personal relationship between the couple – or, perhaps, primarily María Raimúndez – and the royal women. Moreover, the arras charter makes Constanza II essentially doña María's executor for the thousand maravedís she wishes to bequeath, which suggests a tie of patronage or lordship.[70]

---

64   Bianchini, *The Queen's Hand*, esp. 113–15, 121–39.
65   He had previously been married to a doña Estefanía: Lizoain Garrido, *Las Huelgas de Burgos (1116–1230)*, no. 205.
66   Lizoain Garrido, *Las Huelgas de Burgos (1231–1262)*, no. 271. This Infanta Constanza is almost certainly Constanza II; though both she and her niece were technically "daughters of King don Alfonso," a Castilian charter would probably clarify if the Alfonso in question had been the king of León.
67   Lizoain Garrido, *Las Huelgas de Burgos (1231–1262)*, no. 272.
68   Lizoain Garrido, *Las Huelgas de Burgos (1231–1262)*, no. 273.
69   Lizoain Garrido, *Las Huelgas de Burgos (1231–1262)*, no. 274.
70   Reglero de la Fuente, "Las 'señoras' de las Huelgas de Burgos," 13. Cf. Bianchini, *The Queen's Hand*, 228–9.

This April diploma has received some scholarly attention, because "the infantas," who are elsewhere unspecified, confirmed it separately as "Infanta doña Constanza of Castile" and "Infanta doña Constanza of León" – i.e., Constanza II and Constanza III. They also joined the abbess of Las Huelgas in affixing their seals to the charter. This is the only time in the extant documentation that Constanza II and Constanza III employed their seals; by contrast, for example, the abbess and the two Girón brothers each sealed their agreement in 1232, but the infantas did not. Yet the fact that each woman had her own seal indicates that she had regular use for this symbol of independent authority, even if few exemplars have survived. As infantas, then, both Constanzas wielded power and authority entirely separate from their obligations as nuns.

We can see some of this power at work via the lay elites, like don Guiralt and doña María, who appear to have patronage relationships with the infantas. Another example is doña Elvira, who in September 1240 sold various properties to the abbess of Las Huelgas "and to the infantas and the convent" for a total of 600 maravedís.[71] Doña Elvira was clearly a wealthy woman, and her family had well-established bonds of service to the royal family; Elvira's late husband, don Moriel, was Fernando III's *merino mayor*, or chief bailiff, in Castile throughout the 1230s and until his death in the spring of 1240.[72] Perhaps it was her husband's career as a royal client that laid the foundation for doña Elvira's relationship with the infantas. But that relationship ultimately outlived both Constanzas, and centered instead on a younger infanta destined to be more powerful than either of them.

Fernando III had married in 1219 and almost immediately set about having children. Three boys – Alfonso, Fadrique, and Fernando – arrived before his first surviving daughter, named Berenguela in honor of his mother and therefore known as Berenguela Fernández.[73] Born in 1228, Berenguela Fernández would become, as Gayoso calls her, the first of the "Ladies of Las Huelgas"[74] – that is, the first infanta associated with the convent to have something like an institutionalized role.

Carlos Reglero de la Fuente has observed that in the *Cantigas de Santa María,* composed at the direction of Berenguela Fernández's brother Alfonso X, the infanta is described essentially as a child oblate.[75] Cantiga 122 recounts how, as a child, Berenguela had been intended for Las Huelgas. But she fell ill

---

71   Lizoain Garrido, *Las Huelgas de Burgos (1231–1262)*, nos. 320–21.
72   AHN, Clero, 1655/20 (Feb. 3, 1240); Ibid., 982/16 (May 1240).
73   She may have been preceded by his daughter Leonor, who died in childhood, but the chronology of their births is unclear: *Fernando III*, 1: 113; *DrH*, 292.
74   Gayoso, "The Lady of Las Huelgas," 92.
75   Reglero de la Fuente, "Las 'señoras' de las Huelgas de Burgos," 18.

and died. Her mother, Queen Beatriz, placed her at the feet of an image of the Virgin Mary, locked the chapel where she lay, and kept vigil outside the door, trusting in the Virgin to revive her daughter. At last her faith was rewarded; she heard her daughter cry. Along with other gifts promised to the Virgin, Beatriz soon fulfilled her plan to dedicate Berenguela herself to Mary's service, and brought the girl to the monastery of Las Huelgas. As Reglero de la Fuente points out, if Queen Beatriz herself took Berenguela to her new home, the journey must have happened before the queen's own death in 1235, when Berenguela was about eight.[76] Housing and educating girls within Cistercian female houses appears to have been a matter of course, although the Chapter General disapproved.[77]

At Las Huelgas, Berenguela Fernández would have grown up in proximity to her aunt and great-aunt, the infantas Constanza II and Constanza III. She may even have been associated with them in their role as patrons and advocates of the monastery. Two charters from the same date in 1240, in which doña Elvira sells various rights to the monastery, declare themselves to be grants to the abbess, the *infanta*s, and the convent.[78] Berenguela Fernández would have been about twelve at the time of doña Elvira's two sales to Las Huelgas in 1240 – at or on the verge of her majority. She might, therefore, plausibly be identified as one of "the infantas" who acts in the purchases. That Berenguela herself did reside at Las Huelgas and had a spiritual role there is confirmed by the *Historia de rebus Hispanie* of Rodrigo Jiménez de Rada, one of the most valuable narrative sources for this period. Rodrigo reports that Infanta Berenguela "lives in the royal monastery [Las Huelgas] as a virgin consecrated to the Lord."[79] Since Rodrigo completed his chronicle, by his own report, in the spring of 1243, Berenguela had acquired a quasi-religious status by that time.

She was not, however, a nun. This is significant because Rodrigo Jiménez de Rada's description of her as *uirgo Domino consecrata* echoes earlier descriptions of certain *dominae* of the Infantazgo – also not nuns – as *Deo uotae* or *Deo dicatae*, "dedicated to God." In other words, without taking monastic vows, they had assumed a quasi-sacral status.[80] So, at the time Rodrigo wrote this – again, prior to spring 1243 – Berenguela Fernández's position at Las Huelgas could be described by a contemporary as akin to that of earlier infantas who had ruled the Infantazgo.

---

76   Reglero de la Fuente, "Las 'señoras' de las Huelgas de Burgos," 18.
77   Baury, *Les religieuses de Castille*, 81.
78   Lizoain Garrido, *Las Huelgas de Burgos (1231–1262)*, nos. 320–21.
79   *Berengariam, que in regali monasterio degit uirgo Domino consecrata*: DrH, 292; Ibid., 301.
80   Henriet, "*Deo votas*," 195–7; Pick, *Her Father's Daughter*, 62.

Unlike those earlier infantas, Berenguela Fernández did later become a nun. But the circumstances of the event bear scrutiny. The older infantas at Las Huelgas died within a few months of each other: Constanza III in September 1242, and her namesake aunt at the beginning of January 1243. Fernando III and his court were in Burgos when Constanza III died, and may well have remained there the following January.[81] That summer the king returned to the frontier. But in September 1243 he and his heir, the future Alfonso X, returned to Burgos. There, the king "caused his daughter doña Berenguela to be veiled in Las Huelgas," as we are informed in the *Estoria de España*.[82] If Berenguela Fernández had been destined for Las Huelgas since birth, it is suggestive that she did not take vows until after her aunt and great-aunt died. She turned fifteen in 1243. The Cistercian Order instructed that girls not become postulants or novices before age twelve, but even if Berenguela had followed that rule, she could have taken her vows as early as 1241.[83] Perhaps the time of her formal affiliation with the monastery was determined by the previous infantas' deaths, which left Las Huelgas without its royal advocates. But, as in the cases of her aunt and great-aunt, Berenguela Fernández's monastic profession did nothing to circumscribe her secular authority.[84]

However, Berenguela Fernández's entry into monastic life proved controversial. The registers of Pope Innocent IV record that she received the veil from the hand of the abbess of Las Huelgas, in derogation of the episcopal rights of the bishop of Burgos.[85] The curia fired off a series of letters in March 1244, ordering the abbot of Cîteaux to punish the abbess appropriately, forbidding the abbess herself to do such a thing again, and assuring the bishop of Burgos that proper discipline was coming.[86] The register makes clear that the abbess's offense consisted in veiling the infanta specifically: the abbess "presumed to

---

81 *Fernando III*, I: 73–4. Fernando III was in Burgos from late April 1242 (Ibid., III: no. 697) through at least late September and perhaps even early November (Ibid., no. 702; cf. Ibid., no. 703). His location is thereafter not securely attested until early February 1243, when he was in Valladolid, 116 km from Burgos: Pérez Celada, *San Zoilo de Carrión (1047–1300)*, no. 102.
82 *Fernando III*, I: 133; *e fizo [el rey] estonçe poner velo a su fija donna Beringuella en las Huelgas*: PCG, 742.
83 Hoffman Berman, *The White Nuns*, 22–3; Koslin, "The Robe of Simplicity," 265–6.
84 As Rodríguez López aptly puts it, these infantas may have been chaste as nuns were, but they were certainly "neither poor nor obedient": Rodríguez López, *La estirpe de Leonor de Aquitania*, 279. See also Reglero de la Fuente, "Las 'señoras' de las Huelgas de Burgos," 19–20.
85 Reglero de la Fuente, "Las 'señoras' de las Huelgas de Burgos," 18.
86 *Berengariae sanctimoniali sacrum, immo execrandum consecrationis velum praesumpserat imponere*: Berger, *Les Registres d'Innocent IV (1243–1254)*, nos. 589–91.

place the sacred – or, rather, the cursed – veil of consecration upon the nun Berenguela."[87] As this excerpt suggests, the tenor of these letters seems to have been rather heated. They give no reason to suppose that, if the abbess of Las Huelgas had regularly veiled nuns, either Innocent IV or the bishop of Burgos would have looked the other way.[88] Was it because of the infanta's status as a royal woman that the abbess involved herself in this unusual fashion?

By the time the *Estoria de España* was compiled, in the late thirteenth and early fourteenth century, the contretemps over Berenguela's veiling had been either forgotten or deliberately omitted.[89] The passage I cited above reports, in fact, that the king "caused his daughter doña Berenguela to be veiled in Las Huelgas by the hand of don Juan the chancellor."[90] Don Juan the chancellor was also the bishop of Burgos. Innocent IV's letter to Bishop Juan in 1244 had instructed him to (re)veil Berenguela, but if he did, the king was not present.[91] Fernando III never returned to Burgos after September 1243.[92] So the *Estoria de España*'s account of Fernando III and Alfonso X coming to Burgos to celebrate Berenguela's profession as a nun, conducted by Bishop Juan, is at best an idealized version of events.

The first unequivocal reference to Berenguela Fernández in the documentation of Las Huelgas comes in a gift made by one doña Elvira in 1245. Doña Elvira gives her son don Gonzalo Moriel his full share of her property "in the presence of my lady Infanta doña Berenguela and the convent of the monastery of Santa María la Real de Burgos [Las Huelgas]."[93] In the same charter, don Gonzalo requests to be buried at Las Huelgas, and promises to donate a fifth of his maternal inheritance to the monastery. As for the other four-fifths, "I make my lady Infanta doña Berenguela lady and executor of all the rest of the property that pertains to me from my mother, along with whoever shall be abbess

---

87 Berger, *Les Registres d'Innocent IV (1243–1254)*, no. 589.
88 Las Huelgas was in fact cited for disobedience by the Cistercian Chapter General at other times during the 1240s, though not for this particular transgression: Rodríguez López, *La estirpe de Leonor de Aquitania*, 281.
89 Perhaps not surprising, since Las Huelgas was already sufficiently restored to the pope's good graces by 1259 that he permitted the nuns to wear clothing not otherwise allowed by the Benedictine Rule: Rodríguez López, *La estirpe de Leonor de Aquitania*, 281; Lizoain Garrido, *Las Huelgas de Burgos (1231–1262)*, no. 509.
90 *por mano de don Johan el chançeller*: PCG, 742.
91 Berger, *Les Registres d'Innocent IV*, no. 590.
92 *Fernando III*, III: nos. 706–848.
93 *ante mi sennora la iffante donna Berenguela, e antel conuento del monasterio de Sancta Maria la Real de Burgos*: Lizoain Garrido, *Las Huelgas de Burgos (1231–1262)*, no. 354.

of the monastery [when I die], so that they may sell and donate all of it as I instruct, on behalf of my soul."[94]

Berenguela Fernández now emerges as the sole royal woman associated with Las Huelgas. That she had stepped into her aunt and great-aunt's place is partly suggested by the fact that the doña Elvira of this charter, widow of don Moriel, is the same one who conceded property to Las Huelgas, its abbess, and "the infantas" in 1240. Berenguela also appears to have inherited some of the older infantas' household; the 1245 charter is witnessed by, among others, "don Fernando, the infanta's chaplain."[95] This is likely the same Fernando who had served as chaplain to Constanza II and Constanza III in the 1220s and 1230s. Significantly, the charter draws distinctions between the infanta's role and that of the abbess and convent. Although doña Elvira attests to having granted her son his inheritance "in the presence of" Infanta Berenguela and the convent of Las Huelgas, she makes no mention of the abbess, Inés Laínez; and the witnesses to the charter are mostly laymen. Don Gonzalo frequently refers to the abbess, but as an office rather than an individual; since his donation will take effect when he dies, the woman who is abbess at that time will be the one to receive and manage it. But, like his mother, he acknowledges Infanta Berenguela by name and calls her "my lady," indicating a personal tie of lordship with her – not simply with whichever infanta might happen to be at Las Huelgas at the time of his death. Doña Elvira and don Moriel had also been well-established patrons of Las Huelgas, and an undated charter records the couple's gift of a thousand maravedís to the monastery. In that charter, Abbess Inés Laínez, "together with the approval and consent of Infanta doña Berenguela and our whole convent, give and establish" thirty maravedís in rents from certain houses owned by Las Huelgas to fund perpetual masses for don Moriel and doña Elvira's souls.[96] It is difficult to gauge whether the family's connection to Berenguela Fernández originated in their patronage of Las Huelgas or in don

---

94 *e todo lo al que fincare de todel heredamiento qem* [sic] *aperteçe de parte de mi madre fago sennora e poderosa a la iffante donna Berenguella, mi sennora, e al abbatissa que fuere en el monasterio, que lo uendan e que lo den todo por mi alma en los logares que lo yo mandar dar*: Lizoain Garrido, *Las Huelgas de Burgos (1231–1262)*, no. 354.

95 Lizoain Garrido, *Las Huelgas de Burgos (1231–1262)*, no. 354.

96 *en uno con plaçemiento e con otorgamiento de la infante donna Berenguela e de todo nuestro conuiento del mismo logar, damos e estableçemos*: Lizoain Garrido, *Las Huelgas de Burgos (1231–1262)*, no. 355. While the gift was clearly made before don Moriel's death, this charter may not have been; it attests to the funding of the masses, not the original donation, which is described in the past tense. If don Moriel was alive at the time this charter was issued, then the charter must date from between Sep. 13, 1238 (when María Pérez de Guzmán was still the abbess of Las Huelgas (Ibid., no. 310)) and the spring of 1240, when don Moriel died (see above, fn. 95).

Moriel's service to the crown, or both. But the repeated appearances of doña Elvira and her son in proximity to Berenguela Fernández – as well as doña Elvira's earlier association with Constanza II and Constanza III – certainly shows that the family's bond with royal women and with Las Huelgas outlived don Moriel's career at court.

Beginning in the spring of 1246, and for the next fifteen years, any extant charter produced by the abbess and convent of Las Huelgas was co-issued by Berenguela Fernández. Before that, the last charters issued by the abbess and convent *without* the infanta date from the end of 1243; in them, Las Huelgas exchanges two *tierras* in Estépar for another two in Hormaza.[97] Since Berenguela Fernández had already taken the veil, her absence from these charters is somewhat surprising. Property in Estépar had been included in the initial endowment of Las Huelgas, and at least some of it had belonged to the old Infantazgo of Covarrubias.[98] One might expect the infanta in residence at Las Huelgas to take an active role in alienating possessions there – although, of course, it is not clear whether the particular *tierras* at issue had belonged to Covarrubias. However, although Berenguela had taken the veil in September 1243, it had been at the hands of her abbess, and the consequent dispute between the abbess and the see of Burgos was nowhere near a resolution. Perhaps her indeterminate religious status in late 1243 helps to explain her lack of formal protagonism in these documents. By mid-April of 1246, when she becomes regularly visible as a co-issuer, she and the abbey had been restored to the pope's good graces. That month Innocent IV confirmed two privileges that Fernando III had given Las Huelgas, and acknowledged Berenguela in both: "our son most dear in Christ, Fernando, the illustrious king of Castile and León, whose renowned daughter Berenguela serves the Lord of Hosts in your [the abbess's] monastery, having assumed the habit of your Order."[99]

"Co-issuing" charters reflects how a group of people expressed their shared authority in legal acts.[100] In the case of Berenguela Fernández, the co-issued charters begin with one given by the abbess, doña Inés Laínez, "and Infanta doña Berenguela, together with the convent."[101] Berenguela is shown in tandem

---

97 Lizoain Garrido, *Las Huelgas de Burgos (1231–1262)*, nos. 339–40.
98 Walker, "Leonor of England," 361; Lizoain Garrido, *Las Huelgas de Burgos (1116–1230)*, no. 11.
99 *carissimus in Christo filius noster Fernandus, illustris rex Castelle et Legionis, cuius inclita filia Berengaria in monasterio uestro, assumpto uestre religionis habitu uirtutum Domino famulatur*: Lizoain Garrido, *Las Huelgas de Burgos (1231–1262)*, nos. 365–6.
100 Shadis, *Berenguela of Castile*, 35; Bianchini, *The Queen's Hand*, 8–9; Pick, *Her Father's Daughter*, 104–7.
101 *e la iffante donna Berenguela, en uno con el conuento*: Lizoain Garrido, *Las Huelgas de Burgos (1231–1262)*, no. 365.

with the abbess as the principal actors, while the convent is noted secondarily as acting "together with" them. The following month, doña Inés acted "at the command [*mandamiento*] of Infanta doña Berenguela, and with the agreement and consent of our whole convent."[102] This formulation made the abbess the only principal actor, but still drew a distinction between the infanta's role (to command) and that of the convent community (to agree and consent).[103] Later the same year, another charter tried out yet another formula: the abbess acted "at the command and agreement of Infanta doña Berenguela and with the consent of the convent," which implied even more authority for Berenguela than the previous charter had done.[104]

Reglero de la Fuente noted that the language of "command" faded from the charters in 1251, and a new title was established for the infanta. Now the abbess acted "with the agreement and consent of Infanta doña Berenguela, *our lady*, and of our whole convent."[105] That change was short-lived, however. By 1257, the abbess was acting at the infanta's "command" again, sometimes with and sometimes without the title of "our lady."[106] In any case, by the time of her father's death, Berenguela Fernández had assumed a role of significant secular authority at Las Huelgas. This authority sometimes extended into managing the structure and logistics of the monastery's daily functioning, as when she set quotas for the nuns, novices, and laywomen of the convent in 1257 or allocated rents to the infirmary, the sacristy, and other monastic offices in 1263.[107] But it did not infringe on the abbess's prerogatives as the monastery's spiritual head.[108] Berenguela Fernández is more visible in the charters than her predecessors Constanza II and Constanza III, but her role was very much in keeping with theirs. Berenguela Fernández managed Las Huelgas's properties and its relationships with elite clients, just as the Infantas Constanza did. And, like her

---

102   *con mandamiento de la infanta donna Berenguela e con [placimiento] e con otorgamiento de todo nuestro conuento*: Lizoain Garrido, *Las Huelgas de Burgos (1231–1262)*, no. 268; the interpolation is from Lizoain Garrido.
103   Reglero de la Fuente, "Las 'señoras' de las Huelgas de Burgos," 21.
104   *con mandamiento e con plaçemiento de la iffante donna Berenguela e con otorgamiento del conuiento*: Lizoain Garrido, *Las Huelgas de Burgos (1231–1262)*, no. 373.
105   Reglero de la Fuente, "Las 'señoras' de las Huelgas de Burgos," 21. See, e.g., Lizoain Garrido, *Las Huelgas de Burgos (1231–1262)*, nos. 407–408: *con plaçemiento e con otorgamiento de la infanta donna Berenguela, nuestra sennora, e de todo nuestro conuiento*: emphasis mine.
106   *por mandamiento de la infante donna Berenguilla*: Lizoain Garrido, *Las Huelgas de Burgos (1231–1262)*, no. 500; *con mandamiento de nuestra sennora la infante donna Berenguiella*: Ibid., no. 520.
107   Lizoain Garrido, *Las Huelgas de Burgos (1231–1262)*, no. 501; Lizoain Garrido, *Las Huelgas de Burgos (1263–1283)*, no. 534.
108   Reglero de la Fuente, "Las 'señoras' de las Huelgas de Burgos," 27.

aunt and great-aunt, she served as the monastery's liaison with the crown. Her brother Alfonso X made several gifts of property in Seville to "you, doña Berenguela, my sister, and to you, doña Inés, abbess of the monastery of Burgos, and to your monastery and your successors who will come after you."[109] Las Huelgas was perhaps unlikely to have been neglected by the Castilian crown, but the fact that Alfonso X made his donations first to his sister and only then to the abbess and convent underscores the practical value of having an advocate who belonged to the king's lineage.[110] In short, Constanza II and Constanza III sketched out a model for royal women's authority at Las Huelgas, which Berenguela Fernández and her successors subsequently developed.

3 Conclusions

Alfonso VIII and Leonor of England founded Las Huelgas as a symbol of their dynasty's legitimacy – a spiritual touchstone and dynastic pantheon for the crown of their young kingdom. As their children's names suggest, they were keenly aware of the need to link their reign to the prestige of the eleventh- and early-twelfth-century rulers of León-Castile. Las Huelgas, with its echoes of the royal monastery at San Isidoro de León, was part of that project.

But whether they intended to establish one of their daughters at Las Huelgas, in keeping with the older Leonese tradition of the Infantazgo of which San Isidoro was the head, is not clear. Certainly they did not devote one of their elder daughters to the monastic life in Burgos; the daughter who did become a nun, Constanza II, was among their youngest children. And there is no strong evidence for Constanza's dedication at Las Huelgas in her parents' lifetime. She is documented there only several years after their deaths, when her sister Queen Berenguela and her nephew Fernando III ruled Castile. And when she does appear, it is in conjunction with her niece Constanza III. It is possible that the two Constanzas were already destined for the religious life at their christening; Ana Rodríguez López argues, with reason, that the coincidence of their names and their monastic careers was probably deliberate, especially since the name Constanza reappears in a later generation of royal daughters apparently

---

109 *uos, donna Berenguela, mi ermana, e a uos, donna Ygnes, abbadessa del monasterio de Burgos, e a uuestro manasterio* [sic] *e a uuestras successores que depues de uos vernan*: Lizoain Garrido, *Las Huelgas de Burgos (1231–1262)*, no. 442; see also Ibid., nos. 437–38.

110 Reglero de la Fuente, "Las 'señoras' de las Huelgas de Burgos," 22–4; Cayrol Bernardo, "On *Infantas*, *Domnae*, and *Deo Votae*," 139.

intended for Las Huelgas.¹¹¹ But whether Constanza III could have been meant for Las Huelgas as an infant, rather than for some Leonese house, is very much in doubt. And, in any case, neither infanta played a prominent role at the monastery until she was in her twenties.

Their emergence as important figures at Las Huelgas coincided with the resolution of the major internal conflicts that plagued Berenguela and Fernando III's first five years on the throne. It is therefore difficult not to see their careers, or at least their prominence, as a deliberate strategy by the new king and queen to reassert Castile's status and legitimacy vis-à-vis León. Given that Fernando III had been disinherited in his father's kingdom, and that Alfonso IX himself had made a military bid for the Castilian throne in 1217, the spiritual prestige conferred by the Castilian monarchy's association with Las Huelgas was especially desirable. To secure that association, and to make an even more explicit connection between Las Huelgas and the old Infantazgo, Fernando III and Berenguela either created or foregrounded the preeminent position of royal women at the monastery in the persons of the two Constanzas. When these infantas died within a few months of each other, the monarchs supplied a replacement in Fernando III's daughter Berenguela – who may have already been destined for monastic life, but did not take the veil until her aunt and great-aunt had died.

By that point, Fernando III had been king of both Castile and León for many years. Yet neither at his accession in León nor after the death of his mother (who, after all, had lordly rights in much of the Leonese Infantazgo) did he attempt to extend the dominion of royal daughters to include former Infantazgo properties in León. He kept the sacral power of the Castilian infantas focused in Burgos, the *caput Castelle* – a sign, perhaps, of Castilian preeminence over León after 1230. Fernando III put an end to Las Huelgas's role as the royal pantheon, too, when he chose to be buried in Seville. Nevertheless, his son and heir took pains to preserve both the temporal and spiritual prestige of Las Huelgas and its pantheon, as shown by his gifts to the monastery and Pope Innocent IV's concession of remission of sins for anyone who came to Las Huelgas to pray for the kings and queens buried there.¹¹²

To say that the Castilian monarchs sought to create at Las Huelgas a lordship that would evoke the Infantazgo is not to say that they recreated the Infantazgo. As many scholars have observed, there were key differences between the

---

111   Rodríguez López, *La estirpe de Leonor de Aquitania*, 279; Reglero de la Fuente, "Las 'señoras' de las Huelgas de Burgos," 29.
112   Rodríguez López, *La estirpe de Leonor de Aquitania*, 232; Lizoain Garrido, *Las Huelgas de Burgos (1231–1262)*, no. 439.

original *dominae* of the Infantazgo and the *señoras* of Las Huelgas, the most blatant of which is that Las Huelgas's infantas took monastic vows. Yet the effort to recapture some of the numinous power of the Leonese-Castilian Infantazgo indicates the concept's enduring value, even after the partition of the kingdoms and a scarcity of royal daughters had nudged it toward extinction. León-Castile's kings may have been sanctified primarily by the sword.[113] But like their predecessors, its thirteenth-century infantas demonstrate the crucial, and long-lasting, dynastic importance of royal women sanctified to God.[114]

Works Cited

Primary Sources
Unpublished
Archivo Histórico Nacional, Madrid (AHN)
  Clero, 1655/20 (Feb. 3, 1240)
  Clero, 982/16 (May 1240)

Published

Berger, Élie, ed. *Les Registres d'Innocent IV (1243–1254): recueil des bulles de ce pape*. Paris: Thorin, 1881.

Fernández Catón, José María, ed. *Colección documental del archivo de la Catedral de León*. Vol. 5 (1109–1187). León: CSIC-CSEL, Caja de Ahorros y Monte de Piedad, and Archivo Histórico Diocesano, 1990.

González, Julio, ed. *Reinado y diplomas de Fernando III*, 3 vols. Córdoba: Monte de Piedad y Caja de Ahorros de Córdoba, 1983.

Jiménez de Rada, Rodrigo. *Historia de rebus Hispanie, sive Historia Gothica*. Ed. Juan Fernández Valverde. Vol. 72 of *Corpus Christianorum: Continuatio mediaeualis*. Turnhout: Brepols, 1987.

Lizoain Garrido, José Manuel, ed. *Documentación del monasterio de Las Huelgas de Burgos (1116–1230)*. Burgos: Ediciones J.M. Garrido Garrido, 1985.

Lizoain Garrido, José Manuel, ed. *Documentación del monasterio de Las Huelgas de Burgos (1231–1262)*. Burgos: Ediciones J.M. Garrido Garrido, 1985.

Lizoain Garrido, José Manuel, ed. *Documentación del monasterio de Las Huelgas de Burgos (1263–1283)*. Burgos: Ediciones J.M. Garrido Garrido, 1987.

Lucas of Tuy. *Chronicon mundi*. Ed. Emma Falque Rey. Vol. 74 of *Corpus Christianorum: Continuatio mediaeualis*. Turnhout: Brepols, 2003.

---

113   Ruiz, "Unsacred Monarchy," 109–44.
114   Pick, *Her Father's Daughter*, 16–7.

Pérez Celada, Julio, ed. *Documentación del monasterio de San Zoilo de Carrión (1047–1300)*. Burgos: Ediciones J.M. Garrido Garrido, 1986.

Primera crónica general de España. Ed. Ramón Menéndez Pidal et al. Madrid: Gredos, 1955.

Serrano, Luciano, ed. *Cartulario del Infantado de Covarrubias*. Valladolid: Macías Picavea, 1907.

Secondary Sources

Baury, Ghislain. *Les religieuses de Castille au XIIe–XIIIe siècle*. Rennes: Presses universitaires de Rennes, 2012.

Bianchini, Janna. "The Infantazgo in the Reign of Alfonso VIII." In *King Alfonso VIII of Castile: Government, Family, and War*, ed. Damian J. Smith, Miguel Gómez, and Kyle C. Lincoln, 59–79. New York: Fordham University Press, 2019.

Bianchini, Janna. *The Queen's Hand: Power and Authority in the Reign of Berenguela of Castile*. Philadelphia: University of Pennsylvania Press, 2012.

Cavero, Gregoria. "Sancha Raimúndez: An Infanta in the Exercise of Her Power." *Imago Temporis. Medium Aevum* 7 (2013): 271–297.

Cayrol Bernardo, Laura. "El monasterio de San Pelayo de Oviedo: infantado y memoria regia." *Territorio, Sociedad y Poder. Revista de estudios medievales* 8 (2013): 53–66.

Cayrol Bernardo, Laura. "On *Infantas*, *Domnae*, and *Deo Votae*. A Few Remarks on the Infantado and Its Ladies." *SVMMA* 1, no. 3 (2014): 129–146.

Fernández Conde, F. Javier. "La reina Urraca 'la Asturiana'." *Asturiensia medievalia* 2 (1975): 65–94.

García Calles, Luisa. *Doña Sancha, hermana del Emperador*. León: Centro de Estudios e Investigación "San Isidoro," Consejo Superior de Investigaciones Científicas Patronato José María Quadrado, 1972.

Gayoso, Andrea. "The Lady of Las Huelgas. A Royal Abbey and Its Patronage," *Citeaux: Commentarii Cistercienses* 51, no. 1–2 (2000): 91–116.

Henriet, Patrick. "*Deo votas*. L'*Infantado* et la fonction des infantes dans la Castille et le León des Xe–XIIe siècles." In *Au cloître et dans le monde: femmes, hommes et sociétés (IXe–XVe siècle): mélanges en l'honneur de Paulette L'Hermite-Leclercq*, ed. Patrick Henriet and Anne-Marie Legras, 189–203. Paris: Presses de l'Université de Paris-Sorbonne, 2000.

Henriet, Patrick. "Infantes, *Infantaticum*. Remarques introductives." *e-Spania. Revue interdisciplinaire d'études hispaniques médiévales et modernes* 5 (2008).

Hoffman Berman, Constance. *The White Nuns: Cistercian Abbeys for Women in Medieval France*. Philadelphia: University of Pennsylvania Press, 2018.

Koslin, Désirée. "The Robe of Simplicity: Initiation, Robing, and Veiling of Nuns in the Middle Ages." In *Robes and Honor: The Medieval World of Investiture*, ed. Stewart Gordon, 255–274. New York: Palgrave, 2001.

Martin, Georges. "Le testament d'Elvire (Tábara, 1099)." *e-Spania. Revue interdisciplinaire d'études hispaniques médiévales et modernes* 5 (2008).

Martin, Georges. "Sobre mujeres y tumbas. Aproximación a una política femenina de las necrópolis regias y condales (León y Castilla, siglos X al XIII)." *e-Spania. Revue interdisciplinaire d'études hispaniques médiévales et modernes* 17 (2014).

Martin, Therese. "Fuentes de potestad para reinas e infantas: El Infantazgo en los siglos centrales de la Edad Media." *Anuario de Estudios Medievales* 46, no. 1 (2016): 97–136.

Martin, Therese. "Hacia una clarificación del infantazgo en tiempos de la reina Urraca y su hija la infanta Sancha (ca. 1107–1159)." *e-Spania. Revue interdisciplinaire d'études hispaniques médiévales et modernes* 5 (2008).

Martin, Therese. *Queen as King: Politics and Architectural Propaganda in Twelfth-Century Spain*. Leiden: Brill, 2006.

Pick, Lucy K. *Her Father's Daughter: Gender, Power, and Religion in the Early Spanish Kingdoms*. Ithaca, NY: Cornell University Press, 2017.

Reglero de la Fuente, Carlos M. "Las 'señoras' de las Huelgas de Burgos: infantas, monjas y encomenderas." *e-Spania. Revue interdisciplinaire d'études hispaniques médiévales et modernes* 24 (2016).

Reglero de la Fuente, Carlos M. "*Omnia totius regni sui monasteria*: la *Historia Legionense*, llamada *Silense*, y los monasterios de las infantas." *e-Spania. Revue interdisciplinaire d'études hispaniques médiévales et modernes* 14 (2012).

Rodríguez López, Ana. "Dotes y arras en la política territorial de la monarquía feudal castellana: siglos XII–XIII." *Arenal* 2, no. 2 (1995): 271–293.

Rodríguez López, Ana. *La estirpe de Leonor de Aquitania. Mujeres y poder en los siglos XII y XIII*. Barcelona: Crítica, 2014.

Rodríguez López, Ana. "Stratégies matrimoniales, stratégies patrimoniales: Autour du pouvoir des femmes au royaume de Léon-Castille (XIIe–XIIIe siècles)." In *Les stratégies matrimoniales (IXe–XIIIe siècle)*, ed. Martin Aurell, 169–191. Turnhout: Brepols, 2013.

Ruiz, Teófilo. "Unsacred Monarchy: The Kings of Castile in the Late Middle Ages." In *Rites of Power: Symbolism, Ritual, and Politics since the Middle Ages*, ed. Sean Wilentz, 109–144. Philadelphia: University of Pennsylvania Press, 1985.

Sánchez Ameijeiras, Rocío. "The Eventful Life of the Royal Tombs of San Isidoro in León." In *Church, State, Vellum, and Stone: Essays on Medieval Spain in Honor of John Williams*, ed. Therese Martin and Julie A. Harris, 479–520. Leiden: Brill, 2005.

Shadis, Miriam. *Berenguela of Castile (1180–1246) and Political Women in the High Middle Ages*. New York: Palgrave Macmillan, 2009.

Shadis, Miriam. "'Happier in Daughters than in Sons': The Children of Alfonso VIII of Castile and Leonor Plantagenet." In *King Alfonso VIII of Castile: Government, Family, and War*, ed. Miguel Gómez, Kyle C. Lincoln, and Damian J. Smith, 80–101. New York: Fordham University Press, 2019.

Viñayo, González, Antonio. "Reinas e Infantas de León, abadesas y monjas del monasterio de San Pelayo y de San Isidoro." In *Semana de Historia del Monacato Cántabro-Astur-Leonés: XV centenario del nacimiento de San Benito*, 123–135. Oviedo: Monasterio de San Pelayo, 1982.

Walker, Rose. "Leonor of England, Plantagenet Queen of King Alfonso VIII of Castile, and Her Foundation of the Cistercian Abbey of Las Huelgas. In Imitation of Fontevraud?," *Journal of Medieval History* 31, no. 4 (2005): 346–368.

CHAPTER 8

Family and Friends: Women at the Court of Fernando III

Miriam Shadis

Fernando III lived a life surrounded by, dependent upon, and sometimes in conflict with women. This essay surveys the numerous women who were present at or interacted with the court of King Fernando: not only the queens (Berenguela, his mother, and Beatriz and Juana, his wives), other royal and noble women (his many sisters and the wives of his male followers), religious women (notably the abbesses of San Andrés de Arroyo and Las Huelgas de Burgos), but also, albeit briefly, the many women present and working at the Castilian court. Other women were there undoubtedly: Muslim women, some enslaved as a consequence of conquest, others perhaps free peasants who brought produce to sell to household kitchens, or perhaps worked in those kitchens, did laundry, or other domestic tasks.[1] Jewish families, including mothers and daughters, were enticed to settle in the newly conquered Córdoba and regions around Seville by Fernando's administration, and, like other Iberian kings, Fernando employed Jewish courtiers whose wives and daughters undoubtedly therefore had some association with the court.[2] This essay, however, represents only an initial foray of research into the women associated with Fernando's court, and therefore, perforce, starts at the top, and works its way down, with the hopes that new questions will be suggested to scholars thinking about the gendered dynamics of government and conquest in medieval Iberia.

Apart from scholarship on Berenguela, no attention has been paid to the ways in which women formed crucial networks around the king. Rather, Fernando is understood primarily as a great military leader. The court seems highly masculinized, with the militarized projects of the conquest of al-Andalus, on the one hand, and the dominant presence of bishops – who witnessed royal

---

1 Most scholarship on Iberian slavery focuses on the Mediterranean region and later medieval periods, although there are exceptions. For the most part, the presence of slaves must be inferred. Shadis, "Las Navas," 74–5; Echevarría Arsuaga, "Esclavos musulmanes." Barton, *Conquerors, Brides, and Concubines*, 102–3.
2 Ray, *Sephardic Frontier*; Irish, "Castilian Monarchy," 44–5.

charters and controlled the historical record – on the other. Such characterization discourages thinking about women and the roles they played, despite the legal and economic equity dictated by the *fueros* of medieval Castile.[3] However, to take just one example, women religious, particularly of the Cistercian Order, had a strong profile at the Castilian court, and furthermore, given the roles of the king's aunt, sister, and daughter, demonstrated a particularly important intersection of gender, religion, and monarchy.

The court of Fernando III was shaped by women. Their work was reproductive (construed broadly); it was also both religious and commemorative. They supplied key nodes in a network of varied relations: they were administrators, and they were laborers. Women's relationships with the king served to enhance or confirm his status and that of his family. In particular, the king's mother Berenguela reigned supreme, and her influence over the king and her significance to the stability of his realm are widely recognized.[4] Berenguela overshadowed the king's wives, Beatriz and Juana in many ways – though she also worked with them. Other women at the court held significant roles, especially some of the noble and religious women who were either royal relatives or wives of significant court nobles. However, a probable majority of women associated with Fernando are obscured not by Queen Berenguela, but rather, by the processes of historical inquiry. Iberian law made a place for women as familial heirs and full partners with their husbands – this law represented a culture of co-activity, not just a paradigm for solving inheritance claims.[5] Thus when we see men acting at court, or interacting with the king, and being rewarded by the king, and we see their wives or daughters mentioned alongside them, we must consider the strong possibility that these women were also actors in the circles around the king. Finding these women means scouring sources like charters, the records of the *repartimientos*, and literary and archeological sources. Contemporary chronicles also reveal some detail about the lives of the most elite women. Studying the women associated with the court of Fernando III provides an opportunity to think about medieval Iberian women generally, especially how their identities were filtered through their relationships to fathers, brothers, husbands, and sons, as well as mothers, sisters, and daughters.

---

3 Dillard, *Daughters of the Reconquest*.
4 See Shadis, *Berenguela of Castile*; Bianchini, *The Queen's Hand*.
5 Dillard, *Daughters of the Reconquest*, 16–8, 33–5.

1   Queens

Fernando's mother and wives were the queens of his court. Queenship also operated as an identity for other women, such as the former queens of León, Urraca López de Haro and Teresa of Portugal. However, there were also several women destined to queenship who served Fernando's court in this way (or challenged it.) His sister, Berenguela, his aunt Leonor, his daughter Eleanor and his niece Mencía López de Haro all extended Castilian royal identity into the wider world. At the same time, they were absorbed into new socio-political frameworks as a result of marriage (becoming part of the political scenes of Latin Constantinople, Aragón, England, and Portugal respectively), and thus, they did not necessarily take the legal privileges of elite Castilian women with them.

1.1   *Berenguela*

The practice of queenship at Fernando's court was dictated by the king's mother, Berenguela. She had an extraordinary position as a queen by right of inheritance, and was a profound influence on her son.[6] More than any other woman, Berenguela has a notable presence in contemporary chronicles, and throughout her life, Fernando included her when he issued charters. Janna Bianchini has demonstrated her relationships with a powerful following, something which certainly strengthened her ability to govern.[7] Berenguela organized the king's marriages, guarded his chastity, and directed the futures of many of his children. She reinforced the relationship between church and crown, and between dead ancestors and the king through pious patronage. She represented the court internationally, seeking brides for her son first in Germany and then France, arranging a key diplomatic marriage for her sister Leonor in Aragón, and maintaining a correspondence with her sister Blanche, queen of France, and the pope.[8]

Despite all this, there are huge gaps in our information about this important woman – much of her activity has to be inferred from close reading between the lines, and the scrutiny of formulae, such as charter intitulations and witness lists. For example, an ordinary charter of sale made in November 1216, during the reign of Enrique I, from Vela García to García Fernández and his new wife Mayor Arias was witnessed by García Pérez and Domingo Adam, men

---

6   Shadis, *Berenguela of Castile*.
7   Bianchini, *The Queen's Hand*.
8   For example, *Fernando III*, III: no. 661.

identified as the *criazon de la Regina*.⁹ By identifying themselves with the queen's household (which García Fernández and Mayor Arias were part of as well), García Pérez and Domingo Adam help us to appreciate the queen's reach. From the beginning of his reign, moreover, Fernando's diplomas were issued "with the assent and blessing of Queen doña Berenguela, my mother," and some version of this formula appeared in the majority of Fernando's diplomas until Berenguela's death in 1246.¹⁰ Occasionally, Fernando acted "together with" (*una cum*) Berenguela (as his grandfather Alfonso VIII had with Queen Leonor) but mostly this formula was reserved for his brother, Infante Alfonso, and then for his wives, Beatriz and then Juana.¹¹ Similarly, other charters hinted at the queen's status. A March 1228 donation charter from García Fernández and Mayor Arias to Villamayor noted "King Fernando reigning in Castile and Toledo and Extremadura [sic] with Queen Beatriz his wife and his sons Alfonso and Fernando, and his illustrious mother Queen Berenguela."¹²

Those who worked with or for the queen were rewarded for their services to her. After November 1217, García Fernández, formerly Queen Leonor's *mayordomo*, stepped into that role for Berenguela.¹³ While some of Leonor's household appeared in private documents, the queen's *mayordomo* never appeared in royal charters in Alfonso VIII's reign. As Bianchini illustrates, however, Berenguela's *mayordomo* confirmed royal charters when she was queen of León, and this was an innovation, demonstrating her power.¹⁴ Thus it was significant that when García Fernández became Berenguela's *mayordomo* he confirmed royal documents as "García Fernández, *mayordomo* of the lady queen."¹⁵ As the queen's *mayordomo* he sometimes confirmed documents which did not even mention Berenguela. In May 1218, García Fernández was rewarded with houses in Toledo for services to Berenguela and Leonor.¹⁶ In

---

9   Serrano, "Mayordomo mayor," Appendix VII. See below regarding García Fernández and Mayor Arias.
10 *ex assensu et beneplacito dominae Berengariae regina, genetricis meae*: *Fernando III*, II: no. 1.
11 *Fernando III*, II: no. 17. He acted *una cum* Alfonso well through 1221 (up to the time of his son infante Alfonso's birth). Beatriz was added in December of 1219, when Fernando acted *ex assensu et beneplacito domne Berengarie regine, genetricis mee, una cum uxore mea Beatrice regina, et cum fratre meo infante domno Alfonso*: Ibid., no. 93.
12 *regnante rege Fernando in Castella et Toleto et Extrematura cum regina Beatrice uxore sua et filiis suis Alfonso, Frederico, et Fernando et illustrissima matre sua regina Berengaria*: Serrano, "Mayordomo mayor," Appendix XII.
13 *Fernando III*, II: no. 6.
14 Bianchini, *The Queen's Hand*, 62.
15 *Garsie Fernandi, maiordomus domine regine*: *Fernando III*, II: no. 6.
16 *Fernando III*, II: no. 28.

1226, he received the villa of Higueruela near Alarcos "for the many and great services which you performed for me."[17] This charter was given with Berenguela's consent and confirmed by García Fernández as her *mayordomo*, but it seems likely that it actually referred to services to Fernando. In fact, a few years later, García Fernández became Fernando's *mayordomo*; Berenguela's *mayordomo* is not identified thereafter. But in the earliest years of Fernando's reign, he was inseparable from the queen mother, and service to one was service to the other.

Other of the queen's men included Diego Villar, who was rewarded for medical services to Alfonso VIII, Berenguela, Fernando, and "all the feverish men" in a 1218 confirmation of a gift previously given by Alfonso VIII.[18] Rodrigo Ruiz was similarly aided in his construction of a monastery in Saldaña, "for many and freely [given] services which you faithfully executed for my mother in her adversity and which you continue to perform for her and for me."[19] Finally, in 1250 (after Berenguela's death), Pedro Fernández was rewarded with property in Córdoba in a charter that was ostentatious in its gratitude for service to Alfonso VIII, Berenguela, and implicitly, Fernando over the course of the wars against the Muslims in al-Andalus. The charter linked generations of the royal family with generations of Pedro Fernández's family, acknowledging the service of Pedro Fernández, his father Fernando González, and grandfather Gonzalo Pérez, as well as their blood tie to the royal family. Pedro's wife, María Díaz de Haro, as a member of that family (and also mentioned in this charter) may have had a role in the queen's court.[20]

Occasionally, we can see Berenguela's direct influence and personal history through Fernando's charters. She maintained (or regained) control over her original *arras* (awarded to her by Alfonso IX of León in 1198), and continued to acquire properties. In 1219, she exchanged and received property in Burgos from Abbess Sancha of Las Huelgas, acting as the "Queen of Castile and Toledo," as well as property in the city near the Cathedral.[21] A 1220 charter refers to the queen's properties in Talavera in a confirmation of a number of privileges to the Order of Calatrava, including an estate adjacent to one of her farms.[22] Around 1223, Berenguela gave the canons of León a quarter of taxes from Valencia, Valderas, Villalpando, again acting "by the Grace of God, queen

---

17   *pro multis seruiis et magnis que mihi fecistis*: *Fernando III*, II: no. 210.
18   *totis viribus anelatis*: *Fernando III*, II: no. 14.
19   *pro multis et gratis serviciis que serenissime matri mee in suis adversitatibus fideliter exhibuistis et adhuc eidem et michi exhibere non cessatis*: *Fernando III*, II: no. 20.
20   *Fernando III*, III: no. 793.
21   *reginam Castelle et Toleti*: *Fernando III*, II: no. 97.
22   *Fernando III*, II: no. 115.

of Castile and Toledo."[23] In that year also, she made another ordinary gift to Covarrubias of monasteries and lands of Porquera and Berlanga de los Infantes, near Aguilar de Campo.[24] As was typical, those who contravened the charter were threatened with the wrath of God and to be condemned with Judas. More unusually, financial penalties were owed to the queen, possibly because they were part of the Infantazgo. In 1224, she excused Gusendos, in Valencia, from any royal tribute.[25] In 1229, Berenguela, "by the Grace of God queen of Castile and Toledo" gave her castle of Bolaños to Calatrava, acting with the consent and blessing of "my dearest sons" Fernando and Alfonso. This was confirmed by Fernando, whose "dearest mother doña Berenguela" is still identified, despite Fernando's marriage to Beatriz, as the "illustrious queen of Castile and Toledo."[26] In 1238, Fernando gave the castle of Aguilar de Pedrayo to the church of Santiago de Compostela. While the king's charter referred to "my castle," it also noted that the donation was made "at the insistence and with the good will of the venerable queen my mother, Lady Berenguela, to whom this castle belonged by law as a dower;" Bianchini argues that the endowment for Berenguela's soul signals her control over this gift.[27] Four years later, she endowed her son Alfonso de Molina with the monastery of Buenafuente

> with all its populated and unpopulated estates, with cattle and beehives, and with books and chalices, with all the church vestments, and all the furniture and all the servants of the house, and however many rights ... which don Rodrigo the archbishop of Toledo gave to me.[28]

---

23 *Dei gratia regina Castelle et Toleti*: *Fernando III*, II: no. 176. Bianchini, *The Queen's Hand*, 235. Rodríguez López, *Consolidación*, 170.
24 *Fernando III*, II: no. 179.
25 *Fernando III*, III: no. 831. Bianchini, *The Queen's Hand*, 152. Rodríguez López, *Consolidación*, 159.
26 *charissimorum filiorum meorum*: *Fernando III*, II: no. 250; *quam karissima genetrix mea domina Berengaria, illustris regina Castelle et Toleti*: *Fernando III*, II: no. 251. Rodríguez López, *Consolidación*, 171.
27 *sepedicti autem castelli donacio facta est ad instanciam et beneplacitum venerabili regine genetricis mee, domine Berengarie, ad quam idem castellum iure dotalici pertinebat*: *Fernando III*, III: no. 638. Bianchini, *The Queen's Hand*, 233.
28 *con todas sus heredades pobladas et por poblar, et con ganado et con colmenas, et con libros et con cálices, con todas las uestimentas de la eglesia, con todo el mueble et con toda la uassallia de la casa, et con quantos derechos hy he et devo aver ... assí cuemo a mi me lo dio don Rodrigo, arçobispo de Toledo*: *Fernando III*, III: no. 703. In the 19th century, Buenafuente was known for its production of honey and wax. Madoz, *Diccionario geográfico*, t. IV, 473. Shadis, *Berenguela*, 162.

With the exception of Buenafuente and Covarrubias, all of these lands were part of Berenguela's original dower lands. As Bianchini points out, these transactions and others demonstrate Berenguela's extensive, continued, and complete power, especially in the Tierra del Campo, where she enjoyed full regalian rights.[29]

The kinds of limitations encountered in the study of Berenguela apply equally to the study of the other women who were queens at Fernando's court, including his wives, Beatriz and Juana. Their cases, however, are made even more inscrutable by the dominating presence of their mother-in-law. This was especially true in the case of Queen Beatriz of Swabia.

1.2   Beatriz

Beatriz, Fernando's carefully chosen bride, had two primary functions, though we can glimpse others. First, she was to bear the king's children, a task at which she excelled heroically. Married around age fourteen in 1219, Beatriz delivered seven sons and three daughters before dying in 1235, at age 30, likely from puerperal fever or some other postpartum disaster.[30] She had been sick before. *Cantiga* 256 celebrates the miraculous cure of the very pregnant Beatriz, when the "competent doctors from Montpellier" had given up hope. Beatriz's faith in the Virgin restored her health. Alfonso notes that he was an eyewitness to his mother's great fever – "you never saw a sicker woman" – with the doctors saying "she will not live."[31] The refrain "she will not escape this time" suggests that the doctors had seen this before.

Beatriz's motherhood was fundamentally biological – and pragmatic. The *Cantigas* relay the intense story of the miraculous revivification of her small daughter Berenguela, who had become sick and died, a child whom Beatriz had intended for the convent of Las Huelgas. The story focuses on Beatriz's veneration of the Virgin. Although "greatly afflicted" at the infanta's death, she was not the nursemaid, who "grieved ... so greatly all through the night that she thought she would kill herself from sorrow." Rather, Beatriz locked the tiny body in a chapel, insisting that the Virgin accept her oblation one way or another. With the infanta's recovery, "she took the child then and there and gave her to the nuns of Las Huelgas, a worthy place."[32] When she herself died, Beatriz was interred at Las Huelgas, although after becoming king in 1252 and renovating

---

29   Bianchini, *The Queen's Hand*, esp. at 151–2, 235.
30   They were Alfonso, Fadrique, Fernando, Leonor, Berenguela, Enrique, Felipe, Sancho, Manuel, and the infant María, who died shortly after birth – and after her mother's death – in 1235. Shadis, *Berenguela of Castile*, 107.
31   *Cantigas*, no. 256.
32   *Cantigas*, no. 122.

the royal chapel at the Cathedral of Seville, Alfonso X had her body translated there.

Beatriz's other main function as queen, wife, and mother connected the Castilians to the Holy Roman Empire. As the daughter of Philip of Swabia, ward of Otto of Brunswick, and cousin of Frederick II, Beatriz enhanced the Castilians' international reputations and claims. Famously, but unsuccessfully, Alfonso X sought election as the Holy Roman Emperor; it seems likely that Fernando and Beatriz had planned that future for their second son, Fadrique, who was clearly named for Beatriz's Staufen relatives.[33] Furthermore, through her mother Irene Angelos, Beatriz had Byzantine antecedents – her grandfather was the emperor Isaac II Angelos. Although by the time of Beatriz's marriage that dynasty had been ended owing to the Fourth Crusade, the young queen certainly benefited from the association with her prestigious forebears. As for the Castilians, Fernando's marriage to Beatriz enhanced his legitimacy in multiple ways. Archbishop Rodrigo describes Berenguela's concern to find her son an honorable wife – one of appropriate rank – but as Daniel Colmenero López suggests, this could also mean one appropriately *unrelated* to him.[34] Iberian rulers had historically, and recently, faced considerable difficulty with consanguineous unions, exemplified by Berenguela's marriage to Fernando's father, Alfonso IX. Despite the significance of Berenguela's embassy to Frederick II's court to collect Beatriz, undoubtedly negotiations were underway long before the summer of 1219. The first years of Fernando's reign were exceedingly rocky, challenged by his father in León, nobles in Castile and the threat (though not dire) of Almohads to the south. Fernando needed to demonstrate his maturity and secure his position as a viable king, and an appropriate wife would contribute to that. It was no accident that their marriage also coincided with Fernando's knighting and a meeting of the cortes.[35]

Alfonso X's actions underscored Beatriz's bio-political role. Literally appropriating her remains, he removed them from Las Huelgas, took them across the now vast Castilian domain, and reburied them next to Fernando in the newly consecrated Cathedral. In Seville, Alfonso had constructed the *Capilla de los Reyes* in the former mosque in order to elevate his status as a legitimate claimant to imperial (Staufen) rule.[36] Laura Molina López strongly argues for links between this chapel and the aesthetic world of Frederick II, particularly

---

33 Shadis, *Berenguela of Castile*, 57, 107.
34 Colmenero López, "La boda," 14–5.
35 Colmenero López, "La boda," 21. Shadis, *Berenguela*, 106–7.
36 Molina López, "El ajuar funerario," 377. Laguna Paúl, "Mobiliario medieval," 55–6.

the innovation (in Castile) of mortuary statues of the enthroned monarchs in contrast to the traditional recumbent tomb figure. She suggests two sources for Alfonso x's inspiration: his brother, Fadrique, who had spent four years at Frederick's court, and his mother, Beatriz, who in 1215 undoubtedly witnessed Frederick's translation of Charlemagne's remains into a reliquary, which represented a seated king.[37] Beatriz's and Fernando's tombs reflected the king's imperial aspirations. Although the tombs were later rebuilt and so we cannot be absolutely certain of their original appearance, Molina López cites a 1345 description of the queen's seated figure.[38] More securely, Alfonso x himself described Beatriz's and Fernando's tombs in *Cantiga* 292: "he had the body of his mother brought from Burgos to Seville ... he had them both entombed in rich sepulchers, beautifully carved, in their respective likenesses."[39] Although Alfonso describes the statue of his father sitting on a throne, he did not provide the same detail about Beatriz's tomb. The *cantiga* does say that her body was uncorrupted – which would have been typical of the corpses embalmed at Las Huelgas – and certainly helped Alfonso make his case. Much later, an inventory dated to 1500 described the likeness as depicting "the most beautiful woman in the world."[40]

Most fascinating, however, is the cushion on which Beatriz's body was laid. This cushion has been traditionally read as being "completely Christian" in iconography, "interrupting" an otherwise Arabized fashion which dressed the queen's body. Molina López proposes, however, that the scene on the cushion – comprising a knight, a lady, a bird, a flower – is not religious at all, but rather a courtly love scene, or "temática galante," possibly of a wedding, and related to a fresco found in the Palazzo Finco de Bassano in Vicenza, Italy (part of the Empire.)[41] This fresco depicts a troubadour, queen, bird, and flower. Molina López suggests that this cushion was part of Beatriz's original wedding trousseau; Beatriz's tomb itself famously contained, along with the queen's body, the skeleton of a bird, and a flower.[42] These were all items that may or may not have been entombed with Beatriz in Las Huelgas, or, in Seville.

Finally, the famous "Crown of Eagles" which was placed on the contemporary statue of the Virgin Mary in the *Capilla de los Reyes* also connected Beatriz to the world of Frederick II and the Holy Roman Empire. The crown, originally

---

37   Ibid., 380–1.
38   Ibid., 386–7.
39   *Cantigas*, no. 292.
40   Laguna Paúl, "Mobiliario medieval," 64; Laguna Paúl, "El imperio," 232.
41   Molina López, "El ajuar funerario," 384.
42   Molina López, "El ajuar funerario," 384.

made of silver and precious gems, has its own elaborate history: in the fourteenth century, Pedro I replaced some of the gems with false ones, in order to fund his war with Aragón, and then, much later, in in the nineteenth century, the crown was stolen from the chapel and replaced with various reconstructions. Originally, however, the design and workmanship of the crown linked it so closely with the empire that it is almost certain to have arrived in Castile as part of Beatriz's trousseau. Like the cushion described above, it is uncertain whether it was buried with her in Burgos, or brought independently to Seville by her ambitious son.[43]

As I, and others, have argued elsewhere, Iberian queens co-ruled with their royal husbands.[44] In the case of Beatriz, she participated in co-rule with Fernando in a primarily formulaic way, like her predecessor as queen-wife, Leonor of England: she was always included in Fernando's diplomas, where often, she took precedence over the king's mother. But there are other hints of Beatriz's potential activity as a ruler, and if she had lived longer, and perhaps outlived Berenguela, she may have had a greater role.[45]

Beatriz was surrounded by a group of men and women who served her, forming her household. Alfonso X mentioned his sister's nursemaid in *Cantiga* 256. Beatriz must have interacted with her son's known nurses, Urraca Pérez and Sancha, as well as with his tutors, such as García Fernández and his wife Mayor Arias. Other elites, such as the royal niece Mencía López de Haro, discussed below, attended the queen. One charter from October 1226 is confirmed by Beatriz's *mayordomo*, Pedro López.[46] It was possibly the same Pedro López who, with his wife Inés and sons and daughters received a substantial property as a gift in Baeza in 1232.[47] In 1237, a charter clarified that a royal gift to Pedro López and Inés in Tudela should not include monasteries and other possessions of the Church.[48] It cannot be certain that this Pedro López was the figure of the same name who served as Beatriz's *mayordomo*, but if it was, these charters also put his wife Inés within the orbit of the queen and the court.

The appointment of tutors and nurses for her sons gave Beatriz little role in raising them, and after her death, Berenguela managed the details of a number

---

43   Laguna Paúl, "El imperio," 219–21; 227–31.
44   For example, Shadis, *Berenguela of Castile*, 34–9, and Earenfight, "The King's Other Body," 44–50.
45   There is room for greater investigation of Beatriz's relationship to her dower lands, begun by Rodríguez López, *Consolidación*, 156–7.
46   *Fernando III*, II: no. 219.
47   *Fernando III*, II: no. 494.
48   *Fernando III*, III: no. 609; followed by a charter issued to the Bishop of Burgos similarly protecting properties belonging to San Millán: Ibid., no. 610.

of the children's futures.⁴⁹ Beatriz's fecundity suggests that she spent a lot of time with Fernando, and as Berenguela planned, there was no hint of infidelity or straying on the king's part. On the other hand, the source for Berenguela's chastening agenda is Rodrigo Jiménez de Rada, who was writing about Beatriz's marriage, and the fear that Fernando III might "damage his chastity" *after* Beatriz's death, in the light of expressed concerns about Fernando's marriage to Juana.⁵⁰ Beatriz helped found the Cistercian community at Matallana, in the family tradition, although interestingly this was an institution for men, not women.⁵¹ In 1231, she issued a charter protecting a hospital for pilgrims along the *camino* founded by the abbot of Sahagún: it was literally a protection against violence, damage, injury, or extortion (*gravamen in debitum*). Anyone who violated the protection would be subject to the "wrath of the king, and of mine."⁵² She held the tenancy of León in 1231 and 1232, a tenancy which was only assumed by Berenguela in 1236–38, after Beatriz's death.⁵³ Beatriz, already the mother of many, was the king's representative in León in her prime, poised to express her power as a ruler.

1.3 *Juana*

Jeanne de Ponthieu (Juana) demonstrates a simultaneously parallel and divergent portrait of queenship at Fernando's court. She married Fernando in about 1237. Because she was heir to the county of Ponthieu, she was subject to the political schemes of Blanche of Castile – Berenguela's sister. Juana was widowed by Fernando, furthermore, and so we see how a queen might have been rewarded by the king's conquest, through her portion of the *repartimientos*. Being queen of Castile-León was probably not easy for Juana. She became the wife of a king who already had seven sons, and whose mother was a still extremely active co-ruler. Infante Alfonso, the future Alfonso X, was sixteen years old in 1237 and taking on more responsibility, like the tenancy of León, which had been held by Juana's predecessor, Beatriz.⁵⁴ Still, like Beatriz, she also served as the king's companion and guardian of his chastity – over the fifteen

---

49 Shadis, *Berenguela*, 115–7.
50 Shadis, *Berenguela*, 108. On Beatriz, *Set quia indecens erat ut tam magnus princeps extraordinariis petulanciis traheretur, mater sua, que semper uoluit eum ab illicitis custodire, procata est ei uxorem nomine Beatricem*: DrH, 290. On Juana: *Et ne pudicicia alienis comerciis lederetur, regina nobilis mater sua domicellam nobilem ... Iohannem nominee, procurauit in coniugem sibi dari*: DrH, 300.
51 Shadis, *Berenguela of Castile*, 162.
52 *iram regiam et meam*: *Fernando III*, II: no. 368.
53 Shadis, *Berenguela of Castile*, 81.
54 Ibid., 82.

years of their marriage, she bore at least five children, one of whom became the powerful queen of England, Eleanor of Castile, wife of Edward I.[55] In 1251, Juana succeeded her mother as the countess of Ponthieu, and after Fernando's death in 1252, conflict with Alfonso X over her dower left little incentive for her to stay in Castile. She returned to France in 1254, and died in Abbéville in 1279, around the age of sixty.

Like Beatriz, Juana spent a lot of time with her husband, even accompanying him to the frontier. She was present in 1248 at the siege of Seville, when she, with her sons Fernando and Louis, endowed the Order of Calatrava with houses and an estate in Carmona (which had capitulated to Fernando the year before) as well as other property. Anyone who contravened this gift would be subject not only to the wrath of God but to that of the king – and the queen – echoing the language of Beatriz's 1231 charter to Sahagún.[56] In 1252, from conquered Seville, Fernando issued a *fuero* to Carmona, in which the rights and privileges of the queen figured prominently.[57] The fuero clearly indicates that Juana was the lord of the city, and she confirmed the charter:

> And I, Queen doña Juana, authorize all these laws and these things written above, which should be valid and last forever in Carmona and in its *termino*, which the king don Fernando gave me as a benefice: And so that this is firm and stable and endures for all time I put my seal on this charter.[58]

Above all, the queens at Fernando's courts were mothers, but they also partnered with the king and worked in various ways to enhance his status and protect his reputation. The surviving charters of the queens are few, but diverse. They demonstrate queens who were great lords, who administered law and promised justice; who were pious and canny patrons; who were connected to urban environments, such as Burgos, and Carmona. They promoted the Christian

---

55   Eleanor's brothers included Ferdinand, who became count of Aumale, Louis, Simon, and John. The latter two died in childhood.
56   *ira de Dios et la del rey et la mía*: *Fernando III*, II: no. 761. In 1248, Juana also held half of the tenancy Carrión, possibly as part of her arras. Rodríguez López, *Consolidación*, 149–50, 157.
57   *Fernando III*, III: no. 847.
58   *Et yo reyna donna Johanna otorgo todos estos fueros et estas cosas asi commo sobredicho es que valar et duren por siempre en Carmona et en su termino que mio mando el rey don Fernando me dió por bondat: E porque sea firme et estable et dure por todo tiempo mando poner mio sello en esta carta*: Ibid.

conquest of al-Andalus, especially through their patronage of the Order of Calatrava. This is apart from their demonstrable weight as signifiers of legitimacy and corporate monarchy.

2   The Nobility: Countesses, Abbesses, and Others

The royal court must have comprised an enormous number of people: aristocrats who traditionally claimed the most important posts, body guards, clerics, chaplains, itinerant bishops, – these are just the men – and all their servants, the men and women who were necessary to keeping a household running and creating an effective display of power. We ought to think more about the women who were part of this court. We *expect* to see the queens and the royal women there, and we know, or intuit, the presence of a large cohort of women in the households of the queens and their children. The large majority of these women remain unidentified. Yet in some cases, by identifying male members of the royal entourage, we can infer something about the roles of their wives. At the same time, there were many – elites and non-elites alike – who interacted with the court as independent individuals, not as household members. In either case, these women helped shape the court of Fernando III.

2.1   *Mayor Arias*

After the queens, the most powerful secular woman circulating at the court of Fernando III was undoubtedly Mayor Arias.[59] Although she must have come from a noble family, her parentage is unknown.[60] Mayor comes to light – both in the sources and on the Castilian social scene – with her marriage to the powerful García Fernández around 1216. García Fernández had been Queen Leonor's *mayordomo* in 1214. He was probably Berenguela's partisan during the chaotic years of 1216–1220, after which he became Berenguela's *mayordomo*, and then, eventually, Fernando's. He also, along with Mayor Arias, tutored Infante Alfonso. García Fernández had married before – and had three children with Teresa Muñoz – but it would be his many children with Mayor who continued to have influence at the court of Alfonso X. These included Juan, Alfonso, Diego, Teresa, Marina, Urraca, and Mencía García, and possibly Mayor

---

[59]   The best (possibly the only) studies of Mayor Arias's life are embedded in two articles dedicated to García Fernández. Serrano, "Mayordomo mayor," and Álvarez Borge, "García Fernández."

[60]   Serrano, "Mayordomo mayor," 114. Serrano thinks she was Castilian, whereas Álvarez Borge suggests she may have been Galician or Leonese. "García Fernández," 662.

and Elvira Arias.[61] Over the course of his career, García Fernández became a great lord, assembling a vast patrimony of lands stretching from Galicia to Andalucía: Ignacio Álvarez Borge links his ability to build this patrimony with his status as a royal official and courtier.[62] Certainly, he acted with Fernando's knowledge and approval, as when in 1228 abbot Esteban of La Vid sold a property to García and Mayor "with the authorization of the king don Fernando," and Fernando authorized the charter in person, along with his mother Berenguela.[63] Fernando also contributed to the couple's wealth, for example endowing them in 1232 with the villa of Manzaneda in Limia.[64]

Mayor Arias underwrote, enhanced, and exploited her husband's prominence. In 1221, Abbot Pedro of San Pedro of Arlanza sold an estate to García Fernández, which Mayor had previously given to the convent. He also included an estate in Celada, where later Mayor and García would raise the Infante Alfonso.[65] This charter demonstrates Mayor's economic independence, certainly before widowhood, and possibly before marriage. Throughout her marriage, she participated consistently in García's economic activities. She was named as a co-recipient in the gift mentioned above; she was included in a gift from Queen Berenguela in 1227; and eventually, I speculate, she was endowed with the estate known as the "Cortija de Mayor Arias," outside of Córdoba after 1236. The Cortija de Mayor Arias – which can still be found on a map in the environs of Córdoba – while clearly named for Mayor, is generally associated with García Fernández, presumably a reward from Fernando after the conquest of that city. While it is possible that García named this country estate for his wife in some sort of romantic gesture, it seems more likely that the estate (and the implicit reward, whether from husband or king) was hers. It was also a sign of her potency at court.[66] She, along with her husband, was entrusted with the care of the young heir to the throne, the Infante Alfonso. She, along with Alfonso's nurse, Urraca Pérez, was named in the charter recording his wedding to Violante of Aragón in 1246 at Valladolid, and was particularly rewarded by the young king years later in 1255 with the estate of Cecivo de la Torre, "for many services which doña Mayor Arias performed for me."[67] It is ironic then, that

---

61   All of Mayor's sons served at one time or another at Alfonso x's court, but especially Juan, who from 1252–1269 was close to the king. Serrano, "Mayordomo mayor," 139.
62   Álvarez Borge, "García Fernández," 649, 653.
63   Serrano, "Mayordomo mayor," Appendix XIV; González, *Fernando III*, III: no. 237.
64   *Fernando III*, II: no. 479.
65   Serrano, *Cartulario de Arlanza*, no. 155.
66   González, *Repartimientos*, I: 49–50.
67   Serrano, "Mayordomo mayor," 129, note 3; also Appendix XX: *por muchos seruicios que me fizo Donna Mayor Arias*. In 1255, Alfonso X referred to the fact that Mayor *me criaron en*

Mayor Arias appears in so very few of Fernando III's extant charters. Two of his most important gifts to García Fernández do not name her, in contravention with customary formulae. One charter cited above in 1218 includes Mayor but is clearly a gift directed at García, for it rewards services carried out for Leonor, Berenguela, and the king "in the beginning of my reign."[68] However, it was this gift – houses in Toledo and an estate in Aceca – which Mayor would eventually use to establish anniversary masses for García and herself.[69]

García died in 1241. His testament reveals his attachment to Queen Berenguela: he bequeathed her his hawks for hunting herons and ducks.[70] He placed Mayor and Villamayor under the protection of Berenguela, Fernando, and Infante Alfonso (to whom he left a cameo.) Mayor, the abbess of Villamayor, his son Rodrigo García and García Álvarez served as his executors.[71] Both Luciano Serrano and Álvarez Borge point out that it was in widowhood that Mayor Arias "grew in power" – or at least, in wealth. She continued García Fernández's acquisition of property, but on a phenomenal scale. She bought and traded land from Burgos to Córdoba; she was richly endowed by the king in the 1253 *repartimientos* in Seville; she purchased her stepchildren's inheritance (and paid their debts).[72] Álvarez Borge observes that in three short years, Mayor Arias demonstrated the capacity to invest amounts of up to 65% of what her husband had accomplished over his lifetime.[73] Perhaps she was simply following a trajectory established by García, enabled by his status at court. Perhaps, however, it was her own status at court that allowed her to be so successful. Finally, her enormous wealth and family connections, as well as her closeness to the Infante Alfonso, certainly strengthened her position at Fernando's court.

García Fernández is also credited with the reformation of the monastery of San Vicente into the female Cistercian monastery of Villamayor, around 1223. As Álvarez Borge points out, the foundation of Villamayor may have served García's family in much the same way Las Huelgas served the royal family.[74] It was a family pantheon in the care of women, providing a deep bond between

---

Villaldemiro e en Celada. Álvarez Borge, "García Fernández," 689, note 137. Serrano, "Mayordomo mayor," App. XX.

68   *in principio regni mei*: *Fernando III*, II: no. 28.
69   Álvarez Borge, "García Fernández," 660, note 29; Serrano, "Mayordomo mayor," App. XVII.
70   Serrano, "Mayordomo mayor," Appendix XVI. See Bianchini, *The Queen's Hand*, 230.
71   Serrano, "Mayordomo mayor," Appendix XVI. See Bianchini, *The Queen's Hand*, 230.
72   Álvarez Borge, "García Fernández," 670-1. Serrano, "Mayordomo mayor," lists Villasilos, Melgarejo, Villasendino and Villavedón as among her extensive holdings.
73   Álvarez Borge, "García Fernández," 683.
74   Ibid., 678.

the sacred and the everyday life of family, and finally, served as a refuge for women outside of or after marriage (if not for Mayor Arias). It was also, he suggests, another way to manage and grow the patrimony.[75] I think it likely that Villamayor was reformed not only in the fashion of the day (turning to the Cistercian Order) but in direct imitation of the royal family. As Leonor's and Berenguela's *mayordomo*, García Fernández would have been deeply familiar with the purpose and operation of Las Huelgas. But, it seems just as likely that it was marriage to Mayor Arias which encouraged this foundation, since as Serrano has suggested, it permitted Mayor to provide a community over which her sister Marina Arias, almost certainly Villamayor's first abbess, could preside.[76] Mayor's daughters, Mencía García and Mayor Arias, were subsequently abbesses of Villamayor, and other descendants held important offices there, possibly including Mayor García, the daughter of García's first wife Teresa Muñoz.[77] Mayor Arias's religious patronage was also suggested by García's bequest of diamonds to her for the construction of a cross for Villamayor, and her donations to the cathedral chapter at Toledo for anniversary masses for García Fernández and eventually herself.[78]

Mayor herself had a significant household. Her chaplains Rodrigo and Romero witnessed several charters.[79] Her "companía" – some four men – were rewarded in the *repartimientos*, providing a connection between her wealth, her status, and her obligation as a great lord to participate in the king's conquest of Seville. Julio González considered these "minor donations" but as men who were rewarded for their association with a woman, they stand out (others were associated either with royal women or were men whose widows or children were entitled to a *repartimiento*).[80] Mayor's men, Pascual, Andrés Martínez, Marcos, and Fernán Martínez received property in Palmaraya. She also received olive and fig groves in Benacazón in Sanlúcar, wheatfields (*yugadas de pan*) in Alacuás, a tower in Tejada (both in Seville), and a garden in Santa Justa.[81] Mayor's properties in Palmayara, when combined with those given Queen Juana, Queen Violante, and Infanta Leonor, became known as "Las Dueñas."[82]

---

75 Ibid., 678.
76 Serrano, "Mayordomo mayor," 117.
77 Ibid.
78 Serrano, "Mayordomo mayor," Appendix XVII.
79 Serrano, *Cartulario de Arlanza*, CLV; Serrano, "Mayordomo mayor," Appendix XVII.
80 González, *Repartimientos*, I: 275; Ibid., II: 88, 257–8.
81 González, *Repartimientos*, II: 30, 205. Many women named Mayor Arias show up in the *repartimientos*, but they are unlikely to be the same woman.
82 González, *Repartimientos*, I: 275.

2.2 Countess Mencía, Abbess of San Andrés de Arroyo

"Our venerable friend," Countess Mencía, Abbess of San Andrés de Arroyo provided a crucial link between the reign of Alfonso VIII and that of Fernando III – probably through Berenguela's offices. Next to his mother, countess Mencía was likely the most prominent woman active in connection with Fernando's court early in his reign. (His sisters Berenguela and Constanza, while prominent, demonstrated little agency in this period.) While as early as 1173 one Countess Mencía was doing substantial business with the crown, it was really between 1181 and 1214 that Mencía and her foundation of the Cistercian female monastery of San Andrés de Arroyo were significant beneficiaries of royal patronage, receiving seven different gifts or concessions from Alfonso VIII.[83] She was, in all likelihood, the sister of Alfonso's trusted *alférez,* Diego López de Haro.[84] Mencía stepped into the lime-light, however, as one of the executors of Alfonso's will. In 1204, when Alfonso VIII made his will, he named no executors beyond his wife Leonor and his son Fernando.[85] Just before he died in late September of 1214, whatever plans he may have had for his last testament were radically changed by the death of his old friend Diego López: "He had intended to entrust his kingdom and his son, who had not yet reached puberty, and his wife and daughters to the care of that noble and faithful vassal, leaving everything at his command and power…"[86] We know very little about Alfonso's last days: an early charter of Enrique I asserts that Leonor had given custody of the king and kingdom to Berenguela, "just as the lord king of blessed memory had given it to the queen Leonor."[87] It is assumed, based on Alfonso's will of 1204, and Enrique's charter, that Alfonso turned his kingdom (and his son) over to Queen Leonor, but she outlived him by only a few weeks, and the king and kingdom were left in Berenguela's hands. The earliest documents from Enrique I's reign, however, name four executors for Alfonso: Archbishop Rodrigo Jiménez de Rada, Bishop Tello of Palencia, Gonzalo Rodríguez (Alfonso's *mayordomo*)

---

83   *Alfonso VIII*, II: nos. 186, 366; Ibid., III: nos. 528, 553, 680, 870, 925, 935, 941.
84   Canal Sánchez-Pagín, "La Casa de Haro," 60. Canal Sánchez-Pagín identified Mencía as the daughter of Countess Aldonza and Count Lope Díaz de Haro. He suggests that Mencía must have been married (and widowed) by 1174, when she first appears in the documentary record as "countess" – a title, he argues, that could only be achieved through marriage to a count. He proposes, based on a cloister carving at San Andrés, that her husband was a member of the Lara family, most likely Alvaro Pérez de Lara, when he was already quite old. 80–1. Alvaro Pérez died in 1172. Doubleday, *The Lara Family,* 32.
85   *Alfonso VIII*, III: no. 769.
86   O'Callaghan, *Latin Chronicle,* 28, 59.
87   *sicut dominus rex bone memorie dimiserit ipsi Allionori regine. Alfonso VIII,* III: no. 963.

and Countess Mencía of San Andrés de Arroyo.⁸⁸ González describes a charter from the cathedral archive at Osma identifying Mencía, Gonzalo, and the bishop of Palencia as the "trustees of Alfonso of celebrated memory."⁸⁹ In whatever way Mencía became appointed an executor of the defunct king, she was accepted as such, and language from an undated gift from Alfonso to San Andrés suggests he would have approved: "our venerable friend Countess Mencía" is described as faithful and devoted in service.⁹⁰ Mencía's role at Enrique's court was of limited duration. She last appeared in a charter of September, 1215, which gives the effect of pensioning her off: the king confirmed all of the gifts and privileges given by Alfonso VIII to San Andrés de Arroyo, "to you countess Mencía, currently abbess of that same monastery."⁹¹ This happened shortly before Berenguela was forced to leave the king and court in the hands of Álvaro de Lara.

Mencía's attachment to Alfonso VIII, and likely to Berenguela, explains her prominence in the early days of Fernando III's reign. After her death (probably in the late 1220s), San Andrés de Arroyo did not have a significant presence in Fernando's charters, suggesting that it was her individual person, and not the monastery itself that mattered. In November 1217, Fernando invoked Mencía as one of his grandfather's executors; in August 1219 he confirmed an earlier privilege of Alfonso VIII to San Andrés "and to you, my most venerable friend, countess lady M(encía), abbess of the same." This privilege was again confirmed in November 1232, after Mencía's death.⁹² In 1220, Fernando made a direct gift to San Andrés and to "you my most venerable friend" of the villa of Nestar, near Aguilar. This he did not only for services to his grandparents "of happy memory," but also because of help in his youth.⁹³ Here, Fernando (and likely Berenguela) echoed sentiment expressed in gifts to García Fernández and Mayor Arias – gratitude for help and loyalty during the precarious years of Enrique's reign and the beginning of Fernando's. Two more gifts, one concession, and one confirmation were issued by the king to Countess Mencía

---

88 *Alfonso VIII*, III: nos. 963, 969, 970, 971.
89 *fideicomissarios Aldefonsi venerande memorie*: *Alfonso VIII*, I: 221.
90 *que nobis grata sempre extitit, et merito fidelitatis et laudabilis deuotione seruicii* ... : *Alfonso VIII*, III: no. 935.
91 *uobis comitisse dompne Mencie, eiusdem monasterii instant abbatisse*: *Alfonso VIII*, III: no. 986.
92 *uobisque, uenerabili amicissime mee comitisse domine M(encie) eiusdem instant abbatisse*: *Fernando III*, II: nos. 8, 88, 491.
93 *multum suo in tempore placuistis penes quos vestre fidelitatis in ius* (sic) *exigentibus causis* [*tachado y superpuesto "earum"*] *et in summa reverentia habitum mihi constat* ... *cui per omnia a primis cunabulis laudabiliter servistis et servire quotidie non cesatis*: *Fernando III*, II: no. 105.

between 1221 and 1225.[94] In 1226, the king confirmed the purchase of an estate made by Martín Pérez and Elvira Pérez, Martín being identified as the "man of my venerable friend countess doña M(encía)."[95] It was undoubtedly Mencía's status that attracted the king's attention to this otherwise pedestrian purchase, and accounts for his presence at San Andrés.

If Mencía was the sister of Diego López de Haro, then she was also the sister of the former queen of León, Urraca López de Haro.[96] Urraca's story is well known: the third wife of Fernando II of León, she sought determinedly to establish her son Sancho as Fernando's heir, and when Alfonso IX came to the throne in 1188, she fled to Castile to the protection of Alfonso VIII. Urraca founded another dependency of Las Huelgas at Vileña, and secured Fernando III's protection of her foundation in 1224. Fernando's charter reiterated the twenty-first Psalm – "For the kingdom is the Lord's and he shall have dominion over nations" [Ps. 21.29] – and then continued on the fittingness of royal dignity to "increase, defend, and venerate" the devotions of holy women. Addressing the abbess Elvira, Fernando promised to protect "my venerable 'aunt', Queen doña Urraca's" massive donation of multiple properties and exempted several places from obligations of tribute in favor of Vileña.[97] Urraca's foundation coincided with the reform of Villamayor by García Fernández and Mayor Arias.[98] The two foundations (Villamayor and Vileña) not only imitated the patronage of the royal family, but also competed with other, royal, Cistercian foundations, such as San Andrés. In the end, they enhanced female, royal, religious networks, following the model and under the authority of the royal family and Las Huelgas in Burgos.

Over nineteen charters attest to Fernando's attention to the monastery of Las Huelgas. Abbesses Sancha, Ínes, and María Pérez de Guzman received many privileges and exemptions from the king, testifying to the institution's social and economic power. A significant number of Fernando's charters do not address an individual abbess (especially after Sancha's abbacy). This confirms the

---

94 *Fernando III*, II: nos. 140, 159, 186, and 204. Ibid., no. 140, issued in 1221, is directed at *venerabilis amice mee comitisse domne Mencie*, but makes no mention of San Andrés. González offers some potential confusion when he discusses the widow of Gonzalo Núñez de Lara, also a countess Mencía, who "probably retired to San Andrés de Arroyo" upon her husband's death. *Fernando III*, I: 148–9.
95 *homini uenerabilis amice mee comitisse domne M(encie)*: *Fernando III*, II: no. 211.
96 Canal Sánchez-Pagin, "La Casa de Haro," 61.
97 *Quoniam Domini est regnum et ipse gentium dominator, regiam decet dignitatem summopere eius per quem regnant servicio dicata loca misericorditer manu augere, defendere, venerari, ea vero maxime que sanctarum colit devotio feminarum*: *Fernando III*, II: nos. 193, 194.
98 Serrano, "Mayordomo mayor," 117.

idea that it was Las Huelgas itself, and not the women, who held high status at court. In this regard, Las Huelgas and its abbesses demonstrate an inverted relationship, compared to San Andrés de Arroyo and Countess Mencía. The convent was thoroughly imbricated with the court – Fernando's aunt, Constanza, and sister, also called Constanza, were nuns there, serving as the all-important "Ladies" of Las Huelgas, a role that his own daughter Berenguela would also take up.[99] Also living at the convent was Fernando's aunt, Leonor, who had returned to Castile after her marriage to Jaime I of Aragón ended in 1229. But as the pre-eminent Cistercian institution, Las Huelgas served as a core of gendered, religious activity for the court, and the many women interacting with it, coming from San Andrés, Vilena, Villamayor, Cañas, and, after 1230, Villabuena in León.

2.3   His Father's Daughters

Queen Berenguela's story provides the example *par excellence* of the political and personal potential afforded to elite Iberian women as full members of their lineages. As Lucy Pick argues, royal sisters have a deep history and significant role in shoring up monarchical power and legitimacy.[100] In a different context, Jonathan Lyon has demonstrated the power of the sibling bond in twelfth- and thirteenth-century Germany, where brothers and sisters generally cooperated in the interest of the lineage.[101] In Iberia, siblings also had an important role to play. In particular, siblings "from another mother" who were deemed natural or illegitimate could be surprisingly important.[102] As Sara McDougall has shown, by the time of Fernando's reign, canonical and secular rules governing legitimacy were only recently focused on parents' marital status, and gave very little attention to the status of a child herself. McDougall makes the case that Fernando could not be considered "legitimate" (even if recognized by Honorius III as the "legitimate king" of Castile) because his parents' marriage was invalid.[103] The same, then, could be said for the status of his sisters, Sancha and Dulce, never mind his multitudinous other siblings. Certainly, for Fernando, Sancha, and Dulce, a royal inheritance was at stake, which was not the case for their father's other children. In general, the sibling

---

99   For more on the Ladies of Las Huelgas, see in this volume Bianchini, Chapter 7.
100 Pick, *Her Father's Daughters*.
101 Lyon, *Princely Brothers and Sisters*.
102 The cases that follow concern the children of *barraganía* relationships between men and women who were not married to each other or anyone else. Shadis, "Received as a Woman," 9–11.
103 McDougall, *Royal Bastards*, 270–2.

relationship (if not the sibling bond) was a key factor in the structure of Fernando's social and political world.

By the time his father Alfonso IX of León had died in 1230, Fernando had fourteen living siblings (and at least four more had died before that date.) His sisters Berenguela, Constanza, and his brother Alfonso (eventual Lord of Molina) were the children of Berenguela and Alfonso IX. Two of Alfonso IX's children from his marriage to Teresa of Portugal, Sancha and Dulce, survived. Alfonso IX had furthermore produced a number of children with at least five or six *barraganas*, nine of whom survived their father.[104] Of these fifteen siblings living in 1230, ten were women. While Fernando's brothers – especially Alfonso de Molina – were important men, his sisters were not only more numerous, they also provide a clearer view of the variety of challenges and opportunities siblings posed for the king, and in particular, the useful role sisters could play. Female siblings were a particular resource.

Fernando's only sister to enter directly into religious life was Constanza. She helped bind his generation to Las Huelgas, following in the footsteps of their aunt Constanza and paving the way for Fernando's daughter, Berenguela. On the other hand, his sister Berenguela was exploited in an unusual bit of marriage diplomacy in 1224 when she was married to John of Brienne, in a successful effort to prevent that knight from marrying one of Fernando's Leonese sisters, Sancha or Dulce.[105] Berenguela's marriage to John, former titular king of Jerusalem, and then the couple's exodus to Constantinople in 1228 reinforced the link of the Castilians to the prestigious east, initiated by Fernando's own marriage to Beatriz of Swabia. Berenguela also reasserted familial connections to the French court, spending time with her aunt, Blanche, on her way to Constantinople; later, her children sought to exploit their relations in France and Castile.[106] Berenguela thus reinforced the Castilian court's international prestige and connections.

Fernando's half-sisters Sancha and Dulce never married, owing to the fact that his sister Berenguela did. Of all his siblings, Sancha and Dulce were the only ones who ever threatened Fernando's power. Shortly after Fernando received the throne of Castile from his mother, Berenguela, and the two of them secured the realm, Alfonso IX began to work toward establishing Sancha and

---

104 For an overview of these relationships, see Calderon Medina, "Las otras mujeres," 261–70.
105 On this union, see Bianchini, *The Queen's Hand*, 140–79.
106 Marie of Constantinople, "Letter to Blanche of Castile, 1248/49." Marie was eventually buried at St. Denis. She had been betrothed as a young child to the minor king of Jerusalem, Baldwin; her brothers Alphonse, Jean, and Louis were raised at Blanche's court. Grant, *Blanche of Castile*, 65, 72, 78, 115.

Dulce as his heirs in León.¹⁰⁷ Their inheritance might have represented Leonese independence from Castile, but at the time of Alfonso's death in 1230, neither had married, and Fernando had established himself as the king in Castile, as a husband and father, and as a warrior. After Sancha and Dulce's brief attempt to claim León, Fernando and Berenguela settled with his sisters (and their mother, Teresa) in the treaty of Benavente, which Lucas of Tuy characterized as being done "with great reverence."¹⁰⁸ This treaty ensured the sisters of an enormous income of 30,000 maravedís per annum, to be reduced or eliminated in the event that either of them joined a convent or married.¹⁰⁹ Sancha and Dulce, for their part, gave up any claims to the throne of León, and agreed to absolve all homage paid to them by their father's men.

Mostly likely, Sancha and Dulce became Cistercian nuns; they were certainly active on behalf of their mother's foundation of Villabuena in León. In August 1232, Dulce purchased a property from Juan Martínez and his wife María Yañez. The charter noted that "King Fernando reigns in León and Galicia, Castilla and Toledo..." but that "Queen Lady Teresa [is] building the monastery of Villabuena."¹¹⁰ Two years later, Fernando confirmed one of his father's early privileges of protection, authorizing the foundation of Villabuena, but decreed that the monastery should be placed under the obedience of Las Huelgas. He did this at the request of "my dearest sisters" Sancha and Dulce.¹¹¹ At the very least this demonstrates a peaceful, perhaps pragmatic relationship between the siblings. It also confirms Fernando's commitment to the preeminence of Las Huelgas, and the role of that institution in reinforcing the power of the monarchy – and thus, through Villabuena, binding León to Castile. Also in 1234, Fernando and Berenguela were forced to agree to return Castro Toraf to the Order of Santiago, upon the death or change of status (presumably marriage) of either of his sisters, who held it as a part of a long-standing agreement initiated by their father.¹¹² Bianchini points to this concession (or protection) as evidence of Berenguela's role in adjudication, but it also demonstrates Sancha and Dulce's power in León.¹¹³

---

107 Shadis, *Berenguela of Castile*, 110–5; Bianchini, *The Queen's Hand*, 180–207.
108 Lucas cited in Shadis, *Berenguela of Castile*, 115, fn. 99.
109 *Fernando III*, II: no. 270.
110 *Regnante rege domno Fernando in Legione et Gallecia, Castella et Toleti ... Regina Domna Tharasia, faciente monasterio Villabone*: Cavero Domingo, *Villabuena*, no. 10.
111 *carissimarum sororum mearum*: Cavero Dominguez, *Villabuena*, no. 11.
112 *Fernando III*, III: no. 535. According to Jiménez de Rada, Sancha had died by the time he completed his *De Rebus Hispanie* in 1243, but Dulce was still living. *DrH*, 227.
113 Bianchini, *The Queen's Hand*, 215–6.

Sancha and Dulce, in 1230, were in their late 30s, having been born between 1190 and 1194, and this may explain why they never married – perhaps it was too late. Or perhaps, their arrangements with Fernando made marriage a less-than-appealing prospect. But it is interesting in this regard to compare them to Fernando's (and their) other sisters, namely, the daughters of Alfonso IX's *barraganas*. With one exception, these were women who married the most important men in Castile (and then León), sometimes more than once. Their marriages confirmed their places within the highest echelons of society – or raised their husbands to those heights. In his charters, sometimes, Fernando referred to them explicitly as his sisters and other times he did not, but the charter record leaves no doubt about these women's importance.

Very early in his reign, Fernando rewarded Lope Díaz de Haro and his wife, "Urraca Alfonsez, my sister" with the villa of Pedroso on the Tobía river, "for many services" to both himself and his mother.[114] Lope Díaz was the son of Diego López de Haro, the *alférez* of Alfonso VIII, and succeeded his father in that station. This reward, undoubtedly prompted by Berenguela, resulted from his service in aiding Fernando early in his reign. At this point Lope was married to the king's half-sister, Urraca, who was probably barely fourteen years old at the time.[115] How was this marriage arranged? Was it part of Lope's reward? How did Fernando and Berenguela have access to his sister and indeed the ability to arrange such a marriage? (Perhaps the girl's mother, Inés Iñiguez de Mendoza was involved?) Urraca and Lope had a number of children before he died in 1236; she did not remarry. Amongst her children was Mencía, whose marriages were to cause Fernando no small amount of trouble.

Mencía's marriage to the cast-off husband of Aurembiaix of Urgell took place during Fernando's absence from court, and thus without his permission, challenging his perception of himself as king and patriarch.[116] Mencía was the cement in the alliance of embittered nobles, led by her father and her husband, rebels against the king's authority in the early years of his reign. In this rebellion, Lope Díaz sought to "avenge" himself against the king's "disdain and contempt." The *Latin Chronicle* calls this union a "concubinage," signaling the prohibited degrees in which the couple were related. The king was "moved to anger" upon discovering that his ward had been married without his permission. In response, Berenguela and Beatriz encouraged Álvaro Pérez to absent himself from court, flee "to the land of the Saracens or elsewhere," and thereby

---

114 *Urrace Alfonsi, sorori mee … pro multis et gratis serviciis*: *Fernando III*, II: no. 53.
115 Salazar y Acha, *La Casa del Rey*, 433.
116 Shadis, "Received as a Woman," 6, 13.

distract Fernando with worry about a more threatening alliance.[117] Álvaro died in 1240; by 1245, Mencía was married to King Sancho II of Portugal. How this marriage came about is unclear – later Portuguese sources blamed "evil councilors," averring that Sancho acted precisely contrary to Berenguela's advice that he should not marry Mencía.[118] While this marriage brought more grief to Sancho than it did to Fernando – it formed a key pillar of the complaint bringing about his deposition – the Castilian king was none too pleased when his son intervened on Sancho's behalf.[119] Mencía's status, her mobility, her influence, all derived from her mother's relationship to the King of Castile. She was also, however, a pawn to be used against him, effective because of her kinship with him.

Urraca's sister, Aldonza, married twice. Her first husband was Diego Ramírez Froilaz; the second was Pedro Ponce de Cabrera, a prominent noble at both Alfonso IX's and Fernando III's courts.[120] By 1230 he had married Alfonso's daughter Aldonza, who had been born, most likely, between about 1205 and 1220. In 1235, Fernando III confirmed Aldonza's *arras*, in which Pedro endowed her with one half of a tenth of the income from Melgar, Castro Calvón, and Alija, selling the other nine tenths for "mules, cloths, skins and furs of ermine, Moors [Muslims, that is, slaves], and whatever I ought to give in marriage and have not given."[121] Aldonza outlived her husband by at least fifteen, if not twenty years, donating her *arras* to construct a joint tomb at Santa María de Nogales, Pedro's family foundation.[122] Aldonza's son, Juan Pérez Ponce de León, was rewarded in the *repartimientos* and a number of her children continued to hold prominent roles in Castile and León.[123]

A nobleman could also use his sisters to gain access to the king. Simon Doubleday explains clearly how the ambitious Nuño González de Lara, whose family power had been firmly checked in the early days of Fernando's reign, developed a friendship with Infante Alfonso. The infante not only turned over his tenancy of Ecija to Nuño, but persuaded his father to permit Nuño's marriage

---

117   O'Callaghan, *Latin Chronicle*, 125–7. Shadis, *Berenguela of Castile*, 118–9. Rodríguez López, "Linajes nobiliarios," 853–4.
118   Fernandes, *Sancho II*, 325–7.
119   Doubleday, *Lara Family*, 66–7.
120   *Fernando III*, I: 170.
121   *mulas, paños, pieles versa y armiñas, moros y cuanto debió dare en casamiento y no había dado*: *Fernando III*, III: no. 563. Unfortunately, González does not include the actual *arras* charter, but only Fernando's confirmation. González cites AHN Sahagún carp. 914, no. 7.
122   Medina Calderón, "El Impulso nobiliario," 362–5.
123   González, *Repartimientos*, II: 46.

to Teresa Alfonso, Fernando's sister.[124] Nuño's help was likely needed in the siege of Seville, and indeed, he was rewarded in the *repartimientos*. In 1259, Teresa and Nuño donated some mills they had received from Alfonso X to the Order of Santiago.[125] Another sister, Sancha, married Simon Ruiz de Cameros, one of the greater magnates to be rewarded in the *repartimiento*, and a son of Rodrigo Díaz de Cameros.[126] Rodrigo had been one of Queen Berenguela's early partisans, but also a powerful lord who rebelled against Fernando early in his reign. Simon Ruiz was no less ambitious. In 1268 he attempted to compensate Sancha for her *arras*; he refers to her only as the "daughter of the king of León."[127] Two years later he married Malespina Fadrique, the daughter of Fernando's second son, Fadrique; in 1277 Simon and Fadrique were the victims of an execution ordered by Alfonso X.[128] Sancha had a reputation for piety, having entered the convent of Santa Eufemia in Cozuelos de Ojeda after her marriage, but her relationship with Fernando's court is a cipher. It seems nearly certain that her mother was Teresa Gil de Soberosa, Alfonso IX's last *barragana*. Sancha's reputation has probably developed at least in part as a counterpoint to her husband's sad end, execution for rebellion and sodomy.

Fernando's other sisters included María, who married Alvar Fernández de Lara, then Suer Ayres de Valladores; and also another Urraca, who married first García Romero (in Aragón), and then Pedro Nuñez de Guzman (who was rewarded in the *repartimientos*).[129] Like Sancha, María, Urraca, and Teresa have left little personal impact on the record – it is through their husbands that we see their relationship with their brother. Nevertheless, Fernando's relationships with his "natural" sisters, all daughters of Alfonso IX, demonstrate one aspect of royal family structure, which made a place for natural children, simultaneously exploiting and depending upon them.

3   The Working Women

The reproductive work of the women at Fernando's court extended well beyond the maternal obligations and roles of his mother and his wives. Wet-nurses,

---

124   Doubleday, *Lara Family*, 67, and fn 39.
125   González, *Repartimientos*, II: 336.
126   González, *Repartimientos*, I: 261.
127   *fija del rey de León*: Salazar y Castro, *Pruebas*, 39.
128   Doubleday, *The Wise King*, 204–7.
129   González, *Repartimientos*, I: 241; Ibid., II: 323.

nannies, and tutors populated the royal environment. Fernando had fifteen children, most of whom survived. Unlike previous generations, when it seems his grandmother and mother may have at least temporarily nursed their children – or at least their sons – Beatriz's fecundity called for backup.

Urraca, wife of García Álvarez was rewarded in 1231 together with her husband, "for many services (done for me) in nursing (or caring for) my firstborn son Alfonso."[130] Along with their sons and daughters, they received an estate in Portella which the king had confiscated from the archpriest Stephen for issuing false coinage. Later, in 1236, Urraca Pérez (presumably now García's widow) was rewarded as "the nurse of Lord Alfonso" (*nutrici domini Alfonsi*) with an estate in Villalinfierno which had previously belonged to the king's *merino*, Sebastian.[131] The 1236 document suggests that it was Urraca, and not García who was the primary "nurse" of the infante. This same Urraca, along with Mayor Arias, attended Alfonso's wedding to Violante in 1246.[132] In 1242, Sancha Ibáñez was rewarded as nurse ("*ama*") of Infante Fernando; this charter, a later copy, has been poorly transcribed, as it is dated 1242 but says that it was issued with the authorization of Queen Beatriz (who had died in 1235) and Queen Berenguela.[133]

As the cases of Urraca Pérez and García Álvarez, or even García Fernández and Mayor Arias demonstrate, it is not always easy to tell who might be the primary beneficiary or recipient of a charter, although historians have generally assumed (and often rightly) that it was the husband in a married pair to whom a charter was addressed. Still, because of women's particular legal standing as wives in a society of acquisitions, Iberian charters record their names, recognizing their rights, and as a result, reveal a lot of information about all sorts of women. Iberian law lent a particular shape to the structure of society, one which offered women opportunities to exercise their own agency and claim their entitlements. Put another way, they are present in the charters which dictate the privileges of wealth and property, because they were entitled to those privileges. They are not separated from their husbands in the texts of charters, and their husbands, rarely separated from them. This can be obfuscating, but it also presents the opportunity to consider the real presence and real contributions of multiple women who might otherwise be dismissed as formulaic appendages to the identities of their husbands, brothers, or fathers.

---

130   *pro multis itaque seruiciis que mihi in nutriendo Alfonsum, filium meum primogenitum*: *Fernando III*, II: no. 370.
131   *Fernando III*, III: no. 578.
132   Serrano, "Mayordomo mayor," 129n3.
133   *Fernando III*, III: no. 691.

The examples of the nurses, and of Fernando's many sisters, shows how this can work. Mayor Arias provides another important example. Women like María de Almenar, Mencía (wife of Pedro Fernández) and her daughters; Urraca García, Sancha Ordóñez, and Urraca Ordóñez (daughter and sisters respectively of García Ordóñez); Urraca (wife of García Álvarez); Sancha González (sister of Gómez González); Teresa (mother of Juan Fernández Variella, Blasco López, and Blasco Fernández) stand in for at least forty-two individual women named in Fernando's charters (apart from the queens, nobles, and family members discussed above.)[134] Many other women were indicated simply as wives or daughters. One interesting example can only be inferred from two men who are described by their in-law status: unnamed, their sisters or wives are a key piece of their identity.[135] This does not even take into account the hundreds of women – wives, daughters, and widows – associated with the rewards of the *repartimientos*, such as María Pérez, a laundress, and Sol, both members of the *criazon* of Fernando III, awarded land in Genis Cevi.[136]

4 Conclusion

This essay only begins to sketch the women at the court of Fernando III, but consistent themes emerge. The longevity of women like Berenguela and Mayor Arias, combined with their power as matriarchs, lords, and patrons shaped the influence they had and the demands they could make on the monarch. Another important theme is the role of monastic institutions – with Las Huelgas as the center of gravity and point of intersection for the gendered experiences of the court, and abbesses like Countess Mencía or patrons like Queen Urraca performing key legitimizing roles, linking Fernando's reign to his grandfather Alfonso VIII's in Castile and father Alfonso IX's in León. The Lady of Las Huelgas is shadowy figure in this essay, only alluded to, but compels an understanding of the important, gendered role of that institution vis-à-vis dynasty and commemoration.[137] Finally, we see through the example of the Haro elite the many ways in which a family might use women to gain access to the center of power.

---

134 *Fernando III*, II: nos. 187, 208, 240; Ibid., III: nos. 516, 646, 817.
135 *Ferrand Martínez, cunnado de Lope García ... Sancho Pérez, cunnado de Lope García ...* : *Fernando III*, III: no. 743.
136 González, *Repartimientos*, I: 269; Ibid., II: 57, 253, 269.
137 Shadis, "Piety, Politics," 207–9. See in this volume Bianchini, Chapter 7.

More obscure, and deserving of further inquiry, is the part that women like Berenguela played in shaping the gender ideology of the court. Theresa Vann argued some time ago that Queen Leonor, wife of Alfonso VIII, served as a model for the ideal queen in Alfonso X's *Siete Partidas*, but we have seen how Beatriz modeled dynasty and piety for the Wise King.[138] In her fecundity, Beatriz certainly met expectations of a particular kind of queenship. Berenguela herself articulated, without a hint of irony, an ideal of the natural modesty of the female sex when she wrote to Pope Gregory IX in 1239, and she most certainly saw her daughters-in-law as primarily reproductive beings, even as they all negotiated their very public roles.[139] Berenguela extended her expectations of modesty – or chastity – to kingship, but not to all men and women of the court. Fernando was notoriously chaste, and the remarkable absence of *barraganía* in his life may have resulted from a policy of distancing the king from the nobility (*barraganía* could have raised up a whole family, never mind just one woman); this may have been due to Berenguela's expedience in finding her son appropriate brides. She took no such measures for her son Alfonso de Molina, nor was her grandson Alfonso deprived of a female companion before marriage when he came of age. When we look at how Berenguela monitored and organized Fernando's sexual relationships in comparison to those of his brother Alfonso, however, we can see other roles for women. The women associated with Alfonso de Molina – his three wives, *barraganas*, and his daughters María de Molina and Berenguela Alfonso – all have something to teach us about the gendered expectations both by and about women at this court; María in particular must have taken lessons from her formidable grandmother.[140]

In the end, the reign and court of Fernando III was undoubtedly shaped by the experiences of military expansion, clerical framing, and expectations of paternal strength – indeed, patriarchy. But it was also a world in which women held a great deal of agency and influence. From the most powerful queen-mother, to the lowliest washerwoman, they can be seen to give to and to take from the world of the king.

---

138 Vann, "Theory and Practice."
139 *sed propter verecundum quam contraxit sexus femineus a natura* ... : *Fernando III*, III: no. 661.
140 Shadis, *Berenguela*, on Alfonso and his wives, 109, 162. On María de Molina, Ibid., 158–9, 173.

Works Cited

Primary Sources (Published)

González, Julio, ed. *Reinado y diplomas de Fernando III*, 3 vols. Córdoba: Monte de Piedad y Caja de Ahorros de Córdoba, 1983.

González, Julio, ed. *El Reino de Castilla en la época de Alfonso VIII*, 3 vols. Madrid: Consejo Superior de Investigaciones Científicas, 1960.

González, Julio, ed. *Repartimiento de Sevilla*. 2 volumes. Madrid: CSIC, 1951.

Jiménez de Rada, Rodrigo. *Historia de rebus Hispanie, sive Historia Gothica*. Ed. Juan Fernández Valverde. Vol. 72 of *Corpus Christianorum: Continuatio mediaeualis*. Turnhout: Brepols, 1987.

Kulp-Hill, Kathleen, trans. *Songs of Holy Mary of Alfonso X, the wise: a translation of the Cantigas de Santa María*. Tempe: Center for Medieval and Renaissance Studies, 2000.

Marie of Constantinople. "Letter to Blanche, 1248/49." Epistolae. Accessed January 29, 2019. https://epistolae.ctl.columbia.edu/letter/729.html

Martín López, Mª Encarnación and Gregoria Cavero Domínguez, eds. *Colección documental del Monasterio de San Guillermo de Villabuena (1172–1527)*. León: Universidad de León, 2018.

O'Callaghan, Joseph, ed. *The Latin Chronicle of the Kings of Castile*. Tempe: Center for Medieval and Renaissance Studies, 2002.

Serrano, Luciano. *Cartulario de San Pedro de Arlanza*. Madrid: CSIC, 1925.

Secondary Sources

Álvarez Borge, Ignacio. "Los dominios de un noble de la corte castellana en la primera mitad del siglo XIII. García Fernández de Villamayor." *Hispania. Revista Española de Historia* 68, no. 230 (2008): 647–706.

Barton, Simon. *Conquerors, Brides, and Concubines: Interfaith Relations and Social Power in Medieval Iberia*. Philadelphia: Pennsylvania University Press, 2015.

Bianchini, Janna. *The Queen's Hand: Power and Authority in the Reign of Berenguela of Castile*. Philadelphia: Pennsylvania University Press, 2012.

Calderón Medina, Inés. "El Impulso nobiliario en la expansion del Císter en el reino de León: La Parentela de Ponce de Cabrera en los monasterios de Santa María de Moreruela y San Esteban de Nogales." *Medievalismo* 18 (2008): 341–374.

Calderón Medina, Inés. "Las otras mujeres del rey: el concubinato regio en el reino de León (1157–1230)." In *Seminário Medieval, 2009-2011*, 255–287. Oporto: Instituto de Filosofía da Faculdade de Letras da Universidade do Porto, 2011.

Canal Sánchez-Pagín, José Mª. "La Casa de Haro en León y Castilla de 1150 a 1250: Cuestiones histórico-genealógicas en torno a cuatro nobles damas." *Archivo leoneses:*

revista de estudios y documentación de los reinos hispano-occidentales 43, nos. 85–86 (1989): 55–98.

Colmenero López, Daniel. "La boda entre Fernando III el santo y Beatriz de Suabia: motivos y perspectivas de una alianza matrimonial entre la corona de Castilla y los Staufer." *Miscelánea Medieval Murciana* 34 (2010): 9–22.

Dillard, Heath. *Daughters of the Reconquest: Women in Castilian town society, 1100–1300.* Cambridge: Cambridge University Press, 1984.

Doubleday, Simon R. *The Lara Family. Crown and Nobility in Medieval Spain.* Cambridge: Harvard University Press, 2001.

Doubleday, Simon R. *The Wise King: A Christian Prince, Muslim Spain, and the Birth of the Renaissance.* New York: Basic Books, 2015.

Earenfight, Theresa. *The King's Other Body: María of Castile and the Crown of Aragon.* Philadelphia: University of Pennsylvania Press, 2010.

Echevarría Arsuaga, Ana. "Esclavos musulmanes en los hospitales de cautivos de la orden militar de Santiago (siglos XII y XIII)." *Al-Qantara* 28, no. 2 (2007): 465–488.

Fernandes, Hermenegildo. *D. Sancho II: tragédia.* Lisbon: Temas e Debates, 2010.

Grant, Lindy. *Blanche of Castile, Queen of France.* New Haven: Yale University Press, 2016.

Irish, Maya Soifer. "The Castilian Monarchy and the Jews (11th to 13th Centuries)." In *Center and Periphery: Studies on Power in the Medieval World in Honor of William Chester Jordan*, ed. Katherine L. Jansen, G. Geltner, and Anne E. Lester, 39–49. Leiden: Brill, 2013.

Laguna Paúl, Teresa. "El imperio y la corona de Castilla: La visita a la capilla de los reyes de Sevilla en 1500." In *El intercambio artístico entre los reinos hispanos y las cortes europeas en la Baja Edad Media*, ed. María C. Cosmen, María Victoria Herráez Ortega, and María Pellón Gómez-Calcerrada, 217–238. León: Universidad de León, Área de Publicaciones, 2009.

Laguna Paúl, Teresa. "Mobiliario medieval de la capilla de los reyes de la Catedral de Sevilla: aportaciones a los 'Ornamenta Ecclesiae' de su etapa fundacional." *Laboratorio de Arte* 25 (2013): 53–97.

Lyon, Jonathan. *Princely Brothers and Sisters: The Sibling Bond in German Politics, 1100–1250.* Ithaca: Cornell, 2013.

McDougall, Sara. *Royal Bastards: The Birth of Illegitimacy, 800–1230.* Oxford: Oxford University Press, 2017.

Madoz, Pascual. *Diccionario geográfico estadístico-histórico de España y sus posesiones de ultramar.* Volume 4. Madrid: [s.n.], 1846.

Molina López, Laura. "El ajuar funerario de Beatriz de Suabia." *Anales de Historia del Arte* 24 (2014): 373–388.

Pick, Lucy K. *Her Father's Daughter: Gender, Power, and Religion in the Early Spanish Kingdoms.* Ithaca: Cornell University Press, 2017.

Ray, Jonathan. *The Sephardic Frontier: The* Reconquista *and the Jewish Community in Medieval Iberia*. Ithaca: Cornell University Press, 2006.

Rodríguez López, Ana. *La consolidación territorial de la monarquía feudal Castellana: Expansión y fronteras durante el reinado de Fernando III*. Madrid: CSIC, 1994.

Rodríguez López, Ana. "Linajes nobiliarios y monarquía castellano-leonesa en la primera mitad del siglo XIII." *Hispania: revista española de historia* 53, no. 185 (1993): 841–859.

Serrano, Luciano. "El mayordomo mayor de doña Berenguela." *Boletín de la Academia de la Historia* 104 (1934): 101–198.

Shadis, Miriam. *Berenguela of Castile (1180–1246) and Political Women in the High Middle Ages*. New York: Palgrave Macmillan, 2009.

Shadis, Miriam. "Piety, Politics and Power: the Patronage of Leonor of England and her daughters, Blanche of Castile and Berenguela of León." In *The Cultural Patronage of Medieval Women*, ed. June Hall McCash, 202–227. Athens: The University of Georgia Press, 1996.

Shadis, Miriam. "'Received as a Woman': Rethinking the Concubinage of Aurembiaix of Urgell." *Journal of Medieval Iberian Studies* 8, no. 1 (2016): 38–54.

Shadis, Miriam. "Women and Las Navas de Tolosa." *Journal of Medieval Iberian Studies* 4, no. 1 (2012): 71–76.

Vann, Theresa M. "Theory and Practice of medieval Castilian Queenship." In *Queens, Regents, Potentates*, ed. Theresa M. Vann, 125–147. Cambridge: Academia Press, 1993.

CHAPTER 9

The Peculiarities of Frontier Religious Authority in the Age of Fernando III

Francisco García-Serrano

It might have been a coincidence that Suero Gómez, Pedro of Madrid, Domingo of Segovia, and Miguel of Ucero, the four early companions of St. Dominic, arrived in Spain in 1217, the year of Fernando III's accession to the Castilian throne. Likewise, it was in that same year that the Franciscans entered Castile and established their first province in Spain. Legend has it that St. Francis himself came to Spain in the years 1211–1214, during which period he supposedly undertook a pilgrimage to Santiago de Compostela, and St. Dominic had also crossed the Pyrenees into his native land, to establish the first Dominican houses in Iberia. As a result, both great mendicant leaders were in the Castile of Fernando III at a time when both the kingdom itself and the mendicant provinces were in a vibrant period of expansion.

The reign of Fernando III was a period of great territorial change, during which Castile rose to supremacy in the Iberian Peninsula, not only through the unification of Castile and León in 1230 but also due to the staggering expansion of his territories southwards, into the lands of Islamic al-Andalus. In a few decades from the decisive battle of Las Navas de Tolosa in 1212, Almohad power on the Peninsula had been crushed and the crown of Castile had advanced south, conquering the cities of Baeza (1226), Úbeda (1233), Córdoba (1236), Jaén (1246) and Seville (1248), whilst Fernando III had also received the capitulation of the kingdom of Murcia. Scholars of his reign have long contended with the notion of the medieval "frontier" between Christian and Muslim kingdoms, and its various permutations, both in contemporary sources and in a vast range of scholarship.[1] Peter Linehan has suggested that references in Castilian sources to a "frontier" seem to have appeared for the first time in 1222,

---

[1] Discussions around the term "frontier" are numerous. For the key literature on this, see Powers, *A Society Organized for War*; Bishko, *Studies in Medieval Spanish Frontier History*; Ayala Martínez et al., eds., *Identidad y representación de la frontera*; Buresi; "The Appearance of the Frontier Concept in the Iberian Peninsula," 81–99; Burns, *The Crusader Kingdom of Valencia*; Linehan, "At the Spanish Frontier," 37–59, esp. 50–1; and Barton, *Conquerors, Brides and Concubines*, 11–2. See in this volume Boloix-Gallardo, Chp. 3

when Fernando III referred to territories defined by a series of fortresses or the riverbeds of the main rivers.[2]

The role of the Castilian Crown in the process of delimiting the political, military, and economic space of its southern frontier is well-known.[3] Fernando III's frontier policy has been amply discussed with regard to his relations with the papacy, and the predominant role of the military orders.[4] However, the activities, contribution and influence of the mendicant orders on this same frontier have largely escaped scholarly examination.[5] The Dominicans and Franciscans arrived in the Iberian Peninsula as preachers and founders of new houses, and saw rapid success across Castile and the other Christian kingdoms, but it was not long before they had also expanded into frontier territories bordering the lands of the Muslims in southern Iberia and also across the Strait of Gibraltar into the Maghreb. How did the newly formed mendicant orders of St. Dominic and St. Francis relate to the expansion of the Christian kingdom of Castile into Muslim lands? Did the religious frontier influence the expansion of these orders and what impact did it have on their development? This chapter will explore the place of these orders on the frontiers with Islamic al-Andalus and their role within the Castile of Fernando III.

1 The Establishment of the Mendicants

The impact of the friars after their arrival in the Peninsula was rapid and profound. Nonetheless, the mendicant orders were not always welcomed by the traditional Church hierarchy in Castile. The Castilian Church had been impoverished by its financial support for the monarchs in their military campaigns, and was near bankruptcy, and therefore, the arrival of Dominicans and Franciscans, potential competitors of bishops and other clerics, was a threat to the

---

2 *frontarias*: Fernando *III*, II: nos. 154, 157; Linehan, "At the Spanish frontier," 46. Although there is a much earlier reference from Aragón, from 1059, of the term *frontera*; Buresi, "The Appearance of the Frontier Concept in the Iberian Peninsula," 82–3.
3 Rodríguez-Picavea, "The frontier and royal power in medieval Spain."
4 Concerning the papacy, see Mansilla, *Iglesia castellano-leonesa*; Linehan, *The Spanish Church*; Rodríguez López, *Consolidación territorial*. Concerning the military orders, see among other works by these authors, Ayala Martínez and Joserrand, ed., *Identidad y representación de la frontera*.
5 It bears repeating that the study of the mendicants is, at times, problematic due to the scarce sources available. However, one can see García-Serrano, *Preachers*; idem, "Friars and royal authority"; Miura Andrades, *Frailes, monjas, y conventos*; Graña Cid, "Berenguela I y Fernando III"; idem, "The Mendicant Orders."

already fragile social and ecclesiastical balance.[6] The Dominicans in the bishopric of Palencia, for instance, suffered severe opposition and excommunication from Bishop Tello Tellez de Meneses, although this was not the case across the board.[7]

However, from the earliest days, the establishment of the Dominicans went hand in hand with royal support for the order in Castile. As early as 1222, Fernando III issued a letter protecting and promoting the Order of Preachers in the whole kingdom, compelling all Castilians to receive them well.[8] This was an act reiterated by subsequent Castilian rulers, such as Alfonso X, who was never distant from the friars, and Sancho IV and his wife, María de Molina, who helped the Dominicans to an extent unmatched by preceding monarchs.[9] Indeed, it is well known that, from this point onwards, the overwhelming majority of royal confessors were selected from among the mendicant orders, and were most often Dominicans.[10]

The foundation of mendicant houses was also reliant on royal support. It was probably Queen Berenguela, through her son Fernando III, who initiated the donations to the friars when in 1217 they received the generous sum of 1,400 maravedís to establish a house in Toledo.[11] Other convents, such as Santo Domingo of Madrid, founded in around 1217, received a letter of protection from Fernando III in 1228: "I receive under my commendation and protection the house of Santo Domingo of Madrid and the nuns and friars who live there."[12] Aristocratic support also determined the patterns of foundation of mendicant houses, and the Dominicans in particular established strong ties with the

---

6   Linehan, *Partible Inheritance*, 51; idem, "A Tale of Two Cities"; idem, *The Spanish Church*, 162–3.

7   García-Serrano, *Preachers*, 56–7. The disagreement stemmed from a privilege granted by Innocent IV in 1243 authorizing the friars to have conventual churches. AHN Clero 1742/17 (September 3, 1243), AHN Clero 1725/2 (January 20, 1259). In Salamanca, for example, there is no evidence of opposition to the establishment of the friars.

8   *sub protectione et defensione nostra receperimus et ad promotionem supradicti Ordinis*: *Fernando III*, II: no. 152; Linehan, *Partible Inheritance*, 51.

9   García-Serrano, *Preachers*, 39.

10   Nogales, "Confesar al rey"; Arquero, "El confesor real en Castilla."

11   García-Serrano, *Preachers*, 70, 72; AMT: *Libro Becerro del convento de San Pedro Mártir el Real de Toledo* (1806) fol. 2r records this donation. This is confirmed in another document, AHN Clero 3101/10 (July 8, 1293) by King Sancho IV; Hoyos, *Registro Historial*, I: 234.

12   *Sepades que yo recibo en mi comienda et en mio defendimiento la casa de Sancto Domingo de Madrit et las serores et los frayres que y son, et todas sus cosas*: *Fernando III*, II: no. 236. García-Serrano, *Preachers*, 49.

urban aristocracy and nobility, whilst the urban middle classes generated a good portion of the donations received.[13]

The association between the monarchy and the friars was publicized and reiterated in the Gothic iconography of the façade of the imposing cathedral of Burgos, founded in 1221. The Puerta de la Coronería, completed in the 1250s, displays the sculptured images of King Fernando III and Queen Beatriz of Swabia entering heaven, escorted by two mendicants, whom Deknatel has identified as the figures of St. Francis and St. Dominic.[14] Burgos was a fitting place for such a demonstration of closeness between monarchy and mendicants, as the most important political center of the kingdom, the "head of Castile" (*caput Castellae*), and a city in which Fernando III, like his predecessors, resided frequently.[15] In addition, there was an incipient commercial class and an increasingly influential urban aristocracy, the *caballeros villanos,* in the city.[16] This group was of interest to the friars too, as they could provide both material and political support for their foundations. It was also there, as legend has it, that St. Dominic himself, born just a few miles away, in the village of Caleruega, visited his native kingdom in 1218 to present to Fernando III the papal bull confirming the establishment of the Dominican Order.[17]

The early friars were more than successful; by 1250, the Dominicans had founded twenty convents in the most important cities of the Iberian Peninsula, and we know of the existence of about fifty Franciscan foundations for the territory of the kingdom of Castile alone in the thirteenth century.

2   Heresies

In much of the Latin West in the thirteenth century, preaching and the preservation of Christian orthodoxy was the primary consideration that preoccupied Dominican and Franciscan friars. The Dominican order in particular had been confirmed by Pope Honorius III in the bull *Religiosam Vitam* with the express mission of preaching against heresy, most notably in southern France. Heretical movements such as those of the Waldensians and Albigensians gave way to

---

13 See García-Serrano, *Preachers*, 47–73; idem, "Mundo urbano"; Vose, *Dominicans, Muslims, and Jews*; Le Goff, "Apostolat mendicant"; idem, "Ordres mendicants"; Freed, *The Friars and German Society*; Lesnick, *Preaching in Medieval Florence*.
14 Deknatel, "Thirteenth Century Gothic Sculpture," 280–1.
15 Montenegro, *Historia de Burgos*, 138–41. See also Estepa, Álvarez, and Santamarta, *Poder real*, 58–60.
16 Estepa Díez, *Burgos en la Edad Media*; González Díez, *El concejo burgalés*.
17 García-Serrano, *Preachers*, 75.

the anxieties of those who criticized the values of a worldly and increasingly materialistic society and even the Church itself.[18] However, few heretics or heretical movements can be traced in the kingdoms of Castile and León in this period. During the years of the greatest persecution of the Cathars in the south of France, in the first half of the thirteenth century, a few isolated groups of heretics emerged in Palencia, León and Burgos, three important cities on the Camino de Santiago, in which foreigners, pilgrims, adventurers and merchants converged.[19] However, the sources concerning heretics in Castile are as scarce as the heresies themselves. The writings of Lucas, bishop of Tuy, in book three of his *De altera vita*, constitute one of the most significant sources referring to heretical movements in León, although precisely what it was that Lucas was referring to has remained a point of scholarly debate.[20] A Frenchman named Arnold was suspected by Lucas as being something of a ringleader, and he may have been a Cathar-Albigensian from southern France who had travelled the Camino de Santiago, but there is too little evidence to say for sure.

Although small in scope, heresy also concerned the Castilian kingdom and its monarchy. We know that in 1236, Fernando III punished suspected heretics and confiscated their property in Palencia, the same city where St. Dominic had previously studied. This royal intervention was perceived as a clear interference in episcopal affairs, which led the bishop of Palencia, Tello Téllez de Meneses, to complain to Pope Gregory IX about the affair.[21] As a consequence, Pope Gregory ordered the king to return the confiscated goods to the bishop. The incident, and related complaint, seems to have been purely a matter of jurisdictional authority and economic gain, since what mattered most was which party would benefit from the confiscation of goods; little was said about the nature of the heresy and no further conclusions can be drawn about the *heresi infamatis* referred to in the sources.[22]

Finally, in 1238 there were also suspicions of heresy in Burgos, from a confession made before the papacy by a man named Vidal de Arvival.[23] These events

---

18   Little, *Religious Poverty and the Profit Economy in Medieval Europe*.
19   Fernández Conde, "Albigenses en Castilla y León"; idem, "Un noyau actif d'albigeois en León."
20   Lucas of Tuy, *De altera, Libri III*. The principle voices in this debate are Henriet, "Hagiographie léonaise et pédagogie de la foi"; Martínez Casado, "Cátaros en León"; Fernández Conde, "Albigenses en Castilla y León"; and Rucquoi, "La double vie de l'université de Palencia."
21   Abajo Martín, *Catedral de Palencia*, no. 183.
22   Abajo Martín, *Catedral de Palencia*, no. 184.
23   Palacios Martín, "La circulación de los cátaros"; Martínez Casado, "Cátaros en León"; Fernández Conde, "Un noyau actif d'albigeois en León"; Fernández Conde, *La religiosidad medieval en España*, 263–5 and 410–3; Grau, *Cátaros e Inquisición*, 343–59.

are recorded in a bull produced on September 25, 1238, in which Pope Gregory IX ordered Bishop Maurice of Burgos to investigate the heretical group of which Arvival claimed to be part. This man had arrived at the papal curia regretful for having maintained contacts with heretics. It seems that he had meals with them, participated in some of their ceremonies and even donated money to them. Most likely the group was in contact with the numerous foreign merchants that arrived in Burgos due to its thriving commerce.[24] Arvival confessed that he had denounced himself to the Pope for spiritual reasons in order to save his soul, since he was still a believer; however there remains too little evidence to detect the nature of the possible heresy.[25]

There is no evidence of mendicant friars preaching to heretics in Castile, nor of any attempts to pursue heresy there. However, it may be no coincidence that the Dominicans founded houses promptly in Palencia in 1219 and in Burgos in 1224, and later in León, where they delayed until c.1261.[26] Nonetheless, despite their objectives elsewhere in the Latin world to combat Christian heterodoxy, the mendicants in Castile do not appear to have made this their primary mission.[27]

3   Missionary Opportunities in Iberia and Beyond

The lack of major heretical movements could have been one of the main reasons why the early biographers of St. Dominic paid little attention to the events on the Peninsula. Neither Jordan of Saxony nor the handful of other Dominican writers before the mid-1260s, namely Pedro Ferrando, Constantine of Orvieto, Humbert of Romans, and Gerard of Fracheto, have much to say about the efforts of Dominicans to evangelize among Muslims, and neither Islam nor Spain play a preponderant role in the Dominican memory of the thirteenth century.[28] In fact, much more attention is paid to events beyond the Pyrenees, such as the struggle against the Albigensian heresy, the conversion of the Cumans on the Eurasian border, the crusades in the Holy Land or even the Mongols.[29]

---

24   Ruiz, "Castilian Merchants"; Carmen Carlé, "Mercaderes."
25   Smith, *Crusade, Heresy and Inquisition*, 132; Domínguez Sánchez, *Gregorio IX*, no. 79.
26   García-Serrano, *Preachers*, 27.
27   Fernández Conde, "Un noyau actif d'albigeois en León," 43–7.
28   Burman and Walker, "Spain, Islam, and Thirteenth-Century Dominican Memory," 313.
29   Ibid., 326–30.

Nonetheless, the frontier lands to the south of Castile presented the mendicant orders with new challenges, not faced in the same way by their peers elsewhere in Latin Europe. There has been considerable debate about the nature of the mendicants' interactions with Islamic al-Andalus.[30] Were the friars aiming to reach out and convert non-Christians, or were they rather more interested in administering to the faith of those Christians that lived in Islamic lands?

St. Dominic's original intention was to commission his brothers to preach throughout the world, and that is why he sent them to Spain, Paris and Bologna.[31] Famously, the Dominicans instigated the learning of Arabic and Hebrew in Spain in order to preach to the non-believers to the south.[32] Likewise, for the Franciscans, missions to the Islamic south were also important, as clearly stated by the *Regula non bullata* of 1221 (although it should be noted that this was never approved by the pope).[33] According to this early rule, the Franciscan friars who wished to live spiritually among Saracens and among other non-believers should be given permission to do so because they could spread the Word of God among unbelievers in the hope of converting them.[34]

There were opportunities for the friars to go on missions to Muslim territories in Iberia and beyond. In 1229, Fernando III obtained from the Almohad rival caliph al-Ma'mūn, in exchange for his military aid, not only ten fortresses, but also the agreement to build churches in Marrakesh and to give favorable treatment to the Christians who lived in the Maghreb.[35] The agreement did not last for long, but there were other opportunities, such as later in 1245 when the so-called "king of Salé" – identified by Joseph O'Callaghan as one of the sons of Abū Zayd, the king of Valencia – expressed a wish to convert to Christianity.[36] In these instances, the Castilian monarchy, in an attempt to assert power and

---

30   For a summary of the key lines of this debate, see Vose, *Dominicans, Muslims and Jews*; Kedar, *Crusade and Mission*; García-Serrano, *Preachers*.
31   Vones, "Mission et frontière."
32   Burman and Walker, "Spain, Islam, and Thirteenth-Century Dominican Memory"; Altaner, *Die Dominikanermissionen*; Coll, "Escuelas"; Bischoff, "The Study of Foreign Languages"; Ribes Montané, "San Ramón de Penyafort"; Cortabarría Beitía, "El estudio"; idem, "San Ramon," 138; Garcías Palou, *El Miramar*; Urvoy, "Les Musulmans," 416–27; Kedar, *Crusade and Mission*, 189.
33   Francis of Assisi, "Regula non bullata."
34   Tolan, *Saint Francis and the Sultan*, 7–9; Tolan, *Saracens*, 218–9; Tolan, "Taking Gratian to Africa."
35   Ibn Abī Zarʿ, *Rawd al-qirtās*, II: 485–6; González, *Las conquistas*, 58–9; Kedar, *Crusade and Mission*, 137–8. For more on the treaty with al-Ma'mūn, see in this volume Ayala Martínez, Chp. 1.
36   On the identification of this ruler of "Salé," see O'Callaghan, *Reconquest and Crusade*, 119; also Dufourcq, "Les relations"; Lopez, "À propos d'une virgule," 187–8; Muldoon, *Popes, Lawyers, and Infidels*, 40.

influence beyond the military domain, sought to leverage situations in defense of the faith into which the friars could operate.

The "dream of conversion" did not have to be manifested in Islamic lands: mission within the society of Castile would certainly have been another option, since sometimes large populations of Muslims and Jews continued to live in both cities and rural areas of Castile.[37] Indeed, Castilian kings, like their other Iberian counterparts, did not generally enforce papal orders designed to distinguish Jews through distinctive clothing and badges as dictated by the Fourth Lateran Council in 1215. Fernando III's disobedience on this account was something that exasperated Honorius III in 1218, who demanded an immediate explanation both from the Archbishop Jiménez de Rada and from the king. Fernando argued that if he were to impose such restrictions, there would be a massive exodus of Castilian Jews to Nasrid Granada, losing a great source of much-needed revenue for the Crown.[38] Later, the *Siete Partidas*, the law code first compiled under Alfonso X, clearly protected the indispensable Jews from forced conversion.

However, despite this context, and despite the establishment of language schools, there is in fact very little evidence of any real attempt by the mendicant orders to preach to Muslims in the Peninsula. While King Jaime I of Aragón presided over the Barcelona Dispute in 1263, forcing Rabbi Nahmanides to respond to Dominican claims that the Messiah had already arrived, using only the Hebrew Bible and other Jewish sources, we have no record of such disputes between Dominicans, or any other Christian scholars, and Muslims in Iberia in the early thirteenth century.[39] This disinterest in preaching to Muslims seems to contrast with the well-known case of five Franciscan friars who were martyred in Morocco in 1220.[40] However, aside from this, there is equally scarce evidence of Franciscans actively preaching to Muslims in the Peninsula, and their work seems to have been limited to serving the religious needs of Christians (mercenaries, merchants, captives, and other adventurers) who lived in Islamic lands – a population who were commented on by Ramón Lull in the later thirteenth century.[41] In this, the mendicants were supported by the *Redemptor Viri*, the Trinitarians (whose activities were concentrated mainly in the East), and the Mercedarians, originally from Catalonia, whose founder,

---

37 Burman and Walker, "Spain, Islam, and Thirteenth-Century Dominican Memory," 313.
38 Gerber, *Jews of Spain*, 95; Ray, *Sephardic Frontier*, 160–1.
39 Vose, *Dominicans, Muslims and Jews*, 133–5, 139–55, 161–4. See also Smith, "Ramon de Penyafort and his Influence."
40 Tolan, *Saracens*; idem, *Saint Francis and the Sultan*.
41 Ramon Lull noted that those imprisoned in Muslim lands could thus speak with authority about Islamic culture: Szpiech, "Prisons and Polemics."

Pere Nolasco, received alms in Barcelona. These orders were concerned with the fate of Christian prisoners in countries under Islamic domination. Their task was not only limited to the redemption of prisoners of war or the payment of their ransom, but also extended to the care of slaves and Christian mercenaries, Castilian or from elsewhere, who entered the service of Muslim princes.[42]

4 The Reorganization of Religious Authority on the Frontier

Partaking in the military efforts on the frontier and moving to this border-zone was not an appealing prospect to all in Castilian society. Demonstrating great pragmatism, Humbert of Romans, master general of the Dominicans, lamented in 1274 that the conquest of new lands by the Christian kings served little purpose when there was no interest on the part of the Christian populations to migrate to those territories.[43] For the inhabitants of the north of the Peninsula, the conquered south was also a climatic border, often inhospitable, where the heat could be overwhelming, for which reason Alfonso VIII complained to Pope Innocent III that the French knights deserted before the battle of Navas de Tolosa, in mid-July 1212.[44] Fernando III himself feared approaching Córdoba before its conquest in 1236, partly because of his physical weakness and partly because of the weather conditions he would have to endure.[45] It was in these sparsely-populated borderlands that the mendicant orders established their new foundations.

The establishment of the Church in newly conquered territories went hand-in-hand with mendicant expansion. In the aftermath of conquest, Fernando III appointed bishops in Baeza, Jaén, Córdoba and Cartagena and, of course, Seville, a means of territorial consolidation through the imposition of religious authority in this formerly Muslim territory.[46] Although it is worth noting that, with the exception of a few important prelates and members of the chancellery, the Castilian church did not benefit much from the Andalusi *repartimiento*, and the substantial economic efforts made by the Castilian prelates to help

---

42 Brodman, *Ransoming Captives*; idem, "Ransomers or Royal Agents"; Burns, "Christian-Islamic Confrontation"; idem, "Christian-Muslim Confrontation," 80–108, 310–2; idem, *Crusader Kingdom of Valencia*.
43 Linehan, "At the Spanish Frontier," 42.
44 For references to climate in frontier, see García Fitz, "Una frontera caliente," 159; Linehan, "At the Spanish Frontier," 41.
45 Salvador Martínez, *Berenguela la Grande*.
46 Rodríguez López, *Consolidación territorial*.

Fernando III in his Iberian crusades were scarcely recompensated, despite frequent admonitions from the papacy.⁴⁷

When the conquered cities were repopulated, there was a general tendency to leave deserted the neighborhoods *extramura* in order to live in more central locations.⁴⁸ Coincidentally, this tendency is also seen in the process of establishing mendicant houses in newly conquered cities. The first Dominican foundation in conquered territory was in Córdoba, taken by the Castilians in 1236; a Dominican house was founded there sometime before 1241, and in 1246, the city council praised the activities of the Dominicans in establishing Christian society in the city.⁴⁹ Dominicans were also established in Seville by the end of Fernando's reign. While in northern cities the friars had to establish their convents on the periphery of cities due to the lack of space within the walls, and only then moved decades later to more central and secure locations, in cities in newly-conquered territories in al-Andalus, they were allowed to establish themselves in more central locations from the very beginning, a demonstration not only of the value that the monarchy attributed to the presence of the friars in these new cities, but also of the ways in which territorial expansion assisted the mendicant orders in establishing themselves in the heart of Christian Iberian society.

The value of the friars on the frontier can be also seen by the role of some significant individuals. Mendicant bishops, such as Domingo of Baeza (a Dominican) and the Franciscan Pedro Gallego, were trusted by both the monarchy and the papacy. Gallego epitomizes what could be expected from a leading friar on the Iberian frontier. In 1236, he was already the Franciscan Provincial of Castile and soon became the confessor of infante Alfonso (the future Alfonso X). Alfonso would ultimately request Pope Innocent IV to restore the old diocese of Cartagena, for which post the king named his confessor and friend to be the first bishop in 1250.⁵⁰ In 1253, Innocent IV commissioned him to re-establish the episcopal see of Badajoz.

During his episcopate, Gallego was in charge of managing and organizing everything related to the material order of the bishopric, for which he acquired properties for his fellow friars, founded chapters, administered the tithes, and established the limits of his diocese and the bounds of his ecclesiastical jurisdiction, among many other things. He also devoted himself to the Christianization of its inhabitants, and encouraged the development of

---

47   Linehan, *The Spanish Church*, 91; Rodríguez López, *Consolidación territorial*, 19–21.
48   Menjot, "Urbanización fronteriza," 572.
49   Graña Cid, "The Mendicant Orders," 71.
50   See Torres Fontes and Luis Molina, *La diócesis de Cartagena*, 15–6; and Pelzer, "Un traducteur inconnu," 188–240.

sciences and learning in his episcopate, drawing on the Islamic culture that had preceded him in the kingdom of Murcia, which he would try to expand, drawing Castile and Aragón into closer communication with the rest of Latin Europe.[51] Fernando III's religious policy in the newly conquered territories cannot be understood without examining the decisive role played by the mendicant orders in general or by individuals such as Pedro Gallego.

Works Cited

Primary Sources
Unpublished

Archivo Municipal de Toledo (AMT)
   Libro Becerro del convento de San Pedro Mártir el Real de Toledo (1806)
Archivo Histórico Nacional, Madrid (AHN)
   AHN Clero 1742/17 (September 3, 1243)
   AHN Clero 1725/2 (January 20, 1259)

Published

Abajo Martín, Teresa, ed. *Documentación de la Catedral de Palencia*. Palencia: Garrido Garrido, 1986.

Altaner, Berthold. *Die Dominikanermissionen Des 13. Jahrhunderts. Forschungen Zur Geschichte Der Kirchlichen Unionen und Der Mohammedaner- und Heidenmissionen Des Mittelalters*. Habelschwerdt: Frankes, 1924.

Domínguez Sánchez, Santiago. *Documentos de Gregorio IX (1227–1241) referentes a España*. León: Universidad de León, 2004.

Lucas of Tuy. *Lucae Tudensis: De Altera Vita*, ed. Emma Falque Rey. Turnhout: Brepols, 2009.

Francis of Assisi, "Regula non bullata." In *Sources Chrétiennes*, ed. Kajetan Esser, trans. Théophile Desbonnets, Vol. 285, 122–179. Paris: Cerf, 1981.

González, Julio, ed. *El reino de Castilla en la época de Alfonso VIII*. 3 vols. Madrid: CSIC, 1960.

González, Julio, ed. *Reinado y diplomas de Fernando III*, 3 vols. Córdoba: Monte de Piedad y Caja de Ahorros de Córdoba, 1983.

Hoyos, Manuel. *Registro historial (Provincia dominicana de España)*. 3 vols. Salamanca: Editorial San Esteban, 1966–1969.

---

51   Atanasio López, "Fr. Pedro Gallego," 67; Pelzer, "Un traducteur inconnu." See also Adeline Rucquoi, "Autores mendicantes"; Rojo Alique, "Intelectuales franciscanos y monarquía," 303–4.

Ibn Abī Zar'. *Al-anīs al-muṭrib bi-rawḍ al-qirṭās fī akhbār mulūk al-Maghrib wa-ta'rīkh madīnat Fās*. Trans. Ambrosio Huici Miranda. 2 vols. Valencia: Textos Medievales, 1964.

Secondary Sources

Alvira, Martín. "On the term *Albigensians* in 13th century Hispanic Sources." *Imago Temporis. Medium Aevum* 3 (2009): 123–137.

Arquero, Guillermo. "El confesor real en Castilla (siglos XIII al XV): conocimiento sobre el mismo y plateamiento de estudio." In *Incipit 2. Workshop de Estudos Medievais da Universidad de Porto*, ed. Flavio Miranda, Joana Sequeira, and Diogo Faria, 127–140. Oporto: Universidade do Porto, 2014.

Ayala Martínez, Carlos de. "Fernando III y la Cruzada Hispánica." *Bulletin of Spanish and Portuguese Historical Studies* 42, no. 1 (2017): 23–45. DOI: https://doi.org/10.26431/0739-182X.1247.

Ayala Martínez, Carlos de, Pascal Buresi, and Philippe Josserand, ed. *Identidad y representación de la frontera en la España medieval (siglos XI–XIV)*. Madrid: Casa de Velázquez, 2001.

Barkai, Ron. "Diálogo filosófico-religioso en el seno de las tres culturas ibéricas." In *Diálogo filosófico-religioso entre cristianismo, judaísmo e islamismo durante la Edad Media en la Península Ibérica*, ed. Horacio Santiago-Otero, 1–27. Turnhout: Brepols, 1994.

Barton, Simon. *Conquerors, Brides, and Concubines: Interfaith Relations and Social Power in Medieval Iberia*. Philadelphia: University of Pennsylvania Press, 2015.

Bischoff, Bernhard. "The Study of Foreign Languages in the Middle Ages." *Speculum* 36, no. 2 (1961): 209–224.

Buresi, Pascal. "The Appearance of the Frontier Concept in the Iberian Peninsula: at the Crossroads of Local, National and Pontifical Strategies (11th–13th Centuries)." *Quaestiones Medii Aevi Novae* 16 (2011): 81–99.

Burman, Thomas and Lydia M. Walker. "Spain, Islam, and Thirteenth-Century Dominican Memory." In *Convivencia and Medieval Spain: Essays in Honor of Thomas Glick*, ed. Mark T. Abate, 311–339. Cham: Palgrave Macmillan, 2018.

Brett, Edward. *Humbert of Romans: His Life and Views on Thirteenth-Century Society*. Toronto: Pontifical Institute of Mediaeval Studies, 1984.

Brodman, James. *Ransoming Captives in Crusader Spain. The Order of Merced on the Christian-Islamic Frontier*. Philadelphia: University of Pennsylvania Press, 1986.

Brodman, James. "Ransomers or Royal Agents: The Mercedarians and the Aragonese Crown in the Fourteenth Century." In *Iberia and the Mediterranean world of the Middle Ages. Studies in honor of Robert I. Burns, S.J.*, ed. Paul Chevedden, et al., Vol. 2, 239–252. Leiden: Brill, 1996.

Burns, Robert. "Christian-Islamic Confrontation in the West: The Thirteenth-Century Dream of Conversion." *American Historical Review* 76 (1971): 1386–1434.

Burns, Robert. "Christian-Muslim Confrontation: The Thirteenth-Century Dream of Conversion." In *Muslims, Christians, and Jews in the Crusader Kingdom of Valencia: Societies in Symbiosis*, ed. Robert Burns, 80–108. Cambridge: Cambridge University Press, 1984.

Burns, Robert. *The Crusader Kingdom of Valencia: Reconstruction on a Thirteenth-Century Frontier*. 2 vols. Cambridge: Harvard University Press, 1967.

Burns, Robert. "Journey from Islam. Incipient Cultural Transition in the Conquered Kingdom of Valencia (1240–1280)." *Speculum* 35 (1960): 337–356.

Burns, Robert. "Immigrants from Islam: The Crusader's Use of Muslims as Settlers in Thirteenth-Century Spain." *American Historical Review* 80 (1975): 21–42.

Carmen Carlé, Marla del. "Mercaderes en Castilla (1252–1512)." *Cuadernos de Historia de España* 21–22 (1954): 146–328.

Coll, José. "Escuelas de lenguas orientales en los siglos XIII–XIV." *Analecta Sacra Tarraconensis* 17 (1944), 115–138; 18 (1945), 59–87; 19 (1946), 217–240.

Cortabarría Beitía, Angel. "El estudio de las lenguas en la Orden dominicana." *Estudios filosóficos* 19 (1970): 77–127.

Cortabarría Beitía, Angel. "San Ramon de Penyafort y los estudios dominicanos de lenguas." *Escritos del Vedat* 7 (1977): 124–154.

Deknatel, Frederick B. "The Thirteenth Century Gothic Sculpture of the Cathedrals of Burgos and Leon." *The Art Bulletin* 17, no. 3 (1935): 243–389.

Dufourcq, Charles-Emmanuel. "Les relations du Maroc et de la Castille pendant la première moitié du XIIIe siècle." *Revue d'histoire et de civilisation du Maghreb* 5 (1968): 42–53.

Estepa Díez, Carlos, et al. *Burgos en la Edad Media*. Burgos: Junta de Castilla y León, 1984.

Estepa Díez, Carlos, Ignacio Álvarez Borge, and José María Santamarta. *Poder real y sociedad: estudios sobre el reinado de Alfonso VIII (1158–1214)*. León: Universidad de León, 2011.

Fernández Conde, Francisco. "Albigenses en Castilla y León a comienzos del siglo XIII." In *León Medieval. Doce estudios*, 95–114. León: Universidad de León, 1978.

Fernández Conde, Francisco. *La religiosidad medieval en España (siglos XI–XIII)*. Oviedo: Trea, 2005.

Fernández Conde, Francisco. "Un noyau actif d'albigeois a León au commencement du XIIIe siècle. Approximation critique a une oeuvre de Lucas de Tuy écrite entre 1230 et 1240." In *The Church in a Changing Society*, 43–47. Uppsala: Uppsala University, 1978.

Fernández Conde, Francisco. "Un noyau actif d'albigeois en León au commencement du XIIIe siècle? Approche critique d'une oeuvre de Luc de Tuy écrite entre 1230 et 1240." *Heresis* 17 (1991): 35–50.

Freed, John. *The Friars and German Society in the Thirteenth Century*. Cambridge: The Academy, 1977.

García Fitz, Francisco. "Una 'frontera caliente'. La guerra en las fronteras castellano-musulmanas (siglos XI–XIII)." In *Identidad y representación de la frontera en la España medieval (siglos XI–XIV)*, ed. Carlos de Ayala Martínez, Pascal Buresi, and Philippe Josserand, 159–179. Madrid: Casa de Velázquez, 2001.

Garcías Palou, Sebastían. *El Miramar de Ramon Llull*. Palma de Mallorca: Miramar, 1977.

García Sanjuán, Alejandro. "La conquista de Sevilla por Fernando III (646 h/1248). Nuevas propuestas a través de la relectura de las fuentes árabes." *Hispania* 77, no. 255 (2017): 11–41.

García-Serrano, Francisco. "Friars and royal authority in the thirteenth-century Castilian frontier." In *Authority and Spectacle in Medieval and Early Modern Europe*, ed. Yuen-Gen Liang and Jarbel Rodriguez, 104–118. New York: Routledge, 2017.

García-Serrano, Francisco. "Mundo urbano y dominicos en la Castilla medieval." *Archivo Dominicano: Anuario* 18 (1997): 255–274.

García-Serrano, Francisco. *Preachers of the City: The Expansion of the Dominican Order in Castile (1217–1348)*. New Orleans: University Press of the South, 1997.

Gerber, Jane. *The Jews of Spain: A History of the Sephardic Experience*. New York: The Free Press, 1992.

González, Julio. *Las conquistas de Fernando III en Andalucía*. Valladolid: Maxtor, 2006.

González Díez, Emiliano. *El concejo burgalés (884–1369): marco histórico institucional*. Aldecoa: Ayuntamiento de Burgos, 1983.

Graña Cid, María del Mar. "Berenguela I y Fernando III, promotores de las Órdenes mendicantes en Castilla." In *El franciscanismo: identidad y poder. Libro homenaje al P. Enrique Chacón Cabello*, ed. Manuel Peláez del Rosal, 119–142. Córdoba: Asociación Hispánica de Estudios Franciscanos, 2016.

Graña Cid, María del Mar. "The Mendicant Orders and the Castilian Monarchy in the Reign of Ferdinand III." In *The Friars and their Influence in Medieval Spain*, ed. Francisco García-Serrano, 61–83. Amsterdam: Amsterdam University Press, 2018.

Grau, Sergi. *Cátaros e Inquisición en los reinos hispánicos (siglos XII–XIV)*. Madrid: Cátedra, 2012.

Hanlon, David. "Islam and Stereotypical Discourse in Medieval Castile and León." *Journal of Medieval and Early Modern Studies* 30, no. 3 (2000): 479–504.

Henriet, Patrick. "Hagiographie léonaise et pédagogie de la foi: Les miracles de Saint Isidore et la lutte contre la hérésie, XI–XIIe siècles." In *L'enseignement religieux dans la couronne de Castille. Incidences spirituelles et sociales (XIIIe–XVIe siècles)*, ed. D. Baloup, 1–28. Madrid: Casa de Velázquez, 2003.

Kedar, Benjamin Z. *Crusade and Mission. European Approaches toward the Muslims*. Princeton: Princeton University Press, 1988.

Le Goff, Jacques. "Apostolat mendiant et fait urbain dans la France médiévale; l'implantation sociologique et géographique des ordres mendiants, du XIIIe au XIVe siècle." *Revue d'Histoire de l'Eglise de France* 54 (1968): 69–76.

Le Goff, Jacques. "Ordres mendiants et urbanisation dans la France médiévale." *Annales: Économies, Sociétés, Civilisations* 25 (1970): 924–946.

Lesnick, David. *Preaching in Medieval Florence*. Athens: University of Georgia Press, 1989.

Linehan, Peter. "A Tale of Two Cities: Capitular Burgos and Mendicant Burgos in the Thirteenth Century." In *Church and City, 1000–1500: Essays in honour of Christopher Brooke*, ed. David Abulafia, Michael Franklin and Miri Rubin, 81–110. Cambridge: Cambridge University Press, 1992.

Linehan, Peter. "At the Spanish Frontier." In *The Medieval World*, ed. Peter Linehan and Janet Loughland, 37–59. London: Routledge, 2003.

Linehan, Peter. *Spain, 1157–1300: a Partible inheritance*. Oxford: Blackwell Publishing, 2008.

Linehan, Peter. *The Spanish Church and the Papacy in the Thirteenth Century*. Cambridge: Cambridge University Press, 1971.

Little, Lester K. *Religious Poverty and the Profit Economy in Medieval Europe*. Ithaca: Cornell University Press, 1978.

Lohr, Charles. "Ramon Lull and Thirteenth-Century Religious Dialogue." In *Diálogo filosófico-religioso entre Cristianismo, Judaísmo e Islamismo*, ed. Horacio Santiago-Otero, 117–129. Turnhout: Brepols, 1994.

López, Atanasio. "Fr. Pedro Gallego, primer Obispo de Cartagena (1250–1267)." *Archivo Iberoamericano* 12, no. 70 (1925): 65–91.

Lopez, Robert S. "A propos d'une virgule." *Revue historique* 198 (1947): 178–188.

Lourie, Elena. "A Society Organized for War: Medieval Spain," *Past and Present* 35 (1966): 54–76.

Mansilla, Demetrio. *Iglesia castellano-leonesa y Curia romana en los tiempos del Rey San Fernando; estudio documental sacado de los registros vaticanos*. Madrid: Consejo Superior de Investigaciones Científicas, 1945.

Martínez Casado, Ángel. "Cátaros en León: Testimonio de Lucas de Tuy." *Archivos Leoneses: revista de estudios y documentación de los Reinos Hispano-Occidentales* 74 (1983): 263–312.

Menjot, Denis. "La urbanización fronteriza en la Corona de Castilla en la Edad Media: primeros enfoques." In *II Estudios de frontera. Actividad y vida en la frontera. En memoria de Don Claudio Sánchez-Albornoz. Alcalá la Real, 1997*, 563–583. Jaén: Diputación provincial de Jaén, 1998.

Miura Andrades, José. *Frailes, monjas, y conventos: las órdenes mendicantes y la sociedad sevillana bajomedieval*. Seville: Diputación de Sevilla, 1998.

Montenegro, Ángel, ed. *Historia de Burgos. II. Edad Media*. Burgos: Caja de Ahorros Municipal de Burgos, 1986.

Muldoon, James. *Popes, Lawyers, and infidels: The Church and the Non-Christian World, 1250–1550*. Philadelphia: University of Pennsylvania Press, 1979.

Nogales, David. "Confesar al rey en la Castilla bajomedieval (1230–1504)." In *Pecar en la Edad Media*, ed. Ana Carrasco Manchado and María del Pilar Rábede Obradó, 55–80. Madrid: Sílex, 2008.

O'Callaghan, Joseph. *Reconquest and Crusade in Medieval Spain*. Philadelphia: University of Pennsylvania Press, 2003.

Palacios Martín, Bonifacio. "La circulación de los cátaros por el Camino de Santiago y sus implicaciones socioculturales. Una fuente para su conocimiento." *España Medieval* 3 (1982): 219–230.

Pelzer, Auguste. "Un traducteur inconnu: Pierre Gallego. Franciscain et premier évêque de Carthagène (1250–1267)." In *Études d'histoire littéraire sur la scolastique médiévale*, ed. Adrien Pattin and Émile van de Vyver, 188–240. Louvain – Paris: Publications Universitaires – Nauwelaerts, 1964.

Powers, James. *A Society Organized for War. The Iberian Municipal Militias in the Central Middle Ages, 1000–1284*. Berkeley: University of California Press, 1988.

Ray, Jonathan. *The Sephardic Frontier*. Ithaca: Cornell University Press, 2006.

Ribes Montané, Pedro. "San Ramón de Penyafort y los estudios eclesiásticos." *Analecta Sacra Tarraconensis* 48 (1975): 85–142.

Rodríguez López, Ana. *La consolidación territorial de la monarquía feudal castellana. Expansión y fronteras durante el reinado de Fernando III*. Madrid: CSIC, 1994.

Rodríguez-Picavea, Enrique. "The frontier and royal power in medieval Spain: A developmental hypothesis." *The Medieval History Journal* 8, no. 2 (2005): 273–301.

Rojo Alique, Francisco Javier. "Intelectuales franciscanos y monarquía." *SÉMETA* 26 (2014): 297–318.

Rucquoi, Adeline. "Autores mendicants en la cultura hispánica (siglos XIII–XV)." *Cuadernos de Historia de España* 85–86 (2012): 621–643.

Rucquoi, Adeline. "La double vie de l'université de Palencia 1180–1250." *Studia Gratiana* XXIX (1998), 723–748.

Ruiz, Teófilo. "Castilian Merchants in England 1248–1350." In *Order and innovation in the Middle Ages: Essays in Honor of Joseph R. Strayer*, ed. W.C. Jordan, 173–185. Princeton: Princeton University Press, 1976.

Salvador Martínez, H. *Berenguela la Grande y su época (1180–1246)*. Madrid: Polifemo, 2012.

Smith, Damian J. *Crusade, Heresy and Inquisition in the Lands of the Crown of Aragon, c. 1167–1276*. Leiden: Brill, 2010.

Smith, Damian J. "Ramon de Penyafort and his Influence." In *The Friars in Medieval Spain*, ed. Francisco García-Serrano, 45–60. Amsterdam: Amsterdam University Press, 2018.

Szpiech, Ryan. "Prisons and Polemics: Captivity, Confinement, and Medieval Interreligious Encounter." In *Polemical Encounters*, ed. Mercedes García-Arenal, 271–303. University Park: Penn State University Press, 2019.

Tolan, John. *Saint Francis and the Sultan: The Curious History of a Christian-Muslim Encounter.* Oxford: Oxford University Press, 2009.

Tolan, John. *Saracens: Islam in the Medieval European Imagination.* New York: Columbia University Press, 2002.

Tolan, John. "Taking Gratian to Africa: Raymond de Penyafort's Legal Advice to the Dominicans and Franciscans in Tunis (1234)." In *A Faithful Sea: The Religious Cultures of the Mediterranean, 1200–1700,* ed. Adnan Husain and Katherine Fleming, 47–63. Oxford: One World, 2007.

Torres Fontes, Juan and Ángel Luis Molina. *La diócesis de Cartagena en la Edad Media (1250–1502).* Madrid: CSIC, 2013.

Urvoy, Dominique. "Les Musulmans et l'usage de la langue arabe par les missionnaires." *Traditio* 34 (1978) : 416–427.

Vones, Ludwig. "Mission et frontière dans l'espace Méditerranéen: Tentatives d'une société guerrière pour la propagation de la foi." In *Christianizing Peoples and Converting Individuals,* ed. Guyda Armstrong, 203–222. Turnhout: Brepols, 2000.

Vose, Robin. *Dominicans, Muslims and Jews in the Medieval Crown of Aragon.* New York: Cambridge University Press, 2009.

Wacks, David A. *Framing Iberia. Maqāmāt and Frametale Narratives in Medieval Spain.* Leiden: Brill, 2007.

CHAPTER 10

Literary Expressions of Pastoral Reform during the Reign of Fernando III

Cristina Catalina

The efforts of the Holy See to expand papal control over the western Church across the eleventh century were met with some resistance in the Iberian Peninsula. This was particularly the case in Castile, where the ambitious objective of Pope Gregory VII to bring all regional churches within the orbit of Roman obedience was frustrated by the adherence of the Toledan Church to its Hispanic customs.[1] In his letters to Castilian clerics and kings, Gregory demanded that the Hispanic kingdoms adopt the Roman *ordo* and *officium* and abandon Toledan superstition – the so-called Mozarabic Rite.[2] Some three centuries later however, the picture had shifted substantially. From the early fourteenth century, we find a substantial number of treatises on moral theology that are in line with Roman orthodoxy, and the beginnings of a systematic reception of Roman ecumenical norms within Castilian synods and councils.[3]

Between these two snapshots lies the reception of new Roman norms of pastoral care in the kingdom of Fernando III. The Roman See led a process of institutional, sacramental, and moral standardization in Latin Christendom. If the so-called Gregorian Reform of the end of the eleventh century had succeeded in strengthening the disciplinary obedience of regional churches, as well as marking the distinction between lay and clerical members, over the course of the twelfth and early thirteenth centuries the Roman See aimed to go yet further in establishing orthodoxy and orthopraxy; that is, in standardizing doctrine, ecclesiology, and models of Christian behavior. This was effectively a dynamic process, pervaded by the tension between the establishment of a single and defined means of salvation and the multiple forms of resistance that this encountered, from anticlericalism and heresy to independent measures to address the care of souls. Such conditions would typify the ongoing

---

1 On the transition from Hispanic to Roman Rite in Castile, see Walker, *Views of Transition*. Liturgical change was a fundamental event in Aragón also. Baso, "La iglesia aragonesa," 153.
2 See Mansilla, *Inocencio III*, 15–31.
3 Sánchez Herrero, "La legislación conciliar y sinodal," 350.

process of accepting new pastoral norms in the various regions of Latin Christendom.

In the territories that would later make up the kingdom of Castile, the papacy did not begin to exercise effective ecclesiastical power until the late eleventh century, when, in 1088, the Mozarabic or Toledan liturgy (the *Officium toletanum*) was abolished and replaced by the Franco-Roman office, the *Romanorum mysterium* or *Gallicaum mysterium*.[4] However, this did not happen easily. It was a substantive change, and one that would leave an enduring mark on the relationship between the peninsular Church and the Roman pontiff. Over the same period, the territorial expansion of the Christian kingdoms into the Islamic south also conditioned this relationship. Newly conquered territories had to be integrated into the administrative organization of the Church. This formed an important backdrop to the ways in which the Castilian Church related to Rome in the thirteenth century, and would shape Castilian responses to the efforts to impose Roman pastoral norms in the Peninsula, as well as the obstacles that these attempts would face.

The efforts of the Roman pontiff to control what can be described as the "economy of salvation" reached their peak during the papacy of Innocent III (r. 1198–1216). His Fourth Lateran Council of 1215 and the resultant canons of this council aimed to extend the reach of papal norms deeper into the functioning of the Latin Church, and incorporated strategies to bring about their implementation. In line with this, canon ten of the Council, regulating preaching, required that pastoral ministry should be carried out in the vernacular, a purely practical step deployed as a strategy to reach people who were uneducated in Latin.[5] This also invites us to consider, as expressions of this same aim, a variety of literary sources that do not always follow the traditional models of ecclesiastical reform but in which can be identified the echoes of this papal strategy.

The above framework allows for a sociological understanding of the clerical lyric poetry written in the vernacular and preserved in the kingdom of Castile-León during the era of Fernando III.[6] The combination of themes drawn from moral theology, with forms of recitation most commonly associated with the

---

4 Gordo, "Papado y monarquía," 526; and Walker, *Views of Transition*.
5 García y García, *Constitutiones Concilii quarti Lateranensis*, canon x; and Spiegel, *Romancing the past*. One of the effects of Innocent III's pastoral reform was the promotion of vernacular writing, which contributed indirectly to solidifying the Romance languages.
6 We shall make no attempt in this chapter to analyze this poetry. The goal here is rather to interpret it as a sociological phenomenon in relation to the process of assimilating Roman pastoral activity during the era of Fernando III.

troubadours, allows us to suppose that some thirteenth-century poetry in the Romance language was created as a means of responding to these efforts to promote pastoral reform in the Peninsula. The significant number of extant poems contrasts with the scanty evidence for conciliar and synodal acceptance of the Fourth Lateran Council during the same period, as well as with the apparent lack of scholastic treatises produced in the kingdom over this time.[7] My goal in the following pages is to help reconstruct the process by which the papacy attempted to standardize the care of souls in the kingdom of Castile-León, where vernacular lyric poetry appears to express the interplay of Franco-Roman content with the expectations, shaped by the troubadours or *juglares*, of the Castilian "audience" who experienced it.

1   Towards Pastoral Standardization

The expansion of orthodoxy and orthopraxy in the thirteenth century was not always met with straightforward acceptance. We should keep in mind that papal attempts to standardize the conduct and doctrine of the Church unfolded in a context wherein the reach of canon law and papal jurisdiction varied across Latin Christendom. Indeed, in some places, reformists' attempts were faced with the emergence of anti-clerical movements and the construction of counter-narratives of salvation, presenting a new challenge to the obedience claimed by the Roman See.[8] Furthermore, in regions such as Castile, there still survived significant divergences from the ecclesiology, doctrine and praxis of the Roman Church. As such, attempts to establish orthopraxy and orthodoxy across the thirteenth century had to advance in new ways and through channels that went beyond canon law.

The standardization and institutionalization of the care of souls by the papacy brought with it a monopoly on the means of Christian salvation. To the extent that the participation of the individual believer in sacramental services became obligatory – as the only guarantee of salvation – deviations and the failure to obey were thus also increasingly singled out and persecuted. Appropriate methods were developed for identifying and correcting deviation, and for making visible and punishing disobedience. Practices related to catechesis

---

[7] Several scholars agree on this interpretation, among them: García y García, "Primeros reflejos," 249–82; Linehan, *The Spanish Church*; Fernández Conde, *La religiosidad medieval*; Sánchez Herrero, "La legislación conciliar," 349–72; O'Callaghan, "Innocent III."
[8] Cohn, *En pos del milenio*, 44.

and preaching took center stage as the means of achieving the internal conversion of the laity. Without doubt, the deepening of individual Christian devotion would have to prevent the faithful from shunning, or disengaging themselves from, the sacramental and ritual services offered canonically by the ordained clergy. Consequently, the primary vehicle for causing Roman pastoral norms to be obeyed was preaching, accompanied by coercive measures.

2   The Reception of Pastoral Reform in Castile

The prelates of Castile under Fernando III appear to have shown little interest in the papal agenda concerning ecclesiastical discipline, moral reform, or the care of souls. This is illustrated strikingly in their lack of response to the Fourth Lateran Council and the failure to implement the conciliar canons in Castilian territory.[9] Extant documentary evidence suggests that conciliar reforms had almost no effect during the decades immediately after 1215.[10] There is hardly any mention of local synods or councils being celebrated, and even fewer extant acts from the thirteenth century, despite the activity of the papal legate Jean of Abbeville. He was sent to the Hispanic kingdoms by Pope Gregory IX (r. 1227–41), and summoned the Castilian clergy to a reformist synod at Valladolid in 1228, followed by another in Salamanca the following year, at which he lamented the difficulties of implementing the Lateran precepts in Castile.[11] Nevertheless, there is no evidence that his efforts bore fruit in the medium term, as made clear by the lack of subsequent diocesan synods and provincial councils, despite his exhortations for these to be held.[12]

---

9   Scholarship on this matter is widely in agreement on this point. See especially, Linehan, "Councils and Synods," 101; idem, *The Spanish Church*, 10; Kuttner and García y García, "A new eyewitness," 115–78; García y García, "Primeros reflejos de Concilio"; idem, "El concilio IV Lateranense (1215) y la Península Ibérica," 355–76.

10 Tejeda y Ramiro, *Colección de cánones*. See also *Synodicon hispanum*, an edition of local synods of the Iberian Peninsula organized in volumes according to modern-day provinces, with the edition overseen by A. García y García.

11 Jean of Abbeville gives a picture of the Castilian clergy as unlearned and unfamiliar with conciliar and synodal discipline, which made it difficult for the Church to offer canonical pastoral services, criticisms echoed by Pope Honorius III: Linehan, *The Spanish Church*, 10. For a modern edition of the canons of the synod at Valladolid, see García y García, "Legislación de los concilios y sínodos del Reino Leonés," 105–14.

12 See García y García, *Constitutiones Concilii quarti*, 257–335. Two provincial councils were celebrated in Santiago, in 1245 and 1266. Another had been held there immediately after

The primary loyalty of the Castilian episcopate was to the king; they served him at court as counselors and also in military matters.[13] Fernando III himself acted as "lord of the churches of his realm" when it came to managing the Castilian Church and clergy.[14] The loyalty linking the episcopate to the king and his military agenda, in line with papal crusading interests, gave the sovereign a privileged position regarding the management of the Church in Spain, especially after the conquest of Córdoba and Seville by Fernando III; in these unique circumstances, the role of bishops as statesmen and warriors against Islam overrode concern for pastoral reform.[15]

The failure of the Castilian Church to acquiesce to papal discipline can be partially explained as a by-product of the way in which Gregorian reform had interacted with Castilian Christianity. The Holy See had prioritized the suppression of the Hispanic Rite and the acceptance of the Roman, and in so doing, relegated two other central elements of reform to secondary importance: the moral formation of the clergy, and the separation of the lay from the ecclesiastical estate, as typified in the struggle against simony and concubinage, both issues that had been at the center of Jean of Abbeville's criticisms in 1228.[16] The construction of the image of Toledan deviance, even heterodoxy – the *superstitio toledana* – would justify pontifical interventionism in order to "restore" the Petrine Christian tradition and bring the Church to Roman obedience.[17] For Gregory VII, liturgical uniformity was a way of preventing the "resurgence" of any movement derived from an independent Hispanic Church, and of eradicating the religious syncretism of Mozarabic Christianity.[18] As such, the papal curia aspired to create a new Toledo, one that had shed its Mozarabic Christianity, and that would relegate it to oblivion. The change of rite began a process in which Hispanic texts, such as the works of St Isidore or the disciplinary and legislative norms of the Hispanic tradition, simply disappeared from the liturgy of the majority of churches in the Peninsula.

---

      the Lateran Council, between 1216 and 1217. Toledo held a provincial council in 1257. Tejeda y Ramiro, *Colección de cánones*.
13   See in this volume Lincoln, Chp. 4.
14   *señor de las iglesias de su reino*: Rodríguez, "La política eclesiástica," 19. See also Linehan, *The Spanish Church*.
15   Rodríguez, "La política eclesiástica," 36.
16   See above, fn. 11, and also Deswarte, *Une chrétienté romaine*, 356; Fernández Conde, *La religiosidad medieval*; Glick, *Islamic and Christian Spain*.
17   Gonzálvez, "The Persistence of the Mozarabic."
18   See Reilly, *Cristianos y musulmanes*; Guichard, *Al-Andalus*.

3 Routes towards Pastoral Reform

The ecclesiastical monopoly of the path to individual salvation, as synthesized in the canons of the Fourth Lateran Council, instituted a cyclical calendar of pastoral duties.[19] Individual participation in these periodic rituals offered the laity the opportunity to attain salvation. Confession is a good example of this. The criterion for judging lay praxis was guided by an ideal catalogue of vices and virtues, which affected both an individual's participation in ecclesiastical rituals, and their day-to-day behaviors in matters ranging from dress, to sexuality, to food. In general, the ethical rationalization would be written down in texts of moral theology which were to function as guides for clerical pastoral action. In this way, the Church attempted to make certain that such pastoral practices would be in line with Roman orthodoxy.

To this end, the early thirteenth century saw a proliferation of texts instructing the clergy in the art of the care of souls and the catechesis of the faithful, such as sermons, catechisms, confessional manuals, hagiographies, liturgical books, and treatises on the vices and virtues. Originally the products of monastic and cathedral schools, these soon came to be produced in the emerging universities, especially Paris, Bologna, and Toulouse.[20] This is important in our understanding of the reception of pastoral norms in Castile as conveyed through Franco-Roman influences. As part of this process, there would emerge new figures in conjunction with the formation of the clergy, notably, the scholar and the mendicant friar; these figures, with their knowledge of rhetoric, were to play an important role in pastoral reform across Latin Europe.[21]

The new mendicant orders emulated the practices of itinerant preachers emerging in the Languedoc, the Rhineland, and Provence, developing the call to pastoral reform based on their exemplary practices of poverty and humility.[22] The international and intellectual dimensions of these orders made it possible for them to play a key role in parochial administration of the care of souls. In order for the Divine Word to be spread more effectively, the men of the schools and universities received education in the liberal arts, and this included rhetoric. Every indication is that they not only took the lead in high-level scholarly debates but also dedicated themselves to spreading the Holy Scripture among the laity through preaching, including in the vernacular. The mendicant friars' pastoral model was in line with the new practices of ecclesiastical

---

19 Leyser, "Clerical purity," 229.
20 Verger, *Gentes del saber*, 61–89; Wei, *Intellectual Culture in Medieval Paris*, 170–246.
21 Lomax, "Reforma de la Iglesia," 183.
22 Lobrichon, *La religion des laïcs*, 92; Diehl, "Overcoming reluctance," 53.

expiation, in which the idea of gaining salvation through one's own merits was becoming ever more central.[23] All this left a literary legacy.

In Castile, however, scholastic literary responses to this growing culture of pastoral reform were late in appearing, and there are very few extant manuscripts from Castile dating to the first half of the thirteenth century. Indeed, such texts would only become notable towards the end of the century, emerging from the time of the reign of Sancho IV (r. 1284–1295).[24] The *Libro de las confesiones* (1316) by Martín Pérez and the testimony preserved in Guido de Monte Roterio's *Manipulus curatorum* are two important examples that date from the early fourteenth century.[25] Both texts display a notable influence from the *Summa de casibus poenitentiae* (1224–1226) written by the Catalan Raymond of Peñafort, a canonist of the Roman curia.[26] Another peninsular text which also conforms to the new pastoral culture is the catechism of Pedro de Cuéllar; it too is from the early fourteenth century (1325).[27] Its contents are in fact similar to those of contemporary confession manuals, and it is one of the few early fourteenth-century catechisms written in the vernacular. Catechetical treatises contained in synodal and conciliar acts follow a comparable arc. From the eleventh until the beginning of the fourteenth century, catechetical prescriptions produced in Castile were very similar to those established at the Council of Coyanza in 1055, focusing simply on the prayers of the Pater noster and Ave Maria, and the Credo.[28] It is not until the fourteenth century that

---

23   Carozzi, *Visiones apocalípticas*, 158–9.
24   Soto, "Visión y tratamiento," 411–47.
25   Pérez, *Libro de las confesiones*. No information about Martín Pérez exists except that found in this work. It shows that he was educated in canon law, theology, and patristics: for example, one finds numerous citations of papal law, even of recent examples like Book VI of Boniface VIII, or Clement V's constitutions. Its content goes beyond the common topics of *Summae confessorum* – to guide clerics and laity in the sacrament of penance – including many other themes of moral theology; this is illustrated especially by the third part, which concentrates on the sacraments more broadly, not only on penance. This text is also a good representation of how juridical-canonical and moral-theological material overlap. The work enjoyed wide distribution in western regions of the Peninsula. In fact, two of the ten extant manuscripts containing parts of the work are in Portuguese. It is known that two other Portuguese codices existed also, one belonging to King Duarte (1391–1438) and the other in the possession of the abbot of Alcobaça; the second is known to have existed because the Infante Fernando asked for it on loan in a letter dated June 10, 1431. On Guido de Monte Roterio, see Santiago-Otero, "Guido de Monte Roterio," 261.
26   Pérez, "Libro de las confesiones," 13.
27   Martín and Linage, *Religión y sociedad medieval*.
28   For the most important recent work on peninsular catechetical literature between the thirteenth and sixteenth centuries, see: Sánchez Herrero, "La literatura catequética," 1051–115.

they go beyond this basic catechetical model, from which point we see conciliar constitutions and synodal books developing a more complex catechesis, in particular, drawing on the central elements of penance and moral examples.

A similar pattern can be observed with regard to what remains of the evidence for what may be described as scholastic preaching models in Castile; that is, a sermon form that followed a set structure, organized rhetorically around a *thema,* which was systematized in contemporary texts on the *ars praedicandi* as established, for example, by Alain de Lille.[29] This type of sermon first became popular in European intellectual circles at the end of the twelfth century and was given a more concrete form in the nascent universities during the first half of the thirteenth.[30] *Libri Sermonorum* indexed and organized these texts according to different criteria, such as, for example, *ad status* or alphabetically, in order to make them an accessible aid for preachers. Yet, once again, there is very little evidence of sermons following this sort of university model in Castile during the reign of Fernando III. The only comparable examples are linked to the exceptional figure of Juan Gil de Zamora (c.1241–1318). His only extant works are the compilation of sermons found in codex 414 of the library of the Sacro Convento di San Francesco, in Assisi. All the sermons are in the same codex but in two different collections,[31] the *Liber sermonorum* and the *Breviloquium sermonum virtutum et vitiorum*; although it is possible that both once belonged to a single work.[32] In any case, there are no other extant collections of sermons pertaining to Castile-León that follow a scheme and linguistic pattern similar to that deployed in the universities until near the end of the fourteenth century or beginning of the fifteenth, the date of an anonymous sermonary belonging to Ms. 18.54 of the archive of the University of Salamanca.

Besides the university sermon, other texts also reflected the preaching efforts of the late twelfth and early thirteenth centuries, such as compilations of *exempla*, as well as *distintiones*, biblical citations, quotations from the Patristic

---

29 Kienzle, *The Sermon*, 11. The most widely-known model was that of Alain de Lille, the *Summa de arte praedicatoria*, which is preserved in a number of peninsular manuscripts: one from the thirteenth or fourteenth century in Sigüenza, others in Salamanca, Coimbra, and Toledo.

30 Bériou, *L'avènement des maîtres de la Parole*.

31 More manuscripts with sermons by Juan Gil de Zamora have been found, which include some belonging to these two collections and some from others. A. Hamy believes that a single sermonary of Gil de Zamora – an *opus sermonum copiosum* – exists. Hamy, "Juan Gil de Zamora," 74–6.

32 Lillo, "Las colecciones de sermones," 85. Seven of these sermons have been published in a critical edition overseen by F. Lillo Redonet, entitled *Sermonario de Juan Gil de Zamora*.

authors or from other *autoritates*, saints' lives, and others, all of which provided valuable auxiliary material to the preacher and facilitated the standardization of the moral theology and doctrine found in the sermons. One important source for our understanding of the reception of pastoral reform in Castile is the fate of a series of tales drawn from Christian, Jewish and Islamic traditions, and translated into Latin at the beginning of the twelfth century by Pedro Alfonso (*Moshé Sefardí*) in his *Disciplina clericalis*. Once they had been adopted into the cultural world north of the Pyrenees, these stories underwent a process of Christianization, and were used in the development of university sermons; the more than sixty extant manuscripts attest to their wide distribution across Europe.[33] Adapted to the patterns of Christian moral theology, the stories became part of collections of *exempla*, alongside extracts from the Bible and Church Fathers. They are used this way in the *Tractatus de diversis materiis predicabilibus*, written in the mid-thirteenth century by the Dominican Étienne de Bourbon, as well as in Vincent de Beauvais's *Speculum historiale*, also from the mid-century. The *Tabula exemplorum* and the *Speculum laicorum* are both late thirteenth-century texts that also drew on these tales. Significantly, however, in Castile, these texts do not appear to have been used in a parallel manner before their redeployment in scholarly circles north of the Pyrenees. The tales from the *Disciplina clericalis* returned to Castile for use within a Christian moralizing context only after outside influence – their use within the universities of Latin Europe – had given them new meaning and they had been included in the above-mentioned collections of *exempla*. The universities of thirteenth-century Europe, with their ecclesiastically and institutionally supported intellectual endeavors, thus appear to have acted as providers of ecclesiological, canonical, and theological knowledge in the way that the translators of thirteenth century Castile did not. This similarly appears to be the case regarding later thirteenth-century texts of non-sacred wisdom translated at the Castilian court into Latin and/or Castilian without undergoing any previous adaptation to Christian doctrine, including didactical-moral treatises such as *Calila e Dimna* (1251),[34] *Sendebar* or the *Book of Women's Wiles* (1253),[35] or

---

33   Lacarra, *Cuentos*, 13.
34   Produced in c. 1251, this was an Arabic to Castilian translation of the work *Kalila wa-Dimna*, which was itself a translation from Middle Persian to Arabic done by Ibn Al-Muqaffa in the eighth century, which came in turn from the fourth-century Sanskrit work, *Panchatantra*.
35   A collection of tales, or *exempla,* written in Castilian about the middle of the thirteenth century, which brings together Arabic tales derived from the Persian or Hindu storytelling tradition. Lacarra, *Cuentos*; Deyermond, *Historia de la literatura*.

Barlaam and Josaphat[36] (from the end of the thirteenth and beginning of the fourteenth centuries). It would seem, as a result, that scholarly activities in the Castile of Fernando III were not destined to act as a platform for propagating doctrinal, moral or pastoral reform in the kingdom.[37]

4 Pastoral Echoes in Vernacular Clerical Lyric Poetry

If pastoral reform was to be disseminated within and beyond the ecclesiastical institutions of Castile, and to reach populations unversed in Latin – that is, the laity in general – it would require a means of communication beyond what we have already seen. Pope Innocent III himself promoted in various ways what could be described as a strategic approach to reform, motivated by the desire to fit pastoral ministry to the conditions of its reception. It was this desire that lay behind the "vulgarization" of written doctrinal knowledge and its dissemination in the form of vernacular clerical lyric poetry.[38] The existence of such poetry in Castile seems to indicate that Innocent III's purposes produced real effects in the kingdom, even if the tenth canon of the Fourth Lateran Council, *De praedicatoribus instituendis*, was not systematically implemented in the Castilian synods and councils of the thirteenth century.[39] As we shall see, clerical poems could feature pastoral concerns at the same time as drawing on secular troubadour tradition. While, on the one hand, they include themes that are proper to Christian moral theology, at the same time, their versification and rhyme, in mono-rhyme tetrastich form, indicate that they were also the products of oral recitation. The conjunction of pastoral material and the ambition to disseminate this through Romance lyric poetry, through the "vulgarization" and vernacularization of themes drawn from moral theology, suggest that these poems bear witness to a quite different context for the diffusion of pastoral reform, one that diverges from the established models of preaching already discussed.[40] It is worth pointing out here that conciliar and synodal legislation from Castile identifies clerical preaching practices that do not conform to the *ars praedicandi*; in Jean of Abbeville's constitutions issued at the

---

36 On the Iberian Peninsula this work existed in Latin, Arabic, and Hebrew versions, as well as Castilian, Catalan, and Portuguese.
37 Bautista, "El renacimiento alfonsí," 96.
38 Moreno, "Juglaría, clerecía y traducción."
39 Rico, *Predicación y literatura*, 9.
40 Several studies hold to this interpretation, including: Lomax, "Reforma de la Iglesia," 182–6; Rico, "La clerecía," 1–23; Deyermond, *Historia de la literatura;* Gómez Redondo, *Edad Media*; Uría, "Gonzalo de Berceo," 27–54.

Valladolid council of 1228, clergymen are described as being accompanied by *joglares et trasechadores*, and wearing clothing indistinguishable from that of laymen.[41] Negative reception of such practices can be seen, for example, in the testimony of the Catalan Franciscan Francesc Eiximenis, writing in the fourteenth century, who was scandalized by preachers who used the troubadour style: these *trufatores et histriones et verbosi burlatores* abused the *verba picta et rimata*, and their style of delivery was outlandish.[42]

Under these conditions it is possible that official pastoral preaching in its university form was not immediately accepted, whereas an alternate form, adapted to its Castilian audience, found a more ready reception in the Peninsula. Clerical lyric poetry in mono-rhyme tetrastich, the so-called *mester de clerecía* (or "craft of the clergy") may have been the product of this adaptation of Roman pastoral ministry for a Castilian audience. This thirteenth-century clerical lyric poetry in Romance brought together elements of Provençal and Frankish scholastic culture with forms and tones from popular Castilian oral traditions.[43] The resulting verse forms were more complex than those of the *juglares* and troubadours, and imitated the classical poets in its meter, rhythm, and length. They were poems designed for public recitation, being both enjoyable to read and easy to remember. Its prototypical creator is the learned cleric, well-versed in the liberal arts of the *trivium* and *quadrivium*, and keen to distinguish his skills in rhyme and versification from the simple, rustic qualities he attributes to the traditions of the *juglares*. Such figures may well have arrived in Castile by the routes that formed the Camino de Santiago.[44] It is significant that the earliest poem whose meter reveals a Franco-Latin influence, and which marked the beginning of the vernacular poetic form of the *cuaderna vía*, was the song of Roland.[45] The *studium generale* at Palencia, which drew scholars from across Europe, was one of the most important centers of education for Castilian clergy; they also studied in cathedral schools like Osma, canonries such as León, and monastic schools like San Millán de la Cogolla. All these intellectual centers were near the Camino de Santiago.

The Castilian cleric and poet Gonzalo de Berceo could well have been one of these scholars who had a desire for pastoral care, and who tried to bridge the gap between theological book-learning and popular oral culture in his

---

41   Tejada y Ramiro, *Colección de cánones*, 326.
42   Eiximenis, "L'Ars praedicandi," 337. Furthermore, Eximenis advises good preachers not to preach against prelates, princes, or kings, in order not to encourage the people to rebel.
43   Rico, "La clerecía," 19.
44   Gómez Redondo, *Edad Media*, 269.
45   Cacho and Lacarra, *Historia de la literatura*, 328.

wide-ranging poems: four hagiographies, including the lives of San Millán de la Cogolla and Santo Domingo de Silos, three Marian poems, and several other doctrinal texts.[46] Berceo was born in the final years of the twelfth century and lived until the 1260s. He received his education in the monastery at San Millán de la Cogolla and also, seemingly, at Palencia.[47] He fits the model of an educated clergyman with an excellent grasp of Latin and Holy Scripture – well-versed in theological, ecclesiological, and liturgical lore – but who adapted these elements in order to transmit them to the people to whom he preached. This is the pastoral spirit that the Fourth Lateran Council had encouraged. Berceo's output not only offered a catechesis for unlearned people based on moral theology, but also introduced rhetorical devices taken from the troubadour tradition and common in the oral culture of *juglaría*, as has been widely identified throughout his works.[48] These give his writing its unique genial tone that some philological traditions have condemned as vulgar and uncouth.[49] And yet, however, this depiction is contradicted by evidence of Berceo's substantial theological and rhetorical education, as seen, for example, in his poem on the miracles of the Virgin, the *Milagros de Nuestra Señora*, in which his knowledge of the *ars dictandi et praedicandi* are on full display.[50] Thus it would appear that Berceo "vulgarized" learned knowledge for the purpose of reaching the illiterate laity of his diocese, using, for example, the rhetorical device of *captatio benevolentiae* – the effect of false modesty. This didactic strategy seems to have led him to emulate popular speech and troubadour recitation in order to bring himself close to his audience, as seen, for example, at the opening of his *Vida de Santo Domingo de Silos*.[51] This also provides a key to understanding the repeated allusions and references Berceo makes to local rural culture in his works, especially pertaining to the Rioja. His localism and particular interest in the treasury of San Millán monastery do not necessarily imply that he was a

---

46 For the modern scholarly edition of the works of Berceo, see Dutton, *Gonzalo Berceo, Obra Completa*, 5 vols. For the key studies on this important figure, see Ruiz Domínguez, *El mundo espiritual de Gonzalo de Berceo*; and Uría, "Gonzalo de Berceo," 27–54.

47 Dutton and Uría argue that Gonzalo de Berceo must have studied in Palencia. Uría, "Gonzalo de Berceo," 27–54; Dutton, "Gonzalo de Berceo," 249–54. Also Dutton suggests that Berceo acted as notary for the abbot of San Millán during his clerical career. Dutton, "La profesión de Gonzalo de Berceo," 285–95.

48 See Dutton, "Gonzalo de Berceo y los Cantares de Gesta," 407–16; Alvar, "Gonzalo de Berceo como hagiógrafo," 32–8; Dutton, *Gonzalo Berceo, Obra Completa*, I; and idem, IV.

49 For example, Valbuena Prat and Menéndez Pidal. See, Uría, "Gonzalo de Berceo," 8–9.

50 Dutton, *Gonzalo Berceo, Obra Completa*, II.

51 In which Berceo declares that he will write in easily understood Romance: *Quiero fer una prosa en romanz paladino / en que suele el pueblo fablar con so vezino*: Dutton, *Gonzalo Berceo, Obra Completa*, II. Dutton, *Gonzalo Berceo, Obra Completa*, IV.

"provincial" man.[52] The opposite is true: his pastoral praxis in fact place him closer to the *moderni clerici*. If this were not so, it would be hard to explain how his scholastic approach to Marian devotion was so interwoven with the history of Christian salvation. What is more, in his hagiographies, Berceo made use of one of the characteristic resources of the new pastoral activity: illustration by example, with its intense desire to transform popular piety by infusing it with a new *sensus fidelium*.[53]

Another paradigmatic manifestation of the reworking of learned literature is the *Libro de la miseria de ome*.[54] This Castilian poem was a Romance translation in *cuaderna vía* of a work of Latin moral theology, *De contemptu mundi* or *De miseria humanae conditionis*, written in the twelfth century by Lotario dei Conte di Segni (the future pope Innocent III). Innocent III's Latin text was widely distributed on the Iberian Peninsula, and there are various extant manuscript copies from the thirteenth century.[55] It was not, however, a mere translation from Latin to Romance, but introduced a number of modifications in both content and tone, with a new emphasis on penance and repentance, along with formal and linguistic changes. We know that the writer was familiar with scholastic culture because he mentions, for example, scholastic techniques proper to sermon writing.[56] Yet, this Castilian poem, while a work of clearly didactic-moral content, has a jocose quality that goes so far as to become parody. One might suppose this to be a concession of canonical learning to popular rhetorical forms through the imitation of the forms of humor found amongst the troubadours, although its marked parodical tone calls into question the poem's pastoral intentions. It should also be noted that the vernacular-language version introduces a long and detailed allegorical description of Hell not found in *De Contemptu*. This motif is tied to the Christian religious tradition in which apocalyptic eschatology played an important role.[57]

At the end of the twelfth century another romance version appeared – in paired heptasyllabic verses – stemming from the same literary tradition as the *De Contemptu mundi*. In the same way as the *Libro de la miseria de ome*, the

---

52 See, Uría, "Gonzalo de Berceo," 8–9.
53 See Ruiz, *El mundo espiritual*.
54 This is a fifteenth-century codex grouped with eighteen other texts, including *Disciplina clericalis*. There is some suspicion that it was written in the first decade of the fourteenth century because of certain linguistic archaisms it uses. Gómez, *Edad Media*, 421.
55 Rodríguez, "El libro de la Miseria," 203–13. Innocent's text can be found in various Latin copies, as well as a prose translation and another in verse, principally from the thirteenth, fourteenth, and fifteenth centuries.
56 Dutton, *Gonzalo Berceo, Obra Completa*, II: introduction.
57 Gómez, *Edad Media*, 427.

Disputa del alma y el cuerpo ("Disputation between the soul and the body") has a fiercely ironic, parodical tone reminiscent of minstrel tradition. In this case, it should also be noted that the body's response to the soul has been omitted. The tenor of the *Libro* and the *Disputa* stand in contrast to that of another romance-language version, the *Visio Philiberti*, composed at the end of the fourteenth century. This poem is much more serious and dramatic, and has a notable moralizing quality. The same is true of other fourteenth-century versions, such as the prose text known as the *Visión de Filiberti*, which adopts an increasingly devotional tone and take a clear stand in the debate in favor of the salvation of the soul.

Recent scholarship has suggested that the verse form of these poems – the mono-rhyme tetrastich – and their thematic material arose through the influence of Alexandrine verse in Frankish and Provençal poetry, which was in turn the product of Latin lyric poetry that the clergy had developed in the twelfth century via the study of classical poetry in monastery and cathedral schools.[58] The Castilian poem *Disputa del alma y el cuerpo* is itself a Romance version from the end of the twelfth century of a vernacular Frankish poem, *Un samedi par nuit*.[59] It is probable that this Alexandrine verse from the new Frankish and Occitan lyric poetry arrived in Castile via the influence of travelling scholars or monks who traversed the routes of the Camino de Santiago, as well as that of monastic centers, including those linked to Cluny. They carried texts and learning with them. From this viewpoint, the so-called *mester de clerecía* appears to be a Castilian adaptation of a more extensive poetical practice that accompanied the emergence of an intellectual type linked to the new institutions and pastoral culture of the thirteenth century. It would appear that the *moderni clerici* were acquiring cultural hegemony for themselves, while the old pre-eminence of the regular monks was fading.[60]

A good portion of the clerical lyric poetry before the fourteenth century combined theological-moral themes with the popular rhetorical devices and poetic forms found more commonly in the songs of the troubadours, despite the fact that the clergy were distinguished from the *juglares* both by their education and the content of these poems.[61] This combination was a response to the need to reach deeper into Castilian lay society. The clergy thus attempted to make a connection with a populace accustomed to the arts of the troubadours. Poems based on a debating format, such as the *Razón de amor* or *Elena*

---

58   Moreno, *Juglaría*.
59   Gómez, *Edad Media*, 213.
60   Rico, "La clerecía del mester," 8–9.
61   Balestrini and Chicote, "El mester de clerecía," 43–58.

y María – both from the middle of the thirteenth century – were clearly written in order to be "passed": that is, to be performed aloud and in a rhythmical fashion, thanks to the regular syllables of the *cuaderna vía*. Meter infused the recitation not only with rhyme but also rhythm, being a form that made memorization easier and promoted retention by the audience, while at the same time distancing itself from the vulgarity associated with troubadours' songs.[62]

The poem *Razón de amor con los denuestos del agua y del vino* also blends theological-moral themes with the poetic form of the troubadours. It dates from around 1250 and is signed by Lope de Moros – we do not know whether as copyist or author – and was probably written in La Rioja, being composed in an apparent *coiné* that combines Castilian Romance with Aragonese, as well as with some other elements considered by Enzo Franchini to be "Mozarabic."[63] The peculiarity of this poem lies in its similarity to the poetry of the Goliards, which combines the refinement of cultured clerical writing with forms that are inherent to troubadour recitation. The poem's author admits to knowing "much about troubadouring, reading, and singing."[64] The poem plays in jesting fashion with the double meaning of wine: as Christ's blood in the Eucharist – alluding to the question of transubstantiation – but also as a means to drunkenness linked to the profane world of taverns, gaming, and worldly pleasures. It also depicts clerical resistance to celibacy and mocks the ascetic and penitential life; all these are themes common to goliardic literature. The first part of the work, which is distinct from the second in both content and form, is an allegorical-amorous account, figuratively narrating the encounter between two lovers, while the second part unfolds an argument typical of the debates between body and soul, but using the figures of water and wine.[65]

5 Conclusion

The above examples have shown that clerical lyric poetry could act as a vehicle for pastoral reform in Castile, drawing on a range of cultural influences, and, in

---

62 Poems in the Romance language and *cuaderna vía* are not only linked to Latin verse but also show influence from Arabic verse.
63 Franchini, *Abracalabra*, 77–94.
64 *miuio de trovar, de leyer e de cantar*: Gómez, *Edad Media*, 221. A.G. Solalinde studied the relationship between the *Denuestos* and the *Denudata Veritate*, a goliardic text from the twelfth century, and sees connections in twenty-one verses.
65 Lourdes Simó argues for a connection between the two parts of the poem, both having elements in common with Latin compositions of the High Middle Ages. Simó, *Razón de amor*, 276–7.

the process, adapting new Franco-Roman pastoral activity to the context and cultural idiosyncrasies of Castilian society. The themes addressed in this poetry locate it within cultured clerical circles, yet its performative nature and reliance on forms of recitation taken from the troubadour culture demonstrates that it was obliged to adapt to an audience unfamiliar with theological and moral doctrine; these features themselves are in line with a process of religious, moral, doctrinal, and cultural standardization promoted by Rome during this period. This process was supported by the praxis of a new prototype of learned scholar-cleric who, moving beyond the boundaries of diocesan territorial organization, dedicated himself to vulgarizing these new pastoral norms. In this task he was bound to meet with popular Castilian culture far removed from the piety and rhetoric promoted by Rome, and instead drew on the humorous songs of the troubadours. The contrast between the relative abundance of these poems and the scarcity of surviving prose works of a scholarly pastoral nature leads us to suggest that this formed an important route for the entry into the Peninsula of Roman pastoral forms. This need for such adaptation may point to a degree of peninsular resistance to the standardization of the Roman curia, which would be wholly in line with the broader resistance, on a diocesan level, of the Castilian Church and clergy to papal jurisdiction between the eleventh and thirteenth centuries. In this context, these vernacular poetic forms provided an alternative route for the entry of some papal ideas about pastoral reform into thirteenth-century Castile.

Works Cited

Primary Sources (Published)

Dutton, Brian, ed. *Gonzalo de Berceo. Obras completas*, 5 vols. London: Tamesis, 1967–1981.

Eiximenis, Francesc. "L'Ars praedicandi de Francesc Eiximenis." *Analecta sacra tarraconensia* 12 (1936): 301–340.

García y García, Antonio. *Constitutiones Concilii quarti Lateranensis una cum Commentariis Glossatorum*. Monumenta iuris canonici (ed.) Series A: Corpus Glossatorum, vol. 2. Città del Vaticano: Biblioteca Apostólica Vaticana, 1981.

García y García, Antonio. "Legislación de los concilios y sínodos del Reino Leonés," in *El reino de León en la alta edad media, II: Ordenamiento jurídico del reino*, 105–114. Leon: Centro de Estudios e Investigación "San Isidoro," 1992.

García y García, Antonio, ed. *Synodicon Hispanum, VII. Burgos y Palencia*. Madrid: BAC, 1997.

García y García, Antonio, ed. *Synodicon hispanum, X. Cuenca y Toledo*. Madrid: BAC, 2011.
Lillo, Fernando. "Las colecciones de sermones de Juan Gil de Zamora (O.F.M.) (ca. 1241–ca. 1318): *El liber sermonum* y el *Breviloquium sermonum virtutum et vitiorum*." *Erebea* 1 (2011): 83–101.
Lillo, Fernando. *Sermonario de Juan Gil de Zamora. Estudio preliminar, edición, traducción y comentario de siete de sus sermones*. Zamora: Instituto de Estudios Zamoranos, 2011.
Mansilla, Demetrio. *La documentación pontificia hasta Inocencio III (956–1216)*. Rome: Instituto Español de Historia Eclesiástica, 1955.
Tejada y Ramiro, Juan. *Colección de cánones y de todos los concilios de la Iglesia de España y de América (en latín y castellano)*. Vols. 3–4. Madrid: Pedro Montero, 1854–1859.

Secondary Sources

Alvar, Manuel. "Gonzalo de Berceo como hagiógrafo." In *Gonzalo de Berceo, Obra Completa*, ed. Isabel Uría, 29–60. Madrid: Espasa-Calpe, 1992.
Balestrini, María Cristina, and Gloria Chicote. "El mester de clerecía en la encrucijada entre oralidad y escritura." *Anclajes: Revista del Instituto de Análisis Semiótica del Discurso* 1, no. 1 (1997): 43–58.
Baso, Antonio. "La iglesia aragonesa y el rito romano," *Argensoa* 7 (1956): 153–164.
Bautista, Francisco. "El renacimiento alfonsí: renovatio y saber en la producción cultural de Alfonso X (1252–1284)." In *La cultura en la Europa del siglo XIII. Emisión, intermediación, audiencia (Actas de la XL Semana de Estudios Medievales de Estella. 16 al 19 de julio de 2013)*, 85–96. Pamplona: Gobierno de Navarra, 2014.
Bériou, Nicole. *L'avènement des maîtres de la Parole. La prédication à Paris au XIIIe siècle*, 2 vols. Paris: Institut d'études augustiniennes, 1998.
Berman, Harold J. *La formación de la tradición jurídica de Occidente*. Sección de obras de política y derecho. México: Fondo de cultura económica, 1996.
Cacho, Juan Manuel, and María Jesús Lacarra. *Historia de la literatura española, 1. Entre oralidad y escritura: la Edad Media*. Madrid: Crítica, 2012.
Carozzi, Claude. *Visiones apocalípticas en la Edad Media: el fin del mundo y la Salvación del alma*. Madrid: Siglo XXI, 2000.
Cohn, Norman. *En pos del Milenio: revolucionarios, milenaristas y anarquistas místicos de la Edad Media*. Madrid: Alianza, 1985.
Deswarte, Thomas. *Une chrétienté romaine sans pape: l'Espagne et Rome (586–1085)*. Paris: Bibliothèque d'histoire médiévale, 2010.
Deyermond, Alain. *Historia de la literatura española: La Edad Media*. Barcelona: Ariel, 1995.

Dutton, Brian. "Gonzalo de Berceo: unos datos biográficos." In *Actas del Primer Congreso Internacional de Hispanistas,* ed. Frank Pierce and Cyril A. Jones, 249–350. Oxford: Dolphin Book Co., 1964.

Dutton, Brian. "Gonzalo de Berceo y los Cantares de Gesta." *Berceo* 77 (1965): 407–416.

Fernández Conde, Francisco Javier. *La religiosidad medieval en España. Alta Edad Media (siglos VII–X).* Oviedo: Trea, 2008.

Franchini, Enzo. "Abracalabra (Los exorcismos hispanolatinos en el Códice de la *Razón de Amor*)." *Revista de Literatura Medieval* 3 (1991): 77–94.

García y García, Antonio. "Innocent III and the Kingdom of Castille." In *Pope Innocent III and his World,* ed. John Moore and Brenda Bolton, 337–350. Brookfield: Ashgate, 1999.

García y García, Antonio. "Primeros reflejos del Concilio IV Lateranense en Castilla." In *Studia historico-ecclesiastica. Festschrift für Prof. Luchesius G. Spätling,* ed. I. Vasquez, 249–282. Rome: Bibliotheca Pontificii Athenaei Antoniani, 1977.

García y García, Antonio. "El concilio IV Lateranense (1215) y la Península Ibérica." *Revista Española de Teología* 44 (1984): 355–376.

Glick, Thomas. *Islamic and Christian Spain in the Early Middle Ages: Comparative Perspectives on Social and Cultural Formation.* Princeton: Princeton University Press, 1979.

Gómez Redondo, Fernando. *Edad Media. Juglaría, clerecía y romancero.* Vol. 2. Madrid: Visor, 2012.

Gonzálvez, Ramón. "The Persistence of the Mozarabic Liturgy in Toledo after A.D. 1080." In *Santiago, Saint-Denis and Saint Peter. The reception of the Roman Liturgy in León-Castile in 1080,* ed. Bernard Reilly, 157–185. New York: Fordham University Press, 1985.

Gordo, Ángel G. "Papado y monarquía en el reino de León. Las relaciones político religiosas de Gregorio VII y Alfonso VI en el contexto del 'Imperium Legionense' y de la implantación de la reforma pontifical de la Península Ibérica." *Studi medievali* 49, no. 2 (2008): 519–559.

Guichard, Pierre. *Al-Andalus: estructura antropológica de una sociedad islámica en Occidente.* Granada: Universidad de Granada, 1995.

Hamy, Adrienne. "Juan Gil de Zamora, *Apis Dei*: hallazgos homiléticos y propuestas." *Studia Zamorensia* 23 (2014): 71–93.

Henriet, Patrick. "De la recherche d'une idiosyncrasie hispanique à l'étude des échanges culturels intra-chrétiens. En guise d'introduction." *Memini* 18 (2014). http://memini.revues.org/719 [accessed March 19, 2016].

Henriet, Patrick. *"La santidad en la historia de la Hispania medieval: una aproximación político-sociológica." Memoria ecclesiae* 24 (2004): 13–79.

Kienzle, Beverly Mayne, ed. *The Sermon: Typologie des sources du moyen âge occidental.* Turnhout: Brepols, 2000.

Kuttner, Stephan, and Antonio García y García. "A New Eyewitness Account of the Fourth Lateran Councils." *Traditio* 20 (1964): 123–129.

Lacarra, María Jesús. *Cuentos de la Edad Media*. Madrid: Castalia, 2012.

Leyser, Henrietta. "Clerical purity and the re-ordered world." In *The Cambridge History of Christianity*, ed. Miri Rubin and Walter Simons, 11–21. Cambridge: Cambridge University Press 2009.

Linehan, Peter. *The Spanish Church and the Papacy in the Thirteenth Century*. Cambridge: Cambridge University Press, 1971.

Linehan, Peter. "The Spanish Church revisited: the episcopal gravamina of 1279." In *Authority and Power. Studies on Medieval Law and Government Presented to Walter Ullman on his Seventieth Birthday*, ed. Brian Tierney and Peter Linehan, 127–147. Cambridge: Cambridge University Press, 1980.

Linehan, Peter. "Councils and Synods in Thirteenth-century Castile and Aragon." In *Councils and Assemblies* ed. G.J. Cuming and Derek Baker, 101–113. Cambridge: Cambridge University Press, 1971.

Lobrichon, Guy. *La religion des laïcs en Occident: XIe–XVe siècles*. Paris: Hachette, 1994.

Lomax, Derek W. "Reforma de la Iglesia y literatura didáctica." In *Historia y crítica de la literatura española*, vol. 1, ed. Francisco Rico, 182–186. Barcelona: Crítica, 1979.

Martín, José Luis, and Antonio Linage. *Religión y sociedad medieval. El catecismo de Pedro de Cuéllar (1325)*. Salamanca: Junta de Castilla y León. Consejería de Cultura y Bienestar social, 1987.

Moreno, Carlos. "Juglaría, Clerecía y traducción." *Hermeneus: Revista de la Facultad de Traducción e Interpretación de Soria* 5 (2003): 191–214.

Olstein, Diego A. *La era mozárabe: los mozárabes de Toledo (siglos XII–XIII) en la historiografía, las fuentes y la historia*. Salamanca: Ediciones Universidad de Salamanca, 2006.

Pérez, Martín. *Libro de las confesiones. Una radiografía de la sociedad medieval española*. Ed. A. García García, B. Alonso Rodríguez and F. Cantelar Rodríguez. Madrid: BAC, 2002.

Reilly, Bernard F. *Cristianos y musulmanes. 1031–1157*. Barcelona: Crítica, 1992.

Rico, Francisco. "La Clerecía del Mester." *Hispanic Review* 53, no. 1 (1985): 1–23.

Rico, Francisco. *Predicación y literatura en la España medieval*. Cádiz: Universidad Nacional de Educación a Distancia, 1977.

Rodríguez Rivas, Gregorio. "El libro de la Miseria de Omne y su clerecía." In *Medioevo y Literatura. Actas del V Congreso de la Asociación Hispánica de Literatura Medieval*, ed. Juan Paredes, 203–213. Granada: Universidad de Granada, 1995.

Rodríguez López, Ana. "La política eclesiástica de la monarquía castellano-leonesa durante el reinado de Fernando III (1217–1252)." *Hispania* 48, no. 168 (1988): 7–48.

Rodríguez López, Ana. "Légitimation royale et discours sur la croisade en Castille aux XIIe et XIIIe siècles." *Journal des Savants* 1, no. 1 (2004): 129–163.

Ruiz Domínguez, Juan Antonio. *El mundo espiritual de Gonzalo de Berceo*. Logroño: Instituto de Estudios Riojanos, 1999.

Sánchez Herrero, José. "La legislación conciliar y sinodal hispana de los siglos XIII a mediados del XVI y su influencia en la enseñanza de la doctrina cristiana. Los tratados de doctrina cristiana." In *Proceedings of the Seventh International Congress of Medieval Canon Law*, ed. Peter Linehan, 349–372. Città del Vaticano: Biblioteca Apostólica Vaticana, 1988.

Sánchez Herrero, José. "La literatura catequética en la Península Ibérica. 1236–1553." En *La España Medieval* 9 (1986): 1051–1118.

Santiago-Otero, Horacio. "Guido de Monte Roterio y el *Manipulus curatorum*." In *Proceedings of the Fifth International Congress of Medieval Canon Law*, ed. Stephen Kuttner and Kenneth Pennington, 259–265. Città del Vaticano: Biblioteca Apostólica Vaticana, 1980.

Smith, Damian J. "La guerra contra los musulmanes en España «en palabras» del papa Inocencio III." In *Orígenes y desarrollo de la guerra santa en la Península Ibérica*, ed. Carlos de Ayala Martínez, Patrick Henriet and J. Santiago Palacios Ontalva, 207–218. Madrid: Casa de Velázquez, 2016.

Smith, Damian J. "The papacy, the Spanish kingdoms and las Navas de Tolosa." *Anuario de Historia de la Iglesia* 20 (2011): 157–178.

Simó, Lourdes. "'Razón de amor' y la lírica latina medieval." *Revista de literatura medieval* 4 (1992): 197–212.

Soto Rábanos, José María. "Visión y tratamiento del pecado en los manuales de confesión de la baja Edad Media hispana." *Hispania Sacra. Revista española de historia eclesiástica* 58 (2006): 411–447.

Spiegel, Gabrielle. *Romancing the Past: The Rise of Vernacular Prose Historiography in Thirteenth-Century France*. Berkeley: University of California, 1993.

Uría, Isabel. "Gonzalo de Berceo, estudiante en Palencia y colaborador en el Libro de Alexandre." *Berceo* 155 (2008): 27–54.

Verger, Jacques. *Les gens de savoir dans l'Europe de la fin du Moyen Âge*. Paris: PUF, 1997.

Walker, Rose. *Views of Transition: Liturgy and Illumination in Medieval Spain*. Buffalo: University of Toronto Press, 1998.

Waugh, Scott. L. and Diehl, Peter, ed. *Christendom and Its Discontents: Exclusion, Persecution, and Rebellion, 1000–1500*. Cambridge: Cambridge University Press, 2002.

Wei, Ian P. *Intellectual Culture in Medieval Paris: Theologians and the University, c.1100–1330*. Cambridge: Cambridge University Press, 2012.

Index

Adalberon of Laon 15n3
Adelaide (Adèle or Alix) of Brittany, Abbess of Fontevraud 110–115, 121, 129
Adèle of Champagne. *See* Alix of Blois
Agnello, Bishop of Fez 31n64
al-'Adil, Almohad Caliph 52, 54, 57
Alarcos, Battle of 92n36
al-Bayāsī, 'Abd Allah 53–54, 57, 90
Alberic of Trois Fontaines 22, 25
Alcobaça Monastery 147
al-Dabbāj, Abū l-Ḥasan 'Alī b. Jābir b. 'Alī al-Lakhmī 74
Aldonza 216
Alexander III, Pope 86, 96
Alfonso I, King of Aragón 17
Alfonso II, King of Aragón 88
Alfonso III, King of Portugal 33n70
Alfonso V, King of León 16n5
Alfonso VI, King of León-Castile 16–17, 51, 57, 166, 168n19, 173
Alfonso VII, King of León-Castile 17–18, 51, 145, 166, 168n, 9
Alfonso VIII, King of Castile 2–3, 4n14, 18, 21, 87–88, 91, 95, 97n57, 106–107, 121, 125–126, 145, 153–156, 166–170, 173–176, 187, 196, 209–211, 232
Alfonso IX, King of León 1, 3, 4n14, 18–20, 46, 64, 91, 140, 170–172, 174–175, 177, 188, 197, 200, 211, 213–214
Alfonso X, King of Castile-León 2, 23, 27–30, 36–37, 44–47, 56, 58, 74–75, 79–80, 93, 99–100, 155–157, 180, 182, 187, 199, 200–201, 203, 205, 216–217, 220, 226, 231, 233
Alfonso de Molina 198, 213, 220
al-Hasan, Governor of Salé 32, 230
al-Ḥimyarī 71
Alix of Blois, Abbess of Fontevraud 105, 107–112, 115–119, 120–129
Alix of France 108–109, 116
al-Makhlu, 'Abd al Wahid I 54
al-Ma'mūn, Almohad Caliph 34n81, 52–53, 57, 61, 230
al-Ma'mūn, Taifa King of Toledo 51
al-Murtaḍā, Almohad Caliph 36

al-Mustanṣir, Abu Yaqub Yusuf II, Almohad Caliph 53
al-Mu'tamid, Taifa King of Seville 16n9
al-Qadir, Taifa King of Toledo 51
al-Qashtālī, Aḥmad 63
al-Rashīd, Almohad Caliph 31n64
al-Sa'īd al Mu'taḍid, Almohad Caliph 32–34, 73
Álvaro de Lara 210
Arnau Amalric, Abbot 89

Baldric, Bishop of Dol 119
Barlaam and Josaphat 250
Barton, Simon 1n2, 93
Beatriz of Swabia, Queen of Castile-León 4, 21, 24–25, 108, 124–125, 127–129, 154–155, 157, 181, 193–194, 196, 198, 199–204, 217, 220, 227
Bede the Venerable 15n3
Belinchón, *Fuero* of 95
Benavente, Treaty of 214
Benedict of Aniane 144n20
Berenguela, Infanta 153–154, 166, 173n45, 180–188, 195, 199, 212–213
Berenguela of León 4, 174, 195, 209, 213
Berenguela, Queen of León, Queen of Castile 1, 18, 20, 46, 124–125, 129, 154–155, 167–176, 178, 187–188, 193–200, 202–203, 205–207, 209–210, 212–213, 216–217, 226
Bernardo, Bishop of Segovia 98–99
Bertha of Cornouaille 112–113
Bertha of Lorraine, Abbess 111, 115
Blanca (Blanche) of Castile, Queen of France 3, 109, 120, 125–129, 169, 195, 203, 213
Burgos, Cathedral of 4, 21, 108, 157, 227

Calahorra, Cathedral of 156–157
Calatrava, Order of 33, 197–198, 204–205
Calila e Dimna 249
Cantigas de Santa María 180–181, 199, 201–202
Carmona, *fuero* of 204
Carolingian 15, 143–144, 146, 152

Charlemagne   26, 85, 144, 201
Chronicon Mundi   4, 23n37, 26, 49, 141, 171.
   See also Lucas, Bishop of Tuy
Clement X, Pope   2
Conan IV, Duke of Brittany   112–113
Constantine of Orvieto   229
Constanza Alfonso II, Infanta   154, 169–182,
   186–188, 212–213
Constanza Alfonso III, Infanta   154, 172–182,
   186–188, 209, 212–213
Córdoba
   Cathedral of   147–148
   Conquest of   1–2, 27, 45, 49–50, 55–56,
      78–79, 157, 193, 197, 206, 224, 232–233,
      245
Cortes   21, 36, 47–48, 53
Crusade   17–22, 27, 30–32, 47, 54–55, 86–90,
   96, 150n50, 156–158, 231, 233, 245
Cuenca, *Fuero* of   87, 95
Cunegunda   24–25

De Altera Vita   228. *See also* Lucas, Bishop
   of Tuy
Decretum   27, 86
De Rebus Hispanie   28n52, 85, 91–92, 181,
   214n112. *See also* Rodrigo Jiménez
   de Rada
Diego López de Haro   96, 209, 211, 215
Diego Pascual   94
Dominican Order   4–5, 31n63, 31n64,
   224–227, 229–231, 233, 246
Dominic, St.   224, 227, 229, 230
Domingo, Bishop of Baeza   233
Domingo, Bishop of Plasencia   90–93, 95
Domingo of Segovia   224
Dulce, Infanta of León   177, 212, 213–215

Edward I, King of England   45, 204
Eleanor of Aquitaine   108–110, 113–114, 116,
   118, 124, 126, 128
Eleanor of Castile   195, 204
Eleanor of Provence, Queen of England   119
Elvira Alfonso II   168n19
Elvira Fernández   165
Engelbert, Archbishop of Cologne   24n39
Enrique I, King of Castile   18, 106, 121,
   154–155, 170, 195, 209, 210
Étienne de Bourbon   249

Eudes II, Count of Brittany, Viscount of
   Porhoët   112–113
Eugenius III, Pope   119

Fadrique, Infante   25n45, 180, 200–201, 217
Fecho de allende   27–32
Fecho del Imperio   36
Fernando I, King of León-Castile   16, 123,
   165–166, 173
Fernando II, King of León   18, 168, 170, 211
Fernando III, King of Castile-León   33n70,
   97–99, 154, 167, 174–176, 182, 187–188,
   193–194, 196–197, 209–214, 216
   Accession   1, 140–141, 147, 174
   Charters of   105, 107, 119–120, 124, 128–129,
      185, 196, 202, 206, 211, 226
   Conquests   2, 45–47, 56–57, 72–74, 86,
      87–88, 90, 94–95, 146, 156–158, 224, 232
   Crusades   18, 22, 27, 31, 34–35, 48, 233, 245
   Fecho de allende   27–32
   Illegitimacy   19, 212
   Marriage   21, 24–25, 108, 124–125, 180, 198,
      200, 203, 227
   Relations with Muslims   51–55, 62,
      64–65, 67–72, 230–231
   Tomb   1, 44, 46, 75–80, 152, 155–156, 201
Fernando VI, King of Spain   77
Fernando, Infante   169, 171–172
Fernando Pérez de Traba   18n13
Flórez, Henrique   77–78
Fontevraud, Abbey of   105, 107, 111–112, 115,
   118, 121, 124–126, 129
Fourth Lateran Council (1215)   5, 20n23,
   32n64, 96, 97n57, 231, 242–244, 246,
   250, 252
France, Kingdom of   3, 15n3, 45, 113, 124n116,
   125–129, 141, 195, 213
Francesc Eiximenis   251
Franciscan Order   4–5, 31n63, 31n64, 33–34,
   224–225, 227, 230–231, 246
Francis, St.   224, 227
Frederick II, Holy Roman Emperor   21,
   24–25, 30, 45, 125, 200–201
Fuero Juzgo   95

García Fernández, *mayordomo*   97–98,
   195–197, 202, 205–208, 211
Gerald of Wales   141–142
Gerardo, Bishop of Segovia   98–99

INDEX 263

Gerard of Fracheto   229
Gil Torres, Cardinal   99
González, Julio   5
Gonzalo de Berceo   9, 251–252
Gonzalo Rodríguez Girón   178, 180, 209
Granada, Nasrid Kingdom of   2, 46, 55, 62, 64–65, 74, 231
Gregory VII, Pope   241, 245
Gregory IX, Pope   25, 31, 32n64, 33n67, 50, 97–99, 118, 220, 228–229, 244
Guadalajara, Synod of   98
Guido de Vico   18n10
Gutierrez, Bishop of Córdoba   70

Hadrian I, Pope   144n20
Hadrianum   144n20
Henry I, King of Castile. *See* Enrique I
Henry II, King of England   96n52, 99, 112–113, 154n69, 170
Henry III, King of England   29, 118
Henry (VII) of Germany, King of the Romans   25
Hispanic Rite   144–145, 146n30, 241, 242, 245
Honorius III, Pope   19, 20, 21, 22, 31, 54–55, 86, 89, 150n50, 212, 227, 230, 231, 244n11
Humbert of Romans   229, 232

Ibn al-Aḥmar. *See* Muḥammad I
Ibn al-Khaṭīb   65–66, 69–70
Ibn Hūd   52–53, 55, 57, 61–62, 65–66
Ibn Khaldūn   63–64
Ibn Khaṭṭāb, Abū Bakr Muḥammad   75–76
Ibn Maḥfūẓ   53, 56–57, 65
Ibn Manṣūr, *faqih*   73
Ibn Mardanīsh, Muhammad ibn Saʿd (Wolf King)   51
Ibn Mardanīsh, Zayyān   61–62
Ibn Tāsufīn, Yūsuf   16n9
Inés Laínez, prioress of Las Huelgas   176, 184–186, 211
Infantazgo   165–168, 171, 173–179, 181, 185, 188–189, 198
Innocent II, Pope   18
Innocent III, Pope   5, 115, 120, 232, 242, 250, 252
Innocent IV, Pope   30–32, 33–36, 117–118, 182–183, 185, 233
Isabelle of Blois   110, 115, 127
Isidore of Seville   16

Jaén
    Cathedral of (Grand Mosque of)   70–71, 147–148
    Conquest of   1–2, 27, 45, 53, 55, 64–65, 67–71, 78–79, 157, 224, 232
    Treaty of   55, 64–72
Jaime I, King of Aragón   33, 45–46, 89, 212, 231
Jean de Melun, Bishop of Poitiers   127
Jean of Abbeville   244, 245, 250
Jerónimo of Périgord, Bishop of Valencia   85
Joan Plantagenet   114, 116
John of Brienne, King of Jerusalem   4, 213
John of Salisbury   113
Jordan of Saxony   229
Juana (Jeanne) of Ponthieu, Queen of Castile-León   4, 193–194, 196, 203–205, 208
Juan, Bishop of Osma, Chancellor of Castile   19, 21n28, 47–50, 53–54, 183
Juan Gil de Zamora   248
Juan Pérez Ponce de León   216
Juan, Prior of San Zoilo de Carrión   124

Las Huelgas, Burgos   4, 93, 108, 146–147, 153–156, 165–189, 193, 201, 208, 211–212, 214
Las Navas de Tolosa   54
    Battle of   2–3, 21, 61, 66, 85, 93–94, 224, 232
Latin Chronicle of the Kings of Castile   2, 19, 47–50, 140–141, 147, 215. *See also* Juan, Bishop of Osma
León, Cathedral of   157
León, Kingdom of   15–16, 19, 121, 140, 145n26, 166, 169, 174, 214
Leonor Plantagenet, Queen of Castile   106, 125, 154–155, 167–170, 173, 176, 187, 196, 202, 207, 209, 220
Leonor, Queen of Aragón   195, 212
Lope de Moros   255
Lope Díaz de Haro   215
Lope Fernández de Ain, Bishop of Morocco   33–34, 36
Louis VII, King of France   108, 113, 116
Louis VIII, King of France   1, 3
Louis IX, King of France   31, 35, 45, 119, 127, 128
Louis of Blois   115–116, 118

Lucas, Bishop of Tuy   4, 23n37, 26, 49, 141, 171, 214, 228

Mabille de Ferté, Abbess of Fontevraud   117–118, 120, 122, 124, 127
Manrique de Lara   18n13
Marès, Frederic   107, 123
Marès Oriol, Pere   123
Margaret of Provence   127
Marguerite, Countess of Blois   109, 115, 128
Marguerite of Blois, nun   116
María, Fernando III's sister   217
Martín López de Pisuerga   96
Mathilde, Countess of Chartres and Soissons   110, 118
Matthew Paris   29, 35, 45
Maurice, Bishop of Burgos   3–4, 22n29, 124, 147, 229
Mayor Arias   195–196, 202, 205–209, 211, 217
Mencía, Countess and Abbess of San Andrés de Arroyo   193, 209–212
Mencía López de Haro   195, 202, 215–216
Mendizábal, Juan Álvarez   122
Menéndez Pidal, Ramón   123
Menéndez y Pelayo, Marcelino   123
Mester de clerecía   251–254
Miguel of Ucero   224
Missa pro imperatore   147
Missa pro principe   147
Missa pro rege   143–152, 158
Molinism   28n52
Monasterio de Vega. See Santa María de la Vega del Cea (Valladolid)
Moriel   97–98, 180
Morocco, Diocese of   32–36
Mozarabic Rite. Hispanic Rite
Muḥammad I   2, 36–37, 53, 55–57, 61–62, 64–70, 71–72, 74–76, 79
Murcia   1–2, 27, 35, 45, 51, 56, 61–62, 65–66, 75, 78–79, 80n66, 157, 224, 234

Nahmanides, Rabbi   231
Nickson, Tom   78–80
Norbert of Xanten   145
Nuño González de Lara   216–217

Oliver of Cologne (Paderborn)   31n61
Osma, Sacramentary of   148, 151–152

Otto I, Holy Roman Emperor   147
Oviedo, Cathedral of   157

Palazzo Finco de Bassano (Vicenza)   201
Palencia   87, 121
  Cathedral of   97–98, 226, 228–229
  Studium of   4, 251–252
Pedro, Abbot of San Pedro de Gumiel   24
Pedro Alfonso   249
Pedro Fernández   197
Pedro Ferrando   229
Pedro Gallego, Bishop of Cartagena   233
Pedro I, King of Castile-León   202
Pedro López   202
Pedro of Madrid   224
Pedro Ponce de Cabrera   216
Pelayo de Albano, Cardinal   20
Peramán, Monastery of (Zaragoza)
Pero da Ponte   156n78
Petrus de Hyspania, Chaplain and Sacristan   121
Philip II, King of France   125
Premonstratensians   145–146

Quesada, Conquest of   54, 90

Ramón, Bishop of Segovia, Archbishop of Seville   94–95
Ramón de Bonifaz   72
Ramón II de Minerva, Bishop of Palencia   87
Raymond of Peñafort   247
Raymond VI, Count of Toulouse   114
Raymond VII, Count of Toulouse   120
Reconquista   2, 17, 27, 35, 45–46, 49–50, 62, 141, 146, 156–158
Republic, Plato   149
Richard I, King of England   99, 125
Richard of Cornwall   119
Robert d'Arbrissel   119
Rodrigo Díaz de Vivar (El Cid)   85
Rodrigo Jiménez de Rada, Archbishop of Toledo   3–4, 20, 22n29, 31n63, 37, 49–50, 63, 85–86, 88–90, 91–93, 95, 98–99, 141, 172, 181, 198, 200, 203, 209, 231
Rodrigo Rodríguez Girón   178, 180
Rodrigo Ruiz   197

INDEX 265

Salamanca   4
Sahagún, Sacramentary of   146
San Andrés de Arroyo   193, 209–212
Sancha Alfonso II   168n19
Sancha, daughter of Alfonso VIII (died in childhood)   169
Sancha, Infanta of León   177, 212–215
Sancha García, Abbess of Las Huelgas   176, 197, 211
Sancha, Queen of León   166, 173
Sancha Raimúndez   165–166, 168n19, 173
Sancha, sister of Fernando III and wife of Simon Ruiz de Cameros   217
Sancho II, King of León-Castile   166
Sancho II, King of Portugal   45, 216
Sancho III of Pamplona   16
Sancho III, King of Castile   18, 166
Sancho IV, King of Castile-León   97n57, 154, 156, 226
SS Cosmas y Damián de Covarrubias, Monastery of   167–168, 185
SS Pelayo and Isidoro, Monastery of (León)   165, 167, 176
San Salvador de Oña, Monastery of   167–168
Santa María de Carbajal   165
Santa María de Huerta   85, 93
Santa María de la Vega del Cea (Valladolid)   121–122, 124
Santa María de la Vega de Oviedo (Asturias)   121
Santiago, Order of   32, 33, 70, 214, 217
Santiago de Compostela, Cathedral of   198, 224
Santo Domingo of Madrid   226
San Vincente de Sierra (Toledo)   146
Second Vatican Council   2n4
Sendebar (*The Book of Women's Wiles*)   249
Setenario   23, 47
Seville   16, 75–76, 187
   Cathedral of   1, 44, 46, 77–80, 147–148, 152, 155–156, 188, 200–201
   Conquest of   1–2, 27–29, 33n67, 35, 44–47, 50, 55–56, 72–74, 78–79, 94, 157, 193, 204, 207–208, 217, 224, 232, 245
Siete Partidas   93, 95, 220, 231
Simon Ruiz de Cameros   217

Sinbaldo dei Fieschi. *See* Innocent IV, Pope
Song of Roland   85
Stephen, Bishop of Dol   105, 119–120, 124
Suero Gómez   224

Teobald I, King of Navarre   33n70
Tello Téllez de Meneses, Bishop of Palencia   21n24, 55, 97–98, 107–108, 209, 226, 228
Teresa Alfonso, Fernando III's sister   217
Teresa of Portugal, Queen of León   20n22, 195, 213–214
Thibaut V, Count of Blois   108–109
Thibaut VI, Count of Blois   109, 128
Third Lateran Council (1179)   96, 97n57
Thomas Aquinas   149
Toledo, Cathedral of   4, 20n20, 89, 144–146, 157, 167–168, 208, 245
Tortosa, Cathedral of   146–147
Treaty of Cazola   88
Trujillo, Conquest of   90–93
Turpin, Archbishop of Rheims   85

Urraca Alfonso, Queen of Navarre   168
Urraca Fernández   165
Urraca, Fernando III's sister   217
Urraca López de Haro, Queen of León   195, 211
Urraca Pérez   202, 206, 217
Urraca, Queen of León-Castile   17, 165, 173

Valladolid   140, 142, 147, 206, 244
Vermudo II, King of Galicia, King of León   16n5
Vidal de Arvival   118–119
Vincent de Beauvais   249
Vincentius Hispanus   26–27
Violante of Aragón   206, 208, 217
Virgin Mary   35n81, 70, 94, 108, 118, 140, 181, 199, 201, 252–253
Visigoths   16, 17, 26, 46, 49, 146n30

Yaḥyā I, Abū Zakariyāʾ, Emir of Tunis   33

Zafadola   51